My Fall From Grace

CITY HALL TO PRISON WALLS

James J. Laski, Jr.

authorHOUSE®

AuthorHouse™
1663 Liberty Drive, Suite 200
Bloomington, IN 47403
www.authorhouse.com
Phone: 1-800-839-8640

First published by AuthorHouse   5/19/2008

ISBN: 978-1-4343-6279-7 (sc)
ISBN: 978-1-4343-6280-3 (hc)

Library of Congress Control Number: 2008900363

Printed in the United States of America
Bloomington, Indiana

This book is printed on acid-free paper.

Back cover photo, courtesy of Smith/Wright Photography, Chicago

ACKNOWLEDGMENTS

I would like to thank the following people whose support and assistance proved invaluable to me during the writing of this book. First, I would like to thank Professor Dale C. Uhlmann for his expert editing and preparation of the final manuscript, and for his help as a contact liaison. Thanks, too, to Lynda and Amy Blankenship for their editorial help, as well as to the wonderful staff at AuthorHouse. I would also like to thank my good Morgantown friend, supporter, and confidante, Clayton B. Smith. Finally, I wish to extend a special thanks to my four wonderful children, Nina, Jack, Bobby, and Jennifer, for their unwavering love and support.

DEDICATION

This book is dedicated, with all my love, to Kathleen, my wife and best friend, who has never given up on my dreams.

TABLE OF CONTENTS

PREFACE

This book is, in part, the story of a transformation in my life in more than one way. I had always been, prior to my interest in politics, rather introverted—quiet and low-keyed, which would surprise anybody who knows me now. This may have been in part a reaction to growing up with an alcoholic father, resulting in lifelong anxiety and clinical depression, as well as my own battles with alcohol. As a result, much of my early family life I would prefer to forget, although I found a way to partially exorcise those personal demons, at least temporarily.

I started to take an interest in dramatics at St. Laurence High School, on the southwest side of Chicago, in Burbank, Illinois. At St. Laurence, I had a role in the school's production of Rodgers and Hammerstein's *South Pacific*. Stepping into another character's or persona's shoes was liberating, and while I had doubts about becoming a successful actor, I slowly began to consider a career that would similarly allow me to conceal my anxieties behind a totally different mask or face. At the same time, I also wanted to explore an interest I had always had in the law. Thus, I decided to become a lawyer. After graduating from high school, I went to college, and earned a Bachelor of Arts degree from Lewis University in Lockport, Illinois in 1975. I then went to law school, and earned a Juris Doctorate degree from Northern Illinois University in 1978, but, as we'll see later, it would be quite some time before I would actually set up shop with the law license I had so coveted, but that's a story in itself.

I thought I was well on my way to the role of a lifetime—no longer Jim Laski, blue collar, Polish-American kid from the "windy city's" east side, but JAMES J. LASKI, ATTORNEY AT LAW. However, somewhere along the way, my plans changed, and I began to consider a more glamorous role—the role of a lifetime—JAMES J. LASKI, POLITICIAN. That new role, as we'll see, came at a price; one that cost me EVERYTHING—my career, my reputation, my family, and, ultimately, my freedom. This is the story of a profession that has ruined those who came before me, and will continue to ruin others tempted by shortcuts to the American dream. Those shortcuts I know only too well—patronage, corruption, and betrayal of public trust—in short, POLITICS, CHICAGO STYLE.

CHAPTER ONE

THE BEGINNING
November 5, 2006

Here I sit, looking out the window on this lovely fall day while admiring the rolling hills of West Virginia and the bright colors of thousands of mountainside trees losing their leaves. Many deer, wild turkey, geese, and ducks roam the area. A crystal-clear stream cuts through the 300 acre complex, with three narrow walking bridges. This whole area reminds me of a university quad, with separate buildings, a cafeteria, a library, and a chapel, all perfectly balanced on the grounds. For a split second, I almost believed I was back in school. Then, reality set in.

I am at a dormitory in the Bates Unit, one of seven residential units that make up Morgantown Federal Correctional Institute. I've been here for approximately two months of a twenty-four-months' sentence I received for one count of bribery. I sit back and look out the window in disbelief, because, just a short time ago, I was soaring through the clouds as the city clerk of Chicago, entertaining thoughts of running for state treasurer, congress, or mayor. Instead, I am serving the rest of my sentence in a federal prison, and wondering how everything that had seemed so promising and positive for the future had gone so terribly wrong. The answer seems in part to have been the business and career choices I had followed in the nasty business of Chicago politics.

I was fortunate, and I think, blessed, to be involved in public service for about twenty-seven years, over fifteen of which I was an elected official in the third largest city in the country. I had wonderful times and some desperate, heart-wrenching moments that took my family and me down the road of panic and unbearable fear. Many factors, life-altering decisions, and mistakes led me to Morgantown, West Virginia on that morning of September 11, 2006. There, I began a new part of my life, without the fanfare and ill-conceived promises of glory I thought came my way with politics.

To understand my past involvement with the political system, we need to go back to the beginning, to my first introduction to a real-time politician, former Illinois Governor Jim Thompson. I was in law school at the time, when then-candidate for Governor Thompson, dressed in jeans and a flannel shirt, and accompanied by two beautiful golden retrievers, visited Northern Illinois Law School (at the time, Lewis College of Law). His speech was a fiery law and order one that impressed everyone in the auditorium that day. He received a standing ovation when he had finished, and I had the opportunity to meet him and shake his hand. I knew when he had left the school that day that I was going to vote for him, even though he was a Republican, and I had been raised a Democrat by my parents.

Thompson would go on to win one of the closest elections in state history. In Chicago, one of the strongest weapons any local political organization can have is a solid, conscientious, and street-smart precinct captain. Our precinct captain, Mike, was a personable soul forever trying to impress the powers-to-be, at that time, Committeeman and Alderman Bill Lipinski, who would eventually become a U.S. congressman. Mike was a very good captain who had one job, and one job only—to get as many votes as possible for the Democratic candidates that Lipinski had endorsed. Mike also had the responsibility of asking Lipinski's voters what they needed—anything from city services to jobs. When Mike came to my parents' house a few weeks before the gubernatorial elections, he was pushing the party candidates we assured him we would vote for.

At the same time, I needed a summer job while in law school, which he promised he would get for me.

A few months after the November elections, Mike came back to my parents' home to give them his post-election report, and to see if they needed anything else. Before Mike could get a word out, I asked him about the status of my summer job. He stammered and stuttered, and seemed to choke on his words when he told me that there would be no such job. To my amazement, I asked why. Well, Mike, the loyal precinct captain, answered that I wasn't going to receive a summer job because I voted for the wrong candidate for governor. My parents were shocked by the news, and so was I, because I couldn't figure out how he knew, since I had voted by absentee ballot from law school. When I asked him, he explained that all absentee ballots go back to the respective polling places, where the election judges privately put those ballots through a counting machine, unless you live in Chicago, where strong Democratic committee representatives observe the process. Some precinct captains, like Mike, actually assisted in the ballot-counting, by opening the envelopes, looking at the votes, and handing the ballots to the judges. Therefore, Mike knew that I had voted for Republican Jim Thompson, because he saw my absentee ballot. At that moment, I should have walked away from the whole Chicago political scene and its many tricks and false promises, but I didn't. That, unfortunately, was one of the many mistakes I would make.

After graduating from law school, I was all set to pursue what I believed would be a lucrative law career. All that stood in my way was the bar exam. Unfortunately, I failed the first two bar exams I later took, in July 1978, and February 1979. Those were devastating setbacks, because, on both occasions, I failed the multiple choice portion by only a few points. So, now, I was twenty-five years old, had failed the bar exam twice, was living at home with my parents, and, most importantly, was in need of a full-time job.

After reassessing my situation, I called our precinct captain, and again asked if he could speak to the alderman about a full-time position with the city for me. Mike was gracious enough to tell me that he would look into the matter. At the time, I didn't hold much hope that he would be able to help me. However, a few weeks later, he called me, and told me to meet him at the ward headquarters.

When I drove up to the ward office, I have to admit I was petrified. It was a fairly large, two-story building, with huge marquees out front that had the alderman's name, along with the state representative's name, posted in big, black letters. Mike was waiting for me. He told me that he would introduce me to some of Bill Lipinski's inner circle, and that I was going to talk to one of his top guys, John. I remember traveling down a long, dimly lit corridor. As we reached the end of the hall, we came to some brown double doors.

Mike knocked, and all I heard was a rough, guttural, "Come on in."

As we walked in, I saw a short, stocky man in his late fifties, sitting at a desk. He introduced himself as one of Lipinski's top aides. He wore a short-sleeve, white shirt with a little coffee stain on the front, simple, dark green slacks, and plain, black, "old man's" shoes. He had closely cropped, short, black hair and plain black glasses that he had to continuously lift off his nose. When John first spoke to me, it was in a firm, but also fatherly tone. He asked me about my background, education, parents, and my aspirations. All of those questions made me a little nervous, but little did I know that over the next twenty-five years, and even up to the last few months of John's life, he would become a good friend, and an avid supporter of my political career.

Over the next few months, John took me under his wing. As I soon learned, John handled, or was involved in, almost every facet of the alderman's political structure. He handled the precinct captain's requests and their community responsibilities, as well as the organization's financial end. In Chicago, you judge the strength of a ward organization by both its manpower and the money in its coffers. Each precinct captain, depending on his or her salary, had to contribute a percentage back to the organization. Those contributions consisted of buying tickets or purchasing ads for Lipinski. There were usually two fundraisers every year, and each captain was obligated to participate with a certain dollar amount, again, depending on his or her salary.

One of my first volunteer jobs was to count money from a fundraiser that the alderman had just held, so John could deposit the money in the bank. I remember John and me kneeling on the floor and counting thousands of dollars. We eventually had to lock the door, because people kept walking in, and we had one-hundred, and fifty-dollar bills all over the floor. John and I could never agree on the exact amount; if John said his figure was $25,500.00, I would say mine was $27,750.00, and then we would have to start all over again. I actually had quite a bit of fun volunteering for John, which really lasted for a couple of months. Then, John scheduled the meeting I had been waiting for, with Bill Lipinski.

I found myself pacing the whole day. This was my big chance to meet the alderman, and to see what opportunities, if any, would be available. The meeting had been scheduled on a Monday evening, at 7:00 p.m., so I made sure I arrived at least fifteen minutes earlier. As the clock kept ticking 7:00, 7:05, and 7:10 p.m., I became more apprehensive.

Finally, it was 7:15 p.m., and the receptionist, a polite, older woman, invited me in with those magic words, "The alderman will see you now."

She led me down a long hallway towards the back of the building, and up a flight of stairs to a door, which she opened, and asked me to enter the office.

As I walked in, I realized that I was actually in an old apartment that had been converted into an office. There was a huge desk in the middle of the room, with a couple of black chairs in front. Behind the desk was what I would describe as a large, orange sign or marquee, with his initials arranged in a circle. As I sat down, I became more nervous about what to say and how to say it. Then, a tall gentleman entered the room.

With a kind of monotone, almost squeaky voice, he said, "I'm Alderman Bill Lipinski."

He was a middle-aged man, quite tall and thin, with graying hair combed to one side, and a weather-worn, pockmarked appearance, with ears that seemed to be out of proportion to his face.

He sat back in his black executive chair, grabbed one of his Vantage Blue cigarettes, lit it, took a deep drag, and, while exhaling, said, "James, tell me about yourself."

I proceeded to tell him that I just graduated from law school, and sheepishly relayed the fact that I failed the bar exam twice. He responded with questions about what high school I had attended, my parents' occupations, where I lived, and my marital status. I gave short, succinct answers, because I was still nervous, and quite frankly, didn't know how to carry on any kind of small talk with a public official.

After exchanging a few minor pleasantries, including a brief discussion about sports, he asked me a question that totally shocked me, and which, for a split second, left me speechless.

"James, how would you like to be on my personal staff?"

I thought I was in a daze, but I managed to respond with a quick burst of energy that I thought that would be great, and that I would love to be on his staff. With that, he told me to report to his office the next morning (June 16, 1979), at 9:00 a.m., and to see Ray McDonald, whom I would be assisting. I gratefully shook his hand, and thanked him half-a-dozen times. When I left, I was so elated that I could have floated out of his office.

I was so excited that I now had a job working for a Chicago alderman that my lifelong dream of becoming an attorney was at least temporarily, put way on the back burner. It was time for me to start my life in Chicago politics.

The week flew by, and before I knew it, June 16 arrived. I was up, and out of the door by 8:30 a.m. I jumped in my car, and headed to the 23rd Ward office, which was actually only nine or ten blocks from my parents' home. I would jokingly tell myself that the office was one song away on the car radio. While parking the car, I felt as if I were hyperventilating, because I wanted to get started on my first "political" job. As I jumped out of the car and raced to the front door, I told myself this was a great opportunity, and to not screw up.

My first day on the job turned out to be memorable, not for anything I did, as much as for whom I met. When I walked in, I saw an older gentleman scurrying down the hall. He wore an off-white, short-sleeve dress shirt and gray dress slacks that were too big, because the cuffs were dragging along the floor. He was over six feet tall, and stocky; his hair was as white as snow, and for a man in his fifties, his face was so worn, he looked like he was actually in his sixties.

When he noticed me, he quickly came over and asked if he could be of assistance. I extended my hand and introduced myself. I told him I was supposed to start work that day with a Mr. Ray McDonald. He smiled in a gentle, almost fatherly way, and said I had found the person I was looking for.

In my political career, I met thousands of people. However, only a small number would really have an impact on my life, and Ray McDonald would be one of them. He was one of the kindest, most compassionate, and hard working individuals you would ever want to meet. Ray was the alderman's "go-to" guy. He handled all the press for Lipinski, special events and correspondence, and he ran a local newspaper called *The Midway Sentinel,* which Lipinski had founded, and which Ray edited.

It soon became apparent to me that Ray did almost everything in that office, and clearly was in need of some help. I later found out through the grapevine that not only had the alderman and Ray known each other for a number of years, they were the best of friends. As each day went by, I knew my job was to help Ray, and lessen his workload as much as possible. My one regret about my time spent with Ray was its brevity. There were many more things I could have learned from him.

The next two years were busy ones. Ray and I worked together on the newspaper and on such special events as parades, and a host of student programs, including essay contests, spelling bees, track and field competitions, and political rallies. Ray continued day in and day out to provide me with a wealth of information, including how to deal with people, and how to be a good politician. I quickly learned that Ray McDonald was the instrumental figure behind Lipinski's success.

As time went on, Ray and I continued about our business, promoting Lipinski in his newspaper, running his day-to-day operations, and planning all the special events for 1979. While we kept busy, Lipinski was plotting his own future. At that time, he was interested in running for congressperson of the Fifth District. The incumbent was a gentleman by the name of John Fary, a nice enough man who was very much up in years. In fact, the last time he ran for re-election, in 1980, he cut a deal with the local ward committeeperson (a boss who controls votes in his or her respective ward) to step down after that term. However, like many politicians, he became comfortable, and had to either die, or be dragged out of office. Mr. Fary was no exception; he decided to run one more time, in 1982.

Unfortunately for him, Bill Lipinski was not going to wait. He did his homework, and lined up the support of the most influential and powerful politicians on the southwest side of Chicago, including the Daley family from the 11th Ward, Speaker of the State House Mike Madigan from the 13th Ward, Alderman Ed Burke from the 14th Ward, and Committeeman Ted Swinorski from the 12th Ward. By the time Lipinski finished lining up his support, John Fary didn't stand a chance. It was a foregone conclusion that Bill Lipinski was going to be the next congressman.

During this busy and exciting time, my immediate boss and friend, Ray McDonald, came to me with some disturbing news. He was going to have colon surgery, because his doctor had found a tumor. My first thought was about how serious his condition was. My second concern was how long Ray would be out of work. I worked hand-in-hand with Ray, and knew quite a bit about the political operation, but not nearly enough to take over, even on a temporary basis.

After Ray broke the news to Lipinski, the alderman called me into his office. He was very close to Ray, and you could see in his face that he knew there were going to be difficult times ahead. He told me in no uncertain terms that there would be a void in the office, and that he was really uncertain how long Ray would be gone. He then told me it was time for me to step up, and that in Ray's absence, I would handle all of his responsibilities. Although I was excited, I had a tremendous amount of apprehension, because I would be heading up a number of projects, and dealing with the alderman directly, on a one-on-one basis. This was now going to be my opportunity to start setting up my future.

The weeks and months ahead were bittersweet. Ray's tumor was cancerous, and he ended up having a colostomy. His future was uncertain, but Ray made the most of it. There were good days and bad days for Ray. I would spend much of my time going to his house to discuss daily business. When he felt well enough, he would come to the office for a few hours. However, as time went on, you could see what a tremendous toll this ordeal was taking on him, both physically and emotionally. Ray was a fighter, and he was a relatively young man, only in his early fifties, but I began to realize he was on borrowed time.

I was, however, very happy to see Ray share Lipinski's dream of winning the congressional. That whole campaign between Lipinski and Fary was bitter, hard-fought, and received national exposure. When all was said and done, we had a new rising star on the political horizon. Although Lipinski only won the primary against the incumbent Fary, the district was primarily Democratic, so, for all intents and purposes, Lipinski won the general election when he won the primary. Ray worked his fingers to the bone for his long-time friend, and I thought how wonderful it would be for Ray to go with Lipinski to Washington, D.C., just once.

However, one of my saddest days in politics came one morning when I learned that Ray had been rushed to the hospital. During the last few weeks, he had become weaker, his color chalky, and his appetite nonexistent. Later that morning, the call came—Ray McDonald had passed away. He was a mentor, a confidante, and a friend. Ray taught me a great work ethic, but more importantly, how to get along with people and make use of their talents. I will always remember Ray as the most likeable person I'd ever want to meet. No one ever had a bad word to say about him. Ray always believed in me, wanted the best for me, and gave me the tools to succeed.

I still think about him to this day, and I simply say, "Thanks, Ray."

It's often been said that one person's misfortune is another's fortune. I don't know how true that is, but during the months following Ray McDonald's death, I became the editor of Lipinski's newspaper, his press secretary, and most importantly, one of his few "go-to" guys in the organization. This, one of the busiest times of my life, was when I started learning about the dark side of the political game, everything about round-tabling signatures, to tampering with absentee ballots. It was the early 1980s. I was twenty-eight years old, and I was receiving my indoctrination in the "whatever-it-takes-to-get-the-job-done" business of Chicago politics.

CHAPTER 2

TWENTY-THIRD WARD POLITICS I

Back in the 1980s, while moving up the ladder in Lipinski's 23rd Ward democratic organization, I was getting a real education in Chicago politics. If the average citizen thinks that in Chicago, stealing elections, or at least altering numbers to make someone look either good or bad, went out with the days of Al Capone, he or she should think again.

Let's start with nominating petitions. For someone to get on the ballot for a particular office, he or she would have to get a certain number of signatures (depending on the office) on a petition, and submit them to the Board of Elections, along with other required paperwork. If the board agreed that the documents had been properly filed, and that no one had challenged the validity of the petitions within the specified time period, the candidate's name would appear on the ballot for that particular election.

Now, back in the '80s, there was an election for 23rd Ward Committeeperson. Even though a committeeperson's job is supposed to be non-paying (Lipinski, however, paid himself approximately $12,000 a year from his political account, a fact which is a matter of public record), the office did have the control or authority to slate people for various political positions. Lipinski cut a deal to help a gentleman by the name of Tom Ziroli in his race for ward committeeperson, so he could control him. Ziroli would basically do what Lipinski asked him to do. In return, Ziroli would pick up a few city or county jobs from Lipinski, and maybe a few state jobs on his own.

It didn't make much difference either way if Ziroli were in or out, but Lipinski wanted that control. So, petitions were given out, not only to the precinct captains, but also to the office workers. Lipinski ordered Ray, Don, and I to get petitions for Ziroli during the hours Ray and I were on the city payroll clock, and while Don was on the state payroll clock. At the time, Lipinski's Chief of Staff was John Mooney, a nice enough guy, and a World War II veteran, but an Archie Bunker-type, kind of "rough-around-the-edges" guy, who gave us our marching orders to go across the street to the nearby shopping mall, stand in front of Dominick's food store, and collect signatures from shoppers. It sounded easy enough, except that it was the dead of winter. The chill factor was below zero, and it was too damn cold to get people to stop and sign petitions, especially for a candidate like Tom Ziroli, whom most people had never heard of. To make matters worse, after only about thirty or forty minutes, it became so cold that our ink pens froze.

Since I was in charge of the group, I recommended getting out of the cold and coming up with a different plan. Don suggested his house, so we drove over there. Once inside his house, we all sat around his kitchen table and took part in a procedure called "round-tabling," in which we forged people's signatures from the polling sheets. We would randomly select names from the different precincts in the 23rd Ward.

Let's say I started with Precinct 1, and found a particular address with three voters registered at that location. I would sign the name and address of one of those voters on the petition sheet. I would then give the sheet to Ray, who would forge the second name from that address. Then, of course, Don would get the petition and forge the third signature from the polling sheet. This would go on until we filled up all the petitions. It was always best to get five or six people at the table, so we could get a variety of signatures, and in a lot less time. On that particular day, we called one of Lipinski's precinct captains, who hadn't wanted to go door-to-door in the cold, getting signatures, to help us. He joined us in Don's kitchen, where he probably forged 200 signatures alone. I can't tell you how many times over the years Lipinski's organization round-tabled signatures, even for Richard M. Daley, when he first ran for mayor.

Another key ploy was the use of absentee ballots. Those ballots had been geared for senior citizens, disabled people, out-of-town students, vacationers, etc. Any good Chicago Precinct Captain would try to get as many absentee ballots as possible. In most cases, he or she would either help the voters actually fill out the ballot—which meant he or she knew how they voted—or would offer to pick up the ballot and take it directly to the Board of Elections. Now, if that were the case, some of the more devious captains who would not trust certain voters would take those absentee ballots home with them, or back to the ward office, to carefully open them up to see if any of their voters lied to them. There was an art to opening absentee ballots. In most cases, steam would be the way to go, because nobody could tell that the envelope had been tampered with after it had been resealed. Another method was to carefully use a letter opener, which required patience and skill to separate the flap from the glue and the rest of the envelope.

A ballot, as many people know, is like a computer card with holes placed next to numbers representing various candidates. In the case of multiple offices and candidates, a sample ballot would be necessary. For example, if Lipinski's name was on the congressional ballot, chances were his number was low—maybe in the teens. So, for the sake of argument, let's say his number was seventeen, and his opponent's eighteen. If number seventeen was punched out, we would just put the ballot back in the envelope and reseal it. However, if we saw number eighteen, we would have two choices. We could simply punch out number seventeen for Lipinski, and that would cancel out the vote entirely for both candidates, and at least prevent his opponent from receiving the vote. But if we were dedicated, devious, and meticulous, we could punch out the number for Lipinski, take the chad from the punch-out, and, with some tweezers and glue, carefully place that punched-out chad over number eighteen. If we did it properly, with no traces of glue, there would be a good chance that the ballot computer would give Lipinski the vote.

Some precinct captains, though, wouldn't change the vote, but only look at the ballot to see if their voters lied to them. This would become valuable information for the precinct captain, because if that voter needed a future favor, he or she would probably not receive it (remember my own absentee ballot when I was in law school!). Those precincts with the most absentee ballots in the 23rd Ward generally had the best results for Lipinski, and the candidates he supported.

Another important component for less-than-scrupulous precinct captains would be the actions of the Election Day judges. Some of the highest-ranking captains, over the years, had had their own handpicked people at the polling places—usually friends or neighbors who wanted to pick up $100.00 for a long day, and who would help out as judges.

Besides running the ballot chards through the computer, the judges would check out a potential voter's identification, and initial the application and envelope his or her ballot had come in. In the meantime, a precinct captain might intentionally not update his or her own polling sheet, so that people who had moved or died could remain on the voting rolls. Some precinct captains might even purge names from voting rolls and submit the tampered lists to the Board of Elections, who may or may not check their validity. As a result, I saw people vote under the names of the deceased, or under those who had moved. I even saw the same person vote multiple times on the same day at different polling places. The key to this charade would be a judge not checking for the proper identification, or just being part of the overall scheme to begin with.

Some of the final numbers in a particular race would prove astonishing, for example, 300 votes for Lipinski's candidate, to ten for his opponent. Don't get me wrong; there were some very honest precinct captains would do their homework, and get legitimate results. But there were others who would use every trick in the book, for instance, registering voters from an address that was not even a place of residence, such as a tavern. It was amazing how much fraud and vote-stealing went on back then. I was truly part of a culture that felt that the end always justified the means.

CHAPTER 3

TWENTY-THIRD WARD POLITICS II

Around 1989, at the age of thirty-six, I became chief of staff, not only for Congressman Lipinski, but for the entire 23rd Ward Democratic organization. This was when Lipinski was in Washington and I was in Chicago, running day-to-day operations. Both governmental and political work, as well as other business, went on every day.

Many federal investigations have occurred over the years regarding the illegal activities of governmental employees who do political work on taxpayers' time. Some of my actions as Lipinski's chief of staff may have been illegal, but I continued to regard them as normal, or at least, common practice. Unfortunately, this way of thinking eventually resulted in my political downfall.

When I was Lipinski's chief of staff, any number of people came into the office on a host of different issues—everything from trees to be cut down, potholes to be fixed, and alley lights to be replaced, to garbage to be picked up and sewers to be cleaned. Then, of course, there were more specialized services, such as taking care of jury summonses, renewing drivers' licenses, appealing property tax bills, and acquiring building permits, all of which required the help of specific contact people. The process could be as simple as helping people avoid long lines or bureaucratic red tape, or as complex as taking care of a problem without many questions later being asked. On most days, the office was quite busy. If we weren't doing government business, we could take care of precinct work by visiting people and picking up requests, or even cutting down a tree, if necessary—even if it was against the law.

Usually, Lipinski would be in Washington, D.C. from Tuesday through Thursday. Someone would take him to the airport around 6:00 a.m. on Tuesday and pick him up on Thursday evening. Generally, I took him to the airport, and had someone else pick him up. It certainly wasn't unusual for me to receive five or six phone calls a day from Lipinski regarding any number of issues, from business to personal. For example, if it was winter time, and we had had a heavy snow, Lipinski would tell me to send a couple of guys over to his house to shovel his driveway. If he wanted his gutters cleaned, I would send somebody to climb on his roof and clean them. He had a cement wading pool in his back yard, and if it needed re-painting, I would get somebody from the office to buy paint and head over to his house. There were also times when we had to enter his house to clean out a room that needed painting, or to pull up carpeting. One day, Ray and two other employees, Al and Mike, went to Lipinski's house and actually spent the whole day cleaning his son, Dan's bedroom, which was getting painted, and, I think, getting new carpeting laid. In any event, his son (who, by the way, is in Congress now) left his room in total disarray, which meant that Ray and his crew had to pack up boxes, take sheets off the mattress, pull his dirty clothes out from under the bed, and remove all the furniture.

I can't tell you how many times my associate, Ray Drish, I, or someone else from the office, moved his children back and forth, from college or law school, to home. On one particular Saturday, which was a non-working day, we, along with another worker, Mike, moved Lipinski's daughter, Laura, to the University of Illinois, in Champaign, which was an approximate three-hour-drive. We drove there in Ray's mother's van, into which we had loaded Laura's clothes, furniture, etc., while Laura followed and her brother Dan followed us in her car. When we arrived at her apartment complex, we found that she was on the second floor. We noticed that Dan was missing in action, lying across the couch, while we lugged his sister's belongings into the apartment. I told Dan to get off his ass and help us.

Of course, his response was, "Do you know who I am?"

Ray replied, "I don't care who you are. Just start helping!"

I think, just out of embarrassment, he got up and started working. By the time Mike, Dan, and I finished our work, and had gotten something to eat, we didn't arrive back home until around 8:00 p.m.

If anyone knew how difficult it was taking care of Lipinski's family, it was Ray. Whenever Lipinski needed his wife, son, or daughter taken somewhere or picked up, 99 percent of the time, Ray usually had to do it. Don't get me wrong; Ray and I knew this was part of the job. What we never appreciated was the rudeness and arrogance displayed by the family when we did things for them. In 1979, for example, when I began working for Lipinski, one of my first assignments was to drive his son to a little league game. All I remember is, when I pulled the car in front of the field, the boy got out of the car and went merrily on his way, without even a simple thank you. I can't tell you how many times that family failed to show even the slightest bit of courtesy.

Another story worth noting involved the day Lipinski told me to line up three guys from the office to pick up Dan from Northwestern University, and move all his belongings back home. I got Ray and two other guys, Terry and Chuck, who were working at the office that day, to drive down and take care of that task. According to Ray, when they arrived to get him, Dan told them that he forgot to reserve the freight elevator to move his things from one of the upper floors he lived on. Unfortunately, he couldn't reserve a time for the elevator for another three hours, so Ray and the guys had to come back. It was a warm summer day, and the guys had three hours to kill, so they drove down Lakeshore Drive to Oak Street Beach for a couple of hours of swimming, before returning to pick up Lipinski's son—all on taxpayers' money.

During those years, Ray and I laughed, and practically bragged about how we kept Lipinski out of trouble. We always believed in loyalty, and tried to protect him every day. For example, Lipinski's newspaper, *The Midway Sentinel,* which was his political sounding board and public relations community tool—and a key financial and social weapon in his political arsenal—was nearly broke. However, with Ray's help, along with that of some outside volunteers whom Lipinski promised future employment to, I managed to turn the situation around, to the point where within a short period, the newspaper went from a zero balance to over $6,000.00 in profits. One day, Lipinski called me into his office, and told me to bring the newspaper's checkbook with me. At the end of the day, the balance was close to zero again, because Lipinski had written a check that day to Mr. John Rogola for $5,000.00. Ironically, Rogola was one of the initial investors, who along with Lipinski, helped finance the Chicago Congressional office building that Lipinski had a controlling interest in. I heard rumors that Rogola was having financial problems, but I never knew the reason why Lipinski paid him, except, possibly, that the $5,000.00 was Rogola's original investment in the building that he was bought out of, or paid off on. At any rate, *The Midway Sentinel* never did recover financially after that withdrawal. Frankly, Ray and I, after that incident, lost enthusiasm for the paper, and Lipinski never really pushed to jump-start it again. Therefore, it wasn't long after that when I became chief of staff, and *The Midway Sentinel* died a quiet death.

I worked for Lipinski from January 1979 to February 1993. During those years, I learned a great deal about politics, public relations, power orientation, entitlement, and, of course, "Whatever it takes to get the job done." Regrettably, this became my philosophy as I started to move up the political ladder. In my mind, Bill Lipinski had given me the experience, knowledge, and tools to set my own course, and to create my own opportunities without him. I knew that it would be just a matter of time before he and I would have a parting of the ways. What I needed was a plan that would give me a fighting chance against the machine.

CHAPTER 4

KATHLEEN

Throughout my public career, I came to realize that Chicago politics are not only hard-core, but like a roller coaster ride. One day you're up, and the next day, you're down. However, after more than twenty-six years in this business, one thing that I have always been grateful for, and would never change, has been my marriage to my wife, Kathleen. I've had time to reflect on all my trials and tribulations, and the only things that have remained constant have been friends and family, in particular, the true bright spots in my life, Kathleen and my children.

During the summer of 1988, Lipinski placed me in charge of his re-election campaign as congressman, which was not going to be very competitive at all. I was already heading Bill Krystyniak's campaign for state senator. Lipinski had handpicked Krystryiak, who was now the 23rd Ward Alderman, to run against the incumbent first-term Senator Robert Raica, a rising star in the Republican party, who, just a couple of years before, had defeated a long-time incumbent, friend, and organization member, Leroy Lemke. Because Raica lived in the 23rd Ward, he made Lipinski very uncomfortable, especially with his newfound stardom in the state senate. Therefore, Lipinski decided to take him out in the November general election by putting up his strongest horse, Krystyniak. The state senate district covered the entire 23rd Ward and a few precincts in surrounding city wards. The rest of the district consisted of small suburban villages and towns, where although he wasn't as well-known, he still had some name recognition.

The campaign between Krystyniak and Raica was getting state-wide attention, and we were gearing up for a real battle over the next five months. For Krystyniak to make an impact in the suburbs, he needed to join forces with the Democratic incumbent, State Representative John O'Connell, who, in fact, was going to have his own battle in November against his old nemesis Anne Zickus, who previously ran against him two years earlier. John was from Western Springs, and had been the state representative for a number of years in the area, so it had made perfect sense for Krystyniak and O'Connell to run a joint campaign where they could help each other out, in both the city and the suburbs.

As plans got underway, we first established a suburban campaign office in the suburbs, which would be a joint Krystyniak/O'Connell campaign office. Now we needed to man the operation with paid full-time personnel. O'Connell already had someone in mind. However, since this was a joint campaign, several people would get paid by both the State Senate Campaign Committee, headed by Phil Rock, the President of the Senate, and by the Illinois House Campaign Committee, led by Mike Madigan, Speaker of the House. In order to hire someone, that applicant first had to see Lipinski and me at the ward office. If we signed off, that person would then have to go to Springfield for quick meetings with Madigan's and Rock's people, hopefully fill out the necessary papers there, and start working.

It was a nice, warm summer day. I was in Lipinski's office, going over ideas for the campaign, when the front desk buzzed the congressman to inform him that a young lady had arrived for her interview regarding the campaign petition. Since she was hopefully going to be part of the campaign, I thought it only appropriate that I greet her, and escort her to Lipinski's office.

When I walked up and saw her, all I remember her saying was, "Hi, I'm Kathleen Perepechko. I'm here for my interview with Congressman Lipinski."

As corny or crazy as it sounds, I felt as if I were in a fog. I couldn't keep my eyes off her. As I walked back to Lipinski's office, all I saw was this beautiful girl with a dark tan, and a short-sleeve white top. She was about five-foot-six, had blonde hair and blue eyes, a great figure, and a smile that made my legs buckle. She had beautiful, high cheekbones, and a kind of Eastern European look that I could only describe as "drop dead gorgeous." When she met Lipinski and shook his hand, I could immediately tell she had that polish and professional touch to her. After she had talked to us for a few minutes, Lipinski and I both knew she was well educated, aggressive, and perfect for the job.

After the interview, I remember walking Kathleen to the front door and remarking that I looked forward to seeing her soon. I quickly walked back to Lipinski's office with a big smile on my face, and told him that I thought she would fit the job very well. He agreed that she'd be fine. As I took a deep sigh of relief and exhaled, I told Lipinski that this was going to be an interesting campaign.

Soon after our meeting, Kathleen made her one-day trip to Springfield, and met with the staffs of the State Senate President and the Speaker of the House. It wasn't more than a week or so before she had officially joined the campaign.

Over the next few weeks, we opened up our full-time campaign office, which Kathleen actually helped set up and made functional. Quite honestly, she wasn't just a pretty face. Kathleen not only worked hard, but she took pride in everything she did. Since I was still working out of Lipinski's office every day, it became my personal goal to come up with some reason to drive up to that campaign office to check out the operation. Frankly, I knew the office was fine, but I just wanted to visit with Kathleen.

During those visits, I learned that she was twenty-five-years-old, and a graduate of the University of Illinois, with a degree in education. She lived in the 23rd Ward, less than ten minutes from Lipinski's office. Her parents both worked in county government, and she was currently living with them. Over the years, Kathleen's mom, Pat, was a volunteer campaign worker for State Representative John O'Connell. They actually became friends during that time, and he helped Pat by providing Kathleen with an Illinois State Scholarship for the university.

After graduation, Kathleen wasn't sure what direction she had wanted to follow, and began working in the hotel/restaurant business as the assistant director of catering at Oak Brook Hills. She quickly found out how challenging such a job could be, after working sometimes six-to-seven days a week, and ten-to-twelve hours a day. It wasn't long for her to get burned out, but fortunately, at the same time, the campaign spot for their friend, John O'Connell, opened up.

It wasn't long before I decided to ask her out for a drink. I had already learned that she had a boyfriend who was pursuing a job opportunity in Arizona in a few weeks. My opportunity actually presented itself one day at Lipinski's office, when she stopped by to drop something off. As she began walking out the door, I stopped her. I probably fumbled my words; I really can't remember, except that she said yes for Friday night, around 8:00 p.m. I was so excited that I forgot I had a campaign to run. During the next few days, I was so distracted that I couldn't wait for Friday to come, just so I could get back on track after the date.

As I drove to her house that night, I was nervous, but I was also very excited. Over time, we got to know each other fairly well, and I didn't think we'd have a hard time conversing and getting along. When I pulled up in front of the house, I jumped out of my car and skipped over a couple of stairs on the front porch.

After I rang the doorbell, all I remember was that Kathleen answered the door, all dressed up, but with a confused look on her face. My first reaction was to remind her that she had told me to pick her up around eight. She proceeded to apologize, and told me that she had double-booked, and had forgotten about our date. There was no doubt I was disappointed, but I graciously accepted her apology, and told her that I would see her Monday at work. When I got in my car and drove off, I really starting bitching about her having been such an airhead. I was so aggravated that I was starting to think she hadn't really wanted to go out with me after all.

Over the next couple of weeks, I tried to avoid her as much as possible. I was stubborn, and I wanted to prove a point, at least to myself, that being around her wouldn't bother me, even though she hadn't gone out with me. Although in principle my philosophy sounded good, I was going crazy, because I wanted to be around her all the time. Whenever I saw her, it became more apparent to me that I was falling in love with Ms. Kathleen Perepechko. It was right after Labor Day in 1988, and the guy she had been dating had just left for Arizona to pursue a new job opportunity, when I noticed that Kathleen was a little down in the dumps. As a gesture of friendship, I asked her if she wanted to go out for a drink, just to talk. This time, she not only agreed, but promised not to double-book. We actually went out and had a very nice time. For the next couple of weeks, we spent a lot of time together, just hanging out and talking.

One particular night, after she had closed the campaign office, Kathleen and I went out for a drink at a pub just down the street. We sat at a little round table across from each other. I remember this occasion as if it were yesterday. As I was drinking a beer, I had one hand on my glass and I held my cigarette with the other hand, and just nervously began tapping the table. We started to talk about how nice it was to be out, and to relax. Before I knew it, I moved my hand over a couple of inches and gently placed it over hers. I wasn't sure how she would react, but she actually opened her hand, turned it slightly, and grabbed my hand. I could not think of anything else I would rather have been doing at that moment than holding her hand. This was truly the beginning of our romance. With a little more than a month to go before the election, we kept our feelings for each other a secret. Neither one of us told anyone else at the office what was going on.

Every day, we would go about our business and do our jobs. By the end of the day, we would meet at the campaign office, and either go out somewhere, or to her parents' house and sit around. I have to admit that each night we got together we parted later and later, simply because we didn't want to leave each other.

Before long, the election arrived, and the only way I could describe how everything turned out was one word—DISASTER.

Both Krystyniak and O'Connell finished last, and Lipinski experienced his smallest margin of victory in years. What began as such a promising campaign had become a nightmare for most of the Democratic candidates. They lost both the election and the philosophical consensus to the conservative republicans that year. What happened in Chicago in 1988 happened across the country as well, as Republicans won offices everywhere that day. That evening, to say the least, was quiet and sober. Earlier in the day, I was at the ward office with Lipinski and Krystyniak, while Kathleen was at O'Connell's office in the suburbs. Later, Kathleen and I met at her parents' home, to conduct our own post-election analysis. The only positive spin to an absolutely dismal evening was that, at least, I was with Kathleen.

It took a few months after the election to regroup, but we all did. I became chief of staff to Lipinski, and Kathleen went back to the restaurant/hotel business, and became director of catering for the Prairie Restaurant. Although we kept busy, we spent a considerable amount of time together. We took vacations, including trips to Washington, D.C. and Florida, and basically enjoyed life with each other. I moved out of my parents' house in June 1989, and got my own apartment in the 23rd Ward.

By the end of 1989, Kathleen and I were inseparable, and in love. Just before Christmas, we got engaged. The wedding was set for November of the following year, and things couldn't have been better. There was, however, one piece of unfinished business, as far as my fiancée was concerned. That was for me to take the Illinois Bar Exam one more time. Unfortunately, I had failed the exam five times, and had finally stopped taking it back in 1982. It was now seven years later, and I hadn't picked up a law book since then, so what would be any different now?

According to Kathleen, the difference would be that she had a plan, which would include me taking a bar exam review course, and also a leave of absence from my job for about two months. During that leave from Lipinski, I traveled with Kathleen to the Prairie Restaurant around 8:00 a.m. Before she would start work, she would locate an empty boardroom for me for the day. I spent the entire day studying in the room, which didn't have a radio or TV, newspapers, or anything else but a conference table and chairs. Besides eating lunch, the only thing I actually did all day was study. Since the boardroom had a bathroom, I never left until Kathleen came to get me at the end of the day, which sometimes wouldn't be until 8:00 p.m. I spent five to six days a week studying ten-to-twelve hours a day. Passing the bar exam became my new mission in life.

The previous five times I was only able to pass two parts of the test. Each time I had passed the essay portion, but failed the multiple choice part. It was this portion of the test that I now concentrated most of my attention on. Things were going according to plan, but between the bar exam, politics, and the upcoming wedding, I began to feel extreme emotional pressure, and realized I needed help.

For the first time in my life, I saw a psychiatrist, and opened up my life to him. I told him about my childhood and about my lifelong battle with anxiety. My father was a hard-working man who, at times, abused alcohol. When he did, his mean-spirited behavior tore the family apart. I had to share those personal secrets, and I realized that some of those experiences had much to do with my current anxiety and depression.

It was after my visit with my psychiatrist that I was introduced to several new prescription drugs that became part of my life for years to come. To combat my current pressures, I was prescribed Prozac, Klonopin, and Valium. Quite honestly, the new medications helped me prepare for the bar exam, because they calmed me down. Unfortunately, while I was taking those medications, I was also drinking plenty of beer, which enhanced their effects. As time went on, I became more dependent on the pills. The drinking and the pills now were part of my routine, although the night before the test, I cut back on my consumption and drank only a six-pack!

The next morning, I got up, drank a Pepsi, and took each one of my three pills before Kathleen arrived to take me downtown for the test. When we arrived, she literally had to push me out of her car to go and take the exam. As she would later tell the story, she thought she would receive one of two phone calls at lunch time. The first call could be from me telling her that I had gotten through the morning session, and everything was fine. The second call could be from Northwestern Hospital that I had a nervous breakdown. For the record, I called at lunch time to tell her that I had made it through part one of the exams, and that all had gone well.

A couple of months later, I found out the results. The actual letter was mailed to my parents' house, and I told my father a long time ago that he could open the envelope. My father, along with Kathleen, really believed I could pass the bar exam, and he actually supported Kathleen's pushing me take the test again.

As fate would have it, after eight years of struggling, and of not touching a law book for seven years, I passed the Illinois Bar Exam on my sixth try, in April 1990. Immediately, my parents drove to Lipinski's office to give me my congratulatory letter from the State Bar Examiner. I took the letter, went to a florist, and bought a dozen roses. I attached the letter to the flowers, drove downtown to the Prairie, and gave Kathleen the roses and the letter, because she had as much to do with my passing the exam as I did. We went out later that evening with a bunch of our friends, and celebrated at a local bar until 2:00 a.m. Things couldn't have been better. My anxiety was leveling off, my job with Lipinski was as secure as ever, and Kathleen and I were only about six months away from our wedding.

One of the many things we did before the wedding was look for a place to live. Even though I had an apartment, we wanted a home with a backyard and swimming pool. During a fall weekend, Kathleen and I were driving through a little town outside of Chicago called Willow Springs, and we spotted a house for sale. The little town was surrounded by trees and wooded areas, and had quite a few rolling hills, with almost a New England-type atmosphere. Best of all, it was only a few minutes outside of the city, although, because I worked for the congressman, there was no need for me to live in the city anyway. We had to stop and at least check the house out. It was located on a half-acre of land, with a little creek running through the backyard. The house had a rustic look, and was quite large. It was two stories, with a huge master bedroom that had sliding doors to the outside deck which overlooked the backyard. I think there were four bedrooms, three bathrooms, a dining room, and a family room. Needless to say, we fell in love with the house, and reached a purchase agreement with the owners.

We were only a few days from actually signing a contract to buy the house when I had a meeting with Lipinski. It was at that meeting when I found out that I had the opportunity to be the next alderman, which meant Kathleen and I had to stay in the city after all. I had to break the news to Kathleen, who was naturally disappointed, because it meant having to give up our dream house. Still, we were excited about a chance to step into public office. So now, we turned our attention to finding a home in Chicago.

Before long, November 24, 1990 arrived. We were blessed with a magnificent day, with temperatures close to sixty degrees. The ceremony/mass took place right after dusk, at 5:00 p.m., at Old St. Patrick's Church, an historical landmark located right outside downtown. The reception was held at a place called Burhop's, which later became Michael Jordan's restaurant. We had over 200 of our closest friends and family there, including Lipinski and Krystyniak, who had been one of the groomsmen. Everything had gone beautifully, and according to plan.

The following morning we left for an eight-day honeymoon to St. Martin and Barth in the Caribbean. It was finally an opportunity for Kathleen and me to relax, and to enjoy our time on the islands. For the next week, we ate and drank well, basked in the sun, and just took our time sightseeing and shopping.

As soon as we returned home, we were told that in approximately one week, Mayor Daley would appoint me alderman of the 23rd Ward. We had basically just gotten off the plane, all rested and tan, when I learned I had to attend a meeting in two days with Lipinski to announce the appointment to his ward organization. I had opened a new door, filled with love, hope, and opportunity, having begun my life with Kathleen, and ready to start my new career as a public official.

More than sixteen years have gone by since Kathleen and I took our marriage vows, and I can honestly say that we've both been blessed with health and happiness, a good deal of which has centered on our three children, Nina, Bobby, and Jack. They have put smiles on our faces, and have made each day just a little brighter for us. The one saving grace for me during these now darker days continues to be the love and support I receive every day from Kathleen and the kids.

CHAPTER 5

ALDERMEN, VOUCHERS, AND GHOSTS

When I was appointed alderman of the 23rd Ward in December of 1990, I was on cloud nine. I could have started and ended my political career with this office, and still have been happy. A little power and prestige—what else could I have wanted?

Unfortunately, in Chicago politics, very seldom—or never—will the mayor just appoint a new alderman without someone with clout having first given the mayor his or her blessing, in exchange for future appointment privileges from that office.

I was certainly no exception to this rule. All those years with Lipinski paid off for me. When Lipinski decided to make a change in his ward organization late in 1990, he called my predecessor, Bill Krystyniak, into his office. Lipinski was not only the congressman, but also a ward committeeman, or ward boss. He had the political juice to elevate anyone in a political career. Lipinski had already decided that it was time for Krystyniak to move on. Although Krystyniak had been one of the hardest working aldermen in the city, he was also one of the worst politicians on a local level. Lipinski had taken so much heat from his top political operatives regarding his alderman's arrogance and refusal to help them with various requests that he needed to make a change. Lipinski had a new job for him.

Lipinski was a smart enough politician to bullshit Krystyniak into believing anything he would tell him. Lipinski had gotten a huge job from his friend, County Board President Dick Phelan. The job, which would be director of personnel for the Cook County Highway Division, would not only mean a significant pay increase for Krystyniak, but it would allow Lipinski to maneuver his precinct captain through Krystyniak's office, within access of actual county highway jobs. This would be an ideal situation for Lipinski, who could get Krystyniak out of his political office, and put him in a position where he would once again have total control over his every move. Within minutes after that meeting, Lipinski was ready to call Daley's people to proceed with the new alderman's appointment.

Before that call would finally be made, however, Lipinski asked me one more time to stay as his chief of staff. I respectfully declined, because now I had the chance to make a name for myself. Quite honestly, Lipinski was cheap, and didn't offer me any more money to stay. Before long, Daley submitted my name to the city council, which then referred it to the rules committee. After receiving a unanimous approval, the committee sent my nomination back to the full council. On December 10, 1990, they formally approved my place in the Chicago City Council.

With my wife next to me and my parents in the audience, City Clerk Walter Kozubowski swore me in as the new alderman of the 23rd Ward. The real highlight of the day occurred when Mayor Daley formally introduced me during his address to the city council. I basically said the year 1990 had been a most memorable one. I had finally passed the bar exam, gotten married to Kathleen, and had been appointed as the 23rd Ward alderman. I also said I didn't know which of these I was the most nervous about, and received a nice applause for my first speech in the council.

Soon after my appointment, Lipinski and I sat down in his office to take care of some basic housekeeping. In this business, it was no secret that Lipinski was the boss, and that, as ward committeeman, he ran the 23rd Ward democratic organization and called the shots. When he told me what I needed to pay him out of my vouchers, and whom to put on my payroll, there was no question in my mind what to do.

Each alderman at that time received a certain amount of money in the voucher system to pay rent or any other additional city expenses that could be put into the system, and to hire additional employees. Of course, I had to pay rent to Lipinski's family-run partnership that owned the building located at 5838 South Archer Avenue, where the aldermanic, state representative, and senator staffs at one time or another operated. In addition, his political office was located in the same building as the various governmental staffs. At that time, there was no separation or distinction between a political office and a governmental office, which meant that all duties and functions of city, state, and federal offices co-mingled each and every day.

Thus, it was no surprise to me when Lipinski gave me a couple of names to put on my city voucher program. One of those individuals was a man named Ed Malone, an older gentleman, who was probably in his late fifties when I met him. I'm really not sure how he had become friends with Lipinski, but they were more than just acquaintances. Mr. Malone owned a construction company, and his crew handled a number of projects, including the 5838 Building that Lipinski owned, as well as his personal residence. I personally saw the crew remodel Lipinski's basement and repair an outside deck, not to mention they turned a garage into a personal office for Lipinski, which included a skylight and white carpeting. On one or more occasions, when the roof over this office leaked, and stained the white carpet, I backed my car out for Malone's crew to fix the roof. Every major project for Lipinski was essentially done by Ed Malone's men. So there were questions asked when the congressman had told me to put Malone on a monthly stipend from my voucher program, even though he didn't live in Chicago.

Another person I put on my Lipinski voucher account was the wife of one of the organization's top precinct captains. Her inclusion was part of a purely financial arrangement to supplement their income as a young married couple. Her husband's precinct had always been number one, two, or three for Lipinski in votes. Since he had done such a good job politically, and he had just gotten married, that was essentially Lipinski's present to the newlyweds. Those were just two examples of me doing the committeeman's bidding, Chicago style.

Over the years, and after my father retired as a blacksmith from a local steel and manufacturing company, he constantly asked me to get him a part-time political job to supplement his social security. I finally persuaded Lipinski to give him a summer job with the Metropolitan Sanitary District, where he worked in the guard shack checking in trucks. He had that job for at least two summers, and they paid him more than $10.00 an hour. My dad loved that job, even when he worked the afternoon-to-midnight shift. Believe it or not, those were some of the happiest times in his life.

Still, my father often insinuated that I owed him at least a small-paying, genuine political position. It became my mission to find him such a job. It just so happened that the then-alderman, Krystyniak, who happened to serve on the safety committee, obtained small jobs from alderman Laurino, who was chairman of that committee. One day, I went to Krystyniak and started singing the blues about my father, who, for whatever reason, hadn't gotten his usual guard job at the sanitary district that past year. I played on his emotions. I told him, quite truthfully, that my father was giving me all kinds of grief about a part-time political job, and I asked if there was something he could do for him. The one thing I could always say about Bill Krystyniak is that if he liked you, he would try to help you and your family. Bill said there was a spot available on the traffic committee, but that before he could give it to my father, he would first have to get the congressman's approval. For some reason, it really didn't take too long for Lipinski's blessing, and shortly thereafter, in the late 1980s, Jim Laski, Sr. was on the Traffic and Public Safety Committee.

Honestly, I can't remember how long he was on that committee and how much he was paid, but I know it was for a decent period of time, and that he made at least a few thousand dollars. His basic job duties were surveying the 23rd Ward and listing the various locations of any traffic signs that needed to be repaired or replaced. In reality, though, my father's only real obligation (and this wasn't even mandatory) was to donate to the 23rd Ward democratic organization. Again, this was a case of old-time Chicago politics, in which officials were expected to take care of their organization's family members. The real irony was that about five years later, a federal investigation began probing ghost-payrolling at city hall.

Believe it or not, when this investigation hit home for my father and me, I had just recently become city clerk. One evening, I called my parents just to check in and see how things were going. My mom told me that the FBI had come to the house that day to speak to both of them. I was ready to pass out from shock.

My mother said, "It was no big deal. They just came by to ask a few questions."

In this business, if the FBI pays you a visit, you instinctively tell them, "No comment," as you hand them your attorney's card.

In my mom's case, however, not only did she and Dad talk to them, she invited them into the house for coffee and cookies. Although my mom and dad weren't worried, I was frantic. I picked up my phone to call my friend, State Senator Bob Molaro, to ask him to line up an attorney for my parents.

There wasn't much time between the FBI's visit and a federal subpoena handed over to my father, which required him to testify before a federal grand jury about his employment with the City Council Committee on Traffic and Public Safety. Now, for the first time, my parents were starting to get nervous. I immediately scheduled a meeting between them and the attorney Bob Molaro recommended.

During the whole ordeal, I spoke in very little detail with my father regarding his testimony. In fact, the only advice I remember giving was that if he wasn't absolutely certain about a particular answer, then he should say, "I can't recall," or, "I'm not sure." Well, on the day he was supposed to testify, he was not feeling good. In fact, I drove him to the MacNeil Hospital emergency room for heart tests. Although the test results proved negative, he only bought himself a temporary reprieve, because the U.S. Attorney rescheduled his grand jury testimony for the following week. He was, however, going to be given full immunity.

In the meantime, things were heating up at my parents' house, because my mom had not had a clear understanding of what my father had been doing. During that whole time period, my mom thought that he'd been working full-time, and that the money my father had made from the committee was being put into his own personal account. After everyone finally came clean to my mom, she was livid. I think if you were to ask her about it today, she would say the same thing she had said five years ago—we had not only been wrong, but stupid. To her, this was just another example of what was wrong with politics, and why, time and time again, she had asked me to find a different career.

On the day of my father's grand jury appearance, there was also a city council meeting scheduled. As usual, the mayor and the press gathered behind council chambers, and just kind of hung out. On that particular day, the council meeting was already in progress, when I took a break in the back of the chambers.

John Kass, from *The Chicago Tribune*, came up to me and quietly asked, "What's your father going to say today before the grand jury?"

Well, as soon as I heard that, I told John, "No comment," and strategically left the meeting.

No sooner had I gotten back to my office, when other media outlets called asking the same question. Of course, I didn't respond to any of their inquiries, and bunkered down in my office for the remainder of the day.

Before going home from city hall that day, I naturally wanted to stop to see my parents, and find out how my father's testimony had gone. My dad basically told me that he had been extremely nervous, but that he had tried to answer all of their questions to the best of his knowledge. That proved to be the last conversation that he and I had on the subject. It was obvious that we were both uncomfortable about the whole situation, and we felt that most things were probably better off left unsaid. To this day, I can honestly say I still don't what my father told the grand jury that day in the late 1990s.

It was only a day or two after my father's testimony that the U.S. Attorney's office decided to turn up the heat on me. Special FBI agents paid a surprise visit to city hall and dropped off a subpoena for me. The subpoena specifically called for all original documents relating to both part-time and full-time employment from my vouchers, from December 1990, to May 1995. That was clearly in response to my father's grand jury testimony.

On that evening, I met my in-laws, Pat and Wally, at their house for dinner. It was one of those days when no one wanted to cook, so we ordered fast food, and Kathleen had decided to pick up the dinner. I sat with her parents in their living room, watching the news on TV. One of the top stories that evening on Channel 7, ABC News, was about the FBI investigation into Chicago ghost-payrolling that had now shifted to me. The report went on to say that, the FBI had subpoenaed my records as alderman to see if I had participated in an illegal ghost-payrolling scheme.

Needless to say, I almost fell off my in-laws' couch. I remember standing in the kitchen in a state of mental paralysis, and didn't know what to do next, while I waited for Kathleen to return with our dinner. When she returned, I brought her up-to-speed on the situation. In the meantime, I spoke to my attorney, who wanted to review my voucher documents before we turned them over to the FBI.

The next few months were, to say the least, a little tense, as I submitted all my documents to the Feds. It was also the time when they began interviewing individuals, who in the past had been on my voucher lists. Those people included Bobby Byrnes, who was then second in command of the Secretary of State Police for the Illinois Secretary of State, Jessie White. Another person interviewed was Martha Miller, a former part-time employee who replaced my long-time friend and assistant, Janet Nielson, when she retired. I really don't know where the FBI's investigation into my vouchers took them, but fortunately, for me, they didn't have enough to indict me on any impropriety regarding ghost-payrolling.

The one unusual aspect regarding that investigation was that months later, the U.S. Attorney's office called my attorney, Garrett Reidy, and told him to pick up all my original voucher documents that they subpoenaed and reviewed. They indirectly told Reidy that they were finished with them. I certainly felt as if I, along with Lipinski and Krystyniak, had skated away from a situation with potentially serious legal ramifications for us all. Afterwards, besides the Lipinski selections, I was always careful about who would be placed on the voucher system. There may still have been people who had received more money than they had actually earned for the hours they'd worked, but the bottom line was that everyone worked, and there were no more ghosts after I left Lipinski in February of 1993.

CHAPTER 6

THE SPLIT

One of the many problems I always had with Lipinski was the people he surrounded himself with. Under-the-table dealings and other devious tricks, along with power orientation and entitlement were what most of Lipinski's political brain trust partners specialized in.

After two years of being alderman, I was beginning to realize that I could actually make my own decisions in the city council. Unfortunately, because I was appointed by the mayor to fill a vacancy, and my mentor/committeeman's (Congressman Lipinski's) organization supported me in my election, anything less than being a "yes" man would be considered treason, and I knew what the penalty for that was.

When I first got into office at the age of thirty-seven, I learned quickly how the game worked. When Daley needed a vote from me, he would send his people out to request my cooperation. In my case, his number one guy, the Intergovernmental Affairs Chief, Tim Degnan, would more often than not go directly to Lipinski. They told him how I should vote on a particular issue. Degnan, in turn, would call me into his office for my marching orders. I always felt that people should at least ask my opinion about an issue instead of just telling me how to vote.

It was during those first two years that I started to develop my own personality, and when the press corps had begun labeling me a "maverick." I disagreed with the mayor's curfews at Midway Airport, and proposed tax increases; both actions had made for interesting copy in the newspapers, but it also led to Lipinski questioning my motives.

In addition to my cavalier behavior in the council, I also developed a close friendship with Miriam Santos, the city treasurer. At the time, Miriam, a young Hispanic woman and an intelligent, articulate attorney, was a rising star, and attracted media attention, not only across the city, but also from the state, which touted her as a formidable challenger to Mayor Daley. She also had her run-ins with Daley regarding pension fund investments and control over her office. What started out as a very amicable relationship between them (Daley, in fact, had appointed her as city treasurer to fill a vacancy) turned into a bitter rivalry that bordered on hatred. It finally reached a point where they stopped talking to each other altogether.

Thus, as the newspapers began to report the friendship between Miriam and myself, the Daley operatives and Lipinski wondered how close we actually were. In fact, Lipinski twice called me into his office after he spoke with Michael Sneed, a well-informed columnist (for the most part) from *The Sun-Times*. Ms. Sneed asked him if he knew anything about a "Laski and Santos" romantic relationship. When Lipinski asked me about it, I told him it made an interesting story, but that we were just good friends. In fact, I also told him that my wife and Miriam were close friends, and that we occasionally all went out to dinner together. I was beginning to believe that my trustworthiness was now the subject of concern in the Lipinski organization.

Lipinski's organization was run by four guys who were called his "quadrant leaders." The 23rd Ward, at the time, had seventy-four precincts that were divided up among four so-called leaders who were in charge of the precinct captains and their workers. All of them reported to the leaders, respectively—for jobs, promotions, and raises, etc. The four quadrant leaders were his lifeline for getting out the vote. Unfortunately, three out of those four leaders were vindictive political hacks who were responsible for getting rid of former alderman Krystyniak. They had Lipinski's ear and were starting to make my life miserable. When Daley started to cut back on city jobs for Lipinski's organization members, those three blamed that decision on my rebel attitude toward the mayor. In fact, Daley began restricting jobs to all elected officials' organization. Unfortunately, Lipinski's brain trust (which included the Prince of Darkness, Joe Novak, who, in my opinion, was a washed-up hack who made a living tearing people apart on both a political and personal level) had convinced the congressman that I had become a liability.

The fact of the matter was that those individuals were instrumental in my predecessor's political demise. They convinced Lipinski to dump Krystyniak as alderman and to put me in his spot. They felt I would be easier to deal with. Even though Krystyniak was given a higher-paying job, the powers-to-be wanted him out, and they had gotten their wish. As time went on, I expressed my concerns to Lipinski about the quadrant leaders. Quite honestly, I began to worry about my future in his organization.

By the end of my second year in office, I knew that I had to leave Lipinski. All I needed was the right issue on which I could generate some public support. That was an idea I had pondered before, but now I had to wait for the perfect time to execute my plan.

My opportunity presented itself in January 1993, when Daley came out with a proposed property tax increase to pay for hiring additional city police officers. He believed that this was a perfect scenario for him to get away with a tax raise, under the guise of a public safety concern. During my short term as alderman, I always openly advocated collecting the money owed the city, including unpaid parking and business license fees before going to the taxpayers to ask them to dig into their pockets. A tax increase was an issue that many of the aldermen on the city's southwest sides (which were blue collar areas) would have a hard time selling to their constituents. However, this vote was extremely important to Daley, because he needed to flex his political muscle in the city counsel. In his first couple of years as mayor, council votes were always fairly one-sided— in his favor. Out of a possible fifty votes (fifty alderman representing fifty city wards), the closest thing to an anti-Daley vote might have been thirty-five Daley votes against fifteen nay votes. That's exactly the type of stranglehold he had on the council.

Nevertheless, Tim Degnan called Lipinski and informed him that the mayor needed my vote. Shortly thereafter, Lipinski summoned me to his office for my marching orders. However, I told him I had my reservations about voting the mayor's way. Lipinski, who had already taken grief from his own organization members, was now getting it from Daley's inner circle regarding my loyalty. They gave what I had been hoping for—an ultimatum. If I wouldn't vote for the mayor's tax increase, I would be requested to leave his organization and go out on my own. He gave me until the end of the day on Monday to inform him of my decision—that meant that I would have the entire weekend to think the matter over.

What most people didn't know was that I already had made plans in place to move my operation to another location. Over the past year, I started a new law practice in the neighborhood with a friend of mine, Mike Laird, and we rented a large storefront that previously was an auto parts store. I had some good friends in the construction business who had converted 1,700 square feet of nothing into a beautiful building with at least six individual offices and a reception area, with additional space to burn. So my plan was to simply move my aldermanic operation to the law office. I spoke to my partner, who had no problem with the move, because it would eventually bring more business to the practice.

I also lined up my staff. Janet Nielson, my secretary, and Don Zochowski, my legislative assistant, were already working for me at Lipinski's office. During the past few weeks, Janet and Don had come to my home, and given me moral support and encouraged me to move out. There was no question that I felt much more comfortable with them on board. They had both been with me for years, and their loyalty was second-to-none.

Of course, the last piece of the puzzle for my move was Ray Drish, who had been with me in one capacity or another since 1979. He was my political guru and go-to guy, and was currently working in Streets and Sanitation, but was ready to leave as soon as I made the split. In fact, he was going to use his two weeks of vacation to help set up the office.

I made sure that I had everyone up to speed with my plans. There were two more individuals who had volunteered to help with the move—Bob Byrnes, a young, aggressive guy, who to this day has remained loyal, and Al Garza. Although he was on my staff, Garza was being paid by the city's finance committee as a political favor. What I didn't know at the time was that he was a traitor, but since he was never part of the inner circle, he never had any real information to hurt me.

During the course of the past couple weeks, I worked with Ray, Don, and Janet and they helped me get the offices ready for the move to our new location. Ray was already working with the phone company to establish a couple of dedicated lines for the new alderman's office. We actually had an informational flyer regarding my new address already designed by Bob Byrnes, and it was scheduled to be distributed to every resident in the 23rd Ward. My staff also made arrangements to secure a date for my first fundraiser a couple of weeks after the move.

The key to this whole split was for my operation to be up and running as soon as I had moved from Lipinski's building. Even more important was the secrecy, from start to finish, that my entire staff had to maintain during the planning.

All that was left now was for me to actually make the move. If there was one thing I was certain about, it was that I was scared to death. My wife Kathleen and I had recently purchased a home, and she was five months pregnant with our daughter Nina. Any number of seasoned political experts would tell you that I was committing political suicide. I was about to walk out on my so-called mentor, who had been the congressman for the past ten years, as well as ward committeeman of one of the most powerful Democratic districts in the entire city of Chicago. In fact, the true statesmen of the city council, the most eloquent speaker and chairman of the most powerful committee (finance) in city hall, alderman Ed Burke, told me that it would take a miracle for me to survive politically if I left

Lipinski. All this made me wonder if I had taken on too much by trying to climb such a seemingly insurmountable mountain.

That weekend, Kathleen and I went over our options one last time. No matter how much we had already planned, it wasn't too late to pull the plug. I also knew, as time went on, that keeping this whole operation a total secret would be next to impossible. Lipinski had heard a rumor more than once about my intentions to leave. As nervous as my wife and I were, however, we also knew with absolute certainty, that I had no political future with Lipinski. The people around him were poisoning his mind, and it would be just a matter of time when he would relegate me to some obscure administrative job. I didn't want to end up like my predecessor, Bill Krystyniak, who had worked his ass off for Lipinski, but had never gotten the respect he had deserved because of the inner circle's cut-throat mentality.

Although I knew the months ahead would be chaotic, I also found a new energy within me. I really believed I had a purpose now. I believed that I could actually make decisions on my own, and maybe, along the way, help my community's working men and women. Don't get me wrong. I had an ego, and certainly the reputation for being a publicity hound, but I always had the intention of getting something back for my ward. Ultimately, Kathleen and I both knew that we were rolling the dice, but still, we hoped for the best.

Monday quickly arrived, and the mood throughout the office seemed both quiet and a little tense. It was as if everyone was waiting for something to explode. As I sat in my office, I was acting as discreet as possible when I gathered my personal belongings and placed them in certain desk drawers, which only Don knew anything about. Don was handling the moving part of the project, and he had his plans in place for days now, especially since we needed to take important files with us.

I didn't discuss my plans with any other elected official except Miriam Santos. She already knew that I was moving when she called me at the office that day to wish me well. We were already plotting different strategies, such as placing different items in Sneed's *Sun-Times* gossip column, including Miriam and I having dinner together, her plans to run against Daley for mayor, and my becoming her city treasurer. There was no question that she and I were a little devious in our own right, but that was due in large part to our paranoia over Daley's possibly coming after both of us.

As the afternoon progressed, I tried to avoid seeing Lipinski until the absolute end of the day. Even though I thought I knew what I was going to do, a small part of me still had some long-term fears. Regardless of those concerns, I was ready to do what some people had always wanted to do, and what few had ever attempted—to take on Daley, Lipinski, and the Democratic machine. The time had come in this city to take on the establishment.

It was close to 5:00 p.m., and I was taking a final inventory of my belongings when Lipinski appeared in my doorway and told me to report to his office. I anxiously walked down the hallway to the end of the building where his office was located, took a deep breath, and walked in. He was already sitting at his desk as I sat in one of the two chairs directly in front of him. There seemed to be a kind of eerie moment of silence before either of us spoke.

Before I could even get comfortable, Lipinski came right out and asked me how I was going to vote on Daley's tax proposal.

I didn't think I had had it in me, but I looked him directly in the eyes and said, "Congressman, I can't vote for it."

His reaction was kind of a mixed bag. It appeared as if he didn't believe my answer, but it also appeared as if he had half expected it. We didn't spend much time discussing the voting issue. Instead, we spent time discussing how I felt he had unwisely entrusted his organization to a bunch of incompetent, mean-spirited bullies who had made my decision to leave him much easier.

The end of our conversation was civil, except for Lipinski's ominous warning to prepare myself for the day when he would take the aldermanic seat back from me. He snickered when he told me that voters have short memories.

I quickly replied, "Not always, but we'll both know the answer after the next election."

Lipinski then came around to the front of his desk. As I stood up, we firmly shook hands while leaning forward and respectfully embraced each other as our final goodbye. As I started to walk out

46

of his office, he asked me when I would be moving my things out of the building.

I smiled, and answered, "Tonight."

Suddenly, his tone changed, and he arrogantly told me that I couldn't move anything out until 7:00 p.m., when some of his staff members would be present to supervise and approve of what I would take out of the building.

I simply said, "Thank you," and left that building for the last time as a member of his organization.

I then told Don and Janet, both of whom were waiting for me, to gather up everything, because we had to move out that night. I reminded him that when moving the files, not only would Don be supervised, but realistically, we would only get one shot at this, because tomorrow the locks would be changed throughout the building. As I drove home, I had a profound sense of relief. Even though the future was uncertain, I felt as if I had regained control over my life again.

Don proved not only slick and cunning, but gutsy when moving the files. He borrowed a station wagon and enlisted his brother Ken and a friend to move everything. Lipinski's Chief of Staff, George Edwards, told Don exactly what files could be removed. As soon as Don was told he couldn't take something, he took it anyway. He actually grabbed files and political paperwork that really wasn't ours, but since Lipinski's people were giving him such a hard time, he said, "Screw it."

What was so aggravating was that Lipinski's people wanted to keep all the files that related to city business, including all the services provided to ward residents. In addition, those files were zoning permit and favor files I not only wanted, but was entitled to have.

During the actual move, Lipinski called Don and Janet individually back to his office to persuade each of them to stay with the organization. To their credit, they stood up to Lipinski, respectfully declined, and went back to my office to finish moving everything.

While Don and his brother Ken were loading up the station wagon, a CBS Channel 2 news crew had pulled up to film the moving operation. I never found out who actually called the media, but I suspect my friend Miriam Santos was somehow involved. Once word of the move got out, it spread like wildfire through the entire media circuit.

After Janet and Don were finished, they headed to the law office to drop off all the files and my personal belongings. In the meantime, Lipinski's office was up for grabs, with all the precinct captains and staff trying to figure out what my departure would mean politically down the road. Overall, my plan had gone perfectly. I had broken my ties with the congressman, grabbed all the files I needed and then some from his office, and had my new office, with its own phone lines, ready to go by the next day, with the media ready to jump out of their shoes. Most importantly, I had kept Lipinski off balance and in the dark. By the time the smoke cleared and he realized my intentions, it was too late to stop me.

At the end of the evening, my inner circle gathered at my house to watch the 10:00 p.m. news. As we turned on the CBS Channel 2 news report, the top story was, "Laski being kicked out of Lipinski's organization," along with a video of Don loading up the station wagon. Everyone in my basement cheered as the TV anchors reported that I was kicked out of Lipinski's organization because of my refusal to vote for Daley's increase, despite both the mayor's and the congressman's threats. The story couldn't have been more favorable for me if I had written it myself. What made that evening so ironic were the news report's references to loyalty, and to a long-time friend leaving a friend and bucking the establishment. While sitting on my couch, I smiled and basked in my newfound stardom. Sitting right there next to me, and leading the charge for a new beginning, was my loyal friend, Mick Jones, who who had told me years before, to sell out during the Hired Truck Program scandal in 2005.

I couldn't even begin to describe the next morning and the weeks to follow. Every TV and radio station, along with all the print media, called my new office at 6808 West Archer Avenue. That was also part of my plan—to fax all the media outlets my new phone number. The whole story about my having stood up for the taxpayers had created a media frenzy. I soon found myself doing interview after interview to solidify my new position as the true rebel of city council. What probably gave me the most satisfaction was the number of my council colleagues who called not only to congratulate me, but also to tell me that their own offices were being flooded with phone calls from their constituents, telling them to stand up with me and to vote down Daley's tax increase.

Over the next few days, the news reports continued to center on the upcoming city council meeting, when the Daley/Laski feud would come to a head. The real question would be if Daley had enough power to offset the media juggernaut I had put in place against the proposed tax increase. Each time Daley insisted that his proposal had enough votes in the council to pass, the press would reach out for me, and I would simply say that the votes weren't there.

Soon, other aldermen told the media that if Laski wasn't going to vote for the tax increase, neither would they. Finally, elected officials in the Chicago city council stood up and said they weren't going to put their necks on the line for Daley. It came down to their constituents holding them accountable for their vote. The political establishment, even Daley himself, could not convince or strong-arm these aldermen to vote for his measure. Both Daley and I drew our lines in the sand, and we were just waiting to see who would make the next move. Everyone in the city couldn't wait to see how the votes would line up, because now the issue was personal—either they were with the mayor, or they weren't.

Unfortunately, we never found out who had the votes, because on the following Friday afternoon, I received a call from a city hall reporter who informed me that President Clinton's Secretary of Commerce Brown had just spoken to Mayor Daley and promised him the necessary federal funding for additional police, thereby avoiding the need for a tax increase. Of course, every reporter who then called me wanted to portray this as a Laski victory over Daley, and all I kept repeating to them was that the real winners were the taxpayers. Even to the bitter end, Daley arrogantly rambled on to the press that he had enough votes in the city council to pass his ordinance, but that, fortunately, the Clinton administration had helped him out.

When all was said and done, I put myself in a good position with the general public. My two major concerns, however, were the bitterness I would now face from the Daley administration, and the bounty the Lipinski organization would place on my head to destroy me in the next election.

The following months were very exciting, because for the first time in my life, I was totally in control of my political future. Not only did I now have my aldermanic operation in place, but also since the split with Lipinski, I recruited close to one-hundred people to my own organization. The only thing left on my agenda in my immediate future was to make sure that I was securely positioned in the community for my re-election run, which would be less than two years away.

CHAPTER 7

THE DEAL

Following the well-publicized split with Lipinski, my political stock rose city-wide, as the interviews and stories continued. Although the free press I received was worth millions, I was still distracted by the Lipinski/Laski feud in the 23rd Ward. There were back-and-forth accusations by each organization every week in the local newspapers, along with bricks being thrown through office windows, tires being slashed, and threats ushered on the streets. I received so many harassing phone calls at the office that I had the phone company tap my line for two weeks. After those two weeks were up, the phone company sent me information that showed that most, if not all of the harassing calls and hang-ups came from Lipinski's office. I gained one full day of media attention on that issue alone. Soon, however, everyone in the community started to tire of the petty bickering between our offices. I began to think that maybe it was time to come to a temporary truce with Lipinski.

During this whole ordeal, a mutual friend tried to find some common ground whereby Lipinski and I could at least sit down and talk. After a month or so passed, this man, State Senator Bob Molaro, arranged a meeting between Lipinski and me on a Saturday morning at 8:00 a.m. at a place called the Corner Bakery Restaurant, on 79th and Cicero Avenue, in Burbank, a suburb of Chicago. We had both known Bob for some time. He was a personable guy whom everyone liked, and whom I respected for his political insight. The former committeeman of the neighboring 12th Ward had politics in his veins. When he told me that the meeting was set, I was cautiously optimistic that it would be mutually beneficial.

I pulled up to the restaurant about five minutes early, sat in the car, and had a cigarette. At 8:00 a.m. sharp, I went in and got a table in the corner. I wasn't surprised when Lipinski strolled in ten minutes fashionably late. As soon as he sat down, I knew that the meeting was going to be a waste of time. He was arrogant from the get-go, and told me that he was coming after me, and that my days in politics were numbered. Initially, I tried to be respectful, but by the end of our conversation, which wasn't longer than fifteen minutes, we accepted an all-out battle in the ward for my job. He quickly drank the coffee he had ordered, put three dollars on the table, got up from his chair, and, without saying a word, left the restaurant. I took another two minutes to calm down. I sipped my orange juice, and asked the waitress for the check. All I thought about was how arrogant that son of a bitch was, and the satisfaction I would have in winning re-election and defeating his organization. Needless to say, I couldn't wait to see Bob and tell him to get ready for a political blood bath, because it was time for me to bury Lipinski.

A couple of days later, Bob and I met at a local restaurant. Lipinski had already told him about our meeting, and that maybe he had been a little hard on me. Although I had calmed down since that last meeting, I was still reluctant to see Lipinski any time soon. While we sat there, a very good mutual friend and a former colleague of mine, Mark Fary, who, at one time, was the alderman of the 12th Ward when Molaro was committeeman, joined us. Mark, like Bob, was very personable, and was also interested in finding a peaceful solution to the problems Lipinski and I had with each other. It was during this meeting in the spring of 1994 that they floated an interesting idea.

We were sitting around a table talking about politics in general, when Bob reminded us that the city clerk's spot would be open in the next election. The previous clerk, Walter Kozubowski, had been convicted on corruption charges the year before, and Daley appointed businessman Ernie Wish to finish Kozubowski's term, which had had less than two years left. Because of that fact, a special election had not been required. It was widely known that Mr. Wisk, a wealthy entrepreneur, had no real interest in actually running for the city clerk job. For all intents and purposes, that position would be open for someone else. I already knew that following the next election, newly elected officials would receive a salary increase. An alderman's salary would increase from $55,000.00 to $75,000.00, and the city clerk's current $85,000.00 would increase to $105,000.00.

I had to stop and think. I could almost double my salary if I ran and won that spot. Kathleen was no longer working; our daughter Nina had just been born; and the idea of potentially earning over $100,000.00 a year was very enticing. My only problem initially was my ego, because, if I ran for city clerk, I would have to give up the alderman's seat, which I now treasured. I did not intend to ever give back to Lipinski.

As we sat there, Bob and Mark actually presented me with a scenario that at first looked like a win/win situation for everyone. They felt that if I agreed to run for city clerk, Lipinski would support me, and recruit many of his friends from the Democratic Party to help me. In return, I would support his candidate for alderman, and maybe throw him a couple of jobs from the clerk's office. As city clerk, I would have control over at least one hundred jobs or so, which would also help me to build up my own organization. Although they both agreed that I could beat Lipinski's candidate for alderman, they also pointed out that it would take a monumental battle that would cost both sides, financially and emotionally. Their proposal would avoid all that bloodshed and basically allow Lipinski and me to save face, and temporarily bury the hatchet. This was definitely something I needed to talk to Kathleen about as soon as possible.

The next day, Bob came over to my house and spent a good three hours going over the whole scenario, from top to bottom. What intrigued Kathleen the most was the fact I could run citywide, which would allow us to at least consider moving to Chicago's north side, something she had always wanted to do. More importantly, however, was the opportunity to alleviate some of the pressure and anxiety that still existed in the community because of my feud with Lipinski. More than anything else, Kathleen wanted some peace and quiet in the neighborhood. Even before Bob left the house, I had definitely decided to run for city clerk, but before I could formally announce my plans, I needed to talk to my organization's staff and key members. The biggest obstacle ahead of me would be raising some significant money to run a citywide election, because there would still be people who wouldn't know me.

Although the election wasn't until February 1995, I made my formal announcement to run, down at city hall, in June of 1994, with Kathleen, Bob, and my staff standing next to me. It was amusing that before I announced my intention to run for city clerk, several reporters were speculating that I decided to run for mayor. In fact, the day before my announcement, a city hall reporter actually called Loyola Hospital, where I was visiting my daughter who had viral meningitis, to see if she could get the inside scoop before my press conference the next day.

To say the least, the following months were exciting. I reached an agreement or truce with Lipinski, and Bob helped line up support, not only in the city council, but also from elected officials in both county and state government. I campaigned vigorously across Chicago, and rose close to $300,000 for the campaign. I ran against State Senator Ricky Hendon and Ron Jasinski Herbert (a Polish TV and radio personality from the north side) in the Democratic Primary.

Although most political pundits thought I would win, I never let up for a second. Honestly, my campaign manager, Ray Drish, and my media consultant, Eric Adelstein, wouldn't stop pushing me. I actually campaigned all the way through election day. Honestly, along with Molaro, the three of them orchestrated practically my entire campaign.

Election night was spent at the Chicago Hilton Hotel on Michigan Avenue. We went to the Hilton, because Eric knew that was where Daley and his supporters planned to be, which meant that the media would have an opportunity to interview us both, since we would be in the same building.

Kathleen put together most of that evening's festivities, which included renting one of the ballrooms for the anticipated victory announcement and party. In addition, we also rented one of the presidential suites for close friends and family to watch the election results. Kathleen also had the hotel book additional phone lines in the suite, so Ray, Don, and Janet could keep getting up-to-the-minute election results.

Around 10:00 p.m., just after Daley concluded his victory speech, Kathleen, (who was holding our sleeping daughter, Nina), and the rest of my family, along with my staff and close friends, headed to the ballroom. There, hundreds of friends and supporters were waving campaign signs, and the media was waiting for me. Everyone stood and cheered, while the band played "We Are the Champions" as I walked into the ballroom. Those few minutes were the most exhilarating of my entire political career. I really felt that anything else I would accomplish after that would be mere icing on the cake. I made a short victory speech, and partied, all the way back up to the suite, until the wee hours of the morning.

Because I had won the Democratic Primary, I still had to face a Republican opponent, Michael Howlett, in the general election in April of 1995. In Chicago, a truly Democratic city, if you won the Primary, you had a better than 99 percent chance of winning the general election. On the first Tuesday in May of 1995, I was officially elected Chicago City Clerk.

It was during my first few years as city clerk that we really took an antiquated office and moved it into the twenty-first century. I actually took that office from virtual obscurity to one that created programs to assist Chicago's citizens. My carbon monoxide ordinance, the first of its kind in the nation, saved countless lives in Chicago by requiring the installation of detectors in residential units across the city. In addition, we created a children's ID card and a senior citizen's ID card to address safety and health issues for 100,000 children and seniors who received these life-saving cards from my office.

It was probably after my first term as clerk when I became a little more complacent, and maybe even reckless. In 1999, during my first re-election campaign, even though I had run unopposed, I had received more votes than any other candidate that year, including Daley. Soon, various reporters started talking about my possibly becoming a mayoral candidate in 2003. My ego was now sky-high, and I actually started to think I was invincible. During the summer of 1999, I began to spend quite a bit of time on the golf course, either at various outings, or just for the day, with my staff. There, I would cut deals for myself, and for friends like Mick Jones. This was the time I could have spent with my family, building up my law practice, or just taking a step back to re-assess both my personal and political values. Instead, I continued to embrace the culture of Chicago politics that held that I should do anything necessary to acquire more money and power.

CHAPTER 8

DALEY I

Anybody who has grown up in the "windy city" will tell you that you cannot discuss Chicago politics without mentioning the name "Daley." The Daleys are to Chicago what the Kennedys are to Boston—political aristocracy. The king was Richard J. Daley, who served as mayor from 1955 until his death in 1976. His successor to the throne, his eldest son, Richard M. Daley, had to wait thirteen years for his own coronation. However, since his election as mayor in 1989, he can boast of a record that rivaled, if not surpassed, that of his illustrious father.

It all started with Richard J. Daley being widely regarded as the last of America's old-style big city mayors. Daley so dominated city hall that the term "hands-on" administrator could have been invented for him. He deserves credit for the programs that kept Chicago thriving when other Midwestern cities, heavily dependent on the sagging steel industry, were struggling, but his record was not without controversy. As head of Chicago's formidable Democratic machine, with ties to both the Kennedy family and Lyndon B. Johnson, there were constant rumors of patronage abuse and corruption, although he was never accused. In fact, many Chicagoans to this day refer to him fondly as "Boss Daley," "Old Man Daley," or "Daley Senior."

Richard J. Daley served twenty-one years as mayor, a record that his son Richard M. Daley, was fast closing in on. Daley, Jr. was elected in 1989, and re-elected in 1991, 1995, 1999, 2003, and 2007. *Time Magazine's* April 25, 2007 issue praised Daley as the best of five large U.S. city mayors. His achievements include modernizing the Chicago Transit Authority, the construction of Millennium Park, increased environmental legislation, and the development of Chicago's north, south, and west sides.

When I think about Rich Daley, Jr., a few things run through my mind. First and foremost, he is the most powerful mayor in this country. Secondly, he is a dedicated family man. In any conversation I'd ever had with the man, he'd always asked about my family, or talked about his in general. I will always give him credit for his strong respect for family values.

On the other side of the coin, he is a true politician, as clever as a fox, who knows more about what goes on in city hall than what he wants people to believe. In my opinion, he is calculating, short-fused, thin-skinned, and stubborn, as well as an average administrator, and a vengeful politician. I'm not saying that I know Daley's inner secrets, but what I do know is how he and the inner circle had dealt with me over fifteen years, and about some of the policies he had orchestrated and known about.

A good friend of mine who happens to be an elected official, once told me that Daley has three lists in politics. His A list consists of Tim Degnan and maybe a couple of other people, like Jeremiah Jancey, but that's about it. Then you have his C list, which consists of the majority of elected officials that he'll deal with on a periodic basis when he's in a good mood, or when he need a political favor. Of course, there is an F list (or, as some would refer to it, his "shit" list); if anyone is on that list, he or she would have to move mountains to get any cooperation or help from Daley. "F" list members might have to talk to three or four of his people, and wait over six months, before getting an automatic "No." I also believe there may be a B list for people like Victor Reyes, Robert Sorich, John Doerrer, and Shelia O'Grady. He would trust those people to a certain extent, and in my opinion, on a limited basis, depending on the issue.

About five years ago, when I was having a tough go of it with the Channel 2 investigation into alleged time sheet fraud, I needed to sit down with Daley to assure him that I was on solid ground, regardless of any ongoing investigation.

When I met with him in his conference room, he immediately leaned over to me and whispered, "Have you heard anything?"

Quite honestly, I had no clue as to what he was talking about.

When he asked me the same question again, I answered, "Mayor, have I heard anything about *what?*"

He then looked impatiently at me, and kept jerking his head back and forth as he asked, "Have you heard from anybody down the street?"

Finally, the light went off in my head, because I knew he was talking about the U.S. Attorney and the FBI. He always referred to them as "the people down the street."

I then gave him a firm and unequivocal "No!"

Although the FBI was reviewing the Channel 2 tapes, they had never contacted me personally.

It was at that moment that Daley sat back and said, "I want to give you some advice."

To say the least, I was curious about what kind of advice the mayor of Chicago would give me. Although we were in his personal conference room, he spoke quietly, as if he feared his office were bugged. He told me in a very serious tone of voice, that to survive in this business, I had to have a buffer. At that point, he reminded me of Captain Queeg in *The Caine Mutiny*, when he warned me that everyone would try to get me, especially the press. He told me that I needed someone to protect me, and where the buck would stop, implying that everything would end with that person. In my opinion, Daley was forever surrounding himself with his own personal buffers.

The one thing I learned about Daley and his crew was their position on legislative proposals. That position was clearly one that favored entitlement. If an idea had not come from or been cleared by him or his staff, the idea was deemed unworthy of consideration. In other words, it would never see the light of day out of the committee.

I can certainly speak from experience on this issue, and also attest to the ruthlessness and deceit of Daley's office in taking ownership of ideas that quite frankly either had never begun there, or had lain dormant from lack of interest.

Back in 1994, when I was the 23rd Ward alderman, I campaigned for the city clerk's office. At that time, my media coordinator, Eric Adelstein, came up with an idea about child support. Every year the city clerk issues over 100,000 business licenses. It was brought to my attention that some of those business owners were in arrears in child support payments. So my proposal, through Eric, was to deny the issuance of business licenses to owners who were delinquent, or in arrears, in child support payments. Subsequently, the proposal was sent to the finance committee for a hearing, and put on the back burner. After my election as city clerk, I decided to fulfill that campaign promise, and get my child support legislation passed. I spoke to Chairman Burke about resurrecting the idea. He told me that a sufficient amount of time had passed, and no action had been taken. Now it was necessary to re-introduce the proposal as a new idea, and start the ball rolling all over again. When the proposal was once again sent to Burke's committee, Victor Reyes, Daley's intergovernmental affairs guy, respectfully requested that I hold off on any child support legislation hearings. Although the mayor supported the idea, he wanted to join forces with me, and have me be a co-sponsor with him. I agreed, knowing that with Daley's support, the legislation would pass.

Unfortunately, many weeks went by without a word. After I made some inquiries, suddenly one morning my secretary received a call from the mayor's office. They had invited me to a press conference the next morning regarding his announcement introducing "groundbreaking" child-support legislation. Once I heard this, I was livid. I immediately called Victor Reyes, and he told me not to worry, because the mayor would properly acknowledge me at the press conference.

The next day I stood in the mayor's press conference room with about twenty other people, including aldermen and commissioners. My only involvement at the press conference would be to stand there and applaud the mayor. In all fairness, the mayor thanked me publicly for having worked with him on the legislation that he had just taken full credit for. Although some of the media correctly reported the event by noting my involvement in the entire process early on, others simply gave Daley, as usual, praise for everything. In my mind, I felt as if I had received some vindication when, later, NOW, the National Organization of Women, came to my office with a leadership award for having championed child support in the City of Chicago. (I think, as a side bar, it is worth noting that my child support legislation was directly responsible for having collected over one million dollars in back child support.)

Another glaring example of Daley's entitlement issues took place in 1998, when my chief of staff, Ray Drish, came up with a brilliant idea regarding the issue of non-payment of delinquent parking tickets, water bills, and the purchase of vehicle stickers by certain city employees. Ray and I had already known there was a ton of money out there from average citizens who had not paid their obligations to the city. We also agreed that we couldn't publicly ask everyone else to pay their bills when many of our own city employees had not fulfilled their responsibilities. In fact, Ray and I had done some preliminary research with a friend of ours in the city's data department, and had conducted a sampling of city employees. The numbers had been unbelievable, as far as money owed, and that was just the tip of the iceberg.

Meanwhile, we had to plan next year's budget. I, along with my executive staff, met with the mayor's budget director, who, at the time, was Diane Aiogotti, along with her staff. At the meeting, we discussed budget needs for the clerk's office, including raises for some of my key people. As the meeting progressed, Ms. Aigotti asked me about any new ideas for revenue-generating programs. At that point, I told her about my plan for an employee indebtedness program. Surprisingly, she responded by saying we could talk about it later, but for now, we should keep the idea to ourselves, and especially away from the press. She was clearly deathly afraid of repercussions to, and embarrassment for, the mayor.

In the meantime, the covert research Ray and I were doing with our friend was taking longer than I wanted. Every day, Ray would come into my office with a new figure of money owed, which had kept growing. However, with close to 40,000 employees to look at individually, the program was going to take time, and time was something I didn't have. I didn't trust Daley's people, including his budget director. I wanted to get my information out to the press as soon as I thought I had completed enough research. We couldn't possibly check out every single employee, so I told Ray that once his research had showed that there was at least one million dollars owed to the city, I would be good to go.

My paranoia soon forced me to introduce my indebtedness program to the city council, even though it had already been sent to the finance committee for a slow death. I wanted to be on record when I needed to make an announcement. Of course, as soon as my legislation had been introduced, the budget director called the mayor's people. They, in turn, came to see me. One such individual was John McDonough, who had worked for intergovernmental affairs.

When I sat down with McDonough, I didn't beat around the bush or bullshit with him. I told him that Chicago employees owed hundreds of thousands of dollars in unpaid bills to the city. I also told him that I wanted him to forward this information to Victor Reyes and the mayor, and that I wanted to work with the mayor to make a joint announcement of our intention to go after deadbeat city employees. Of course, McDonough took notes as I spoke, but I think he just threw them out when he left the office. In any event, he told me that he would get back to me on the issue, which he never did.

In the meantime, our research went on. About two months later, Ray told me what I'd been waiting to hear.

"Clerk, we're over one million dollars, and that's just the tip of the iceberg!"

As soon as I heard that, I called McDonough, and asked him to come to my office. When he arrived, I told him that I was over one million dollars in my research, and that this was his last chance to talk to Victor Reyes or Pat Huels, the floor leader. I told him that in approximately two days, I would go before the city council budget committee. I further informed him that if any alderman on the committee asked me about my indebtedness program, I'd reveal all. I was frustrated by the lack of interest on the part of Reyes and the rest of the powers-to-be. I warned McDonough that this issue would explode right in the mayor's face.

Two days later, in October 1998, during a city budget meeting, I was sitting at the front of the council chamber on the rostrum, at the table below the mayor's chair and desk. It had been a quiet day, with maybe only fifteen aldermen and about fifty in attendance, including Pat Huels. As far as the press was concerned, the only representative present was Bob Crawford from WBB Radio, who had been hounding me for weeks after I told him that I had a huge story for him, and that today might be the day.

While I sat there, some of the aldermen asked me basic questions about my budget, and requests I had made regarding funding additional projects. I had not intended to grandstand by just throwing out my information at the meeting, but if an alderman asked me a question about the issue, that would be a different story. I remember Alderman Huels sitting in his usual seat in the first row, just staring at me and wondering what I was going to do.

Soon, the questions started to wind down, and I began to think that my opportunity was in danger of slipping away. Then, all of a sudden, Alderman Ricardo Munoz of the 22nd Ward raised his hand to speak. He thanked me for having attended and answering all their questions. He complemented me on my office for its efficiency.

After those kind remarks, Munoz asked, "By the way, City Clerk Laski, how is your indebtedness program going? Have you found out anything?"

My eyes lit up. At last, my opportunity had arrived.

I told Munoz, "You bet I have."

I proceeded to tell him that my research showed that city employees owed over one million dollars and that they had failed to pay for past due parking tickets, water bills, and vehicle stickers. The aldermen at the meeting (who had been barely awake) quickly got an adrenalin rush. Meanwhile, Bob Crawford ran from the chambers to the press room to break the story over the radio station.

Afterwards, wherever Daley went in the city, the press corps followed, asking him about the scandal. At one point, some of the media asked him how he felt about City Clerk Laski's having disclosed the information and bringing the situation to the public's attention.

Quite angrily, he responded, "It's not about credit, Laski, or Daley. It's about the taxpayers of this city. Trust me, everyone who works for the city will pay their debts."

Everyone knew that he meant business. However, everyone in the media knew that I had shown him up, and that didn't sit well with him.

I continued doing interviews across the city, and I scheduled a half-hour TV interview with WTTW, Channel 11, Chicago's public broadcasting station. What would make this interview so different from the rest was that I would be joined by three other guests, including Diane Aigotti, Steve Neal from *The Sun-Times*, and a professor from DePaul University. The taped interview would occur on October 29, 1996, the day after my forty-third birthday, at 4:00 p.m. It would air at 7:00 p.m. that evening.

I remember being ready to leave the house for the interview, when suddenly the phone rang. On the line was Alderman Pat Huels. Quite honestly, I was shocked, because the word had been that Daley's people had been writing my obituary, and that they would not lift a finger to help me. However, when I answered the phone that evening, I couldn't have been more pleasant. The alderman was an astute politician who had always been honest and upfront with me. I really had never had a problem with him personally, nor did I want one now. He had called to tell me that this was one hell of a story, but that the mayor was not angry with me. They mentioned that he wanted to help me with anything I needed for my budget. As nice as all of that sounded, I knew there was a catch, and a catch there was. Huels then reminded me of the interview I was getting ready to leave for, and he asked me to do him and the mayor a favor—to lay low on the show, not attack the budget director personally during the taping, and under any circumstances, I was not to be critical of Daley. In return, he promised to take care of me. He told me that we would meet the following week, on Election Day morning, at his club downtown.

The show itself went very well. The moderator was Phil Ponce, a seasoned veteran of Chicago politics who had known the right questions to ask. Every chance he got, however, he tried to play the Daley-Laski feud card. Unfortunately for him, I wouldn't bite. If anything, I tried to give the mayor some credit.

As much as I wanted to go after the budget director, I didn't. In retrospect, I wish I had. Toward the show's end, Phil Ponce attempted to clarify what the mayor and I had done regarding this issue, and they wanted to know who had been at the forefront. The evidence had been clear that I had introduced the legislation, had done the research, and that I had brought it to the budget director's attention months prior to the show. Anyone who knew the story had no doubt who had held the city workers' feet to the fire for not paying their debts.

Sadly, Diane Aigoitti made a feeble attempt to credit Daley for the legislation, and went so far as to say that his administration had made plans months before to crack down on city scofflaws. She proved to be a very good actress in spouting off one exaggeration after another. It got so bad that I bit down on my tongue, because, otherwise, I would have ended the show by having told her that her story was bullshit!

As hard as it was, the budget director and I departed the studio on friendly terms.

I met Alderman Huels a few days later, on November 5, 1996, at his club downtown. It was early Tuesday morning, Election Day, and both of us were planning to stop at several polling places during the day to shake hands with people. Even though it was a state election, the citywide election was less than four months away, and it was always nice to see people when you didn't have to ask them for a vote.

When we sat down, Pat asked me if I wanted breakfast, but I politely declined, since I rarely ate anything in the morning. I did, though, out of courtesy, order orange juice and toast. Although he complimented me for my performance on the TV show, he told me how pissed Daley was about the whole indebtedness story. The mayor had thrown things in his office, and had actually broken a lamp, or something similar, next to a fish tank. Huels also said that Daley was prepared to fire Victor Reyes, but he had convinced him not to, even though they both agreed that Reyes should have worked with me instead of ignoring the information I had given his assistant.

In any event, Huels wanted me to quiet down, and to let the mayor's people handle the employee indebtedness scandal from that point forward. He then told me that Daley had signed off on my budget requests, including a couple of $15,000 raises for Ray and Don, and for another police bodyguard to assist Tom Lally. By the time we finished, Huels assured me that everything would be fine between the mayor and me. The only problem was that I didn't believe a word of that promise, because I knew that Daley had a long memory.

As John Kass, a reporter for *The Chicago Tribune* told me, "Revenge is a dish best served cold!"

CHAPTER 9

DALEY II

Probably one of the best examples of Daley's power orientation, manipulation, and ego involved a change in how business licenses were processed in the city of Chicago. As city clerk, one of my responsibilities was the issuance of over 100,000 business licenses each year in the city. On the license would be the name of the business, the type of license, the license fee, etc., and, at the bottom, two signatures, Daley's and mine. During my tenure as clerk, I received a number of complaints from business owners regarding delays or mistakes in the process. Unfortunately, I had to explain that my office simply issued the license; it was the Department of Revenue that actually processed the paperwork and signed off before anything was sent to my office for issuance. There were, in fact, many hurdles to jump over, depending on the type of business to obtain a license for in Chicago. In many cases, other city departments, such as Buildings, Fire, Health, Liquor, and Zoning, would have to place their stamps of approval on the paperwork before Revenue could sign off. It was a process that could be very tedious and time-consuming, and one that I believed could be changed and streamlined.

Soon after my first re-election as clerk, I began receiving numerous complaints regarding business licenses, and unfortunately, had to take the blame for all mistakes. It became necessary to put Ray on the problem, to find out what the hell was going on. What I discovered was shocking: In addition to simple clerical misspellings of names and addresses, many businesses across the city had gotten the wrong types of licenses. For example, a heating and air conditioning service had gotten a liquor license, a beauty salon, a food license, and a restaurant, a home license. In addition, there were rumors that some people might have taken kickbacks to issue illegal licenses. This was a real time bomb waiting to explode, and all my office could do was to be a checks-and-balances operation for the Department of Revenue, and to collect the money owed to the city.

I knew something had to be done, so I proposed taking over the entire business license operation from the Department of Revenue, and appointing liaisons to provide "one-stop-shopping" for business owners, so that all of their paperwork could be handled at one central location. My idea would not only speed up the process, but would also clean up those suspect areas by assigning total responsibility for the operation to the city clerk.

My plan to orchestrate the takeover of the entire business license operation needed Daley's approval. I wasn't going to take this to anyone else but him. I certainly wanted to avoid any breakdowns in communication, or misunderstandings. The way to do that, I thought, was to have a one-on-one meeting with the man.

I spoke with him at the city council and told him I needed to see him. Less than a week later, I had my audience with Daley. When we sat down in his conference room, he took off his suit coat and rolled up his sleeves slightly, while holding a black pen and legal pad. I could tell he was interested in what I had to say. I proceeded to tell him about all the serious problems he had had with the Department or Revenue handling business licensees. I explained to him the many mistakes that had been made, both accidentally, and on purpose, and the potential problems and embarrassment both he and I could face in the future. I also informed him of my discussions with the Illinois Restaurant Association and the Chicagoland Chamber of Commerce, both of whom supported my proposal to take over the entire business license operation. In fact, I had a personal conversation with Colleen McShane, President of the Association, who not only expressed her concerns over current license-issuing problems, but assured me of her confidence in my plan to take over the entire operation from start to finish.

During our conversation, I did about 95 percent of the talking, and he spent most of the time taking notes. One of the things that upset him was my referring to the businesspeople and elected officials' complaints about the Department of Revenue. Daley did not like to hear abut complaints from people who he respected in one way or another. I told him that the former revenue commissioner and his former budget director, who was the current CEO of the Chicago Board of Education, Paul Vallas, also supported my office's taking total control of business licensing. I intended to present Daley with enough positive information to encourage him to support my proposal. Before I left his office, we shook hands, and he told me that he would definitely get back to me as soon as possible. As I walked out of his office, I could sense both frustration and maybe a little anger in his face, which had become red during the meeting. Although I felt cautiously optimistic about our conversation, I was also a little apprehensive.

After the meeting, I went directly to my office, and brought Ray up to speed about my conversation with Daley. I gave Ray the okay to call Michael Sneed of *The Sun-Times* to tell her that the mayor and I had just had a secret meeting, and to drop a hint that it had been held to discuss my proposal to take over the processing of the city's business licenses. When I told Ray to make that call, I knew I was running the risk of pissing off Daley, who always hated reading about meetings in his office that he wanted to keep secret from the media. Since our conversation was about problems in the Department of Revenue that were potentially embarrassing to the mayor, holding off on that call to Sneed may have been more prudent. Unfortunately, Daley and I did not trust each other, so I wanted to back him up into a corner by disclosing a small part of my proposal to the media.

About a day after my piece appeared in the Sneed column, Ray and I were in my office, going over business, when Janet buzzed me on the phone. I generally put her on the speaker phone when Ray was in my office, because, I could first ask Ray about whatever message

I'd be getting, or have him take the call instead. But this time, Janet had shocked us both by telling us that Victor Reyes and his assistant Shelia O'Grady (soon to become Daley's chief of staff) were on their way downstairs to see me in person.

Before Ray and I could even guess what this meeting was about, Janet was escorting both of them into my office. When they walked in, I got up from my chair and walked around my desk to greet them. Ray, who had been seated in front of my desk, also got up and shook hands. Reyes immediately said he didn't want to take up much of our time, but that Mayor Daley wanted him to read me a note he had written. Ray then sat in a chair next to an adjacent coffee table, while Shelia O'Grady, who hadn't said a word since she had walked into my office, sat on the office couch, right next to Reyes.

As soon as I sat down behind my desk, Reyes began reading Daley's letter, which turned out to be both a political threat and an ultimatum. The note started off by stating that the business license process would remain with the Department of Revenue, and if I didn't like that decision, he would have the State General Assembly introduce legislation to take away my statutory powers to issue business licenses. He warned me that he would consider my pursuing this issue with the media or the city council a personal attack, and would go to war with me—providing absolutely no help with any problems or requests I may have in the future. His last warning was that his staff would call all fifty aldermen in Chicago, and every state legislator in Springfield, about this issue, which would be portrayed as a Daley vs. Laski feud. Daley's people would then tell everyone they called that there would be no middle ground, and that either they would be with the mayor, or against him.

When he finished reading the note, Reyes neatly folded the paper, stood up, and slid it into his pocket. He didn't say one word as he and Shelia O'Grady walked out of my office. There was total silence for at least one minute before I had regained my composure and closed my mouth, which had been open because of shock. I turned to Ray, who looked like a deer caught in a car's headlights, and asked him what the hell that had been all about. I told Ray that I literally felt as if I had just gotten the shit beaten out of me. We must have sat there for at least twenty minutes just mumbling to each other. I had been caught totally off guard, and was just trying to take a few minutes to gather my thoughts. Frankly, I think Ray and I spent the rest of that afternoon shaking our heads in disbelief at what had just happened.

Later that day, I received a phone call from State Representative Dan Burke, who was in Springfield. He wanted to inform me that he had just received a call from Victor Reyes, who had told him that there might be an upcoming battle between the mayor and Laski, and he wanted to know if Daley could count on his support. Reyes hadn't even explained the details of the whole situation; he had just wanted to know what side of the fence Dan would be on. Of course, Dan had told Reyes he needed to call his brother Ed to get clarification on where he should stand. Over the next couple of days, Reyes and his staff made calls to other elected officials, including some aldermen who called right after they had received their own marching orders.

In the past, I had picked and chosen my battles with the mayor carefully. For example, when I opposed him on property taxes back in 1992, and more recently on the city scofflaw issue, I felt confident and secure in my position. However, this time, I had a bad feeling that he was going to use all of his powers to destroy me over an issue that I wasn't sure the average citizen would really be concerned about. I just didn't think that a fight with Daley over who issued business licenses was important enough to most voters to warrant my putting my political career on the line. Frankly, I was expecting one more issue to take him to task on before he and I would be going head-to-head with each other, because I knew we'd be unable to work with each other in the future.

Needless to say, I sat back for awhile and did nothing, in order to defuse the situation. It took months before I got a return call from Reyes or any other member of Daley's staff. Reyes admitted to me later that the mayor had ordered him not to lift a finger to help me, let alone talk to me. It wasn't until I had later broken the ice during a city council meeting by assuring him privately of my support that I was again able to receive budgetary help for my office.

I learned an important lesson—if I wanted to take on Daley, I needed to build on the support that I already had from the police and fire unions, and to include other city labor unions. More importantly, I needed to find an issue that would not only resonate throughout the entire city for Chicago, but which would allow me to build a citywide platform for the future.

CHAPTER 10

DALEY III

One of the hotter issues involving Chicago politics of late has involved the city's hiring practices. In fact, during this past year, the federal government convicted Daley's patronage chief, Robert Sorich, for what the U.S. Attorney termed "fraudulent and/or corrupt hiring practices." It is worth noting that before, during, and after his trial, Sorich never, to my knowledge, implicated anyone else in the mayor's administration regarding his or her involvement in this issue.

I'd personally dealt with Sorich on a number of issues that went back to the 1990s. He was a quiet and accommodating gentleman who dealt with department heads across the city. In my opinion, he had a tremendous amount of power, but in my numerous conversations with him, he told me that certain requests I needed expedited had to be approved by the fifth floor—I took that to mean by Daley.

Over the years, Sorich worked as an assistant to Victor Reyes, and, later, to John Doerrer. I don't know what happened, but Doerrer eventually relinquished his power or control over jobs. Ever since Victor Reyes left government employment for the private sector, there was only one person to see regarding jobs, and that was Robert Sorich. When I say "jobs," I also mean such issues as granting raises for people, changing titles, and moving someone from a union spot to an exempt position. In my opinion, anyone in city hall could hire someone for a political job without an interview, or without regard to qualifications.

There were many occasions when city administrators found their offices short-handed. For example, I once needed to fill a position entitled "Payment Service Representative," which was, for all intents and purposes, a cashier-type job selling vehicle stickers and dog licenses. Since this position was a union job, its hiring required an interview and a selection of candidates from a list held by the department of personnel. Applicants could get on the list legitimately by filling out an application with the personnel department. If they met the position's qualifications, and if that department recommended them, they would be put on a list as qualified and eligible candidates for that particular job. However, in many cases, lists did not stay open all year round. In fact, if a number of candidates were on a particular list, personnel would keep that list closed. Since I would be required to conduct interviews, I would pick ten or so candidates from the existing list, and chances were that I would select someone from those interviews for the job.

What would an administrator do, though, if he or she needed to hire a particular person as a political favor to his or her sponsor, but that applicant's name was not on the existing list? What if the list was closed? Suppose hiring freezes were in place? The answer would be to see Robert Sorich.

Hypothetically, "John Doe" would fill out an application and hand it in with his resume, which had to meet all the criteria for that particular job. Then Doe would give the administrator's "go-to" guy the resume, which he, in turn, would take to Mr. X in the personnel department. If the resume didn't meet the necessary criteria, Mr. X would return the resume to Doe and tell him what changes to make. The "go-to" guy would tell applicant Doe about these changes, and then, after they had been made, and Mr. X in personnel had signed off, the administrator would get both the application and resume in his or hands, and call Sorich. In most cases, somebody from Sorich's office would pick up the paperwork and take it back to personnel. Within one week, Doe's name would appear on the "Qualified" list, along with the ten interview candidates. The key to the whole process was first to get Doe's name on the list. The rest would be a done deal, with the interview nothing more than a sham. This practice was, in my opinion, used in all city hall departments.

What if an executive needed to maneuver payroll and job titles in his or her office? For example, one administrator I knew received a call from a high-ranking state official who needed a big-paying job—somewhere around $80,000.00, for someone. He told him if his applicant wanted the job, he would have to first start in the upper forties. To increase the salary, that official would have to call Sorich personally, because he needed him to authorize the necessary changes in title, and to provide the executive with additional money in his budget.

About two weeks later, the new budget director called the administrator into his office, where he quietly told him, "Your friend called my friend," which meant that the state official called Sorich.

He then said the mayor would help with whatever was needed to fulfill the hiring request, and that the administrator would receive additional appropriations for his office. Within a week or so, he was able to afford an $80,000 position in his office for the state official's person.

On many occasions, administrators needed to change titles, or move positions from one person to another— just to take care of another elected official who was looking for a job for an associate. There was no doubt in my mind that under those circumstances, whenever those executives went to Sorich, he would at least mention their requests to the mayor, if not get his blessing to move forward.

Before meeting Kathleen, I was briefly married from 1983 to 1985. On one occasion, my oldest daughter, Jennifer, from my first marriage, needed a job. She was living in Arkansas, but wanted to move back to Chicago. When I asked him about that possibility, he told me in no uncertain terms that I would have to talk to the mayor personally. When I did speak to Daley, he couldn't have been kinder. He asked me about her skills and education. Jennifer had just graduated from high school, and we needed to be careful about where we would place her. Daley felt, because she was my daughter, it might be better to get something outside of city employment. Initially, he thought about one of the airlines, but later said that someone from his office would look into other areas and let me know. Within a day, I received a call from Sorich, telling me that someone from the mayor's office, who dealt with the city's aviation department, would be calling me.

Within two weeks, I managed to schedule an interview for my daughter with Turner Construction, who had done a ton of work for the city of Chicago, including O'Hare Airport. I took Jennifer for her interview at the airport in one of Turner Construction's mobile-trailers. Turner offered her a job for approximately $24,000.00, which was more than generous for an applicant right out of high school, and with no skills. There was also plenty of overtime available, along with a host of benefits. She would be reviewed in thirty days. At the end of the day, however, Jennifer got cold feet, and decided to stay in Arkansas. Sometimes I wonder what she would be doing now if she had taken the job.

Even today, I still hear the mayor, repeatedly pleading ignorance about the latest Chicago political scandal. I was in government service for twenty-seven years; sixteen of those as an elected official. In my opinion, the mayor knows everything that goes on in city hall. Over the years, I dealt with many of his top people, such as, Tim Degnan, Pat Huels, Victor Reyes, John Doerrer, Shelia O'Grady, Paul Vallas, and John Harris. Quite honestly, each and every one of those people, at one time or another, told me they would need to check with the mayor before assisting me with any program or request. A perfect example of this close contact came about in 2003, when I was seeking re-election, and shaking the trees for money to build up my war chest. On one particular morning, I met with Victor Reyes who was now a very successful lobbyist/consultant. During the course of our conversation, I disclosed my re-election intentions, and mentioned that the mayor and I would be working together as a team in an upcoming election. I then asked him to contribute to my campaign, and to help me with some fundraising, especially in the Hispanic business districts. His answer summed up Daley's knowledge, or alleged lack thereof, of city business, which included political hiring in Chicago.

Reyes told me in no uncertain terms, that even as a lobbyist, he still owed everything to the mayor. To help me with fundraising or anything else, he would do what he had always done. He would contact the mayor, and whatever Daley would tell him, that was what he would do. Reyes said he would help me as soon as Daley had given him his okay. Well, four years later, in 2007, I'm still waiting for Reyes' help, and for a check from his firm. Maybe I still will get that check, though I doubt it.

Daley is a hands-on sort of guy, and I would find it hard to believe that when it came down to important issues, both politically and administratively, he could plead ignorance, or plead the Fifth. He didn't become this country's most powerful mayor by simply turning things over to, or not following up with his staff. He is too shrewd and insecure for that, because he feels he needs to know what's going on at all times. When I was an alderman and went on tour with him in the 23rd Ward, I was amazed by his eye for detail. He pointed out potholes, faded traffic signs, trees that needed trimming, and streets that needed cleaned. That's why I think it's highly unlikely that he would not have a handle on the most important issues in the city, because he certainly always paid attention to many of the smaller ones.

Besides his administrative skills as mayor, he is also one of the most astute politicians I've ever met. He knows the players (shakers and movers) in this business, and according to that old adage, keeps his friends close, and his enemies closer. I saw him at city council meetings, keeping the majority of the aldermen in line with his agenda. Since I sat only a few feet from the mayor, I could attest to the number of aldermen who would try to get his permission for a quick audience at the rostrum in the city council chambers, about everything from public works projects to jobs. For someone who claimed he didn't know what had been going on, he sure took a lot of notes when talking to other elected officials.

Daley is a man who receives personal, handwritten birthday cards from sitting presidents (he was especially proud of the one in 2005, from President George Bush). Anyone who wants to run for political office in the state of Illinois will sit down with him, and presidential hopefuls from across the country will not leave this city without an audience with Daley. A man with this stature and power would not have been where he is today without having known about certain people's actions or behavior that could continue to hurt him.

In May 2003, on inauguration day in Chicago, Daley, me, City Treasurer Rice, and fifty aldermen were sworn in for our new terms. I was in my office with Kathleen, Nina, and our sons, Jack and Bobby, where we were all celebrating, and taking pictures with staff and friends. One of our Chicago Inaugural Day traditions was to take a picture with the mayor. However, his office had told us that he might not be able to do so that year, because of a conflict in his schedule. As the afternoon progressed, the family was just hanging around, so we could all go home together. Then, out of the clear blue sky, I received a call that the mayor was waiting for my family in his office. Kathleen combed the boys' hair, Nina checked herself out in the mirror, and I gave all the kids instructions about their behavior.

I particularly told Bobby that when he met Daley, he should shake his hand and say, "Congratulations, Mr. Mayor."

Bobby was very excited about this opportunity, and because he is, for the most part, dependable, I was confident about his ability to congratulate the mayor.

When we arrived on the fifth floor, we checked in with the two police officers at the front desk. They, in turn, called to the back, to let the mayor's staff know that we were waiting. Only a couple of minutes later, his personal secretary, Kathy, came up front to greet us. She led us back to his outer office, where she and two other assistants were located. Daley's outer office was splendid, with a couple leather couches, approximately four comfortable, upholstered chairs, and all kinds of magazines and newspapers to read.

Less than five minutes later, I heard Daley coming out of his private office, talking to someone else. However, his office was off to one corner, so I couldn't see anything from where we were seated. Suddenly, Daley entered with a tall, distinguished gentleman whom I instantly recognized as Massachusetts Senator John Kerry, one of the Democratic candidates for president. Of course, since he was campaigning in Chicago that day, he needed to pay his respects to Daley, to get his support down the road.

My son, Bobby, then darted out in front of us to do his part by formerly congratulating the mayor. Bobby was so excited, he ran up to both gentlemen.

Smiling, he extended his hand to Senator Kerry and said, "Congratulations, Mr. Mayor."

Everyone in the room started laughing hysterically. Senator Kerry actually picked Bobby up and hugged him. He kept holding him while the photographers took picture after picture. Daley, with his hearty laughter echoing throughout the room, patted Bobby on the back. It was, to say the least, a precious moment.

Everyone in the family, including Bobby, congratulated Daley. As soon as Senator Kerry departed, we all went to the mayor's private office for photographs. Daley was always very kind and personable with my family. I think he has a soft spot when it comes to a close-knit family, especially one like ours, with three young children.

As far as Bobby was concerned, he could always show his friends and family the pictures of him being held by the man who would become the Democratic nominee for president of the United States, and getting patted on the back by unquestionably the most powerful mayor in this country. I guess my only concern will be how all my children will view and react to politicians in general when they finally understand the true meaning of Chicago politics. I will let them judge for themselves.

CHAPTER 11

THE HIRED TRUCK PROGRAM SCANDAL:
THE BEGINNING

At the end of 2003 and the beginning of 2004, a story broke in *The Sun-Times* that would change my life forever. Just before New Years, I decided to go to a 7-Eleven, as I usually did in the morning, to pick up a large coffee for Kathleen and a *Sun-Times.* However, I had vowed some day never to buy that paper again because of the continued hatchet job I thought they had been doing on me and other elected officials. When I picked up the paper from the rack, I immediately saw the words "Hired Truck Program," which caught my attention. As I read the story, I experienced a burning and nauseous feeling in my stomach. What I always feared in the back of my mind was now actually happening—someone was looking into the city's Hired Truck Program's operations.

Not only was there a media inquiry, but information was leaking out about preferential treatment, politics, and bribes. I quickly headed home, where I dropped off the coffee to Kathleen. I told her I had to stop at the law office to see Bob Molaro, but what I really did was get into my car and call Mick Jones. I reached him on the two-way Nextel and told him to meet me in about twenty minutes at Valley Forge, a neighborhood park that was only a couple of blocks from his house, as soon as possible. I could tell by the tone of his voice that he knew exactly what we were going to talk about.

I pulled up short of the park field house, and parked in front of the field where the kids played football or soccer, just so I could be conspicuous. I don't know why, but I started to feel uncomfortable when Mick pulled up in his truck. We then both jumped out of our vehicles and walked towards each other. During this meeting, we spoke basically in general terms, except when the name "Angelo Torres," the director of the entire program, came up. For whatever reason, Torres wasn't being kind to "Get Plowed, Inc.," the company that Mick and his wife, Traci, owned with their friends John and Mary Novak. One has to know some basic facts about the city's trucking operations to understand why *The Sun-Times* was turning up the heat. Let's go back to late 1994.

I was campaigning for city clerk at that time, and one day, Mick told me about a program he was interested in for himself and his partners. At that point in my life, I had known Mick Jones for over sixteen years. We played softball together, drank together, celebrated our birthdays together, spent time at each other's homes, and became the best of friends. Besides working for the city as a housing inspector, Mick also had a snow-plowing business with his friend, John Novak. Whenever there was a snowstorm, Mick took time off from his city job to plow many of the local business parking lots. In those years, it was easy for him to manipulate his time off by taking sick days or administrative leave days, especially since his direct supervisor was a friend.

One late afternoon, Mick showed up at the alderman's office. I'd just returned from a campaign stop on the north side, and had stopped at my office to catch my breath. When I walked in, I saw him and immediately invited him into my office, because he was in my inner circle, and I enjoyed bullshitting with him. After a short conversation regarding the city clerk campaign, Mick asked me for a favor. He told me that the city had a Hired Truck Program that employed private trucking companies to work for various city departments, such as Streets and Sanitation, and the Department of Water. A company's trucks would report to a certain job site and load materials from the project, and take them to another location. As I began to learn, the whole truck program was a gravy train for these companies, and Mick wanted to hop on. Let's say the city paid a company $40.00 per hour for its truck and driver for a day. That company was paid regardless if the crew worked or not. So even while just sitting and waiting to be called, they would still get paid. Drivers would make between $8.00 and $10.00 per hour. Even with the cost of insurance, gas, and upkeep, there would still be plenty of money to make. Mick told me this was a great opportunity for him, and that he needed my help to get his foot in the door. He also mentioned that when things got moving, he would take care of me. I didn't know what he meant—or I should say, I didn't *want* to know, even though I really did, but didn't want to admit it. After he gave me the lowdown, I knew exactly whom to see.

The following week, I had an appointment with Alderman Pat Huels, who was not only chairman of the transportation committee, but the mayor's number one guy. If anyone needed anything from the mayor and his office, Alderman Huels was the one to see. He was not only Daley's floor leader in the council, but he had the mayor's eyes and ears for everything else.

Pat was a heavyset gentleman, maybe around five-foot-eight, with short, salt-and-pepper-colored hair. He was well-groomed, and an immaculate dresser—so much so that he may have walked out of *GQ Magazine.* We talked briefly about the election, and he expressed his confidence in my chances of winning. I then talked to him about pay raises for all the elected officials. He asked me if I would like to double my own salary. The current clerk was making $85,000.00; however, a current proposal supported by the mayor would raise that salary to $105,000.00. As alderman, I was then making $55,000.00, and although that salary would increase to $75,000.00, as the next city clerk, I would be getting a $50,000.00 increase, which to me would be like winning the lottery.

After these pleasantries, I asked Pat about the Hired Truck Program, and told him I had a very good friend who was interested in being part of the program. I also told him that this would be a personal favor to me if he could put some of Mick's trucks on the payroll.

When I finished, the alderman answered nonchalantly, "No problem."

I gave him Mick's phone number. Before long, "Get Plowed, Inc." was working for the city.

It wasn't long after the trucks were on, maybe a month or so, that Mick stopped by the house one evening. He was his usual jovial self, as we sat down on the basement couch and drank a few beers together.

Before too long, he leaned over to shake my hand, and said, "Take care of the family."

As I extended my hand and we shook, I knew, though we never spoke about it in any detail, he had just handed me money—how much, I didn't know. As soon as we transferred the money, I quickly put it in my pocket. During the course of the evening, Mick used my bathroom, and I went into my pocket and counted five $100.00 bills. I knew at this point that we were starting a wonderful, but illegal, business relationship, because this was technically bribery. However, I told myself the money wasn't for me, but for my family—my loved ones.

During the next few years, through the end of the '90s, "Get Plowed" always had one or two trucks working on and off. There were times, however, either when "Get Plowed" would be knocked off, because of the program's seasonal aspects, or because Angelo Torres wasn't happy. Perhaps certain insurance paperwork wasn't in order, or something mechanical on the trucks was in question, which would result in the company's being laid off temporarily. When that would happen, I would get a call from Mick, and, in turn, I would call my people, either Victor Reyes or Robert Sorich.

As time went on, and the 1990s came to a close, new developments took place. Pat Huels resigned as alderman after the media had brought up issues concerning his security business, and favorable loans he had received from a certain individual doing business with the city. Huels' resignation was problematic for me, because I had such a good relationship with him that I knew whomever I dealt with in the future would not be the same. Pat Huels was the type of man who, if he could do something for you, he would, and if he couldn't, he would tell you. I knew that this changing of the guard would not be helpful to me.

It was no surprise to me when I found out that Victor Reyes would now be in charge. He had basically been Pat's guy, and prior to that, Tim Degnan's assistant. Although Victor was a nice enough guy, he wasn't Huels—both in terms of personality and in getting things done.

As I completed my first term in office, things were going well. I was running unopposed, since I had knocked off my only challenger for an insufficient number of signatures. Moreover, my office was moving forward in generating revenue, and had created a new safety program, known as "The Kids' ID Program." My political career could not have been better. I was on cloud nine, along with my ego.

One day, right after the election, I was waiting in front of St. Daniel, the Prophet Catholic School to pick up my kids when another friend of mine, Randy Aderman, came up to me. I met Randy when I started working for Lipinski back in 1979. He was a nice guy, and married, with four children; as a matter of fact, his youngest son went to school with my boys. Like Mick, Randy and I played softball together, and Mick and Randy had long known each other (Mick had actually stood with Randy at his wedding). The ironic thing about their relationship was that they were both extremely jealous of each other. Furthermore, their wives, Traci Jones and Noreen Aderman, did not like one another at all. To complicate matters still further, Randy also had a snow-plowing business, and he would constantly be at odds with Mick over plowing contracts with local businesspeople. Their love-hate relationship eventually would destroy whatever friendship they had.

Randy had worked for the city his entire life. He started when he was eighteen years old, and was currently working for the water department. Over the years, Randy and I had worked together in some business enterprises. For example, after I left Lipinski and went on my own, Randy and I started a local newspaper called

The Midway Times. Unfortunately, we had financial troubles. Our advertising was not covering printing costs and salaries. A couple of times we were ready to close the doors, but because the paper served as a valuable tool for my political agenda, I did everything in my power to keep it afloat. The only way I could continue to do that was to get some additional financial backing from Randy, to the tune of about $20,000.00. Despite our valiant efforts, we had to shut down the operation in less than a year.

I felt I needed to help Randy. Quite honestly, besides investing money in the newspaper, he had also invested in an insurance policy with me. Randy had recently had an office job with the sewer department, but wanted to make more money as a caulker—a union position that required him to be in a ditch or hole for projects to lay pipe. He had absolutely no knowledge or experience in that field, but he wanted the job. So I called a truce with Lipinski, because I needed his help with this favor. We proceeded to call Victor Reyes and Robert Sorich, and eventually got Randy his caulker's job, which boosted his salary around $20,000.00. It wasn't long, however, before Randy grew tired of being in a ditch during the winter and summer, and he wanted another job change.

This time, we were able to get him a job inside the water filtration plant, as a project coordinator. He was now capable of wheeling and dealing with people, and could schmooze with the big shots down there. Randy had gotten that job through the 11th Ward and John Daley, because of a relative who had been involved politically with that organization. So he knew politics and what it would take to move up the ladder. That was why Randy had come to me again, to tell him about his boss, Don Tomczak, the Water Department's Deputy Commissioner.

While we were talking in front of the school, Randy now had a lot of questions about his buddy Mick and the truck program. I immediately pleaded ignorance, hoping he wouldn't pursue the conversation. Then, he began talking about Tomczak. It was amazing what Randy told me about this guy, including the political army he had built to do the bidding for Mayor Daley's inner circle. He told me some of his new responsibilities under Tomczak included working phone banks, circulating petitions, buying fundraiser tickets, being a bag man, picking up envelopes across the filtration plant and city hall for Tomczak, and taking care of his birthday and Christmas employees. Randy admitted he routinely picked up thousands of dollars in cash for him.

I knew, however, that all this talk about his job and Tomczak was just general bullshit, and that he actually was going to ask me for a favor. First, Randy wanted me to set up an appointment to see Tomczak. Randy already told him about our relationship, and Tomczak, who was also of Polish descent, told Randy to have me stop by and talk to him. Randy's mind was racing, because he knew that any kind of relationship with Tomczak would benefit him, but I didn't know that it would have something to do with the truck program. After I agreed to set up the meeting, Randy asked me to do one more thing for him. He wanted me to help a friend of his get a truck contract with the city. I'd learned quickly that there were no secrets in this business, and that Randy wanted to jump into my business relationship with Mick. I was almost embarrassed to admit anything to him. However, as the conversation continued, Randy came right out and told me that I would get a piece of the pie if I helped his friend. He again asked me what I was getting from Mick. Instead of just telling him, I thought I would appear less guilty if I used sign language. I put five fingers in the air for each truck, meaning $500.00.

Randy looked at me with disbelief, and said, "If you get one truck on for my friend, I'll double that and give you $2,000.00, and the other guy should be doing the same thing for everything you've ever done for him."

Honestly, I was shocked to hear Randy talk like that, but I was even more nervous about having disclosed that information about my relationship with Mick in the first place. I was starting to think that the more people who were involved with this deal, meant more possibilities of something going wrong, but I also thought about the money, and my relationship with the both of them. I told myself, "I trust them, and I'll go for it!"

The next day was a Thursday, and since I was not going to city hall on Friday, I called Robert Sorich on my cell phone to hopefully take care of the Randy situation. In matters like this, I had learned to not even bother Victor Reyes, because he would only tell me to call Sorich anyway. His secretary told me that Robert would be in meetings most of the day, so I left both my cell phone and home phone number, and asked for a return call on Friday. The next morning after I dropped the kids off at school around 8:00 a.m. and walked into the house, my phone rang. It was Robert. I thanked him for the return call, and immediately jumped into business. I told him that my friend Randy (whom Sorich knew from his earlier job requests) had a friend who owned a trucking company, and he wanted to contract with the city. For the sake of anonymity, let's call Randy's friend "Mr. C.," and his company "ABC Trucking." Sorich seemed hesitant, because he apparently knew about this particular company. Still, he basically told me in so many words, that the matter would be taken care of, and to tell Randy and his friend to relax. About two weeks later, "ABC Trucking" was working for the city.

Now, things were really moving. I had both Mick and Randy taking care of me. It proved a great arrangement, even though each of them would ask me daily how the other one was doing, to keep tabs on one another. It was the calm before the storm that no one knew was coming. The arrangement with Randy and his friend ended after one year. To this day, I'm not sure what happened, except that Randy later told me his friend's trucks had gotten knocked off the list during the winter months, and had never been put back to work.

As soon as that relationship ended, Randy was working on something else, and that "something else" was Tomczak. Little did I know at the time that Randy and Mick were talking (or should I say, "scheming?") about putting more trucks on with the city. However, they both needed me to talk to Tomczak, who controlled every truck with Chicago's water department.

Early one morning, while I was on my way downtown, my cell phone rang. It was Randy. He always asked me what I was doing, which made me nervous, because I knew he needed something. He wanted me to meet him in about two hours at the water filtration plant, because he had set up a meeting between Tomczak and me. I had never met the man before, and I knew the first time would be a little awkward, because I was going to ask him to add a truck to his department for me.

The water filtration plant was like an island unto itself, hidden along the lakefront behind Navy Pier and Lake Point Towers (which was a forty-story-high condo complex). The filtration plant gate reminded me of a drive-through bank, because it had about five different gates and guardhouses. As I pulled up, my security guard, Tom Lally, with the Chicago Police, quickly announced my arrival to meet with Tomczak. It was only a matter of seconds before the white security gate lifted, and we were on our way driving down several winding roads to the plant. On one side, we could see Lake Michigan, and on the other side, Navy Pier, a family amusement center with restaurants, shops, and rides, and also right on the lake. As we pulled up to the large facility, we circled around to the back entrance, where Randy was waiting. I jumped out of the car and told Tom to take off, and that I would two-way him on our Nextels when I was ready to leave.

When I walked in, I could not help but be impressed, not only by the building's size, but also by all the activity going on inside. It reminded me of a combination of a chemistry lab and something out of NASA, with long tubes, tanks with gauges, and big, meal wheels. As Randy led me to metal grated stairs a couple of floors up, a number of employees recognized me and said "hello." When we got to the top floor, I could tell this was the building's administrative portion, with a number of little cubicles with employees shuffling paperwork. As we headed to the building's other side, I could see all the way down the hallway, where there was one big office, which Randy told me was Tomczak's. At the front office, a nice young woman greeted us, and quickly notified Tomczak by phone of our arrival. She then told us to go straight through the door directly in front of us. When Randy and I walked through the front door, we found ourselves in another office altogether, which I assumed was part of Tomczak's inner circle. Two guys attired in dress shirts and pants were at their desks. As soon as I walked in, they stood up, introduced themselves, and asked me if I wanted something to drink, but I declined. Then, one gentleman opened another door, stepped into the office next to him, came out, and asked Randy and me to enter. When I walked in, the first thing I noticed was the beautiful view, and windows along one entire side of the office. Directly to my right, Tomczak stood behind his desk, waiting to shake my hand. He wasted no time telling Randy that he would meet with me privately. As soon as he left and closed the door, I sat down in one of the nicely upholstered chairs directly in front of Tomczak.

Don Tomczak was an older-looking gentleman, in his mid-to-late sixties. His face looked quite worn from what I believe was a combination of stress, weather, and drinking. He had grayish, medium-length, thin hair, and a larger-than-life nose that was quite red, with visible blood vessels protruding from both sides. His ears were large and flopped about. The one feature that most stood out was his piercing eyes, and a mean look on his face, despite his half-ass smile when we had shaken hands. I could tell that, over the years, he had been through some real political wards, and that I would rather have him as a friend than as an enemy. The first thing out of his mouth, surprisingly, was his prediction that I would quickly climb the political ladder. At first, he gloated over the fact that we were both of Polish ancestry, and insisted that Daley would not be around forever. He also asked me about my fundraising and political war chest, which at that time was around $300,000.00. He told me to have Randy let him know about my next fundraiser (at which time, in fact, Tomczak bought a table and gave me $1,500.00 in cash).

The conversation quickly shifted gears on my part, and I asked him about putting trucks on with the city. Specifically, I mentioned Randy, who prior to this meeting, had told me that he had been told that Mick's company, "Get Plowed," was Randy's, because he believed that Tomczak would be more receptive to helping him, than outsiders like Mick. At that time, I should have called off the whole thing, but I was already in too deep to even consider that option. What I did realize was that Randy and Mick, despite their mutual jealousy and mistrust, were still cutting deals with each other, but that these last few under-the-table arrangements would come back to hurt everyone.

Soon after the Tomczak meeting, Mick and "Get Plowed" got another truck on with the city. Tomczak would put trucks on for awhile, and then take them off, so as to make room for someone else's trucks. It was a good way for Tomczak to keep his operation in place. My only problem was that each time a "Get Plowed" truck would call me, I would have to run over and see Tomczak and ask him to do me a favor, and put a truck back on. Of course, he would play dumb, and pretend he didn't know anything about such an arrangement. But, trust me, Tomczak knew everything about which trucks were working for the city, and which were not.

I learned that the people who worked for Tomczak feared him, and that Daley's people needed him. I don't know how many times I was in Tomczak's office when he would take calls from Victor Reyes or Robert Sorich. The conversations were always short, but Tomczak would tell me about meetings he would have to raise money, or to send his army out to gather petitions, either for Daley, or for a candidate of Daley's. It was no secret that Daley and Tomczak hated each other. The hatred dated back to former Mayor Jane Byrne's administration, but Tomczak had one friend that even Daley couldn't say "no" to, and that was former Congressman Dan Rostenkowski. At one time, he was the most powerful congressperson in the country. Because of Rostenkowski, Tomczak continued to work for the Daley administration, and provided those services that the Reyeses and the Sorichs needed.

Although Tomczak hated Daley, he certainly knew where his bread was buttered, as he continued to follow his marching orders on a daily basis from Reyes or Sorich. Tomczak told me on more than one occasion that when he received instructions regarding the Daley campaign, or an aldermanic race that the powers-to-be were interested in, those instructions always came from the top of the ladder. There was never any doubt about that.

Tomczak and I, though, met a couple of times to talk about something other than trucks. He always kept pumping me about running for a higher office, but he didn't want me to leave the city for a county or state office. He also spent much of his time talking about his sons, one of whom, Jeff, was the State Attorney of Will County. There was no doubt in my mind that Tomczak would do anything to help his sons, especially Jeff. In fact, Randy, on more than one occasion, asked me to find a trucking company or two that would donate money to Jeff's re-election campaign. Unfortunately, all of the eventual negative publicity from the Hired Truck Program scandal helped end his re-election bid.

Tomczak also had a few other people in his life whom he wanted me to help. According to Randy, Tomczak had a girlfriend in one of Chicago's north side neighborhoods. Randy also told me there were times during the day when he would drive Tomczak from the filtration plant to an undisclosed location and drop him off to meet her. Randy would then return in a couple of hours to pick him up. It was no secret at the water department about his relationship, and I should not have been surprised when, one day, Randy brought me her resume, and told me that Tomczak needed my help. Fortunately or unfortunately, that résumé just sat on my desk, and one of the reasons it did was because this young lady did not have any office skills. On another occasion, he sent me an older gentleman he wanted me to hire. That individual did have some skills, and he probably could have helped the office, except for the fact that he lived on the city's north side, and didn't want to travel to city hall. In addition, he didn't want to work full-time. In fact, he wanted to decide what hours he should work. Needless to say, I knew he wouldn't work out!

During all this time, Randy was a loyal soldier to Tomczak. He drove him to political rallies and dinners, raised and collected money for him, conducted phone banks, and did anything else his boss wanted. Despite all Randy did for Tomczak, it still amazed me that he questioned Randy's ability to keep his mouth shut. Tomczak continuously told me to remind Randy to keep quiet, especially after he would put a "Get Plowed" truck on with the water department. It made me nervous to hear Tomczak talk about what a nice guy Randy was, and how he always followed orders, but how worried he was about his talking to too many people.

The irony of this whole Tomczak story was his propensity for bragging about his toughness and loyalty, both of which he attributed to having been from the so-called "old school." He used to bask in the glory of his many tales of having stood up to various past investigations and having kept his mouth shut, or of even having told certain law enforcement people to fuck themselves. After having listened to these stories, I believed that even under extreme torture, or the threat of death, Tomczak would not give up a soul in order to save himself. He told me once how much he despised "rats" (informants) and how, if it weren't for them, the Feds would never have the slightest clue about what was *really* going on in city hall.

CHAPTER 12

THE HIRED TRUCK PROGRAM SCANDAL:
COMPLICATIONS

With that background now set, we can return to those troubled days of early 2004. Mick and I hoped that the story would just go away, but two weeks after the first "Hired Truck" article had appeared in *The Sun-Times*, new trouble erupted. I decided to make a pit stop at Ray Drish's house to talk about politics, fundraising, and employment issues. Ray was still my number one advisor, even though he was no longer on the city's payroll. About ten minutes into our conversation, my cell phone rang. On the other end was Joe Panarese, my new chief of staff, who replaced Ray in 2001. Joe (who is now a Cook County Circuit Court judge) immediately cut to the chase, and told me that a *Sun-Times* reporter had called, and asked me to speak about Mick and Traci Jones, and "Get Plowed, Inc." Unfortunately, my political campaign recently received a recent donation from "Get Plowed." In addition, those checks were signed by Traci, even though she was supposed to have been off the books and working for me for several months, at my southwest side satellite office. In addition, Mick had allegedly divested himself from any ownership or monetary interest in "Get Plowed," yet the company's business address in the phone book was 5711 S. Sayre, which was the Jones family's home address. *The Sun-Times'* information implied that the Joneses still had a financial ownership interest.

I immediately called Mick, and told him to pick me up at Ray's house ASAP. Even though it took him only ten minutes to get there, it seemed like ten hours. When Mick pulled up and I jumped into his truck, the first thing he said was that he knew very little about what was going on with the whole *Sun-Times* story. However, before we can consider Mick's whole explanation of innocence, we must again go back in time to understand how the Joneses tried to conceal their still active involvement with "Get Plowed."

Back in the '90s, Mick asked me to give his wife Traci a job. I explained that as long as "Get Plowed" still paid her, I couldn't hire her. Mick assured me that had changed soon after the city's ethics department had reversed its previous decision on the matter by now allowing city employees' spouses to have financial interests with trucking companies working for Chicago.

Mick grew concerned over Traci's ownership role in the company when his trucks, at one point, were knocked off the Hired Truck Program. As a safeguard, Mick made a formal inquiry to the Board of Ethics. After a thorough investigation, they ruled that there was absolutely nothing illegal, or any type of ethics violation, in Traci Jones having an ownership interest in "Get Plowed." Soon after that ruling, I called Reyes and Sorich to notify them of what had taken place, and requested that the "Get Plowed" trucks be put back on with the city, which they were. However, within months, the Ethics Board reversed its original ruling, and prohibited any spouse from having a financial interest in a trucking company employed by the city of Chicago.

Following that news, Mick authorized his attorney and accountant to draw up new paperwork, divesting Traci of an ownership in "Get Plowed." In the meantime, Mick met with his partner, John Novak, to make other money-making arrangements with him. When the divestiture paperwork was completed, Mick assured me that neither he nor his wife now had any interest in the company—at least on paper. I then forwarded Mick's request (or plan) to hire his wife for my satellite office. The real kick in the ass to this whole idea, though, was that Traci, a prima donna who wore the pants in the family, really wanted to work only part-time hours during the summer at my satellite office, which was only about five minutes from their home. Because of Mick, I paid her around $20,000.00 a year for a part-time job. Traci only had a high school education, with no real clerical skills whatsoever, but it didn't matter; that was our plan.

Due to the Ethics Board's scrutiny, Mick could no longer depend on city income from "Get Plowed," and with education costs rising for their three kids, it was soon necessary for Traci to work full-time. Therefore, when Carla, my satellite officer supervisor, retired, Traci took over her close-to-$50,000.00-per-year position. In addition, although Mick and Traci technically divested themselves of the company, he made an arrangement with his partner for some type of secret assistance, by which the company would pay certain expenses for him and his wife. The whole scheme was working perfectly, until *The Chicago Sun-Times* turned up the heat.

As soon as I jumped into Mick's truck, I asked him point blank, "Is there anything you haven't told me?"

He confidently answered, "No!"

Over the years, during my political career, I was always quite good at—or at least lucky with—handling damage control. Still, I was very nervous about where all of this was headed.

Since *The Sun-Times* had called my office, I knew they were waiting for a response from me. I was also aware that if I didn't respond that afternoon, a weekend story was likely to be unfavorable. Joe Panarese called back to ask for some direction regarding my response. I abruptly told him to be patient, and that I was working on it.

As Mick and I continued to aimlessly drive around the Garfield Ridge Community neighborhood, I came up with a plan that I believed would temporarily stop the bleeding. I told Mick to go home and pick up all the documents regarding the decisions made by the Board of Ethics that had allowed Traci to have an ownership interest in "Get Plowed." In addition, he needed to get the remaining documentation that showed an eventual total divestiture of control, both on a financial and management level, on the part of him and

Traci. We also needed supporting documents that could further show their relinquishment of any ownership rights. I then told Mick to drop me off at home, pick up all the paperwork we had discussed, and head to city hall to meet with Joe Panarese. They were to meet at the front doors on the Washington side of the Hall. Mick was to have called Joe ahead of time, to tell him to jump in the car, and as they were driving around, he would explain the significance of the paperwork he'd be giving him, along with any other information that would help him understand the story. When I returned home, I immediately called Joe at city hall to update him on what was happening. I told him that as soon as he had finished his conversation with Mick, to call me on my cell phone, so we could go over a plan of attack with *The Sun-Times.*

About two hours later, Joe called back, and told me that he had just finished talking with Mick. Joe was a little cynical about most of my employees. He always felt that they were trying to take advantage of me. However, in this case, he knew how close Mick and I were, so he was extremely careful not to crucify him around me. I instructed Joe to tell *The Sun-Times* that before we had hired either Mick or Traci Jones, we had received documentation that clearly showed they had given up all interest in "Get Plowed, Inc." The fact that a phone number and address were the same as the Jones's residence was purely a coincidence, and that calls had been made to the phone company to remove that business address from the phone book and replace it with one at which their former partner's wife lived. At that point in time, I felt Joe had enough information to adequately respond to *The Sun-Times.* I simply told him to call me back after he had finished his phone conversation with the paper.

Less than thirty minutes later, Joe called me again. He sounded very upbeat, and told me that he gave *The Sun-Times* all the information I specified, and also tried to insulate me and my office from the entire situation. Even though the paper was happy with the information, it still expected a forthcoming story about the Joneses.

As the weekend approached, I realized there was nothing further I could do regarding *The Sun-Times.* The weekend came and went, with no story on "Get Plowed," and I was now starting to feel that maybe, just maybe, I would be lucky, and that suspicions about the trucking program would go away.

On Monday, I was back at city hall feeling very good about the weekend and the lack of news. However, that false sense of security ended quickly when Mick called and told me that *The Sun-Times* had called downtown looking for him. They had also called the satellite office, asking for Traci. It was quite evident that Mick was shaken up, so I told him to get off the street, just in case he was being followed, and head for home. I told him I would drop by the house on my way home from city hall.

I left city hall around three in the afternoon, and told Tom Lally to drive me straight to Mick's house. I remembered thinking that as long as *The Sun-Times* continued to track Mick and Traci, this would be a story that was not going to go away. When we pulled up to Mick's house, he was waiting at the front door. I told Tom I would call him in an hour or so to have him pick me up.

As I entered the house, I could immediately see that Mick was worried, which didn't help my nerves. He seemed very concerned that the press had contacted Traci, and he didn't want her to be upset. I asked him again if there was anything else out there we needed to address, and he kept saying no, that he had covered everything.

As we sat on the couch trying to stay calm, I glanced out the front window. I saw two individuals, one with a camera, walking toward the front of the house. I quickly dove on the floor to avoid being seen, and Mick ran to the kitchen. I still had on my full-length overcoat, as I crawled out the front room into the kitchen. Mick and I quickly moved toward the back of the house to get out of sight. Mick then called his wife, and told her not to come home until he had called to give her the okay. He also told her to get a hold of the kids, to make sure they wouldn't be coming home from school soon. When he got off the phone, the doorbell rang, and I could see panic in his face. We knew it was a *Sun-Times* reporter. It rang maybe three more times, followed by a couple of firm knocks on the front door. We decided to sit in the back bedroom, and wait to see how long they would camp out.

Mick and I then stood in the kitchen, looking at each other in disbelief. Mick leaned over and whispered that he was scared. We both knew that there was going to be a story, and we were betting it would come out tomorrow. He then called Traci again, and I called Tom, to let him know that the coast was now clear. Tom showed up within five minutes, and I quickly left through the back door and jumped in the car. Before I did, I'd told Mick to call me on my cell phone about 5:00 a.m., or as soon as he got his hands on the paper.

Tom drove me home as quickly as possible, because I just wanted to hide in my basement. I knew that this night was going to be a long one. When I walked in the door, Kathleen, as usual, could tell that something was wrong by just looking at my face. I tried to tell her as little as possible. After fourteen years of marriage, we had gone through our share of political controversies and investigations. All of which were finally starting to take an emotional toll on her. The rest of the evening, thankfully, turned out to be relatively quiet. Kathleen put Jack and Bobby to bed early with her, and I let Nina watch TV downstairs with me until 10:30 p.m. As soon as Nina went upstairs, I finished off my last beer, took a sedative, and went to bed. I knew, though, that I would only sleep a few hours.

I tossed and turned most of the night. When I finally got out of bed, it was 4:30 a.m. I quickly went downstairs and decided to call Mick on his cell phone. The phone only rang once, and Mick picked up. Before I could say a word, he informed me that the story was indeed in the paper. Surprisingly, he told me that it could have been worse. The headline did not mention his name, but simply referred to him as "Laski aide." Still, the story did have facts and figures about how much "Get Plowed" had made over the years. It also went into some detail about the company's contribution to my campaign fund, along with the company's address and phone number being the same as those of the Jones's home residence. For dramatic effect, the story left enough space for a nice-sized picture of the Jones's home. For some reason, a number of people who saw that picture later in the day thought it was my house. In any event, the story was now out, and starting an avalanche of problems for a number of people.

After that initial story, I knew there would be follow-ups, and there were. The Hired Truck Program was turning into the "Hired Truck Scandal." Every day, indictments followed, and every news story found a way to include Mick's relationship with me.

What developed next was no surprise. The FBI and the U.S. Attorney's office were all over city hall and various departments, pulling various records and documents regarding the truck program. Right after that, Mick called me, desperate to meet with me. I left early from downtown, and had Tom drive directly to Mick's house, where he had been waiting for me in his truck. I then told Tom to drive my car back home, and that I would get a ride back to my house.

When I got into his truck, Mick wasted no time telling me something that would not only further complicate the problem, but would eventually change both of our lives. He simply said that Randy was involved in the trucking scheme, and that we all needed to talk. Well, I got that nauseous feeling in my stomach again as I picked up my cell phone and called Randy, who was already at home. I told him that we would pick him up in five minutes behind his garage. Randy was waiting for us when we pulled up, and he quickly jumped into the back seat of Mick's truck. The three of us talked as we drove around the neighborhood.

Apparently, Randy recently got another two trucks on with the city for Mick—one of them for his own financial benefit. Randy bought one truck from a friend whose company also did business with the city's truck program. Mick agreed to buy the truck from Randy, and in turn, Randy would get that truck on for himself, along with another for Mick, through Tomczak's office. Each of them would then keep their respective profits from those trucks. Unfortunately, Mick registered the title of the truck he secretly bought from Randy under his in-laws' name and address.

Our whole explanation to *The Sun-Times* was that Mick and Traci Jones now had no interest whatsoever in either "Get Plowed," or the truck program. Then why had a new "Get Plowed" truck been put on with the city less than two months ago, and registered to Mick's in-laws, when he and his wife were no longer involved with the company? Furthermore, why did Randy, who worked for the water department, buy a truck from a company that also would be under investigation, and sell the vehicle to a long-time friend's in-laws in the first place?

The more information they gave me, the worse I felt. I knew this was now a problem that could have criminal consequences. The conversation soon started heating up as Mick and Randy played the blame game with each other. Before they got completely out of control, I jumped in and asked how long had the truck that Randy sold to Mick been on the payroll. They both said approximately one month. I then asked whether the original invoice was paid, and where the original paperwork on the new truck was filed. Randy told me that the paperwork was filed with the water department's office for accounts receivable and accounts payable, which was woefully behind in its processing. The bottom line, according to Randy, was that the truck's original invoice was still on someone's desk, along with a copy of the registration, and all other pertinent information regarding the new truck purchased by "Get Plowed" —Mick.

With that information now on the table, the next question was whether anyone had gotten their hands on those documents. Randy was absolutely certain that the FBI had not been in that office yet, because they were pulling only those invoices that had already been paid, and not those yet to be processed. Randy offered to see someone he knew in that office, to try to grab all the information and paperwork relating to the truck that the FBI had no idea existed yet. Randy also agreed to destroy all the documents once he got his hands on them. Thus, there would be no paper trail, except for the title that Mick's in-laws would receive from the Secretary of State, but there would be no red flag raised that would warn any investigative agency to look in that direction.

As soon as we all agreed on the plan, I warned Randy to be careful. I told him if something didn't appear to look right, to try to get out of there, because now he was potentially risking being charged with destroying evidence in a federal investigation. After we dropped Randy off at his home, Mick and I became cautiously optimistic. We felt that Randy would know exactly whom to see and where the paperwork was located.

The next day, I decided to stay in the neighborhood, instead of going downtown. It was payday, and Tom had already dropped off my paycheck. Around 1:00 p.m., I headed to the bank, which was only five minutes from the house. As I pulled into the bank, my cell phone rang. I picked up. It was Randy. He told me he could meet me in ten minutes.

About fifteen minutes later, Randy pulled up in his family's green Caravan. As we got out of our vehicles in the back of the bank's parking lot and started walking toward each other, I could see a smile on his face. He told me that everything had gone well. The only question I asked him was where he had disposed of the paperwork. He said he had thrown the shredded materials into a dumpster on the city's north side, where his business did some sweeping and snowplowing. We both sighed in relief, and I called Mick to share the news with him. When I called Mick on his cell phone, I was very short and obscure in my conversation, and simply told him that all the lost paperwork was found and properly filed.

The next day, Mick and I got together, and I reminded him that one other loose end needed to be taken care of, and that was the truck his in-laws now allegedly owned. He immediately informed me that his partner, John Novak, would take care of that business, which he later told me involved stripping the truck for sellable parts, while destroying the rest of the vehicle. I knew we weren't out of the woods yet, but I felt that we had at least dodged a few bullets. I began to feel a little more relaxed, even if only temporarily.

Besides a few references to "Get Plowed" in *The Sun-Times'* continuing investigation of the Hired Truck Program, the following months were relatively quiet, until just before Easter. I was at home doing some odds and ends when my cell phone rang. It was Mick, who said he was stopping over to see me. My first reaction was that some new problem had come up. I was doing some basic cleaning and straightening up in my backyard when Mick pulled up behind my garage. He was all smiles, and said Novak had called, and had just left a meeting with the FBI. Of course, my mouth instantly froze shut, and my legs felt paralyzed. Mick, though, assured me everything was fine, and proceeded to tell me the story, while I tried to keep my wits about me.

John Novak was driving to check out a job site when his cell phone went off. A man on the other end identified himself as an FBI agent, and proceeded to tell John that he needed to meet with him as soon as possible to ask him some questions about his truck company.

The agent asked him when they could schedule a sit-down, and John answered, "How about now?"

I could only imagine his reaction when John assured him he could be at his FBI office near Timken Park, a suburb of Chicago, in approximately one hour. My first reaction was, "Is he crazy?—meeting with an FBI agent without an attorney present?"

Mick ignored my questions, and calmly informed me that John spent almost two hours answering questions from a couple of agents. Those questions ran the gambit from who actually ran and had interest in his company to any payoffs or kickbacks John had made to anyone. Specifically, they questioned him about his relationship with me. John said he met me through Mick at some party, and that we had only spoken a couple of times over the past ten years. In fact, he indicated that any political contributions he might have made to me were out of loyalty to his mom, who was a big supporter of mine. The agents then grilled him about the amount of money given me, which John said he didn't think was much. At that point, they supposedly threatened him with a "come clean" attitude, claiming that the company was just a shell game for him and Mick. Mick told me that John was not worried, and that he had given them absolutely nothing to implicate any of us. Mick said that John had a lot of balls, and that maybe, just maybe, the Feds believed him. However, as I would continue to learn, the Jones family had many questionable deals with various people. Once again, we have to go back in time for more historical background on some of these relationships.

Mick Jones and John Novak had long been friends, but because of personal issues in Novak's life, they hadn't been as close lately. When John married his neighborhood sweetheart, Mary, many years before, one or both of the Jones's was in their bridal party. As time went on, the two families became inseparable. Mary was godmother to one of the Jones children, and both families took vacations together.

Kathleen and I knew Mary Novak through the Joneses. She was quite petite (only five-feet tall), and weighed about one-hundred pounds. A very nice lady, she was also quite an intelligent woman who had taught second grade for over twenty-five years at a neighborhood Catholic school that my children attended. In fact, Mary taught our daughter Nina, and now was doing the same for our twins, Jack and Bobby. Mary was not only a very good teacher, but also a caring and compassionate person who always treated our kids as her own. I can't tell you how much interest she took in all of our children. She was also a counselor for Catholic charities, and a dance instructor after school. Her day didn't end until 10:00 p.m., every night during the week. A few years ago, John built Mary a magnificent suburban home, only about a thirty-minute drive on the expressway from the neighborhood. The home had a couple of levels, rooms everywhere, and a beautiful wooded area in the back. If I had to guess, I'd say the house was worth over $600,000.00. It seemed that John and Mary had everything they ever needed, or at least I thought.

What I didn't know was that over the past few years, John had been losing interest in his marriage. According to Mick, because Mary was always so busy, John became lonely. It wasn't long before John had met another woman and moved out on Mary. Naturally, Mary was devastated, and they separated.

That entire situation complicated Mick's life, because he wanted to continue to be friends with both John and Mary. Mick knew that if anyone could bury him with the Feds regarding his business dealings and other arrangements with "Get Plowed," it would be John and Mary Novak. Thus, Mick tried to walk a fine line between the two of them, especially since John ran the trucking operation with the city, and Mary wrote checks out of the "Get Plowed" account.

At one point, while trying to find John, the FBI called Mary on her cell phone, and asked her where he was living. She had supposedly told them they were separated, but that she had his cell phone number. My understanding was that the FBI never arranged or requested a meeting with her about the business, which I still find incredible, even until this day.

Another individual I believed played a role in this whole complicated story was a man named Phil, a next-door neighbor whom, I'd been told, had watched out for Mary after she and John had separated. Since Mary had such a big house, there were always times when she needed Mick to come over to fix something. So, over the years, Mick became very good friends with Phil.

Under ordinary circumstances, Mick's friendship with Phil would have been no big deal—except for the fact that Phil had been employed for over twenty years as an FBI agent, and was currently working out of Chicago. Once the Hired Truck investigation started, Mick told me that he would talk to Phil to try to find out if he knew what was going on with the Feds. Sure enough, Phil allegedly told Mick that his fellow agents came to both his house and Mary's house, looking for information about John and Mick. Mick later met with Phil, who told him about the FBI visit and their questions. According to Mick, Phil said that his colleagues were interested in how long John had been separated from Mary, and the last time he had been seen at his own house. The agents also wanted to know how many times he had actually seen Mick at Mary's house, and what, if anything, Phil knew about their relationship. Mick chuckled when he told me that Phil informed his agents about what a good guy Mick was, how Mick helped Mary all the time, and that he had seen Mick and his family over at the house on many occasions.

Mick never hid his relationship with Phil. On the contrary, he bragged to our mutual friends about having an FBI agent in his back pocket. He would also boast that when he and Phil would get drunk on occasion, Phil would share professional secrets with him. For example, according to Mick, Phil told him that, after 9/11, FBI agents posed as janitors in the Sears Tower in Chicago, because of possible terrorist attacks. Phil also referred to possible future subway attacks, and to the FBI's checking of various off-street maintenance entrances to the downtown subway system. Every time there was a heightened security alert, Mick would seem to know about it, and comment on how that would keep other agents from looking into the

Hired Truck Program. Although Mick told me that Phil's expertise was in bank robberies, he assured Mick he would always keep his ear to the ground on other matters that Mick might want to know about in the future.

Kathleen and I had an opportunity to meet Phil one time at Mary's house. Mick and Traci had convinced Mary to hold a graduation party for their oldest daughter, Ashley. When we arrived, we discovered a number of guests standing in Mary's garage drinking, including Mick, who was waiting for us. He promptly took us into the garage where all the coolers were placed, to introduce us to a tall, medium-built, middle-aged, very polite, and personable man named Phil. During the evening, we also met Phil's wife and daughter, and my children got a chance to see their dog, which jumped on one of the boys, accidentally scratching him to the point where he started crying.

During one part of the evening, while standing in the garage, drinking and smoking, Mick and I started talking about the advantages of living in the suburbs. Then, some of our friends began commenting on Daley and the truck program. The longer this conversation went on, the more uncomfortable, it seemed, Phil became. Finally, he threw what was left of his cigarette in a beer can that was used as an ashtray, excused himself, and went back into the house. The conversation evidently touched a raw nerve with Phil. Although he always kept his feelings under wraps, he later told Mick privately that in cases like the Hired Truck Program scandal, the Feds generally started by looking up the food chain, in order to catch a big fish. Those words, as I learned later, became gospel for Mick and Traci Jones.

Not long after John's meeting with the FBI, unexpected visitors dropped off subpoenas for both Mick and him to appear before the Inspector General of Chicago regarding their involvement in the truck program. In addition, they were ordered to bring the necessary paperwork regarding their divesture form "Get Plowed." As in the past, whenever anyone close to me had a problem with an investigatory agency and needed legal representation, I would call my friend, Bob Molaro. Bobby and I went back many years. Every time he helped someone in my world, I would always stay out of the process so that Bobby would maintain the integrity of the attorney/ client privilege with his client. This case was no exception, and Mick and Traci went to see Molaro at his office to prepare for their meeting with the inspector general.

The meeting took place quickly. Mick and Traci went in separately, for about forty-five minutes each, answered all questions asked, and then returned to my office. Both of them seemed relieved, and felt relatively confident about the meeting's outcome.

During my years in public office, I learned that dealing with the U.S. Attorney and the FBI was entirely different from dealing with the Chicago Inspector General. As I mentioned earlier, above this agency was the mayor's enforcement arm. The inspector general answered only to the mayor, and any information from an investigation was provided only to the mayor's office, and not to city council. I've always wondered what would happen in the event of a pending investigation of Mayor Daley or his staff. Would the inspector general inform the mayor that he was a target of its investigation? I would think not! This became apparent a few years ago during a budget hearing, when the inspector general told the city that he was answerable only to the mayor, including notifications of any pending investigations. The city council distrusted and despised the special alliance between the agency and the mayor. The inspector general's office skills had long been amateurish, at best, with a distinctly unimpressive track record of breaking cases or uncovering scandals. The most that office ever did was to jump on the coattails of a TV expose.

Honestly, I had always been a little suspicious of the inspector general's motives over the years. I probably was the target of at least four different investigations from that office that I knew of, and I wondered how many of those had been sanctioned by either the mayor or his staff. I still suspect that not only did someone on the fifth floor know about those investigations, but they also had tremendous input in their exposure to the press.

In any event, following the inspector general's investigations, I took it upon myself to find out anything I could about the "Get Plowed" investigation. I spoke to a friend over at police headquarters who had done his own research. He found out that a couple of police officers assigned to the inspector general's office were the lead investigators in Mick's case. Eventually, he learned that after a preliminary investigation, they had found nothing of a criminal nature, nor any city ethics violations. As far as they were concerned, their job was finished, except for sending their report to the FBI.

During that time period, there were further indictments, including that of Don Tomczak, who was charged with a truckload of counts, along with a couple of his underlings, who the government had listed as his "bag men." After the Tomczak indictment, Randy called, and asked me to meet him at Valley Forge Park, which was about four blocks from his house. When we met, the only thing he wanted to tell me was that as long as Mick or John Novak hadn't bribed anyone from the water department, or anywhere else, neither one would have anything to worry about. For some reason, Randy thought that Tomczak received some money, which to my knowledge, never happened. One thing Randy said he did know was that Tomczak would NEVER cooperate with the FBI.

As the rest of 2004 moved quickly by, Mick and I constantly re-assured each other that everything was going to be fine. With so many other investigations going on in the city, unless there were some informant in our inner circle with some solid information, there was no way the U.S. Attorney could ever indict either Mick or me on just speculation or hearsay.

Believe it or not, the holidays were quiet and uneventful. For the first time in months, I began to relax and enjoy life again with my family. As we moved into 2005, little did I realize how short-lived that serenity would be.

CHAPTER 13

THE HIRED TRUCK PROGRAM SCANDAL:
THE CALM BEFORE THE STORM

As the new year started, I tried to push the whole truck scandal behind me. It was time to concentrate on my political career, and the opportunities that would be worth pursuing. Of course, I wouldn't consider any political moves without first discussing them with Kathleen and Ray, who were my closest advisors and biggest influences in my life. If the three of us would sign off on making a move to run for another office, it would be a done deal, and we could let the rest of the world know.

During discussions with my wife, there was one office of mutual interest to us, and that was Bill Lipinski's congressional seat. Although my ego in past years wanted me to run against him, I decided not to. It wasn't that I couldn't win, but I was reluctant to spend hundreds of thousands of dollars that I wasn't even certain I could raise. I was also afraid of potentially damaging my relationships with Mike Madigan, Ed Burke, and John Daley, to name a few people—all of whom had helped me, and who felt comfortable with me as city clerk. More importantly, I wasn't sure if either my wife or I could stand up to the pressures of such an intensely personal campaign.

Well, before I could even re-consider that option, the news came out that Lipinski would not run in November. Lipinski won the

Democratic primary in March, and would be a shoe-in in November. He would complete his twenty-second year in Congress, and there was no one out there who would have been able to challenge him.

However, with his surprising announcement came the arrogance and lack of respect that I'd grown to know Lipinski by over the years. Although he wasn't going to run again for re-election, he would gather all his committeemen friends from the Congressional district, who would select a replacement for him on the November ballot. It was a virtual certainty that whoever would be picked would be the next congressman. It was no surprise when Lipinski announced that he would lobby for, and ask his fellow committeemen, to appoint his son, Dan Lipinski, as the Democratic candidate. Since the committeemen's votes were based on voter population (weighted vote), Lipinski's 23rd Ward, Mike Madigan's 13th Ward, and John Daley's 11th Ward had been enough to have put Dan over the top.

Needless to say, there was much public criticism from not only the community, but most of the Chicago media. Everyone was talking nepotism, and dirty, backroom politics, but if the Madigans and others could put in their kids, why couldn't Lipinski? Knowing Lipinski as I did, there was no way, barring an Act of Congress, he would ever change his mind.

I called David Axelrod, the most highly respected political consultant in the state of Illinois, if not the entire country. Our meeting, which was set for about two weeks later, on a Friday, was held in Axelrod's office, and consisted of only three people—Axelrod, myself, and Kathleen. After some preliminary small talk, we got down to business. Axelrod said he knew why I had come, and told me he thought I would be a logical choice to run against Lipinski's son, and that I could beat him in the next primary. Clearly, Axelrod believed that this election would be one of the most highly watched races in the country.

Now, after all those positives came the negatives. Axelrod asked me if I could prepare myself to lose, because in this type of election, which would be a bloodbath, I would need to anticipate that possibility. He also informed me that Bill Lipinski would raise a ton of money for his son, and would dry up any potential money I would go after. He conceded, however, that Dan Lipinski's advisors would have their hands full trying to cultivate his personality, and to position him politically to run against me in less than a year. I then asked David if he would be willing to join my campaign. I told him that I had around $400,000.00 in my campaign account. He quickly answered that I would probably need close to $1,000,000.00 to be competitive in the primary. At the end of the day, he told me he would love a good fight, but needed to get back to me, because he had a contract pending with the National Democratic Committee to work for incumbent Democrats. Handling my campaign would certainly be a conflict of interest. However, he promised me that in the event he couldn't handle it, he would give me the names of a couple of consultants he would recommend. After we left, Kathleen and I knew we had a lot to talk over on the way home.

A couple of days later, I checked back with Axelrod, who told me what my wife and I had already suspected. Since he had committed himself to the Democratic National Party, he couldn't get involved in my campaign. I told him I appreciated his honesty, and that my wife and I would have to do some soul-searching before I could call him back about the other consultants he mentioned.

For the next two weeks, I talked the matter over with my wife, Ray, Sam Gammicchia, and Mick Jones, just trying to figure out what I should do or not do. I then came up with another idea. One night, while I was at home smoking on my stoop, and thinking about the future, it dawned on me that my friend, State Treasurer Judy Topinka, was considering running for governor. Since she was a Republican and I was a Democrat, any conversation with her would give me a wide-open slot from the other side in a Democratic primary. Running statewide would be a great challenge for me, and no elected official of Polish ancestry had ever won a statewide office. The best part of all was that no other Democrat was even thinking about running for State Treasurer.

I finished my cigarette and ran into the house to tell Kathleen my idea.

I have to admit I wasn't looking for a positive response, but I was pleasantly surprised when she had said, "Let's take a look at it."

I knew Kathleen was tired of city politics, tired of the investigations, and tired of people stopping at our house, complaining about a raise, promotions, or wanting a new job. It wasn't that I was tired of helping people; I was simply tired of helping the *same* people over and over again. The more I gave them and their families, the more they always wanted. Already, there were plenty of people who worked for me downtown who were being paid anywhere between $50,000.00 and $100,000.00. In some cases, multiple members of a family received jobs from me.

Nevertheless, when I started talking about the treasurer's office, I received mixed reviews from my staff downtown. Regardless of their views, I proceeded with the necessary publicity to announce my intention to run for State Treasurer. When the story appeared in both major Chicago newspapers, I began to field questions about what I was going to do in the office if elected, and about any new developments in the Hired Truck Program story. Although I felt comfortable about running for a new office, I still had some anxiety about future investigations.

Over the following days, I made a number of phone calls to other elected officials to gather their support. There were friends such as Bill Banks, a powerful alderman from the north side, who told me that he had been the first official who had endorsed me for city clerk, and that he would be the first to endorse me for State Treasurer. Of course, I reached out to the Speaker of the State House, Mike Madigan, who, as usual, was non-committal, playing his cards close to the vest. He implied that he was happy with me being city clerk and with everything I had done to help his organization, and that my future was in the city of Chicago.

The next meeting I arranged was with Mayor Daley. Surprisingly, it didn't take long to set up that meeting, possibly because of the publicity over my running for State Treasurer. I believe Daley wanted to know how serious I was about running statewide.

I probably waited less than five minutes in the outer office, before he came strolling out with a big smile. He shook my hand and told me to come back to his office. We actually went to his conference room, and we sat at the head of the table. We started by exchanging our usual pleasantries. One thing about Daley is that he is a true family man, and he never missed an opportunity to talk about my family, always showing an interest, which I believe was sincere.

When we got down to business, I came right out and asked him what he thought about my possibly running statewide.

He immediately answered, "Why not?"

Daley usually would take a slower approach, analyze the situation, and get back to me, but this time he said it was a good idea, and that I should go for it. I then asked if he would support me, and actually endorse me politically.

He didn't waste one second before answering with a firm, and unequivocal, "Yes!"

I was actually shocked by his answer, so just to make sure I had heard right, I asked him again; his answer was the same. Honestly, I now had mixed emotions, because I knew he always wanted to get rid of me as city clerk, since he considered me a thorn in his side, but I would gain a tremendous leg up in the state race with his support.

Daley then took the opportunity to remind me that people in politics should never forget where they had come from. He quickly directed those comments to Governor Blagojevich, whom he referred to as an ingrate. He told me that Blagojevich was becoming arrogant, and did not mince words when he said that if the governor didn't change his ways, he would have a problem. Daley had not liked the fact that Blagojevich had been quoted in the newspapers as having disagreed with him on some issues like gambling. Trust me, no one—and I mean no one—can tell this mayor how to run Chicago, not even the governor of the state. By the time I left his office, there was no doubt in my mind who was the most powerful Democrat in Illinois.

Even though I had not made a final decision regarding the state race, I knew I had to make a trip to Springfield to meet some of the legislators and lobbyists, and get a sense from them about my future. I also needed to tell them about the mayor's support. I quickly planned my Springfield visit around my daughter's own trip there, because she had been selected as one of the state finalists for her history project.

Since the family was going to be there anyway, I figured I would go down a day early to meet with some people.

The trip, which was set for early May 2005, included an appointment with the current Treasurer, Judy Topinka, and a possible dinner with State Speaker Madigan. At the same time that I was going to Springfield, so were the investigators from my office, going for a training seminar on the laptop computers they would use to write tickets in Chicago. Since Mick Jones headed that unit for my office, he scheduled the whole seminar for that time. When he found out that I was also heading there, he immediately offered to drive me down, and said he would take me to my various meetings.

I knew that Mick had a vested interest in my decision to run for treasurer, because of his pension. He only needed about three years to be fully vested with the City of Chicago, and if I won the treasurer's race, he wanted me to persuade the next city clerk to keep him on until his pension had vested, and then he would join me on the state payroll. In any event, many other things needed to happen before we could start worrying about pensions.

The trip to Springfield allowed me to meet quite a few new faces. I had the opportunity to talk to legislators from all over the state of Illinois. I was surprised at how many of them knew about me, and my political plans. The weather was incredibly hot, and by the end of the day, I was soaking, having worn a suit. On that first night, Mick and I couldn't wait to change clothes, and take my investigators out to dinner, after their all-day seminar. Our plan included after-dinner meetings with Dan Burke and a few other people, a few parties, and then back to the bar of the Renaissance Hotel for a nightcap.

About 7:00 p.m., Dan Burke met us at the bar/restaurant for a drink, and he told me about the people we had to meet at the beer distributors' party that was taking place somewhere in Springfield that evening. We all piled into Dan's car and headed to the party. It was about a fifteen-minute ride. When we arrived, wall-to-wall people were drinking beer and having a good time. Dan took me around to meet everyone. I couldn't even tell you how many people I met, let alone who they were, but if one of them gave me a business card, I handed it to Mick, who held onto it until we had gotten back to Chicago. That allowed me to send that person a thank you note asking for his or her future support. Quite honestly, most of the people I met were not only receptive to my plans, but asked me to meet them in the near future, in their local communities, for some preliminary campaigning. The only problem with a beer distributors' party was that everyone kept giving me a beer. So, only more than an hour after I had arrived, I told Mick to plan my exit, and we grabbed Dan and headed back to the hotel.

When we got back to the Renaissance, the bar was fairly crowded. I found myself talking to at least half of the Hispanic Caucus of the General Assembly, so what I thought was going to be a short evening was turning into a marathon. I ended up asking many of the Hispanic legislators for their help, in return for my supporting one of their members as the next Chicago city clerk.

By this time, I had enough drinking and campaigning for the evening. Every time I thought I had seen an opening to sneak back to my room, someone else would stop by to talk to me. We closed the bar at 2:00 a.m. Every legislator and lobbyist who left that building should thank God there were no police officers driving around, because every one of them could have been arrested for drunk driving.

At approximately 2:30 a.m., I finally went to bed. I was excited about meeting Kathleen and the kids around 11:00 a.m., but I would first see State Treasurer Judy Topinka in her office around 9:30 a.m. With the front desk's help, I woke up around 8:00 a.m. I quickly showered and dressed, and knocked on the door of the adjoining room where Mick had spent the night. After we ate, Mick and I got into his car, and headed to Judy's office. As walked in, the first thing we noticed was how happy and relaxed everyone on her staff was. A couple of her staff immediately took Mick to a room where he could wait until my meeting was over, while her office manager directed me to the treasurer's office. Her office, although somewhat large, seemed old, as if it could use a good cleaning and a paint job, although I felt comfortable, because I saw ashtrays everywhere, along with the fresh smell of tobacco.

Judy was sitting at her desk when I walked in, and before I could run over to her, we kind of met in the middle of the room, where we hugged each other. I have to say that Judy is one of the nicest, most sincere people I'd ever met in politics. Don't let her nice personality fool you, though. She has the tenacity of a bulldog. Judy is both articulate and well-versed on the issues—traits that would make her a formidable governor.

Our meeting lasted about forty-five minutes, and we spoke about everything from our favoring the same cigarettes (Marlboros) to our mutual interest in running for different offices. The bottom line for Judy was the money issue. She was concerned about the amount of money her opponent would force her to spend. The other wild card was the rumor of former Governor Jim Edgar's running again, which neither of us believed would happen.

At the end of the day, she would not commit herself either way, but I knew she was leaning towards running, because she kept saying that I would be an excellent replacement, and that she would go over everything with me during the transition. The last thing she told me was that I would be the very first Democrat she would call when she decided to run. After hearing that, I knew she was serious about the governorship, and we both expected her announcement to be made around Labor Day.

I spent the rest of my time in Springfield with my family. My daughter's history fair had gone well, and she had received second honors for her project. We also did a little sightseeing of the capital before heading home. During the ride home, I wondered if Springfield would become my usual home. Little did I know that this would be my last trip to Springfield.

I spent the next couple of months planning my annual fundraisers. The first would be my annual golf outing at Oak Brook Hills Resort. Shortly after that, we would plan a downtown fundraiser in September or October, which could be the kickoff for my state treasurer campaign.

The beginning of summer in 2005 was quiet for the most part, except for one article by Fran Spielman of *The Chicago Sun-Times*. The article accused me of giving summer jobs to influential politicians, in order to get their support for my state treasurer campaign. I have to be honest when I say that was a little paranoid about Spielman and *The Sun-Times*, because over the past few years, I believed they were trying to persecute me for anything I did. The summer job story was a joke, because I went to the aldermen and other elected officials about such jobs when I first became city clerk in 1995, over ten years ago. For the most part, the program worked well for everyone. I would usually pick up a very qualified high school or college student whom one of my colleagues had wanted to help, from his or her community. In turn, I would get an energetic student to work in my office during those crazy summer days when we usually sold over one million vehicle stickers. What bothered me the most about this story was that Spielman also insinuated that maybe some of those students, especially those who were related to elected officials, were not actually working, but still getting paid. The one thing I always took pride in was my office's efficiency. My directors and supervisors kept a close eye on our summer interns. If someone didn't work out, I signed the paperwork to terminate that person. Although the media could blame me for certain issues down the road, they couldn't, in good conscience, attack my achievements, including my office's revenue-generating aspects. I think that record speaks for itself.

Soon, it was August of 2005. The family and I had just returned from our yearly two-week vacation at my in-laws' home in Eagle River, Wisconsin, which is in the northern part of the state, about 337 miles from Chicago. I thought about the fun we had every year up north—the boys' diving off the platform into the lake and swimming, Nina's attempts at tubing and water skiing, and Kathleen just relaxing while watching our kids have fun. I took great pleasure in grilling every night on the deck. I made everything from ribs, to chicken, to brats, and, of course, all of it marinated in beer. The nights were so peaceful that off the lake, we could hear a pin drop. Our deck was no more than fifty yards away from the lake, and if I weren't sitting out there, I would be at one of the neighbor's homes, playing poker. My in-laws' house was surrounded by trees, and there were plenty of deer, raccoons, and eagles, of course. For the avid outdoors person, the fishing was excellent, and my son Jack took full advantage by catching one-hundred fish in two weeks, many of which we fried and ate.

No matter how stressful the year could be, everything seemed to even off in Wisconsin for Kathleen and me. Even now, I can just sit back and pretend I'm on the deck, sipping, a beer, and just looking at the lake, imagining what the future is going to hold—then I snap out of my pleasant dream, and I'm back in my cube at Morgantown, looking out the window. Dark and rainy, it's the last week of the year, 2006, and I'm getting ready to recall the worst time of my life, and how it led me here.

CHAPTER 14

THE HIRED TRUCK PROGRAM SCANDAL:
DECEIT AND LOSS

It was Thursday, August 11, 2005. We had just finished dinner. Jack and Bobby were in the back room watching television. Nina was downstairs in the basement, on the computer, and Kathleen was upstairs, putting laundry away. The evening was warm and sunny, and Kathleen and I were discussing my golf outing, and how disappointed we had been so far with the response. With the outing only eight days away, we were especially concerned because of the disappointing response to the event so far, and about our plans for a new campaign, and my staff's lack of enthusiasm over its direction. In addition, Mick, who ran the outing, was on his annual family vacation in Florida. In previous years, his vacation was never time-sensitive, but this year, when he moved the date forward to August 19, we didn't take into account his vacation. He would return home earlier than the rest of his family, probably on Monday or Tuesday, which would give him at least three days to tie up any loose ends.

Despite our overall concern, Kathleen and I were having fun that night, agreeing facetiously to the idea of golfing ourselves, if no one showed up, and selling raffle tickets and serving, but not eating, the meals in order to save money on the event. I laughed so hard, I had tears in my eyes. Just at that moment, the doorbell rang.

Wondering who could be ringing our doorbell at 7:00 p.m., I took my time going downstairs. I was hoping whoever was there would get impatient and leave. Before opening the door, I quickly peeked out the corner of the front door window, and saw a man and a woman, both dressed up, and holding what appeared to be leather satchels. I thought they were Jehovah Witnesses, or members of some other religious group. It wasn't uncommon in our neighborhood to have what I called "Bible beaters" going door-to-door and soliciting money for the various religious materials, they were selling to try to convert people. I knew as I opened the door, that whatever the case was, I wanted no part of it.

I stepped outside planing to politely tell them I wasn't interested, but before I could say a word, the young man, dressed in a gray business suit, asked me if I was Jim Laski.

I swallowed hard, exhaled, and said, "Yes."

He quickly replied that he was a special FBI agent. The young lady stepped up, handed me her business card, and told me the same thing about herself. He said they needed to speak to me regarding their ongoing investigation of the Hired Truck Program. I remember the female agent walking toward my front door and asking if she could come into the house just to talk to me for a few minutes. She said she wanted to ask me a couple of questions. Although I had been completely caught off guard, I kept my political wits about me and told both of them that I would be happy to answer any of their questions, but that I needed my attorney present. I could tell that they both had been down this road before, as they handed me their cards. I said that my attorney would call them back to set up an appointment, although, quite frankly, I didn't know whom to use as counsel. The male agent pulled out his pen and some papers, and quickly wrote something down on one of the pages, and handed me the whole set. Then, he wrote my name on a grand jury subpoena, which required my appearance on August 18, the day before my golf outing. There was no doubt that my appearing before a grand jury would not be a good situation. I could possibly be setting myself up to be charged with perjury. I politely thanked them, and assured them that my attorney would be in touch. As soon as they turned to leave, I went into the house and watched them walk to their car, which had been parked three blocks away. I waited until they actually drove away.

I can't even explain how I felt when they left. I guess it was a feeling of numbness and terror. No matter how I looked at this situation, the U.S. Attorney and the FBI had received information from some source, which put me in the middle of this whole scandal.

I ran upstairs, and with what I thought was a blank look on my face, told my wife, "You won't believe who was here."

I thought at first she may have thought I was playing a joke on her, but that changed when with a grim look on my face, I told her the FBI had stopped by to talk to me. Honestly, I thought that with all the time that had passed, I was now in the clear. In the back of my mind, I always knew that the Feds had both time and unlimited resources on their side to pursue anyone they wanted.

For the first time, I could tell that Kathleen was afraid. I could see the fear and anxiety in her eyes. The only comfort I could give her was to tell her they wouldn't do anything to me until they had talked to my attorney. The next question was who should represent me?

Before I could answer that question, my cell phone rang, and the name "Aderman" appeared on the cell ID. I immediately knew this call was not a good sign, and those fears were confirmed when I answered the phone. It was Randy, who told me that the FBI had just left his house. He said he didn't go to the door, but hid in the basement while his oldest son answered the door and took the necessary information from the two FBI agents—who, by the way, were not the same agents who came to see me.

Of course, Randy was looking for advice, but the last thing I wanted to do was to talk to him on the phone. Basically, I told him to sit tight, and not to talk to anyone else, because I would have an attorney contact him. Unfortunately, Kathleen was standing by me when I answered Randy's call, so I told her I needed to talk to some people, and that in the meantime, she should just go about her business, and try not to worry.

I then went downstairs to call Bob Molaro. Whenever I needed an attorney for someone else, I would always call Bob. I told him the basics, and asked him to call Randy. I already suspected that all my phones were probably being tapped. Afterwards, I called Mary Pat Burns, one of my attorneys from the Fireman's Pension Fund. Over the past couple of years, Mary Pat and her partners, Vince Pinelli and Ed Burke (not to be confused with Alderman Ed Burke) were very good friends of mine, and they always told me to just give them a call. At first, I got Mary Pat's answering machine. I left a message, but a half-hour later, she returned my call. I immediately told her what had happened. She asked me if I had talked to them.

When I answered, "Of course not!" she told me to relax, and to meet her at her office the next day.

I was scheduled to speak with Vince Pinelli, who handled criminal matters for the firm.

Not surprisingly, I didn't sleep much that night. The next morning when I arrived at the law office, the only thing I could think about was how to get a hold of Mick in Florida, or even if I should. He would be home in another few days. As soon as I told the receptionist at the law office who I was, she escorted me to the conference room, where Mary Pat and Vince were waiting for me. Both of them told me not to worry, and that everything would be fine.

Before I could start explaining myself, Vince told me he had already spoken to someone at the U.S. Attorney's office, and been informed that the FBI needed to set up an interview with me. He also told me not to worry about next Thursday's grand jury date, as long as I agreed to the FBI interview.

My mind raced a mile a minute when Vince and Mary Pat told me that it would be advisable to find another attorney to handle this matter for me. Who would represent me? How much would he or she charge? Could I, on top of all of the other legal fees I would be sure to incur, afford it? I was reluctant to trust anybody else, but Vince and Pat explained that because they had already represented me in my role as president of the pension fund, I should retain other legal help to avoid the appearance of any conflict of interest.

Then, Vince said, "Look, Jim, my brother Tony has handled hundreds of criminal matters for our firm, and he's dealt with the U.S. Attorney before."

When I heard that, I became more interested, and wanted to know more. Vince told me that Tony had even recently represented a client involved in the truck scandal.

"Tony's got over twenty-five years experience in this field, Jim."

"Well, how can I get a hold of him?" I asked.

"You don't have to, "Vince replied. "I called him earlier, and asked him to come over. Why don't you just talk with him, Jim?"

"Please?" Mary Pat added. "Then you can decide whether or not you want to retain him."

There was no doubt I had my back against the wall, and needed to make some quick decisions. I agreed to at least talk with Tony. Then, Vince stepped out, and quickly returned with his brother. The introductions were brief, as Mary Pat and Vince wasted no time excusing themselves so Tony and I could get down to business.

My first impression of Tony was that he could have played a role on the series *The Sopranos.* He was short and stocky, and maybe fifty or so pounds overweight, all in the stomach. With black hair, an olive complexion, a five o'clock shadow, and a round, chubby nose, he just looked like a rough guy. Still, he was one of the nicest guys I would want to meet.

We probably met for about an hour, and went over basic information regarding the truck program and my involvement with Mick and Randy. Never in our conversation did I ever tell Tony that I had taken any money; in fact, I was very defensive, and played the victim the whole way. He did believe, however, that the former Deputy Water Commissioner, Don Tomczak, whom Randy and a number of other misguided souls believed was as solid as a rock, was singing like a canary to the Feds.

I have to admit that after our initial meeting, I felt very comfortable with Tony, and decided to retain him as my attorney. Since the weekend was quickly upon us, Tony didn't know when he would speak to the U.S. Attorney, but he assured me that I would have to appear before the grand jury on August 18. Based on the information I gave Tony, he believed that I had nothing to hide, and should therefore submit to the questioning. He did warn me, however, that anything I would tell them could be used against me, including information that could later be proven untruthful. Tony kept emphasizing that as long as there was nothing else out there I could think of, he saw no problem with my talking to the Feds.

Still, I was a nervous wreck over the weekend. On top of everything else, I had my golf outing on Friday. It was late Monday morning when Tony called me. He told me that we would meet with Assistant U.S. Attorney Patrick Collins one week from that day, at 9:00 a.m. He was happy to inform me that Collins had agreed to come to Tony's office, which he thought was a good sign. Any time a public figure under investigation didn't have to walk into the Federal building and be spotted by the press was good, Tony said. We agreed to meet on Monday, August 18, at 8:00 a.m. —an hour before Collins would arrive—to go over our game plan. Meanwhile, I needed to ask Tony about his retainer fee. He asked me to bring a check for $25,000.00.

For some reason, I felt better after talking to Tony, because I believed he was experienced enough to get me through this ordeal, regardless if I didn't tell him everything. In the meantime, Bob Molaro told me that Ron Belmonte from his office would be sitting down with Aderman about scheduling a meeting with the Feds.

Meanwhile, Mick was hopping on a plane back to Chicago. I had not spoken to him since our visit Thursday. However, Kathleen had talked to him a couple of times regarding the golf outing, but had been very careful on the phone not to say anything about the Feds. She really believed that Mick had no clue about what had been going on back home.

After his plane landed, I was on a cell phone with him. He was his usual jovial self when I told him abruptly to come to my house, because I was concerned about the numbers for the outing. He said he had just gotten off the plane, and needed to stop at home after he returned his luggage. I thought I may have sounded a little angry when I again told him to come over ASAP.

Less than an hour later, Mick knocked on the side door. My wife and I were very happy to see him. We were all like family as we embraced, and then sat down at the dining room table. It was around dinner time, so we ordered a pizza, and I went downstairs to grab a couple of beers for the two of us, trying to hold off as long as possible before breaking the news to him. When I returned with the pizza, and the two of us were sitting in the basement (since I needed to talk to him), eating our share, I couldn't wait another minute.

I said, "Mick, I have some shitty news."

I then told him the whole story, from start to finish, including Randy's visit. His former relaxed and happy mood quickly turned somber, as he fired question after question at me. Mick told me he had done nothing wrong, and that there was nothing to worry about, However, he didn't express those same sentiments when it came to Randy.

As much as we now tried to keep busy with the golf outing, it was hard not to think about what was ahead, especially with my interview on Monday. In any event, we had to put our best face forward, and pretend to everyone there, including my own staff, that everything was fine.

The weather for the outing turned out to be beautiful. It was going to be about ninety degrees, and everything was in place, both on the resort's end and my own. One check area was right behind the Pro Shop at one end of the resort, next to the parking lot, where everyone could pull their cars in and register for golf. Weeks later, I learned that FBI agents had been sitting in the parking lot that day, keeping track of everyone who attended the event.

As a whole, the outing went fairly well. Everyone seemed to have had a good time. My only thought was to get the whole thing over with, and jump into the pool. The one thing that did happen that afternoon was that Randy stopped by, along with his youngest son, Kevin, who was in the same class as my boys. So, for the next hour, we let Jack and Kevin golf together, while Mick, Randy, and I spoke almost in code about our situation. It was almost as if we were afraid to talk openly about anything that day. What I didn't know was that this was going to be the last time the three of us would ever get together again to talk.

Now, during that whole day, I had to put on an Academy Award performance for my other guests. The only exceptions, of course, were Ray Drish and Sam Gammicchia, both of whom knew exactly what was going on, and who kept an eye on everyone else, to try to discover anything suspicious.

When the event was over, the Laski and the Jones families hung around the pool that warm evening, just trying to relax. Although we didn't talk much about our legal concerns, we did assure each other of our mutual loyalty, and of our plans to keep our futures together intact. The next morning we all had breakfast at the resort, and we let the kids go the pool one more time. I have to say I had a tight feeling in my stomach that whole morning. I just felt as if something was ending that day, and I wasn't sure what.

The rest of the weekend I stayed to myself, just trying to figure out what possible questions the U.S. Attorney would ask me, and what my answers would be. I also knew that there was one particular question I would be asked, to which I was already prepared not to answer truthfully.

I woke up early Monday morning, about 6:30 a.m. I took my Lorezpan and Lexapro, just to get started. Since the weather was warm, I wore a light sport coat and a white crew neck top over khakis, and went outside on the backstop to have my Pepsi, as usual, along with my Marlboro. I told Tom to pick me up around 7:00 a.m., to give me enough time to get to Tony's office by 8:00 a.m. Kathleen told me to stay clam, and to think before answering a question. Before I knew it, Tom arrived, and Kathleen gave me a hug and a kiss as I jumped into the car.

As we drove downtown, I was very quiet. Tom, who was usually very talkative, knew what I was going through, so he respected my silence and my space. It was 7:45 a.m. when we pulled in front of the building that housed not only Tony's office, but other top Chicago attorneys. Before I went in, I had another cigarette, and told Tom that I would call him when I was finished, but that I would probably be at least three hours. When I entered, the hallway was dimly lit, as in the Paul Newman movie, *The Verdict*. I remember Newman's clients coming to see him in the film, and the surroundings seemed very similar—dark, dingy, quiet, and old.

Tony shared an office at the other end of the hallway with two or three other attorneys. When I arrived, I was so early that the receptionist hadn't even been in yet, but I saw one of those bells that you hit with your hand, which I did. In response, Tony walked nervously to the front office, and invited me in. We then went directly to the conference room we would use for the FBI interview. As we sat down, he told me that if I wasn't sure how to answer a particular question, to stop the interview and confer with him. In fact, if I were in doubt about anything, I should always turn to him for advice and clarity.

Around 9:00 a.m., Tony's receptionist, who had arrived about an hour earlier, notified him that our guests were now there. While Tony walked out of the waiting room to meet them, I rose from my chair and walked directly toward the entrance, where I stopped about ten feet from the door and positioned myself to one side of the conference table. It was only two minutes, but seemed like two hours before they walked in the room.

Patrick Collins entered first, and immediately introduced himself. Mr. Collins was impeccably dressed in a dark business suit and conservative red tie. He was over six feet tall, and at the risk of sounding corny, he had a John F. Kennedy look about him. Poised and confident, he appeared ready to begin the interview as soon as he entered the room. It was clear why he was the lead prosecutor for U. S. Attorney Patrick Fitzgerald in the upcoming trials of former Illinois Governor George Ryan and Mayor Daley's patronage chief, Robert Sorich.

Mr. Collins was not alone. His entourage included the two agents, who had visited my home earlier, along with another individual, whom I think was an assistant U.S. Attorney. After they all introduced themselves, we sat down. I sat at the end of the table closest to the window, with Tony directly to my right, and with everyone else seated around us. Mr. Collins was two seats over to my left, with an agent between him and me.

Before we actually began, Collins and Tony conferred on some basic rules about the interview, including the fact that anything I would say could and would be used against me in a court of law, and that I had agreed to be interviewed, and understood the consequences of not answering every single question truthfully. This whole process was incredibly nerve-wracking. Nothing seemed more terrible than this ordeal.

The interview began with a few basic questions—name, address, and employment history—but right after that, Collins began probing. He asked me straight out who was in my inner circle.

I answered, "Ray Drish, Sam Gammicchia, and Mick Jones."

He then quickly asked me about Randy Aderman's position in the organizational structure. I told him he was a very good friend, but only second tier in the political decision-making process. Every time I thought there was a pattern to his questions, he would switch gears and go into a different area. For example, he spent a considerable amount of time on my relationship with Tomczak. He asked me about my visits, and details about our discussions. Then, suddenly, he would ask me about my relationships with Lipinski and Daley, and about my falling out with them. There was no doubt he was trying to keep me off balance.

Collins concentrated on my friendships with Jones and Aderman, and how those relationships led to my contacting Tomczak. Some of those questions, I had the feeling, Collins already knew the answers to, and because the person whom everyone regarded as such a loyal soldier, Mr. Tomczak, had obviously been talking, big time.

There were also many questions regarding my initial inquiries into the truck program. Collins clearly knew that former Alderman Pat Huels was my first contact. Collins also threw out such names as Angelo Torres, Victor Reyes, Tim Degnan, and Robert Sorich. He asked me about their roles with the city and my relationships with them.

In addition, Mr. Collins inquired about my conversations with Mick and Randy following the FBI's initial visit to my home. They already knew that Mick was in Florida, but asked me if I had spoken with him. I hadn't, but Kathleen had, about the golf outing. He also asked me about Randy, and when I spoke with him. I told him that he called me shortly after receiving a visit from the FBI. The one thing I didn't tell him was that Randy was hiding in his basement, and never talked to the agents that evening. Collins pursued that issue with me, asking me where Randy was when he called me. I told him I thought he was home, but Collins reminded me that Randy was in his basement. I then knew that all our phones were tapped. He asked me again about Randy's whereabouts, but this time his voice carried a tone of frustration and fire. Although I was intimidated, I tried not to show it when I answered I wasn't sure, or that I couldn't recall.

Another surprising piece of information Collins had was his knowledge of my meeting with Mick and Randy after the Hired Truck scandal broke in the paper. He asked me why I called the meeting, and what we discussed. I don't remember ever telling him about such a meeting, and if I didn't tell him, who did? Regardless, I now said I was concerned about both of my friends, and that I had wanted to make sure I wouldn't be blindsided by anything they may have done in the past.

Mr. Collins again switched subjects, and asked me if my golf outing, which took place three days earlier, was a success. He came right out and asked how much money the event raised, and approximately how many people attended. He also inquired about my political accounts, from the amount of money in each one, to what I used the money for. Collins also had a list of certain names and businesses that he read to me, and asked me to identify anyone I knew from that list, and what role he or she played in my life.

There was a point toward the end of the interview when Mr. Collins paused and told me, almost apologetically, that he now had special questions he needed to ask me. In the same breath, he warned me that over the years, many individuals had ended up in big trouble for not answering them fully. Collins advised me to take my time before answering each and every question. Again, in retrospect, these were questions he probably already knew the answers to.

Collins asked a round of questions in rapid fire.

"Did you ever take any money from Mr. Jones for any reason?"

"No."

"Did you ever take any money from Mr. Aderman for any reason?"

"No."

128

"As long as you have been an elected official, have you ever taken any money from anyone, for any reason?"

"No."

I remember taking a big swallow of water before looking into Collins' eyes and answering every question with an emphatic "No!" There may have been a few other questions about taking or giving money, but at that point, they didn't seem that important anymore. I now realized I could no longer turn back the clock.

At about two hours into the interview, Collins asked Tony if he could give him a few minutes with his staff. Tony and I got up and went to the outer office. Roughly five minutes later, Collins came out of the conference room and told us that he had to attend another meeting, but that his staff had a few more questions for me. He thanked me for my cooperation, but in kind of an ominous tone, he reminded me that if I thought of anything else I needed to tell him, to let Tony know. With that, he shook hands, and left.

The rest of the interview lasted only about twenty minutes, with some general housekeeping questions, which I knew were only a ploy to ask me one more final important question, or questions. Earlier, Tony had made it clear that there would be no questions whatsoever about my hiring practices and Robert Sorich. However, as the interview was winding down, they tried to ask some questions about my staff. Naturally, Tony reminded them that I would not answer such questions. Then, for all intents and purposes, the interview was finished. Everyone quickly packed up their notes and belongings, said their goodbyes, and left.

I then spent about ten minutes alone with Tony, just briefly going over some of my answers. He praised the fine job he thought I did, and told me that, minus any secret witness or hidden information the Feds might uncover, I was basically done with the U.S. Attorney, although they might still want to look at some of my financial records. At that point, I was mentally exhausted.

The ride home with Tom was a little more upbeat than the one during the morning, as we discussed the interview in general terms. We were both suspicious of the city cars being bugged, so we were extremely cautious about our conversation. As we pulled off the expressway and got closer to home, I contacted Mick on the Nextel, and told him to meet me at the Bethel Reform Church in five minutes. Tom only took about two minutes to get there. As soon as we pulled up, Mick was right behind us. I told Tom that I would see him tomorrow, and made the quick switch to Mick's vehicle.

As we quickly pulled away and headed out of the neighborhood, I started to tell Mick abut the interview. Every time I told him about one of Collins's questions, Mick would ask me ten of his own questions. The one remark I made to Mick that I would later be reminded of was that Collins seemed arrogant and vindictive, and to be careful. Unfortunately for all of us, the heat was about to be turned up.

Meanwhile, I was happy to be done with my interview. I forgot that Randy had one scheduled for next week, and Mick, I assumed, would have one coming up. Soon after John Novak's experience with the FBI, Bobby Molaro had urged Mick and Traci to retain a top-notch criminal attorney by the name of Mike Ettinger, who represented a number of former elected officials and political big shots, including Roger Stanley, a major republican lobbyist/entrepreneur. Ettinger, I later found out, was famous for cutting plea agreements in order to save his clients from significant prison time. This would become an important issue for the Joneses.

Randy's interview took place approximately two weeks after mine. Only about an hour after the interview was over, I learned that a potential avalanche was coming to bury all of us in the truck program. Around lunch time, I took a call from a good friend (let's call him "Don"). He told me that he needed to see me right away, and since we were both downtown, we agreed to meet on Clark Street, in front of the County Building, in ten minutes.

When I arrived, Don was already there. Since we were in downtown Chicago at lunch time, and standing in front of the County Building, there were at least a half-dozen people stopping to say hello to us, so we had to start walking. It didn't take long for Don to give me the bad news.

Supposedly, when Randy and his attorney, Ron Belmonte, met with the U.S. Attorney, Pat Collins did not mince words. Collins informed Aderman that they had enough information to already prosecute him, and that if he wanted to see his wife and four children in the foreseeable future, and have any chance of keeping his pension, he had better cooperate with his office now!

After Randy was given his options (or lack thereof), he said he was ready to talk. Randy then admitted to not only helping Mick Jones get additional trucks on with the city, but passing payoffs from Mick to a former water department supervisor. I was amazed by this story, because I knew nothing about their side deals. I guess it goes back to that old saying, "There's no honor among thieves."

At that point, things looked as if they were beginning to unravel. When I got back to the neighborhood, I stopped at a 7-Eleven. Who did I see there but Mick, Traci, and Mike Stec, who was a police officer assigned to my detail through the recommendations of Tom Lally and Mick Jones. Stec happened to be Mick's best friend, having both grown up together. I immediately told them what I had learned. Of course, Mr. and Mrs. Jones were not surprised; they used a number of expletives, and called Randy a traitor. Right now, I was only worried about how to stop the bleeding. Again, for the hundredth time, the Joneses assured me they were solid, and that we all needed to stick together. I guess I had no other choice. Still, I was really concerned about how solid they would be, because I had absolutely no clue about their other business dealings, let alone their financial records. The wild card was that Traci Jones now did quite a bit of check writing for "Get Plowed."

I'm not sure how many times Mick and Traci then met with their attorney, and how many times with the Feds to cut a deal. I do know that during the month of September 2005, the Joneses began "treating" me to their Academy Award-winning performances. In September, each time Mick said he had an upcoming meeting with his attorney, we would talk in my garage. I actually would turn my stereo radio up quite loudly, and pat him around his waist and chest, which really insulted him. When he was in my garage one last time, he angrily told me that he was going to drop his pants, so that I could check his balls for a wire. I guess I should have listened to him.

One day, during mid-September, I had Mike Stec drive me to check out a location for my office at a satellite site. Before heading to the north side, we picked up Mick, because he was familiar with the location—a vacant shopping mall. When we arrived, Mick and I got out of the car and started walking. Mick began to tell me that his wife had suddenly started to recall having given me some envelopes with money.

I reminded him of what he told me when this whole business started. "This is between you and me. Nobody else knows anything, including my partner—not even Traci."

He explained that Traci wasn't stupid and that she had written many checks and figured things out. At that point, I started to get annoyed and upset, and asked Mick what that meant. He said he needed to protect Traci, and that if she could get immunity by testifying before the grand jury, she couldn't lie, and that we would have to figure something out. I couldn't understand what he wanted me to do, because a week earlier he told me that the FBI had every financial record on him and Traci, not only from the business, but copies of his boat purchases, and his Vegas gambling receipts. He said he thought he had a slight tax problem, and that to protect everyone else, he would probably have to take a short prison sentence. He was mostly concerned about whether I could take care of Traci, and pay the remaining balance on his daughter Ashley's beauty school tuition. If I could do both of those things, he said, everything would be fine until he got out, and then he and his partner John would kick everything into high gear. Of course, I agreed. I had earlier resolved to take care of his family if something went wrong for him.

I now realized that I had to prepare for almost anything, including my own defense, if everyone else went south. It was during this time that Tony Pinelli received a lengthy subpoena requesting all of my political financial records from the years 1999 through 2003. This order included all statements, cancelled checks, accounts receivable, and accounts payable, plus any other notes, and a roster of organization members with their names and phone numbers. The Feds also wanted all paperwork for my political accounts. Trust me;

there was a ton of paperwork. I had two checking accounts and three CDs, all totaling close to $400,000.00.

Unfortunately, I now had to get my closest friend and advisor Ray Drish involved, because he was the treasurer and chairman of my accounts. Although he was slightly nervous, Ray had been through the wars with me before. However, with that subpoena pending, and all the paperwork Ray had to get together, we needed outside help. We decided, with Tony Pinelli's approval, to hire another attorney, Craig Tobin, who had represented Ray on another FBI matter five years before. Tobin would not only go through all my records, but would be Ray's legal representative, and protect my financial interests.

Honestly, with everything going on with the Feds, I still had my other responsibilities downtown as city clerk, and at home, as a husband and father. I couldn't wait until the end of each day, where I could be in my basement, late at night by myself, and just drink, in order to forget everything and put myself to sleep. I was beginning to think that I might be having a nervous breakdown.

On the home front, my dad's health was failing, and my father-in-law's diabetes had heated up to a point where he could no longer drive. A couple of weeks before, my brother-in-law Gary had driven Pat and Wally up to their summer home in Eagle River, Wisconsin one last time that year, to close the place up for the winter. My plan was to go to Wisconsin with a friend on Sunday morning, and stay overnight. I would then drive one car, while my friend would drive the other that was up there, and bring it home on Monday.

My whole problem that week was whom I would take to Wisconsin. My buddy Ray said weeks ago to stay away from Mick; he no longer trusted him, and warned me not drive seven hours with him to Eagle River. Bob Molaro told me to follow my attorney's advice, which was simply not to discuss my situation with anyone else, especially with a government target like Mick Jones. I then spoke with my inner circle, and I don't think anyone thought I should be in a car alone with Mick for that amount of time.

My dilemma was simple—I had a serious trust problem with Mick, but I also wanted to keep him close to me, not only to keep tabs on him, but to keep him loyal. During that week, I also spent time with Stec, who knew Mick better than anyone else. He told me that Mick considered me like family, and would never do anything to hurt my wife and kids. Stec did, however, offer to drive me to Wisconsin if it would make me feel more comfortable. That gave me two or three people from my world who would drive me on Sunday. I just didn't know what to do. One side of me said, "Don't take Mick with you." The other side said, "He would never hurt you; your kids call him 'Uncle Mick,'" and you two have taken vacations together." In addition, my son Jack once asked Mick to go to his school and speak to his class as his hero. Moreover, the Joneses, Kathleen, and I always celebrated our birthdays together, along with every other family occasion. So, in my heart of hearts, I couldn't believe that Mick, whom I'd known for over twenty-six years, would ever turn on me.

By Friday, Mick was calling me. Over the past week or so we hadn't spoken much, but I knew I had to decide whether or not to let him go with me to Eagle River. When I finally called him back, he was his old, jovial self, assuring me that everything looked good, that he really wanted to spend some time with me, and that it would be a perfect occasion for both of us to get away, and to see Pat and Wally's place.

In life, I think everyone regrets at least one decision he or she has made. In this case, my closest friends and advisors told me not to do it, but instead of following my gut feeling, I followed my heart, and I agreed to have Mick drive with me to Wisconsin. Even after I agreed to have him go, he still insisted on driving his Ford Escape out there. Although I didn't trust him, and should have cancelled all the plans at that moment, I told him I was taking my in-laws' other car, and that he should just forget about taking his car; I had everything set. He then reluctantly agreed to meet me at my house, Sunday morning, at 6:00 a.m. Now, all I had to worry about was my dad's health being stable enough for me to travel to Wisconsin with a clear conscience.

On Saturday morning, I headed over to my parents' house to see how they were both doing. I guess I was so into myself and my own problems that I never realized how sick my father was. When my mom answered the front door, she looked tired, but had a smile on her face, as she told me everything was fine. As I walked to the back of the house, there was a bedroom that was off of the kitchen, where Mom and I were going to sit. As I looked into the bedroom, I saw my father, sitting in his reclining chair. He had his pajamas on, along with his heavy robe, socks and slippers. He was sleeping when I went up to him and kissed him on his forehead. The touch of his skin to my lips seemed cold. My dad looked tired, not like a beaten man, but like a man struggling to hang on.

My mom woke him, and, as usual when he saw me, he smiled and said, "Oh, it's Jimmy. How are you?"

I would always tell him I was fine, and that politics were fine.

He would smile and say, "That's good."

I don't know how many times we all thought we were going to lose my dad. He once had a bout with stomach cancer, and the doctors removed three-fourths of his stomach; he had a pacemaker put in to help his heart, which was now only functioning at about 39 percent. He had had two or three battles with pneumonia, and a few blood transfusions, but always possessed a strong constitution. Kathleen often told me that my dad always reminded her of the Energizer Bunny—he just kept on going. When I was young, I thought my dad was going to be around forever. Now, it seemed that most of his time was spent in his recliner, sleeping.

I spoke with my mom, and told her I was stressed out, so I was going to go golfing in Lake Geneva with Mick. I didn't want her to worry that I was traveling all the way up to Eagle River, Wisconsin, while my dad was so ill. The bottom line was that I felt guilty about leaving now, and the only way to make me feel any better was to lie to her about where I was going. My mom was confident that my dad was stable, and she really wanted me to relax. When I left, I felt comfortable enough to tell them both I would see them on Monday.

That night, Kathleen and I talked about the trip up north. Although I normally told her almost everything that went on in my life, I had never revealed my shady dealings with Mick and Randy. Whenever she would question me too much about either one of them,

I would simply tell her that it was in her best interests not to know everything. In any event, I would always minimize the situation, so Kathleen would never really think that anything that serious was going on. I told her that I would call her on the road, and that before I left, I would give her and the kids a kiss goodbye. My plan was to meet Mick around 6:00 a.m. at my house, where he would put his cooler-full of soda and beer in my car's trunk. We would then go back to his house to drop off his car before getting on our way.

I woke up around 5:30 a.m. Sunday morning, took a quick shower, and drove over to 7-Eleven to pick up some snacks for the road and leave a coffee for my wife. I was standing in front of my yard when Mick pulled up. I don't know how to describe it, but he somehow looked different, although that perception could have been due to my own paranoia. We quickly transferred Mick's bag and cooler over to Pat and Wally's car, and in less than five minutes, we were back at his house, where he promptly parked his car. I then slid over to the passenger seat. Mick jumped in, and we were on our way.

We had only driven about five minutes, when we both realized we needed gas. I used my credit card for the purchase while Mick pumped the gas.

As soon as we were both done, and were getting into the car, he turned to me and said, "Traci has to testify before the grand jury, and she doesn't want to lie. What should she do?"

I just sat there silently, looking at him in disbelief.

Soon after, while on the highway, I thought how convenient it was for him to lay that shit on me then! I did, however, ask him what he wanted me to do.

Mick said, "You know what went on. What's my wife supposed to say?"

As each and every word came out of his mouth, I started to wonder if Ray's suspicions about him were true after all. I know it sounds crazy, but I turned the volume on the radio way up, and began leaning over to talk to him. I told him there was a lot at stake here, and what did he want me to accomplish? Mick turned to me and said he needed to protect his wife, and that we'd have to figure out something.

The next five or six miles were brutal. The conversation grew intense, as we both went back and forth about our friendship and loyalty, but more importantly, our mutual concern for our families. Because of the circumstances, the ride seemed exceptionally longer than usual, but I decided to take a shortcut along Route 45, but because Mick and I weren't concentrating, we got lost twice. The longer we drove, the more pressure he exerted on me regarding what we should do.

I already had a headache from the radio's loud volume, but my response continued to be, "What do you want me to do?"

At that point, Mick broke down in tears, insisting, "I don't want to do this! This is so hard for me, nobody knows!"

Now I was choking up with emotion, and I told him that I was worried about my own family and that if something would happen to me, who would take care of them?

The last hour of the trip was quieter. I had a terrific headache, but I was hoping that when I got to Pat and Wally's, I could relax, even though my stomach was tossing and turning.

We pulled up to their house around 3:00 p.m. It was a beautiful day, sunny and warm, around seventy-five degrees. We pulled down a sandy dirt road. Among all the tall trees were about eight homes sitting next to Cranberry Lake. As soon as we reached the side of the house, I saw Pat and Wally sitting on their deck. As soon as they saw us, they came over to the car, with big hugs and smiles. I have to admit I was drained, both physically and emotionally, from the drive. We all sat on the deck as we looked at the lake, which was approximately fifty yards straight ahead. Meanwhile, Mick started talking a bunch of bullshit, as if nothing was wrong.

We planned to relax for about an hour or so, and then head off to town for dinner. Hopefully by then, I could eat, and enjoy the rest of the evening. As soon as I got into the house to sit in the recliner and close my eyes, my cell phone went off. When I looked at the caller ID and saw my parents' phone number, I started to panic, because I knew my mom would not have called me unless there was an emergency. I quickly picked up the phone and heard my sister Linda's voice. She said that nobody wanted to bother me, but that I needed to know that Daddy had taken a turn for the worse. In fact, hospice had brought in a hospital bed. He was semi-conscious, and had stopped eating and drinking. The hospice nurse told the family that his body was shutting down, and that it would just be a matter of time—possibly as quickly as tonight, or within the next forty-eight hours. Our mom was too upset to talk, but I told Linda that I would call her back in a few minutes.

What would happen next between Mick and me would be something I would never forget as long as I live! After the call, my body was shaking. I felt as if I were hyperventilating while I ran down toward the lake to gather my thoughts. When I reached the pier, I fell to my knees. With my hands over my face, I began crying. Mick followed me down, and stood right next to me on the pier. I looked at him and told him my dad was dying, and that I couldn't handle the pressure and stress.

He just looked at me and said, "You need to talk to Traci and tell her what to say to the grand jury. She doesn't know what do. All I'm asking you to do is come up with a plan to protect her. In the meantime, I'll try to postpone her testimony until you get everything straightened out with your dad, so don't worry about that. I don't know what kind of dealings you had with Randy, but I'm telling you now, I'm going to bring him down for what he did!"

While I tried to compose myself, and to make sense out of what Mick unexpectedly had just told me, Wally came down to the pier to check up on me, and then he went back to the house. Honestly, I didn't how I felt—relieved, scared, or if I had just received a temporary stay of execution. Whatever my feelings were, I needed to leave for Chicago. At 4:00 p.m., Kathleen and I decided that I should start driving back. Meanwhile, she would call Mike Stec and his friend and fellow officer Ron O. (his real last name is so long that I've decided to simplify matters for the reader) to have them start driving toward Wisconsin. Somewhere in the middle we could meet, and one of them would drive me home. My only concern with the driving was my night vision, and the darkness along the Wisconsin highways in the northern part of that state. Over the past couple of years, I'd had some difficulty with night-time driving on rural roads. However, I knew I had to get back on the road, so I gave Mick his overnight bag and cooler. Pat and Wally told me to be careful, as I got into the car, at about 4:30 p.m., for another seven-hour drive to Chicago. In the meantime, Mick would stay overnight, and then drive Pat and Wally back home the next day.

After I left, the three of them went out to dinner. Afterwards, Mick went down to the pier to drink a few beers by the lake. Later, he watched a little TV. During this whole time, he never changed clothes. The next morning, he washed his face, but never took off the sweatshirt and pants he had worn from Sunday morning, nor would he, even after dropping my in-laws off at their house on Monday morning after driving them home. In all the years I had known Mick, I had never seen or heard of him exhibiting that kind of behavior.

Meanwhile, as I drove to Chicago, I felt as if a one-hundred-pound weight were on my shoulders. I thought about my dad, my mom, Mick, Kathleen and the kids. My goal was to get as close to Illinois as possible before dark. I remember driving around seventy miles per hour most of the time. I also kept calling Kathleen who had already contacted Mike and Ron; they were on their way. Unfortunately, I missed the cut-off where they were waiting, so I had to pull off to the side of the highway, put on my flashers, and yell on the two-way radio to Mike to let him know where I was located. Within five minutes, they picked me up. Mike jumped into my car and drove, while I instantly collapsed from exhaustion in the front seat. Ron followed us in the other car.

We pulled into my parents' house around 10:45 p.m. I rang the doorbell. When my mom came to the door, I could tell she was having a rough day. Her eyes were swollen from tears, but amazingly, she managed to put a smile on her face. She immediately apologized for having Linda call me, but I told her not to worry about that. I then turned, stepped into the doorway, and saw my father lying in a hospital bed. In the afternoon, my brother-in-law, Art, and Mike moved some furniture around, so the bed would fit better. It was a shocking sight to see. In only thirty-six hours, he had deteriorated so much. He didn't even recognize me, even though his eyes were open. His breathing was labored, and he was being given regular doses of morphine for his pain. One thing I'll always remember was how he, while lying on his side, stretched his hand through the bed railings to touch the white stucco bedroom wall, whose finish, to the eye, glittered. So, my father, almost like an innocent, curious child, was trying to feel its glitter. That, by far, was the most helpless and saddest condition I'd ever seen my dad in.

I decided to stay overnight with Mom, just in case she needed me. I thanked Mike and Ron for all their help before they left. I also called Kathleen to check on her and the kids. I guess she was the one who insisted I stay at my parents' house. By the time I changed clothes and settled in, it was around midnight. My mom and I sat on the living room couch and just talked about anything and everything, including my trip, for about an hour. I think she was glad that I was staying with her that night. It was about 1:00 a.m. when my head finally hit the pillow.

The next morning, about 8:00 a.m., I woke up, and noticed how quiet the house was. My mom was sitting at the kitchen table, reading the newspaper. I asked her how the night had gone, and she told me she had been up most of the night, just checking on Dad. I peeked into his bedroom; he was sleeping, but breathing heavily. The hospice nurses would be coming by in the morning and afternoon to check on his vital signs.

Although my mom wanted to make me a full breakfast, I usually didn't have anything that early—just a can of Pepsi to go along with my two cigarettes. However, I compromised, and had a piece of toast and a glass of milk. After I ate, I told her I was going home to see Kathleen, but that I would come back in the afternoon. In the meantime, despite my father's worsening condition, I was still thinking about little else than my situation with Mick—a fact that I would feel guilty about for the rest of my life.

After checking in with Kathleen, I decided to stay one more night with my mom and dad. I woke up early Tuesday morning so I could go back home, shower, and see if the kids needed a ride to school. Nina, I found out, had a ride, so I decided to drive with Kathleen to take the boys to school. After we dropped them off, we picked up a newspaper and a coffee, and headed back home. We sat at the dining room table, just reminiscing about everything. It was so quiet and calm in the house with Kathleen that I didn't want to leave, because I felt so safe. However, I knew I had to get back to my parents' house. I had already called the office and spoken with my office girls, Martha and Toni, just to check in, and let them know I wasn't planning to come to city hall for the rest of the week. I then took a quick shower, got dressed, and headed out again.

I arrived at my parents' home at about 11:00 a.m. As usual, my mother was happy to see me. My dad was the same; he would come in and out of sleep. When he looked at us, we weren't sure what he was thinking, but I felt he knew we were with him. My mom needed something to do, so she opened a can of soup for me, because it was lunch time. After she heated up the soup, she started wiping up the stove and counters, just to keep busy. I asked her to sit down and rest. After lunch, I went into the bedroom to check on my dad. His eyes were pointed towards the ceiling, as his breathing continued to be labored. Since it was so nice out (sunny, and about seventy-five degrees), Mom asked if I would stay with my dad, so she could sit in the backyard for a little bit, on the recliner swing. She wanted me to listen for the doorbell because one of the nurses was scheduled to stop by at 1:00 p.m.

A couple of minutes past 1:00 p.m., while I stood in the bedroom and watched my dad, the doorbell rang. I quickly walked to the front door and let the nurse into the house. As we walked toward the bedroom, I told her he was hanging in there, but that his breathing seemed a little shallow. When we walked into the bedroom, my dad was still looking at the ceiling, and I remarked to the nurse how peaceful he seemed.

She then placed her hand on his wrist, removed it, turned to me, and said, "I believe your father is gone."

She put her hand on his forehead, and then next to his mouth.

She turned to me again, and said, with even greater certainty, "He passed away."

I was stunned, because I had left the room for only a minute to answer the door. She assured me that he knew I was in the room with him when he finally decided to let go. I immediately thought about my mom, and went out to the backyard. I hated to bother her, because she looked so peaceful in her swing, but I had to tell her that the nurse was here.

When Mom walked into the bedroom, the nurse put her arms around her and softly broke the news to her. My mom turned and looked at me in disbelief, as I nodded my head up and down, confirming what the nurse had just told her. With tears in her eyes, my mom leaned over my dad to give him a hug and a kiss, and to say goodbye. I really thought that when my mom had decided to go outside, my dad had felt secure enough within himself, and with God, to say goodbye, and to leave his wife of almost sixty years. I gave my mom a few minutes before turning to her. We hugged each other and cried. The nurse leaned over my dad and closed his eyes. Then, she reminded us of some phone calls we had to make, so I left my mom with the nurse, and went to the living room to make those difficult calls.

I called Linda at school to tell her. When she answered the phone, it was almost as if she already knew, due to the sadness and fear in her voice. I remember telling her to be careful driving, and to take her time. Next, I called my wife, and she quickly drove over to see me. I then made a call to my office, and spoke with Martha and Toni, who would follow protocol and let the appropriate people at the Hall know about my father's death. Lastly, believe it or not, I reached out to Mick on his cell phone, to tell him. He answered very abruptly, and told me he was with his attorney. In a quiet and very sad voice, I then simply informed him that my dad had just died. He immediately apologized, and asked if he could come by the house later.

I said, "No problem. I'll see you later."

Now, I was done for awhile with the phone calls.

A few minutes later, Kathleen came to the house to see how everyone was doing. Before she had left, Kathleen whispered to me that Mick called her to tell her how bad he felt when I told him the news earlier. He apologized to Kathleen, too, and told her he wanted to come by later, just to hang out with me, drink, talk about sports, and relax. I was so shell-shocked by all that just happened that I really didn't care.

Before the afternoon ended, my sister and brother-in-law, along with some friends and neighbors, came over. I then remembered to call the funeral parlor; we had already made preliminary arrangements. We all said goodbye to Dad one more time before going back into the living room, and letting them take care of business. They took him away on a gurney, in a black body bag, and placed him in the back of the hearse.

My mom actually wanted to be alone that evening, but we all planned to get together the next morning at the funeral parlor to make final arrangements. My mom wanted Kathleen and Art to help with the arrangements the next day, so we agreed to meet them around 10:00 a.m.

It was a very somber evening for me, as I thought about my dad. I decided I would also write a letter to him, which I would have someone else read at the funeral. I pulled out a book that Kathleen had bought me about a father-son relationship, and thought that would be a perfect place to start. As I started to write some initial thoughts down, there was a tap on the basement window, which was the code from a close friend that he was standing at the side door. In my business, when you have people coming over at all hours of the evening, and you have young children, it's best to have a system where you don't have to ring the doorbell, and wake up the entire house. I walked upstairs and opened the side door. I saw my friend Mick standing there. He immediately extended his hand and gave me a big hug. Mick knew how I felt, because he had lost his own father over ten years before, from cancer. His dad would come to all of our softball games, and he used to call me "Crazy Legs," because I would run like crazy when playing left field.

For the next couple of hours, we sat in my basement and just talked about family, friends, and sports. As we sat there, it seemed like the good old days, with two best friends just sitting, drinking, and having a few laughs together. Around midnight, Mick finally left. Since the next day was going to be spent running around and making arrangements, we planned to meet again Thursday, at the wake.

The following day, we all got together as a family at the funeral parlor, to finalize arrangements. It was amazing how many details needed to be worked out—readings, music, holy cards, flowers, the suit my dad would wear, who would be the pallbearers, etc. The most difficult part of the day for me was going with my mom to the funeral parlor's lower level, to choose a casket. Afterwards, we all went home. I then picked up the boys and Nina. That evening was very quiet. I put the finishing touches on my goodbye letter to my dad, and I let Kathleen read the letter to see if she could handle its reading Friday morning at the church. All that was left now was trying to keep it together at the wake the next day.

As difficult as a parent's funeral can be, everything went fairly smooth. First of all, the weather was sunny and warm, and the service was beautiful. Kathleen did a wonderful job of reading my final goodbye to my dad, which, by the way, did not leave a dry eye in the house. My family then had a private moment with Dad at the cemetery before heading over to Ray's place for the luncheon. All in all, I thought everything went as well as could be expected for my mom and the rest of the family. Especially touching was the fact that my dad, a World War II veteran, had a proper military burial, with the local VFW Post that he belonged to, which provided a gun salute, taps, and of course, the American flag draped over his coffin. At the memorial service, veterans performed the proper folding of the flag and presented it to my mom.

She, in turn, handed me the flag, and told me, "I love you, and Dad would want you to have this."

I kissed my mom and thanked her, as I wiped the tears that were rolling down my cheeks. I will never forget that moment for as long as I live.

The afternoon we all ended up at Ray's bar, where Mick and many of my friends stopped after the luncheon. Everyone in the group drank, and became fairly drunk, to excess. I, however, was emotionally drained, and left early for home with Kathleen.

In retrospect, I think I will always feel guilty about not properly mourning my father's passing. From the day he died to the day we buried him, I felt as if my mind had been a million miles away, worrying about what Mick and Traci were going to do. I could have helped my mom more by comforting her, instead of being so totally wrapped up in my own web of deceit. Some day, I will need to apologize in my own way to my mom, and in a spiritual way, to my dad.

CHAPTER 15

THE HIRED TRUCK PROGRAM SCANDAL:
THE HOUSE OF CARDS FALLS

Not long after my dad's funeral, Mick started calling me (I should say, "harassing" me) regarding talking to Traci about her grand jury testimony. I grew more cautious about talking to them, so I now decided to talk to Sam first. If anyone would take a bullet for me, it was Sam, who ran my organization, including collecting dues and ticket money. Whenever my family or I needed anything, he was always there to help. The people I could trust in politics I could count on one hand, and Sam was right there. I wanted him to talk to Mick to get a sense of what was going on, and to find out if Mick could still be trusted.

Over the next several weeks, Sam and I sat down with Mick and Traci on numerous occasions. In fact, Sam was becoming the liaison between Mick and me. At first, Sam felt very comfortable about the whole situation. When Mick said he needed money for his attorney fees, I had Sam give him $5,000.00. However, it wasn't long before Mick started asking for more and more.

Besides talking to Sam about money, Mick kept trying to call me about Traci's grand jury date, which was Thursday. He said I needed to tell her what she should say. At that point, Sam and I decided to simply let Mick and Traci do what they thought they had to do, because neither one of us was going to talk to them anymore.

Unfortunately, Mick stopped by my house on Tuesday evening, and trapped me. I agreed to go to his house Wednesday evening to talk to Traci. When Wednesday evening came, Sam and I got together. We agreed again that I wasn't going to talk to them. As the evening progressed, and I didn't show up, Mick kept calling me on my cell phone, and leaving messages. To keep Mick in the dark, I called him back and told him I was at my mom's house, helping her with a plumbing problem that had flooded her basement, and was cleaning things up. I also told him she was down in the dumps about my dad, and that I would stay overnight. Mick was so desperate on the phone that he said Traci and he would stay up and wait for me. At that point, I said I'd get back to him.

Well, Sam and I stayed at my mom's for another hour, until about 10:30 p.m., when Mick called her house. I answered the phone, and told him I was still cleaning the basement. As soon as we left my mom's, Sam drove me home. I told Sam that I planned to be "sick" the next morning, and that I would not go downtown, but instead fake a visit to Northwest Hospital.

When I got home, I turned off all the lights in the house and shut off my cell phone, on which Mick had already left two messages since I had left my mom's. Unfortunately, now I needed to tell my wife something, because things were starting to unravel. I told Kathleen that I helped Mick with some business with the city that I really shouldn't have. I also told her that I was worried that he could put me in a very bad spot. I told her that I had decided, because he was acting so strangely, to stay away from him. Kathleen was terrified by the whole situation, and didn't ask many questions.

The next morning Ron Stec picked me up, and as we headed downtown, I told him I wasn't feeling well, and asked him to drive me to Northwestern Hospital. I said I had been up most of the night with stomach pains, and that my doctor was waiting for me at the hospital. Meanwhile, Kathleen called Mick, and told him what happened. Of course, he told her to call him as soon as she heard something, because he had to pick up Traci at 11:00 a.m. and take her somewhere.

I told Ron to call my office, and tell my staff where I was, and that I would call him on his cell phone when I was done. The bottom line was that I sat by myself at Northwestern Hospital, from 9:00 a.m. to 3:00 p.m. in the lobby, reading magazines and walking around. After enough time had passed, I called Ron to pick me up. I told him that my doctor had run a number of tests, and had given me medication for my stomach, and for stress. Because my daughter had a volleyball game at a school in Hyde Park, I ended my day by going to watch her play. When the game was over, and Nina and I were getting ready to go home, Ron told me that Mick had called to see how I was doing. He told Mick that everything was fine, and that he could see me tomorrow. That evening, I asked Kathleen to call Mick, and to tell him I still wasn't feeling good.

That next day, Mick came by the house. Since it was Friday and a beautiful day, I stayed home, except for having run a few errands. When he did stop by in the afternoon, I was sitting on my front step. He was in a very good mood, and told me that Traci's testimony went well, and that my name didn't come up. Initially, I felt relieved, and thought that maybe this would all blow over. Then, Mick said she had to go back in a couple of weeks, to finish off her testimony, and that we could all get together before that time.

During the next few weeks, I talked less and less to Mick. I asked Sam to be the intermediary between us. Sam said that if this situation had just involved Mick, he didn't see a problem, but Mick, according to Sam, would say or do anything to protect Traci, and that was what he was worried about. Sam also told me that he was going to have a private meeting with them on Saturday morning. He told me he would be very honest and upfront with them about loyalty, and "protecting the quarterback."

At that meeting, Sam supposedly threatened them with something like, "If you screw us, you'd better get into the Witness Protection Program."

For each day that went by, Sam and I felt differently about the whole situation. One day, we were convinced Mick was loyal, while on the next, we were careful about what we said to him. Once, Sam came over and told me that Mick kept calling him on his phone and asking him about my having taken money from him. He had also said that I pressured him for money for such expenses as vacations. I was livid, but Sam assured me that he told Mick that he knew nothing about that, and he had never seen me take money from anyone. I was now very apprehensive about even talking to the Joneses. Since another grand jury date had been scheduled for Traci, Mick was pressuring Sam for a meeting to coach her on her testimony.

Finally, Sam convinced me to meet with them in his basement. The meeting would take place approximately three days before her actual appearance. I would arrive as Sam's about an hour before them. I told Sam right away that I wouldn't be speaking much in specifics. Sam said that he would do most of the talking anyway, and he told me not to worry.

While we waited for Mick, Sam turned the TV on, and I told him to raise the volume when they arrived. Ironically, on one of the stations, Sam had found the movie, *The Godfather*, so we decided not only to watch it, but to leave it on when the meeting had started.

The Joneses arrived at about 7:30 p.m. They seemed very nervous, especially Traci. We all exchanged pleasantries, handshakes, hugs, and kisses before sitting down. While we all got situated, Sam sat in his recliner; to his left was a two-seat couch. Mick sat closest to Sam, with Traci sitting next to Mick. To her immediate left was the bigger couch, where I sat down only two or three feet from her. She had a big purse that was more like a duffle canvas or straw-tie bag that people would normally take to the beach. She placed it closer to me than to her. At that moment, I should have realized that this item was big enough to place all kinds of items in—including a hidden camera or tape recorder—and that there was a reason why she had placed it so close to me. At that moment, I had a strange feeling that I should just leave Sam's basement and go immediately home, but I decided to stay. Quite honestly, I really didn't know what to do, since many thoughts were going through my mind.

Immediately, Mick started the conversation, and asked what the game plan for Traci was.

Well, I answered, "You should tell the truth, of course."

Mick then asked, "Okay, then, what does she *really* tell them?"

Sam tried to help by jumping in and saying we all had to protect me.

Mick, who was now becoming irritated, told Sam, "You don't know everything about this situation, and it's best you don't get totally involved."

Up to that point, Traci had not said anything, but she talked about the issue of signing checks. She told us she wrote and cashed checks for snow salt in June, July, and August. When Sam asked why, she said she couldn't remember. Obviously, Mick and Traci were now trying to push every check she had written from the "Get Plowed" account on to me. What's more, they were still paying for their gas out of that same business account they supposedly had nothing to do with anymore. In fact, I once saw Mick use his business card at a gas station. He used to brag to me that his partner John Novak's cash from various city trucking jobs would still take care of him and Traci.

Each time the conversation would get hot and heavy between Sam and Mick, or when a specific question would come to me, I would excuse myself and use the bathroom. Finally, there was some discussion about the money Traci said they gave me as political donations instead of what they had told Sam were kickbacks. Now, we would have to go back to Ray and indirectly ask him for dates when "Get Plowed, Inc." gave my office donations, and have Traci use those dates in her grand jury testimony. During the whole evening, either Mick or Traci would constantly ask what she should say to the U.S. Attorney, while that big purse never moved one inch from her side. Again, in retrospect, I should have been more suspicious about its size, position, and contents, but I guess, deep down, I wanted to believe (and probably Sam, too), that neither one would ever really betray me.

As the evening wore on, Mick grew more impatient with Sam and me—more so with me, because Sam was doing most of the talking. By the time they were ready to leave, we still hadn't resolved the issue, at least not in the Joneses' eyes, because I had never come right out and directly told Traci what to say. Sam merely told Mick that we would get back to them in the next day or so, in any event, certainly before Traci would have to go before the grand jury again.

Meanwhile, I leaned over and whispered to Traci, "Don't worry, I'll figure it out; you just need to trust Sam and me."

When they finally left Sam's house, Mick had a look of frustration on his face, and Traci had an expression of panic on hers. I then told Sam I was through talking with both of them.

The next day was a free one for me, because I had to spend most of my time preparing for my colonoscopy and endoscopy, both of which were scheduled for the next morning at Northwestern Hospital. I was supposed to have both procedures two years ago, when I turned fifty, but I backed out at the last minute. Now, with all the stress and stomach pains I was experiencing, this would be a perfect opportunity to check things out. In addition, the tests would be the day before Traci's grand jury appearance, which would give me a perfect excuse to avoid speaking to both of them the night before.

Sam called me that night to wish me well on the tests, and to let me know that Mick had phoned him, bitching about how I wasn't helping his wife out before she had to appear before the grand jury again. Sam told him he would call him tomorrow, because I would be tied up at the hospital, and he would advise him about what to tell Traci.

The next morning I had somebody drop me off at the hospital around 9:00 a.m. By the time I checked in and put on my gown, the nurse had hooked up my IV. It was right around 11:30 a.m.; both procedures took less than an hour that day to complete. I do remember waking up in the recovery room around 1:30 p.m., because I looked at my watch. When I actually opened my eyes, I felt as if I had just had a full night's sleep. Over the past year, I had not slept well, but that short two-hour nap re-energized me. The nurse came over to me and offered me orange juice and crackers, both of which I eagerly consumed because I hadn't eaten since the morning before. Soon after that, another nurse, who had assisted the doctor, came in to tell me that both tests had gone well, and that there were no stomach or colon abnormalities. She then gave me a form that stated that I needed to take it easy for the rest of the day. That meant no driving, and no alcohol that evening—just rest.

By the time I got my ride home, and arrived at my house, it was about 3:00 p.m. I was beginning to feel tired again, so I went down to the basement with my blanket and stretched out on the couch. Around 6:00 p.m., I heard Kathleen open the back door. It was Sam. He wanted to know how I was feeling, and he wanted to know about the test results. As soon as he walked down to the basement to see me, I gave him the good news. Then, we both heard the back screen door open again, and people were actually entering the house. It was only seconds before Mick and Traci Jones walked down to the basement. I could see Kathleen's face, as she rolled her eyes with an expression that said, "There was nothing I could do." My wife told me later that she was in the kitchen when the screen door opened, and she unexpectedly met Mick and Traci at the back door landing. She tried to tell them that I was resting downstairs, but they ignored her, and quickly walked past her. They insisted that they would only stay a few minutes.

As soon as Kathleen saw everyone else standing around me, she made a strategic exit upstairs. Sam looked at me with utter amazement. I was just tired, and really didn't feel like socializing. A couple of minutes followed with small talk, when, to my surprise, Sam announced that he was going home.

My first reaction was, "Don't leave me alone with them!" But Sam thought that if he left, they wouldn't stay long, because they were supposed to talk to him later.

I now felt ill, and actually pulled the blanket, which had been at my legs, up to my chin. Mick didn't waste a second.

He immediately asked, "What should Traci say?"

Neither one of them even asked how I felt. Both of them just launched into their full-court press on me, peppering me with questions concerning political donations and money Traci said she had handed me once or twice before (an incident that I still can't remember). It was like watching a tennis ball volleying back and forth on a court. Mick insisted that I had to give her some advice on what to say, because we needed to protect her. I probably dodged and ducked them for about an hour-and-a-half, just telling them I wasn't feeling good, and I reminded them that the political records would authenticate the donations, and that Sam would let them know what to say.

During this time, my daughter Nina needed to use the downstairs computer, so I tried to keep my voice down when I was talking to them. Jack and Bobby, both of whom idolized Mick, came down to see him. I knew with them downstairs it would be difficult to talk, but for the first time, he ignored my sons, and kept talking about what Traci should say. I asked the boys to go upstairs for a few minutes until we were finished, and I could tell from the look in their eyes that they knew something was not right.

I finally had enough of their cat-and-mouse game, and told them that if Traci felt comfortable with the political donations story, then she should use that testimony, because that's what I truthfully remembered they told me in the first place.

Well, Mick was extremely aggravated as he jumped off the couch, and told Traci, "Let's go!"

At the same time, she grabbed that same big duffle bag or purse and moved it right next to me after Sam left. As they walked out of my house, they didn't say goodbye to any of my family.

I remember Mick looking at his wife and saying, "Don't worry. You have immunity anyway, so do what you have to do."

With that, they both walked out the back door.

I talked to Sam again later that evening, and told him, for all intents and purposes, I was done with any further conversations with Mick regarding the whole truck thing. Sam agreed, but he also said that Mick had just called him, and wanted to do the right thing, but was nervous because I hadn't been talking to him. I told Sam I had no problem with Mick, except I would not talk to him about his or his wife's pending legal matters. With that, we both agreed to let Mick and Traci do what they had to do before the grand jury, and to see what would happen tomorrow. At that point, I felt mentally drained, and called it a night.

The next morning, I got up bright and early, and rode with Kathleen to take the boys to school. As soon as I got back, Tom Lally was waiting for me, and we headed downtown. I was less than five minutes from city hall when Sam called me on my cell phone. Sam said he had just spoken to Mick, who told him that Traci was going to use the story of political donations in her testimony. Mick said that he and his wife were team players and they would protect the organization and me.

My first question to Sam was, "What do you think?"

Before he could answer me, Tom pulled up in front of city hall, so I told Sam to hold on, as I got out of the car stood outside in front of the building. When I told him I was now free to talk, Sam said he had a very good conversation with Mick, and felt that we could trust him.

I again asked, "Are you sure?"

He told me the worst that would happen would be trying to match up all the dates for political donations, and for Sam to create a scenario in which I had given Mick cash for the Joneses, for organizational purposes, but had never recorded it, because Mick had never given it to Ray to deposit. I told Sam I was still standing in front of city hall, and that not only was it noisy, but a number of people had recognized me, so I needed to go to my office. Sam then told me there was one more thing he needed to tell me.

With a huge sigh, I said, "Go ahead."

Sam proceeded to tell me that Mick needed assurances that we would all stick to the political donation story, so one of us had to call him back. I was trying to get out of it when Sam said Mick would really like to hear it from me. So, reluctantly, I agreed, except there was one more catch.

Mick was going to be with his investigators all morning, so I had to call him on the Nextel two-way radio and just say, "Go Cubs!" which would mean that everything was okay, and that he could then call his wife.

I asked Sam, "Why 'Go Cubs?'"

The answer was simple—the White Sox were in the playoffs, and if anyone on Mick's end heard, "Go Cubs," they would think it was a joke, because Mick was a Sox fan. At that point, I was so frustrated that I agreed to call Mick in a couple of minutes, after I got situated in my office.

I took the next twenty minutes checking my phone messages in my office, and then spoke briefly with my staff in the main area.

Then, I went back into my office, closed the door, picked up my Nextel, clicked Mick on the two-way, and asked, "Are you there? Hello?"

Quickly, Mick replied, "Yes, I'm here."

I then said the words that thousands of people would come to know in about three months—and which would have such a dramatic future impact on my life—"Go Cubs!"

As soon as I said that, the immediate response on the other end was a relieved, "Thank you. Thank you!"

For some reason, I laughed and said, "No problem," and repeated, "Go Cubs!"

After that, we both said goodbye, promising each other that we would talk later.

I don't remember if we actually spoke with each other later that evening, or the next day, but we did get together. Sam, Mick, and I all met at Mick's house. Mick assured Sam and me that everything went well before the grand jury that day, and that Traci did a great job. He told us that he believed that they were now done with the Feds, and he thought that Traci was granted immunity. Furthermore, his attorney believed Mick might not have to testify himself, since Traci already had. Mick did remind us, though, that he needed certain dates from Sam that he would give to his own attorney to substantiate Traci's testimony. Those dates covered three, four-year periods when either "Get Plowed" or the Joneses personally made political contributions to me, and would be given to the U.S. Attorney for evidence.

It was now about the middle of October 2005. The White Sox were on their way in the playoffs, and I promised myself that no matter what, I was finished talking about the Hired Truck Program scandal with either Mick or Traci. If our friendship was going to stay intact, we needed to move on and hope for the best. Kathleen and I, along with Mick and Traci, got together one last time for my birthday (October 28), which fell on a Friday that year. They both came over and brought me a birthday gift, which happened to be a beautiful, black and white, White Sox hooded sweatshirt. That evening reminded me of times past, when the four of us would sit around, drink, and just enjoy each other's company. After they left, I told Kathleen that I thought maybe everything would work out after all.

The last few days of October and the month of November were fairly quiet. However, the U.S. Attorney's office moved full speed ahead on additional subpoenas, for my political account. They were now looking for specific checks from various trucking companies, and a list of names, addresses, and phone numbers of all the members of my organization—a fact that Sam and I discussed in detail before turning this information over to my attorney, Tony Pinelli.

Although I hadn't spoken with the U.S. Attorney since August, I had been in constant touch with Tony each and every week. Sometimes I would call Tony just to bullshit with him, and at other times, to ask him to speculate on the U.S. Attorney's next move. I was always hoping that he would tell me they were done with the investigation, but that, of course, was wishful thinking.

On Thanksgiving, we would always go to my in-laws' house for dinner. I tried to supply the turkey every year, and Pat got up bright and early every Thanksgiving morning to put the turkey in her oven, so that we could eat around 4:00 p.m.. Well, that morning, I ran to the garage to grab some soda that I had stored, and to have a quick cigarette. For some reason, I decided to call Mick, to wish him a happy Thanksgiving. When I got him on the phone, he was at breakfast, but we briefly wished each other a happy holiday. I will never forget telling him that I just wanted to have a nice Thanksgiving, and a happy Christmas and New Year.

His response (which today has much meaning) was, "Jim, let's take one holiday at a time."

How true his remarks would prove for my family.

The following week I was busy at work, just trying to catch up mentally with everything that had been going on in the office. I had abandoned my run for State Treasurer, and just really wanted one last term as city clerk. I was really tired of all the pressure, scrutiny, and countless investigations over the past ten years. I could recall three FBI investigations alone, including this last one, and at least four different inspector general inquiries. Every day, I was getting more tired, and I told my inner circle that I was only going to run for city clerk one more time for re-election, in February of 2007. I wanted the people in my world to know I would not be in politics forever, and that they would have four more years to plan their futures.

It was now Wednesday, the last day of November 2005. I was becoming more comfortable about my decision to get out of politics over the next four years, and to start collecting my pension. Quite honestly, though, I wasn't even sure I was going to finish my last term. I would be fifty-five years old and fully vested in pension. That would allow me to receive 80 percent of my salary, which came out to approximately $107,000.00 per year, for the rest of my life. I was ready to change my life, and quietly end my career as city clerk in the next couple of years. As I was finding some inner peace in these thoughts, Martha contacted me on the intercom, to ask me if I wanted to talk to Don Zochowski, my former legislative assistant during my alderman days. I was in politics with Don for over twenty years, and maybe, I thought, I should share my thoughts with him now. When I picked up the phone, he asked me if he could stop by my house to talk. I really didn't know why Don wanted to stop, but I thought it would be nice, just before Christmas, to sit down and have a few beers with him.

Around 8:00 p.m., Don tapped on the window and came downstairs. It was always nice to see him, especially since we hadn't been as close the last couple of years as we should have been. One trait about Don I never questioned was his loyalty. What he was about to tell me would confirm my worst fears over the past couple of months.

Although Don seemed relaxed, I knew he had come over for a reason. After I grabbed a couple of beers for us, we sat on the couch. I asked him what was on his mind.

Don was never one to beat around the bush, so he came right out and said, "The word on the street is that Mick's been wearing a wire."

I wanted to say that I was shocked, but honestly, I wasn't. I was more hurt than anything else. Needless to say, I asked him where he heard that claim. He told me he heard the story from more than one source, including some people from the satellite office who heard Traci talking about it, and from someone working downtown who had a previous relationship with one of Mick's brothers.

My first dilemma was considering what would be my next step. Even though I thought about Mick betraying me, I still didn't know if it were true, and if it were, how long had he been cooperating with the Feds? Don stayed for about an hour. We mostly talked about Mick, and if it were possible for him to betray me. I knew that tomorrow I had to confront Mick. I thanked Don for giving me this information, and promised to keep him updated.

I probably stayed up until about midnight, drinking and just going back and forth in my mind about Mick. If in fact he had cooperated with the Feds, I wondered how I would defend myself, depending upon what he may have told them. Even though lately I had been very careful about talking to either Mick or Traci, I was scared to death of them now!

That morning, December 1, I promised to take my mom to the store for groceries. Originally, I planned to go downtown, since it was the first of the month, and payday, but after last evening's events, I decided to stay close to home. I was sitting in the parking lot, waiting for Mom. Because my nerves were getting the best of me, I had decided to run into the store to see how far she was with her shopping. Since she wasn't even in line yet to check out, I called Mick in the store, on the two-way. I asked him what was going on, and where he was. He told me he was writing tickets on the north side with Mike Stec.

I didn't waste any time, and said, "Mick, according to Don, the word on the street is that you've been wearing a wire."

There was a short moment of silence before Mick replied, "I heard that, too."

He then said that as soon as the two of them finished writing tickets, they would stop by my house to talk. I felt a little better, but what I didn't know was that Mick and I had just talked together for the final time!

About 5:00 p.m., there came a knock at my back door. To my surprise, Mike Stec was standing there, by himself. When he came into the house, I asked him where Mick was. He told me Mick had to stop somewhere, and that he would call me that night, or see me tomorrow. I then took the opportunity to ask Mike if Mick was himself lately; he just seemed preoccupied, and kind of out of it. He attributed all of that to the investigation, but admitted that he was concerned about Mick. In any event, I agreed to get together with Mick the next day, and told Mike that it would be a better day.

During this whole mess, I continued to talk to Kathleen in general terms, letting her know that there could be potential problems, but I never discussed any business dealings I had had. Kathleen had high blood pressure and diverticulitis, so, the less stress for her, the better.

Around 6:00 p.m., I sat down to a dinner of breaded pork chops. I was just about finished when my cell phone went off. During times like these, I always kept my cell close. When I looked at the caller ID and discovered it was my attorney, I immediately picked up. As soon as I heard Tony's voice on the other end, I knew there was a problem. He asked me what I would be doing tomorrow morning, and I told him that I'd be taking my daughter to school. He then told me, firmly, that I needed to find someone else to take her. Now I was getting nervous, and asked what was up. Tony vaguely replied that he had received some new information and that we needed to discuss it immediately. He told me that I should meet him at 7:00 a.m. in his office.

At that point, because of his serious tone, I knew that any further questions would be futile, so I simply said, "I'll see you in the morning."

I could see the fear on Kathleen's face as she asked me what was wrong. I told her I needed to meet with Tony early in the morning, and that we would have to ask one of our friends to take Nina to school.

For some reason, and I don't know why, I looked at my wife and said, "I think there's a problem."

I wasn't sure what it was, but I felt something was terribly wrong.

The rest of the evening was quiet, to say the least. It was difficult to talk to Kathleen about anything, because of the uncertainty of the situation. After she went to bed, I drank about six beers, just to relax, because I knew I'd have a hard enough time falling asleep. When the alarm went off at 5:30 a.m., I showered, put on a sport coat, turtleneck, and khakis, and gave my wife a hug, as if I were leaving home for a war, and headed downtown.

At about 6:55 a.m., Tom and I pulled up to the building that housed a number of offices, including Tony's. I told Tom I would call him when I had finished, and headed inside. Since it was so early in the morning, there were very few people around. Quite frankly, walking down the hallway was a little eerie; there was only one light on, which was coming from Tony's office. As soon as I opened the front door, Tony walked out to greet me, and let me into his office from the foyer. With a look of total concern on his face, Tony told me that around 5:00 p.m. yesterday, Patrick Collins had called him. Collins told him that he had had some new information or evidence, and that he wanted Tony and me to see him, ASAP. What I found out later was that Tony had rescheduled that meeting from last night to this morning.

There really wasn't much time to talk. Tony simply suggested that we head over to the Federal building, because he had promised Collins we would be there by 7:30 a.m. Our subsequent walk to the building was very quiet, as I tried to figure how bad this situation had possibly become.

At the Federal building, Tony and I boarded the elevator. After we disembarked, and started walking down the corridor, all I could remember seeing was the office of U.S. Senator Dick Durbin staring at us, about forty feet away. Tony then stopped in the middle of the hallway, and in front of an office with no name listed, just a number.

Tony knocked on the door. Within seconds, Assistant U.S. Attorney Patrick Collins opened the door and invited us in. I felt as if all my blood had rushed to my head. My knees were shaking, and my hands were dripping with perspiration as we walked into the office. Standing with Mr. Collins were the two agents who had come to my house earlier, and the other, a member of Collins's team. They all introduced themselves by name, but I couldn't tell anyone what they'd even said, because I was in a total daze, getting ready, I knew, for the fight of my life. Mr. Collins said that before we could get started, he needed to meet with his people for a few minutes alone, so he asked Tony and me to sit down at the conference table, and to wait for them.

After they walked out, I started looking around. In front of the brightly lit, decent-sized room was a conference table on which there were stacks of what appeared to be audio and visual tapes, and a couple of photocopies of actual pictures. File cabinets and paperwork were everywhere. I then strolled toward the back of the room, where there was a small table, with the morning edition of *The Chicago Sun-Times* on top. The headlines read, "Laski Friend Wore a Wire." As I walked back to the conference table, I started looking at the various paraphernalia. Every single tape had been labeled with a different informational heading, such as "Laski and Jones," and "Gammicchia," along with different dates, times, and places. I then started examining the copies of the pictures. I saw myself sitting in my basement on the day I came home from the hospital after my tests, with a blanket pulled up to my chin. During that time, and with my children around, either Mick or Traci had brought some type of hidden camera (probably in that big purse of Traci's) to take pictures of me. Now, I didn't know what to do. I felt as if Mick and Traci had ripped my heart out. As I walked to the back of the room, I looked out a huge window, which provided a beautiful view of Lake Michigan, and my whole political life just passed before me. I knew there was going to be a bad time ahead—I just didn't know how bad. Then, Patrick Collins and his people returned to the room.

Collins sat directly across from me at the conference table. Tony, of course, sat next to me, and the rest of the FBI agents, along with various U.S. Attorneys, sat on either side of Collins. The meeting started with Collins just turning to his right and having one agent present the government's evidence against me. He started with a chronological set of events going back to when I first called former Alderman Pat Huels. The most aggravating part of this process was him accusing me of shaking Mick down for money; in fact, the indictment stipulated that I wouldn't make the first phone call to Huels unless Mick first paid me $500.00. Had I taken money? I sure had! But I had never—and I mean NEVER—shaken either Mick or anyone else down. In fact, Mick was trying to save his own ass, and Traci's, too, by embellishing his story and creating more lies as he went along.

The agent also selected three or four tapes from probably a dozen or so from the table. The first tape he played was an excerpt of Mick's conversation with me in the car on the way up to Wisconsin on September 20, 2005. He had been very emotional and almost in tears, and had told me how hard everything was for him, and how we needed to help Traci and protect our families. At one point, this agent admitted to following us up to Wisconsin, and with a smirk, gave me a list of the highways we took up there. He also told me that I passed them on the way back that evening, on one of those highways. He never did mention that I went home because my father was dying—this was all business to him!

I also heard another tape, recorded at Sam's house. On that tape was a lot of back and forth conversation about what Traci should say, and Sam's comments on protecting me. At that point, the agent stopped the tape and commented how brazen and callous Sam and I had been for having had *The Godfather* on TV while we had been busy obstructing justice.

He then played parts of two more tapes—one was of me, talking in my basement about political donations I may have received from the Joneses. That conversation had taken place the evening after the hospital tests, when I'd been on the couch, with the blanket to my chin. In fact, that's when the agent showed me copies of the photos that either Mick or Traci had taken of me with a hidden camera.

The last tape he played, and the most damaging of all, was that portion of my conversation with Mick on the two-way, when I was recorded as saying, "Go Cubs!" According to the Feds, that was the go-ahead for Mick to instruct his wife to lie to the grand jury.

After the last tape, Mr. Collins took over the meeting and told me that I was now under arrest. He gave Tony and me a copy of the indictment, and then laid out his terms. He said he was not out to crucify me, but that I needed to cooperate with them by providing information about "Get Plowed," as well as about my own hiring practices and my relationship with the Daley administration. If I decided to talk that day, and if Collins believed I was being truthful, the U.S. Attorney would keep my indictment sealed for a period of time, as long as I continued to cooperate. However, if I chose to remain silent, and to fight them by going to court, Collins promised to take me down the street to the Dirksen Building, and with all the media fanfare possible, formally indict me. With that, he handed Tony and me a copy of the indictment. The entire entourage of agents and U.S. attorneys got up, and Collins told us they would give us some privacy for awhile, and for Tony to come out of the office to notify them of our decision.

As soon as they left the office, I got out of my chair and walked slowly over to the window, just to look at the lake and the skyline. Right then and there, I knew, without having even talked to Tony, that I would probably be going to prison. I guess what I needed to know was if I had any options at all. I had a moment of panic and terror, as I looked aimlessly out the window. I thought, as I was screaming inside to myself, about Kathleen and the kids, and their emotional survival. I thought about my job, about money, about the house, and about private school tuition. Most of all, I was thinking, "How in the hell had I screwed up so badly?"—and the question I'll be asking myself for the rest of my life—"Why?"

By the time I finally sat down, Tony had already read part of the indictment.

His expression was both serious and somber, as I asked him the one million dollar question, "What should I do?"

Tony paused for a second, and then looked me straight in the eye and answered, "I don't think you have a choice. You need to consider Collins's offer."

Tony explained that because of the growing public anger and disgust over the Hired Truck Program in general, even if I had wanted to carry on the fight in Federal Court, I would probably lose. I replied that I didn't think there was that much in the way of incriminating evidence from the tapes. He informed me that just the part involving the Jones's cooperation was enough to convict me. Even though I felt like delaying the outcome forever, I needed to make a decision. This was a time in my life when no one else could help me. Certainly, Tony could advise me, and he assured me he was with me no matter what I chose to do, but that it would have to be my decision. At that point, I told Tony to have Collins and his group come back, because I knew what I had to do.

Everyone then returned to the room and sat down. I looked across the table at Collins, and with my voice cracking, told him that I would cooperate. He then told me that he didn't enjoying crucifying people, and that he wasn't arrogant, but just doing his job. What Mr. Collins was referring to was my conversation with Mick, following my first FBI interview. I told Mick that I thought Collins was slick and arrogant, and someone who would enjoy sticking it to me. Clearly, Mick was sharing a lot of our mutual conversations with the U.S. Attorney. After Collins got his little dig in, he gave me another little lecture. He told me that I should not blame Mick for anything, because what he had been merely protecting his family, as I would be doing now by cooperating (I wanted to ask Collins if that meant lying, as Mick did when he told the Feds that I shook him down for money). In addition, both Collins and the FBI agent who talked to me earlier warned me about the consequences of threatening or harming the Jones family's safety (apparently, Mick told the Feds that he was worried about what Sam might do to his family when he had found out about his and Traci's cooperation with the U.S. Attorney). They also warned me not to have any future contact with Sam, and that, again, if anything should happen to the Joneses, the government would (and I'm paraphrasing) "come down on me like a ton of bricks." The FBI agent then asked me how dangerous Sam was. I told him that he had a number of health issues, and would never hurt anyone, because his bark was worse than his bite. Collins then reminded me of Sam's past criminal record, including a charge that I didn't know anything about.

Tony and Collins next discussed the ground rules for the rest of the day, which would determine whether I could go home after the meeting, or be taken for a formal arraignment at the Federal building. They both told me that I had to be totally truthful with the U.S. Attorney from that point forward. Basically, by cooperating, I would be accepting responsibility for my past actions—a fact that a judge would look favorably upon, and which would lower the criminal points determining how much time I would spend in federal prison. At that point, Collins informed us he had to leave and that his assistant, Manish Shah, would be taking over the questions.

I now needed to use the washroom, which was about fifty feet down the hallway. Collins and the FBI agent told me, since I was technically under arrest, I couldn't go anywhere without an escort. So the same agent who had played the tapes walked with me. While I stood in front of the urinal, he was not more than ten feet behind me. During that whole time in the washroom, he didn't say a word. I felt like a terrorist, or a major flight risk.

Finally, on the way back to the conference room, the FBI agent leaned towards me and said, "I'll bet you're glad this is finally over."

I didn't know what to say, except, "I guess."

When we returned to the conference room, Collins left, and his entourage of assistants and agents started pouncing on me, with Manish Shah leading the charge. Shah was five-foot-nine, and a thin young man of either Middle Eastern or Pakistani descent. He had neatly groomed hair, and wore a suit that was at least two sizes too big. He had a cold and arrogant look that as time went on, would aggravate me. There were times that day when he spoke to me almost as if I were a child. He constantly reminded me of the consequences if I didn't tell the truth, including time away from my family.

The first couple of hours of questioning concerned the foundation of my guilt. He asked, as Collins had, if I received money from Mr. Jones.

Again I answered, "Yes."

He then asked me if that money was for helping "Get Plowed" and the Joneses. I again answered "Yes."

There was one question after another concerning my relationship with Jones. Shah wanted every single detail about the bribe money given me. When did the payoffs start? Were the payments weekly or monthly? How long had that arrangement lasted? Did Jones ever give me cash? If so, was it in an envelope? Did anyone else know? What did I do with that money? They also asked questions about my relationship with Tomczak. In fact, hundreds of questions were asked and answered over the next several hours. At one point, everyone stopped their questions about Jones and the truck program and jumped into those about my hiring practices. They specifically asked me how I went about hiring people and about my relationship with the mayor's people. Did I go to them for help or approval in getting people hired? I certainly had quite a bit of information, but I didn't throw it all out at once.

When they seemed to be zeroing in on one topic, they would keep me off balance and start asking me about my political account and fundraising. Every topic and every question always led to inquiries about possible legal activities on my part. Although I believed that the U.S. Attorney now had more than enough evidence to convict me, Manish Shah wanted to hammer in as many nails as possible into my coffin.

During the course of the interview, another gentleman from the U.S. Attorney's office commented on my previous political aspirations.

With a smirk on his face, he said, "There was talk about you running for mayor some day. Was that true?"

I simply answered there had been ongoing discussions regarding a number of different political offices.

Around 3:00 p.m., everyone decided to take a break. Tony and I had been sitting in that room for about eight hours, and without lunch, although I did have two bottles of water. Shah then told us that he had to call his boss and inform him of the extent of my cooperation, and then they would have to decide what would happen next. As crazy as it was, there was still the possibility that they could drag me into Federal Court at the last minute and arraign me. Everyone else then got up from the table to stretch their legs. I, though, didn't move, and neither did Tony. I think we both felt physically, mentally, and emotionally drained. As much I had wanted this part of the day to be over, I surely wasn't looking forward to going home and facing Kathleen with the truth.

When Shah returned to the room, he informed me that the U.S. Attorney's office wanted to keep our dialogue going. Of course, he reminded me again about the importance of telling the truth, and of staying away from anyone directly involved in the case, including Mick, Traci, Sam, and Randy. He also told me that the only person I could discuss this matter with was my wife. If I violated any of these agreements, I would be in Federal Court the very next day. I then told Shah and his associates that tomorrow (Saturday, December 3) was my annual Christmas party, which my wife and I had held for the past twelve years. I needed advice on what I should do. After a few minutes of discussion, everyone agreed that I would be ill and unable to attend, but that Kathleen would put on the smiley face and be the hostess. We agreed that we could meet again at least a couple of days next week, at the same location. We then scheduled the next interview for Monday morning, around 9:00 a.m. With that, I was told that I was free to go home under the previously agreed-upon stipulations.

As Tony and I left the building, we kept a watchful eye out to make sure that no one from the media was watching. Instead of going back to his office, Tony and I agreed to meet on Monday morning, to confer together before the next interview. I had already called Tom to pick me up right outside of Tony's building. By the time we got there, he was already waiting for me. I then climbed into the car to head back south.

Around 4:15 p.m., we arrived at my house. Kathleen was still waiting in the front room for Nina, who would get a ride home from school. I knew that Kathleen would be very concerned, because I had never been able to call her all day. Kathleen opened the front door, looked at me with a very sad expression, and asked me if everything was okay. I told her that we needed to talk after Nina had gotten home. However, Kathleen told me that Nina would be home later, and that Jack and Bobby were watching TV in the back room, so we could sit down now and talk.

We went directly to the dining room and sat directly across from each other. I'll never forget the look of panic on my wife's face when she asked me again if everything was okay. I don't know really know how to describe my feeling, except to say that I felt as if a part of me had just died, and that I was now saying goodbye to my family. I looked at Kathleen and told her that I had been arrested by the FBI and indicted by the U.S. Attorney's office. I gave her all the gory details about the tapes and the day's events.

I also looked right into her teary eyes, and told her, "Kathleen, I'm going to prison."

With that, she broke down, and began to cry. She asked what she and the kids would do without me. I can't remember a more difficult time that Kathleen and I were about to experience than what was ahead of us. For the next hour or so, I tried to explain what had transpired, and what was possibly ahead for me. Besides this whole mess, we had three very intelligent and inquisitive children who could sense when something in our home was not quite right.

Kathleen and I did the best we could for the rest of the day just going through the motions. Every opportunity when the kids were occupied, we sat down to talk. My immediate concern was to have Kathleen handle the organization of our Christmas party by herself. Kathleen knew that I was in no condition to attend, so she would try to put on a happy face and represent both of us in wishing all our friends and supporters a Merry Christmas. The story would be that I had the flu. She would not tell a soul what was really going on, including Ray and Sam. If those two were to be told anything, it would be from me, personally, and in a couple of days.

Before we went to bed that evening, Kathleen wanted to know exactly what went on between Mick and me, and what I was charged with. I could barely stand the pain and disappointment in her face when I explained in detail the arrangement Mick and I had with the trucks, for which he had regularly given me money.

When I finished, she asked me one simple question—"Why?"

She reminded me that I had a great job, and that I was an attorney. What, then, had I been thinking of? Over the years, Kathleen and I always agreed that nothing worthwhile in life comes easily, and that for us, success would continue to only result from hard, honest work. She considered the whole scheme between Mick and me a shortcut to hard work, and that, unfortunately, I took the easy way out. I did explain to her, however, that when Mick started giving me the money, he presented it as a gift, and said it was for the family.

Whenever I had a financial problem at home, Mick always prefaced any money he gave me with, "Here, use this to pay that bill."

I tried to soften the blow for Kathleen, but although what I was telling her was true, I used bad judgment in putting myself in that predicament to begin with. I knew, right then and there, that my wife would experience an emotional roller coaster. My only hope was that she would hang on to her faith and stick with me, because none of what was going to happen would make any sense to me without my wife and children.

The next day, I didn't leave the house. I hid out, because I didn't want anyone to see me out and about if we were telling people I was ill for the Christmas party. Also, there were big stories in one of the major newspapers describing how a long-time friend of mine had betrayed me, and how the FBI now had incriminating evidence on tape. I didn't want to discuss that situation with anyone else, so my best bet was to remain secluded at home.

That evening, Kathleen got all dressed up, and headed for the party. I stayed home to watch the kids, while one of our friends picked her up at about 8:00 p.m. Since the party would last from 7:30 p.m. to midnight, she would be there for the main period of time, when most people would be attending. After Kathleen had left, I went downstairs with Nina, Jack, and Bobby, to watch TV together. Fortunately for me, the kids had been tired from a full week of school, because I was so depressed that I could hardly talk at all. When I looked at the kids and saw how innocent they were, and how much love they had in their eyes for me, it took every ounce of my emotional strength not to break down and cry. There were times, however, when I did feel tears running down my cheeks, and that's when I had to run into the bathroom to compose myself.

At about 11:00 p.m., Kathleen returned home from the party. As she walked through the back door, Tom Lally followed her. It was at that time I knew I needed to tell him something, which I did. I gave Tom the basic information about my predicament, with the hope that he would keep his mouth shut. I always regarded Tom as a loyal friend. I had known him since I was alderman, back in 1990. In the fifteen years since then, he had been on my detail for the past ten, during which time we shared many personal issues with each other. I felt I always did whatever I could for him and his family. Once, when there was a ton of overtime approved, Tom enjoyed the distinction of being the second-highest-paid police officer in the city of Chicago that year. He also always had all sorts of job perks, and his daughter received a summer job, and his sister-in-law a full-time position. Well, as time went on, it became apparent that Mr. Lally had his own agenda, since he would soon totally abandon ship.

After my brief explanation to Lally, I turned to Kathleen, who looked ready to pass out. She said that everyone at the party was wonderful and supportive. She also told me that Ray made a speech that didn't leave a dry eye in the house. He talked about loyalty, about how much I'd done for people, and how it was their turn now to support and help me. Although hosting that party was extremely difficult for Kathleen, I believed that being around our friends and supporters comforted her. At the party, Ray and Sam were both concerned about me. All she told them was I was sick, and feeling very stressed-out. A few people came up to Kathleen to tell her they had also heard about Mick wearing a wire and fully cooperating with the Feds. She said she just shook her head and walked away. Of course, everyone at the party was looking for the Joneses to dispel any rumors of betrayals, but they were no-shows.

Tom left around midnight, and Kathleen stayed up with me for about another hour, just to talk about the party and our future. We agreed to do whatever it would take for Nina, Jack, and Bobby to have a wonderful Christmas. We also agreed to start saving money by not buying each other gifts, and for none of the adults in our immediate families. We both knew that when I lost my job, there would be serious financial problems that we would need to address. I was hoping during the holidays to speak to my brother-in-law about some financial assistance. During the rest of the weekend, I kept a low profile and just tried to relax, because on Monday, I would be back with Tony and the U.S. Attorney and his entourage to continue my interrogation.

On Monday, Tony and I returned to the same unmarked office as on Friday. There to greet us were Manish Shah and the rest of the same group, except for Patrick Collins, who had turned the remainder of the questioning over to them. Once we sat down, Shah and the same FBI agent who started the interview on Friday quickly reminded me about telling the truth and keeping the interview process going. Shah began by asking me questions about specific hiring practices and how the system worked. I discussed in detail the process from A to Z, from applicants changing their resumes before having field applications, to putting certain individuals on already closed lists. During the course of the interview, Shah switched gears, and began asking me about my political accounts. He wanted to know how I had used that money. For some reason, Shah believed that my guys, Ray Drish and Sam Gammicchia, were guilty of kickbacking to me the money they had given me, for my own personal use, and for my daughter's tuition. That was a flat-out lie, and in my opinion, Mr. Jones told the Feds that bullshit to try to help himself and his wife out. In fact, someone from my organization later told me that the Joneses personally asked him that same question regarding such alleged kickbacks.

During that Monday interview, I was amazed by how much information the Feds had. They asked me about my Christmas party, even though they knew I wasn't there. They also asked what my wife said to the people who attended. What really floored me was the fact that they knew in detail the content of Ray's speech. So, either Ray's place had been bugged, or someone at the party was wired, which meant there'd been another informant working for them.

Unfortunately for me, the interviews continued for the next three weeks in December, two-to-three-days-a-week, for three-to-four-hours-a-session. There would be days when I would feel so drained that I would just want to quit, but I knew that by talking, I could have a quiet and peaceful Christmas with my family, and wait until January 2006 for the actual public indictment.

On some days, they would specifically ask me about meetings, conversations, and any incriminating information I could provide about other elected officials, including Mayor Daley, County Commissioner John Daley, Governor Blagojevich, State House Speaker Mike Madigan, and a host of others, including all current sitting aldermen in the city council. Shah continuously reminded me that any information about other elected officials the U.S. Attorney's office deemed useful could be helpful to me when I would be sentenced, because they would throw in a good word about my cooperation to the judge.

During those interviews, Shah and the FBI agents were arrogant and mean-spirited, and showed very little compassion for my family.

At the end of each interview, when Tony would ask Shah about a break for the holidays, his standard response would always be, "We'll see how the rest of the interviews go."

Meanwhile, practically every document, cancelled check, list of employees, financial report, anything else subpoenaed was thrown in my face. In fact, I had to go through each of my approximately 140 or so employees, and explain how they had been hired, and if he or she had political sponsors, been part of my organization, or had supported me financially.

One of the questions they kept asking me was what I did with the money from Mick. My answer was, and continues to be, I spent it. They also asked if I took money from anyone else. In an effort to cut my losses and work out my own deal, I admitted to taking money from Randy for having helped him out. I then had to go through the details of how much money I was talking about, over what period of time I received it, how often, and at what locations the meetings to drop off the cash were held. In return for one trucking company I had gotten on the city payroll, Randy gave me $2,000.00 in cash over an approximate one-year period, for a total of $24,000.00. So, at that point, the FBI wanted to know what I did with all that money. Besides some vacations and big home remodeling projects, they still believed I had spent more money than I so far admitted to.

When I first started accepting money from Mick and Randy, I kept it at home, but as soon as the amount grew larger, I decided to keep it in a safety deposit box, which I had maintained up until the time the FBI had started its investigation. After my first meeting with Patrick Collins in August, I pulled the money out and brought it back home. The most I had ever had at any one time at the bank was $30,000.00.

After that one particular interview, I told Tony that there was still some money from the paybacks around. He asked me how much, and I told him approximately $15,000.00. I would have another meeting with the Feds in two days, so we agreed I would bring that money to the next session.

Before the next meeting, I went to Tony's office first, and brought a thick envelope with me containing $15,400.00 in one-hundred bills. Tony, in turn, counted the money, so he would know exactly the amount I would be turning over.

After we arrived at our next meeting, and all of us sat down, Tony told Manish Shah and the FBI agents that I had something to disclose to them. Tony handed me my envelope, which I then laid on the table. I told Mr. Shah that there was $15,400.00 in cash in that envelope, representing the remainder of the money from Mick and Randy. I think, at that point, everyone around the table was shocked, including Shah, who just stared at the envelope. For a couple of minutes, they didn't know what to do. In fact, Shah asked the chief FBI agent there what they normally did in such situations. They both agreed to give the envelope to another agent to take, who would do an actual accounting or inventory, and provide Tony with a receipt. The agent left with the envelope, and that was the last I would see of that money. I think both the U.S. Attorney's office and the FBI had been embarrassed by the revelation of that remaining money having been, unbeknownst to them, in a safety deposit box all that time. The next day, the government issued subpoenas for not only all my safety deposit boxes and bank records, but for an inventory of my in-laws' box, which happened to be at the same bank. Needless to say, I never heard anymore about either my or my in-laws' safety deposit boxes after that.

As we got closer to the holidays, the U.S. Attorney's office and the FBI seemed to be putting more pressure on me to give them additional information. They actually told Tony that they believed I was holding back on them. So, just before the holidays, I disclosed information about Mick Jones and his friend Phil, along with other details regarding Traci Jones, and certain allegations I had learned regarding her role as supervisor of the city satellite office. I also told them about illegal merchandise I knew the Joneses once brought into this country from China. Still, though, I knew that unless I talked about some other elected official, all of those other revelations would fall on deaf ears.

At the end of one day, less than a week before Christmas, Manish Shah told me that I would be getting a holiday break. He also told me that they were basically done with me, and that I should use the break to think of anything else that might be helpful to him, because that would be my last opportunity to help myself. Then, the FBI agent who had been with me from day one of the interviews reminded me that time was running out, and implied that any additional information I had could help my family now, but not after the indictment had been sealed. Ironically, everyone then told me to enjoy the holidays the best I could, under the circumstances, with my family. With that, Tony and I wished each other well, and agreed to talk after Christmas, at which time he would tell me the date of our next meeting, which would be in January.

It was during that holiday break that I saw Sam. I had been avoiding him ever since the FBI arrested me. Just before Christmas, as at every holiday over the years, he would stop over with gifts. He would always buy saving bonds for the kids and Kathleen, and

I would get a very nice gift certificate for a department store. This year, Sam already knew something was wrong. As soon as he stepped into the house, he told me that the word on the street was that Mick was indeed wired up. I just nodded my head affirmatively, and advised him to be careful. Sam's stepdaughter, who also worked at my satellite office, had overheard Traci telling people on the phone that her husband was wearing a wire. I again told him to exercise care by watching every move he made, and every word he said, especially over the phone. I also told him the most important thing he could do to protect himself was to stay away from the Joneses. I was hoping that some day Sam and I would be able to get together again, but I knew for the time being, that would be impossible.

Right after Christmas, I talked to Tony. He told me that our next meeting with the U.S. Attorney's office would be during the first week of January. We both agreed that unless I could give them something else, the interviews would probably reach the end of the line. Manish Shah told us early on that he expected input about when and how I would leave the clerk's office, and that he wanted that information prior to the unsealing of my indictment. However, I wasn't yet sure I really wanted to resign. I wanted to hold on to my position as long as possible, which would be contingent on what kind of sentencing deal the government would offer me. I was still considering fighting the government charges in court, because I still had doubts about all those tapes, which I had never really heard in their entirety, except for those few excerpts. I was also pissed off about Mick's falsely telling the Feds that I shook him down for $500.00. I wanted both of us to take a polygraph. Tony, however, reminded me that it didn't matter if I shook him down or not; the crime was taking the money in the first place. However, I was still aggravated, because I knew the Joneses would continue to use desperate tactics to try to manipulate the system to their advantage.

Without anymore fanfare or controversy, my family and I then quietly spent New Year's Eve at home. We brought in the New Year by watching the celebration on TV after watching a movie we had rented. At midnight, Kathleen and I hugged and kissed the kids. We

CHAPTER 16

THE HIRED TRUCK PROGRAM SCANDAL: INDICTMENT, CONVICTION, AND SENTENCING

The year 2006 started with another interview with the Feds. Little did I know this would be my last interview with them. The questions primarily focused on the conversations I could recall having had with the mayor or his people regarding, basically, any issue at all. They were looking for any dirt I could throw out there about any other elected official. Of course, I again mentioned the Joneses' relationship with the FBI agent and his partner, John Novak, but by the end of the day, they were no longer interested in that kind of information. By the time Tony and I had left the office, everything was still up in the air regarding future interviews, my resignation, and the indictment's unsealing. As difficult as it was, I had to wait.

Surprisingly, the next ten days or so were relatively quiet. I did the best I could at work, trying to stay focused on my job. As trying as it was, it was extremely helpful to be directly involved again with my office's day-to-day operations. During this whole time, there was only one person in the entire office who knew anything about my legal problems, and that was Deputy Clerk Ed Kantor. I think it was around mid-December when I had told Kantor everything. There were times when I had to leave early, or arrive late, so it was imperative that either Ed or I would always be at the office to run things. Quite frankly, he made my life much more tolerable during those difficult times. I learned who my real friends were. That list may have been short, but Ed Kantor was certainly on it. As the days moved on, I asked myself, "Could I actually fight this case and hold on to my office?" I knew it would be an uphill battle, but I hadn't yet given up hope.

Soon, it was Friday, January 13. I woke up Friday morning to get dressed, and to take Jack and Bobby to school. The day was dark and gloomy. Little did I know how dark that day would actually be.

As I went downstairs to grab my phone, I noticed a voice mail message. Since it was only 7:00 a.m., I figured it had probably been a late night call from Ray. However, during those crazy times, I wanted to make sure it wasn't some type of emergency involving my case or my mom. The message was from Sam Gammicchia's wife, Arlene. Although she was quite composed, I could sense a fear in her voice as she informed me that the FBI was at their house around 6:00 a.m. to arrest Sam. The only other thing she had said was that Sam needed an attorney, and asked me to call her back. I immediately picked up the phone and called; it rang only once before Arlene answered. She believed at least a half-dozen agents were at their front door that night to whisk Sam off in one of their vehicles. Although I was a little shocked, I told Arlene to relax the best she could while I got on the phone to Bob Molaro about getting an attorney down at the Federal building ASAP.

I was, to say the least, very concerned about the whole situation as Kathleen and I dropped the boys off at school. We then stopped to pick up a newspaper and some coffee, and headed back home. For the next hour or so, we sat at the dining room table, trying to figure out why Sam was arrested and what that would mean for me. I was hoping that Sam hadn't tried to contact Mick or Traci, or said something crazy.

In any event, I told Kathleen I wasn't going downtown, but that I was going to take a shower, and just stay by the phone the rest of the day. After I showered, and was in a robe in front of the mirror combing my hair, Kathleen opened the bathroom door, holding our cordless phone. She told me that Tony was on the other end of the line, and that he needed to talk to me immediately. As soon as I answered the phone, Tony, in a very somber tone, informed me he had just gotten off the phone with Manish Shah, who told him that I needed to be at the Federal building that very day, at 2:30 p.m. sharp, and that if I weren't there, the FBI would apprehend me and lock me up.

My first question was, "What the hell have I done now?"

Tony simply told me to meet him at his office by 2:00 p.m., and that we would walk down to the Federal building together. He then came right out and told me that this was not going to be pleasant, and to be prepared for an indictment.

As soon as I hung up the phone, I turned to Kathleen, and told her that this was it—that I was going to be indicted, and to get the kids out of school and stay at her parents' house. I then picked up my cell phone to call Ed Kantor downtown. He quickly said that it was all over the radio and TV about Sam and other possible indictments today, including mine. I simply told Ed to hold down the fort, and that I would call him later.

The other phone call I needed to make was to Tom Lally. I let him know not only what time to pick me up, but to tell him to call my mom and ask her to go to my sister's house, because of the media attention this was going to bring, not only to me, but very possibly to her as well.

The last call I asked Kathleen to make was to Father Marc, the pastor of my church, to inform him of my situation. I told her to ask him to stop by the house, because I wanted to see him before I went downtown to meet with Tony. Father Marc said he would be here in about half an hour. Kathleen asked me if I wanted to eat something for lunch, but I politely declined, as I waited and tried to imagine how bad the afternoon was going to be.

Soon, Father Marc arrived. The three of us actually took the next forty-five minutes or so to reflect and pray. Father Marc was wonderful, as he encouraged me to have the necessary strength and courage to face the tough times ahead. He also reminded me of all the positive things I had done, not only for the community and the city as a whole, but for the people, who would never forget those accomplishments. Before he left, we all held hands in the living room and said an "Our Father" prayer. He then gave Kathleen and me a blessing before he left. As he walked out to his car, there was a reporter and camera crew waiting. Father Marc stopped for a couple of seconds to say something to them. Then, he got into his car and drove away.

Back in the house, I was getting my coat on. I had stationed Tom in the alley, so I could exit through my back door and go through the garage to the car. As Kathleen and I said goodbye to each other, we both had tears in our eyes.

I remember the subsequent ride downtown as both tense and quiet. Because of the situation, Mike Stec, despite the fact he was on the clock, rode with us. Tom wanted another police officer with us, just in case he had to walk with me, and he didn't want to park the car. All the radio stations claimed that there would be further indictments involving that day in the Hired Truck Program scandal, and that mine might be one of them.

When we were one block away from both Tony's law office and the Federal building, I told Tom to stop the car and park. I got out of the car, because I needed a cigarette desperately. While I was smoking, snow began to fall. I still had about fifteen minutes before my meeting with Tony, so I lit up another cigarette. As I stood and looked around, I couldn't see one vacant parking spot. As I looked down the next block, toward the Federal building, I saw TV trucks from all the major stations parked on both sides of the street. Clearly, this was going to be a major news story.

As much as I wanted to avoid the entire situation, I had to get back in the car and tell Tom to drive to the law office. When we pulled up, Mike Stec jumped in the driver's seat, while Tom walked me to the elevator, and up to Tony's office. When we got to his office, I immediately told Tom to go back to the car, and that I would call him when I was ready to leave. When I talked to Tony, there wasn't much he could say to me now, except to take a deep breath. He also told me, very frankly, that we were going to face a tough afternoon, but that he would be with me every step of the way.

We quickly exited from the front of the building and made an immediate right turn to the corner, which was only a few feet away. We then crossed the street, and at the corner, turned left, which put us maybe fifty or sixty feet from the Federal building. I felt as if I were in a haze, and walking to the end of a cliff. As we got closer to the building's front doors, we saw a couple of people standing outside as lookouts. As soon as they identified me, they ran inside to inform the entire media delegation that I had arrived.

As I walked behind Tony through the revolving doors, all I could see were flashing lights and cameras. It was unbelievable how many media people turned out. All of them were roped off to one section of the hallway, facing the front metal detectors, and positioned between the elevators that were located on either side.

Before I left Tom, I gave him everything from my pockets (credit cards, business cards, cash), except my driver's license, since I wanted as little as possible on the conveyor through the metal detector. As I checked in, I handed a middle-aged lady my driver's license. She smiled and told me that she lived in my community, and that I had helped her when I was alderman. She wished me well, and I politely thanked her. As I continued to walk past the detector, another employee was waiting with a device that looked like a paddle, which he ran over my clothes to check for other objects. When he finished, I waited for my overcoat, which had been passed through the detector, and was now directly at the end of the conveyor belt. When I turned to my left toward the elevators, all I could see were flashing, almost blinding, lights again, while reporters were yelling questions to me. On the elevator, I could still see the little white dots from all those camera lights. While Tony and I headed toward the courtroom, I could have heard a pin drop. That silence seemed like an omen.

As I walked into the courtroom, Tony told me to sit in the first row of what resembled church pews, and to wait for him while he tried to find the U.S. Attorney, either Collins or Shah, to find out why the government had decided to unseal the indictment. I sat down, and noticed, through the huge windows to my left, that the snow was really starting to come down hard.

A federal courtroom looks quite different from a larger local or circuit courtroom. This was not a big courtroom; there were only five pews behind me, and in front, two long conference tables facing parallel to each other, and about the length of the entire room. In front of the tables was a podium with a microphone, a few feet in front of which was the slightly elevated judge's bench. To my right was the jury box. While I waited, I saw reporters from *The Sun-Times, Tribune,* and most of the TV stations. I put my head down as I heard them whispering my name. When I did look up, two artists, one to my left, and the other to my right, were sitting in chairs toward the front of the courtroom and just impassively staring at me as they sketched my likeness on a big pad of white paper that each had been hiding. I didn't know which way to look, so I turned toward the window and peered again at the snow, which had become even heavier. I couldn't imagine a more uncomfortable situation in my life than those minutes when the whole world had seemed to be watching me.

After a few minutes, Tony walked in. Following him were Patrick Collins, Manish Shah, and a few FBI agents, along with other members of the U.S. Attorney's office. Tony came over to me and whispered that as soon as the case had been announced, I should meet him at the podium. In the meantime, he told me that I should remain seated in the same spot. As Tony sat at one of the tables, Collins and Shah walked right in front of me, with icy, stony glares. It seemed like hours before the judge entered the room.

The courtroom was packed, as the bailiff called the matter of *U.S. v. James Laski.*" Manish Shah, Tony, and I then approached the podium. I quietly stood there while Shah requested the unsealing of the indictment. He then began reading its gory details. As hard as it was, I tried to block most of what I heard out, except for the part referring to what I had been charged with—two counts of bribery and two counts of obstruction of justice. The judge asked me if I understood the charges, and reminded me that each count carried a maximum sentence of ten years in prison, and if I understood that fact, too.

I firmly answered both questions with, "Yes, your Honor."

There was now an additional courtroom housekeeping detail that took place. Shah asked the judge to put me under some type of home confinement, with a monitoring device, because the government was concerned about the safety of the Jones family. To this day, I don't know exactly what happened, except that the government either fabricated that concern, or someone lied to them, and led them to believe there were actual threats against the Joneses.

Tony was going to argue that part with the judge, but we had another duty to attend to—my processing. If I weren't processed within the next hour, I would have to be locked up until someone could process me, and since this was Friday, and Monday would be the Martin Luther King, Jr. holiday, I wouldn't be released until Tuesday.

In any event, because we felt we didn't have time to argue the government's motion, the judge ruled in their favor, requiring me to wear a monitoring device on my wrist or ankle for an undetermined amount of time. At that point, Tony and I went to a private room to talk. He basically read me the riot act, and said that the government informed him that I gave an order to threaten Mick and Traci, and that Sam and I were talking with each other on a regular basis. I never issued an order against Mick and Traci, but couldn't deny talking to Sam about other matters pertaining to the case during all this time. Tony then told me that I was now ordered to stay away from all co-defendants in the indictment, including the Joneses, Randy Aderman, Sam, and John Briatta. This was all part of my personal recognizance bond, and if I would violate any part, I would immediately be held without bond. Tony then pleaded with me not to talk to anyone I trusted, because now they would all be cutting their own deals, and sticking it to me in order to save their own asses. I later learned that Sam's stepdaughter had gotten into a verbal confrontation with Traci at the office over the issue of Mick and the wire. In my opinion, the government pulled the plug on the sealed indictment because the Joneses weren't able to keep their mouths shut. What was once a highly kept secret was now public knowledge, especially since other parts of the investigation were leaked to the newspapers, due, in my opinion, to deliberate leaks in the Feds' own office, because that's how they do business.

While heading out of the office and making our way to the elevators, we were confronted by the media from every direction. Along the way, I continued to defend myself, while Tony told them that someone was lying to the government, and that it wasn't me, because I never ordered any threats against anyone.

As we literally pushed our way on to the elevator, a few reporters boarded with us, and continued to ask questions, to which Tony had the same answer, "No comment."

We then got out and walked to the big steel door of the processing office, where we were buzzed in, with reporters still following us. Inside was like a currency exchange or bank, with some chairs and glass windows; behind each window was a U.S. Marshal. I had to give one of them my driver's license, while another marshal gave me some papers to fill out, which included information about me and my family, parents, siblings, home, and medical history. This process was quite extensive, and I remember my hand shaking as we were getting closer to the 5:00 p.m. deadline, and I was still filling out paperwork. Tony sat with me to calm my nerves, and he helped me with providing the necessary information.

When I returned the paperwork to the marshal, he told me to walk over to another steel door, directly to my left, and that he would buzz me in. At that point, I could go by myself, so Tony said he'd wait for me. I was terrified as I walked into another room, in which there were three cameras and a fingerprint machine. Two marshals then started taking my fingerprints. I had to keep wiping my fingers, because of all of my perspiration, as they first printed each digit, and then the fourth digit, of each hand together. This was all done on an inkless computer. One marshal then punched up my name on the computer, to see if any of the fingerprints had not turned out. In fact, one finger on each hand needed to be redone.

After the fingerprinting, I sat down, and they began getting the camera ready for pictures. While I sat there, I noticed metal benches with locks on both the top and bottom, for the inmates who had been jailed or taken from another location, and who had to be locked to the benches with their shackles. When it was time to take my pictures, the marshals told me to stand against a backdrop, and then they gave me instructions on the different poses they needed. These included a frontal shot, with me holding a plastic I.D. card under my chin, just as in the movies. I also had to give them both right and left profile shots, and some more head-on photos.

Both of the marshals who attended to me in that room were decent guys who told me, "Let's get this over with, so we can all go home."

They actually asked me how I was doing, along with some general questions about being a politician, such as how long I'd been in office, and my responsibilities. When we had finished, they escorted me back to the steel door I had entered, and where Tony was still waiting.

By that time, I was exhausted, both emotionally and physically. Tony told me that we now had to go to another part of the building, to meet my pre-trial officer, and to fill out more paperwork. After we sat down in the pre-trial office, a young man, dressed casually, told me to follow him to another room, which almost looked like a medical office. There, a lady seated at a desk met us, and asked me to sit down. I again gave my name and other pertinent information. She then told me that I would be providing a urine sample. I quickly told her what medication I was on, because the last thing I wanted was some type of drug charge after the test. As soon as I finished answering questions, the same young man who had escorted me in took me to the workroom, where he handed me a lid-covered plastic cup. As uncomfortable as it was, I had to urinate in that cup with that guy watching me. When I finished, we walked out together, and I turned in the specimen.

The next step on the merry-go-round was to sit down with my pre-trial officer. Tony and I walked into another office, where I found out that my officer would be a young lady by the name of Tiffany Millard. However, at that moment, I had to meet with someone else, who would go over more paperwork, including my financial status. I began answering questions about savings and checking accounts, IRAs, cash payments, and on and on, when everything that had been happening that day had just caught up with me, and I broke down and started crying. I needed to take a break for just a couple of minutes, to regain my composure. When I continued, I disclosed all of my assets and liabilities, as on a balance sheet. All of this information would be included in my file, which I assumed would be used against me if I had any type of forfeiture or penalties levied against me in the future.

Once that was over, I had to see one more person before I could leave—a relatively nice young man who would place the monitoring device on me. He explained to me that once it was attached, it could not be removed without proper authorization. I agreed to have it placed on my ankle, instead of on my wrist, so that my clothing would conceal it in public. It resembled a watch with a big, black plastic band. I pulled my pants leg up, over the knee, while he hooked the band onto my right ankle. He then gave me what looked like a small receptor tower that had to be plugged into a phone line. This second device would not only monitor me, but would be the government's means of keeping track of my whereabouts at all times. This phone line could not have any type of call-waiting or voice mail, so I was fortunate to have a fax line that I could use for the monitor. The monitor couldn't be too loose, so it seemed a little snug. It was waterproof, but quite honestly, I couldn't dry it very well after a shower, and it just felt uncomfortable.

After I was hooked up, I asked about the weekend, because Saturday would be my dad's first birthday since he had passed away in September. My mom had scheduled a special Mass in his memory on Sunday morning. On Monday, the Martin Luther King, Jr. holiday, my family and I had tickets for a Bulls game.

The answer to the entire weekend, and to Monday, was, "No!"

I would be confined strictly to my home for at least the first week, with the exception of going to and from work. At that point, at about 6:00 p.m., I was finally done, and ready to leave the Federal building.

I had already called Tom to pick me up at the law office. Tony told me to stay right next to him, while he would push his way through the media, and then across the street, back to his office. As soon as we got off the elevators and had headed towards the doors, the entire media contingent rushed towards us. The camera lights went on and microphones were shoved in my face, while reporters screamed out question after question. Tony did the best he could, under the circumstances, but he didn't know about a construction project right outside the building whose barricades were blocking an exit across the street. In addition, because it was so dark, and the camera lights were in our faces, all we were doing was walking in a circle, especially since the media obstructed our view of our one and only exit. Tony, who was as frazzled as I was, pushed a cameraman aside, as we darted across the street.

The only question I answered concerned my resignation, to which I unequivocally responded, "No," and that, in fact, I would be at my office on Tuesday morning.

As soon as Tony and I crossed the street and went through his building's revolving doors, the media onslaught ended. I thanked him for his assistance as we walked down the hallway to the other end of the building, where Tom, along with Mike Stec, were waiting for me. Tom told me to try to relax. I replied I didn't know when I'd ever be able to relax again. I then quickly jumped into the car, as we headed home.

Tom asked me if I wanted the news on, and I said it would be okay. However, there was nothing else on the news except my name being repeated, and how I had been dragged into court and indicted on two counts of bribery and two counts of obstruction of justice. I soon told Tom to turn on some music instead. I then called Kathleen at her parents' house to let her know I was coming home. She asked me if I were going home to sleep, or over to her parents' home. I decided to go home, or to at least try to sneak into the back of the house. I then called Don, who lived only two blocks away from my home, and asked him to drive past my house to see if the media were still out front. Don quickly called back to tell me that everything was clear for the moment. When Tom arrived at my house, he drove around back and opened the garage door, while I ran through the garage to my back door. With a sense of relief, I walked into my house.

I went straight to my basement, and flopped right down on the couch. In the meantime, Don was at the back door where Tom and Mike now met him. I hadn't eaten anything all day, so Mike volunteered to pick me up a hot dog, while Tom and Don hooked up the monitor tower to my phone line downstairs. It took a couple of minutes to figure everything out, but finally it was set up. I knew I could only go as far as right outside my back door and no further.

By the time I got situated, changed clothes, and ate, it was close to 10:00 p.m. I told the guys, in a tearful, but angry voice, that I couldn't believe Mick's betrayal, I wanted to know what the hell Sam had said to cause the government to have come after me so viciously. At that point, I implied that I needed some time alone, so Tom, Mike, and Don left. I then called Kathleen, and she reluctantly agreed to return home that night with the kids, although she waited until almost 11:00 p.m., just to play it safe.

Of course, I finished the evening off by drinking, so I could relax and put myself into a stupor. Quite honestly, Kathleen was upset, and I wondered how much she could take, and if she would stay with me. I'm sure Kathleen couldn't believe how stupid her husband was. All I could do was apologize. I tried to reassure both her and myself that somehow or some way, we would get through this nightmare, and that we could start all over again. That was—and is—the most painful thing of all—realizing what I actually did to my family.

The next morning I woke up around 9:00 a.m., and felt as if I had been in a car wreck. My body just ached from head to toe, due to yesterday's intense emotional stress. As I got out of bed and glanced at the monitoring device on my ankle, I just wanted to climb back in and pull the covers over my head until the nightmare was over. When I came downstairs, Kathleen was reading *The Chicago Sun-Times*. When I asked her how bad it was, all she did was show me the front page, with my picture and story plastered all over. Because of all the media attention, we closed every blind on every window. Kathleen and I actually felt as if we were prisoners in our own home.

During that whole weekend, TV trucks were out in front of the house, just trying to get a glimpse of me or someone from the family either going in or out. My mom and sister stopped by the house on

Saturday after visiting my dad's grave. They brought us lunch, since I couldn't leave the house. Just seeing the pain in their eyes when they looked at me was heartbreaking.

I stayed bunkered down for the next two days with Kathleen and the kids, just trying to find some semblance of peace and quiet in our lives, even if for a short time. In fact, I didn't even go to church on Sunday, because some of the TV crews camped out there, waiting for me in the parking lot, until the associate pastor booted them out. Since Monday was a federal holiday—Martin Luther King, Jr.'s birthday—I couldn't go downtown to work, so I again stayed in the house, and gave my ticket to a friend, whom I asked to take my entire family to the Bulls game. I wanted Kathleen and the kids to get out of the house and enjoy themselves as much as they could at the game.

That whole holiday weekend was unbelievably difficult, just because of the enormous stress both Kathleen and I were under, and with no foreseeable light at the end of the tunnel. In a way, I was happy that the long weekend was finally ending, but I knew I was in for another media circus on Tuesday morning at city hall.

The next morning I called my pre-trial officer to let her know I was leaving home, and heading downtown. I reached a younger, pleasant-sounding gentleman on the other end, who told me I needed to provide him with the approximate time I was leaving home, and how long I thought it would take me to get to city hall. He reminded me that if I left city hall to attend another event, or to go home, I had to call again, to receive permission. The travel times on the expressways varied each and every day, based upon traffic, and when I would at last return home, I would have to phone my pre-trial office.

When we neared city hall, I called my office to find out if the media had camped outside my door. My deputy informed me that the reporters and camera people had positioned themselves outside my private door in the hallway. I certainly didn't want to hide from them, because I wanted everyone to see that no monitoring device or indictment would prevent me from going to my office and doing my job. I at least wanted to convey confidence, even though I was, in fact, scared to death.

When I pulled up at city hall, a member of the media who was acting as a lookout gave the high sign. As I got out of my car and walked up to the main doors, the camera lights began flashing. Thankfully, my private door was to my immediate left, only ten feet away. I couldn't hear all of the questions they were asking as I pushed my way through the crowd of media people. However, just before I entered my office, I turned around, and told them that I had no intention of resigning, and that I planned to be at work all week. During that week, the media would wait in the hallways of city hall until I arrived in the morning; then, they would leave, only to return at the end of the day, around 4:00 p.m., to try to catch me going home. At that point, I would walk with one of my chiefs of staff, underground, to the parking garage.

I was now losing patience with the monitoring device. On days when I had to leave city hall for a meeting, I first had to call in to report my whereabouts. Then I had to tell them how long I would be gone. I even needed permission to pick up my daughter from school!

One week after the bracelet was put on my ankle, Tony was able to get a court order, without the U.S. Attorney's objection, to remove the device. Tony told me to come downtown that day, and we would walk over to the Federal building where someone would remove it. When I got to Tony's office around 11:00 a.m., he immediately called the guy who put the bracelet on my ankle in the first place. He told Tony that he was leaving for the weekend, but that because we had the court order, we could just take a pair of scissors, cut the band off by ourselves, and return the device the next week. Tony then found a pair of scissors for me. It only took a minute or two, and it was like cutting a thick watch band. I can't tell you how good it felt to be finally free of that contraption!

Although I got back to work on what I would call a normal schedule, I still had to stay in touch with Tony regularly, because I had not yet decided whether or not to take this matter to trial. Even though Tony was not confident about a trial's outcome, I had not given up hope of fighting these charges in Federal Court.

During this whole time, I was also in touch with my good friend, Miriam Santos, who had been offering me advice along the way. At one point, she gave me the numbers of a couple of other attorneys to speak with regarding my chances in court. (I later spoke to a number of these people, but they said that until they could actually review the evidence, offering me a worthwhile opinion at this point would be difficult.) I respected Miriam's opinion because she had already gone through what I was struggling with now. More than five years ago, she was indicted on corruption charges. She fought the case in court. Unfortunately, she lost. The judge was Charles Norgle (remember that name!), who had earlier made a number of controversial, and appealable rulings. Norgle gave her forty-one months, just short of the maximum she could have received. But there's more to the story than that, and it's one of the most disturbing I've ever heard about Richard Daley's vindictiveness.

A city employee whom I will call "J.J.," worked during the spring of 1999, at Navy Pier, where Daley christened a coastguard float. After the ceremony, J.J. was standing in an open-air stairwell lobby at the east end of the pier. Directly below him, on the stairwell, was the mayor, talking with a gentleman named Gavin, the site's security head. According to J.J., he overheard Daley assuring Gavin that the judge in Miriam's case was on "their" side, and that he was going to "throw the book at her." J.J., who shared this story with a couple of his co-workers at the time, feared the mayor's wrath, and never again mentioned this conversation to anyone else for over eight years, until recently sharing the story with me. He currently holds a supervisory position in the city, and hopes to retire in the future. Based on what J.J. told me, I guess I would be nervous about disclosing my identity and want to remain anonymous, too. Clearly, this story speaks for itself.

Even though Norgle, as Daley predicted, "threw the book" at Miriam, she wound up serving only four-and-a-half months in federal prison before seeing her conviction overturned. I remember that, about a week or two later, Kathleen and I were invited to her house, along with a group of close friends, to celebrate her release.

However, even though she was free, the U.S. Attorney threatened to re-try her. As a result, Miriam and her attorneys agreed to plead guilty to one count of wire fraud, so that her sentence would count as time already served, and she would not have to go back to prison. Still, she had to pay a substantial fine, as well as outstanding legal fees that I believe she is still paying. More importantly, to this day, she suffers from the emotional scars caused by the same nightmare I was presently experiencing at Morgantown.

Thus, with Miriam's troubles still fresh in my mind, I asked Tony to try to determine how much time I could be spending in prison. Meanwhile, Kathleen decided to meet with him on a Saturday afternoon, just the two of them, so she could better understand where we might be heading. Kathleen and I were not sure of Tony's desire to go to trial. We were both of the opinion that he didn't anticipate how complicated this whole matter had become.

During their meeting, I anxiously waited at home, hoping that Kathleen would have some positive news, or at least would feel better about my possibly fighting the charges. I don't think I'll ever forget her expression as she walked into the house, took off her coat, and sat on the living room couch. I couldn't stand the suspense, and asked what had happened. She just kind of stared at me, and said she felt totally flattened. I asked her again what Tony had said. Kathleen proceeded to tell me that Tony believed that if I fought this case, I would lose. He assured Kathleen that he would take it to trial if I wanted, but that the result would still probably be the same. He also told her that if we did go to trial, and I was found guilty on all four counts, I could receive a sentence of eight-to-ten years. The exact sentence would depend on the judge, but he believed that due to the negative public perception of the Hired Truck Program, there was no way we could get a fair trial. Kathleen then asked him what I would be looking at if I cooperated, and pled guilty. He said he couldn't answer that until he sat down with the Assistant U.S. District Attorney, but he thought maybe around three years.

After that news, Kathleen confessed she wouldn't know what to do if I would receive an eight-year sentence. I was already fifty-two years old, and I'd be close to sixty when I would get out. That alone was an awful thought. What about the emotional impact on my entire family? These questions were becoming too overwhelming for me, so I told Kathleen that I wished I could either receive a vision from God, telling me what to do, or actually wake up, and discover that all this had just been a bad dream. Although I didn't believe either was likely, I did need time to myself to really think about what decision would be best for my family.

As the days started to quickly move on, my attorney was becoming impatient with me. We were approaching the end of January, and he was still trying to negotiate a plea agreement while I was still holding on to my office as city clerk. Tony kept telling me that he couldn't finalize any kind of agreement with Manish Shah while I was still clerk. The Feds insisted that resigning my office should be a mandatory prerequisite to any deal, since my resignation would signify the acknowledgment of my "acceptance of responsibility," an act which would lower my sentence.

My own stumbling block was my continued obsession with both Mick and Traci's still working at the jobs I gave them. He had already been indicted for bribery, while his wife, who played such a significant role in the business, probably violated some city ethics laws. Both, though, were still collecting pay checks. Why, I asked myself, should I resign my position when these two individuals, whom I believed were as guilty as sin, were still free, and being paid? I know my concern about the Joneses infuriated Tony, who kept telling me I wasn't making my job any easier. If all that weren't bad enough, we found out that Judge Norgle was appointed to my case. As soon as I received that news, I actually started to believe that there was a government conspiracy to get me. To make matters worse, Tony informed me that Norgle once held him in contempt of court, and that there was no love lost between them.

Well, I certainly thought that a motion was in order for a change of judges, since I believed that Tony would have a difficult time with Norgle. Also, I feared that because of my friendship with

Miriam, getting a fair trial with him on the bench would be next to impossible. Moreover, if I decided to plead guilty, Norgle would be the sentencing judge; he wouldn't have to follow any plea agreement. In fact, he could issue a sentence that could be either above or below the sentencing guidelines. This was, to say the least, a frightening dilemma for both me and Tony, who was already drafting a motion for Norgle to step down, and for a new judge to be appointed. So, as we were pondering what our next move would be, Tony reminded me that time was running out, and that I had to decide whether I was going to resign, or go to trial. Tony warned me that, soon, all offers would be pulled off the table, and there would be a point of no return. Before the next morning, by 10:00 a.m., he needed an answer. He would also be ready to file his motion to remove Norgle from the case.

That evening, all Kathleen and I did was talk in circles about what I should or should not do. There was no clear-cut answer, because I felt if I resigned, I would be giving up my last bargaining chip with the Feds. On the other hand, if I stayed in office, the U.S. Attorney could hit me with additional charges superseding the four counts already filed against me. Furthermore, if we lost our motion, and Norgle remained on the case, I could really catch hell from him. Even after I went to bed that night, I still wasn't sure what I was going to tell Tony the next day.

That morning, I arrived at Tony's office promptly at 10:00 a.m. As soon as I sat down, I knew something was wrong. Tony began to tell me how difficult this case was, about his sympathy for both me and my family, and the troubles he was currently having with the U.S. Attorney's office over Norgle's removal. The bottom line, Tony said, was that with my February 13 arraignment quickly approaching, he felt it would be in everyone's best interests if he stepped down as my attorney. Tony believed that at this point, I would be better served by a specialist or expert in plea agreements. Also, he was worried about any repercussions from Norgle if we lost our motion. So he handed me a copy of the letter he was going to send to Manish Shah regarding his withdrawal as my attorney, which he believed would buy me a couple of extra days to make my decision to either resign or go to trial. He also handed me a sheet of paper with the names of two top plea bargain attorneys. The one name I didn't recognize, but the other was Jeff Steinback, whom I first met over twenty years ago. Jeff was undoubtedly considered one of the best negotiators, not only in the Northern District of Illinois, but across the country. He represented me when I tried to sue the Illinois State Board of Law Examiners over their refusal to let me see my test scores on the Bar Exam. Although we eventually lost, we had taken the matter all the way to the State Appellate Court.

This time, I needed Jeff's expertise on a far more serious matter. I immediately told Tony I wanted Jeff, and he said he would contact him right away. He also gave me Jeff's number, so I could call him myself. Tony said if Jeff took the case, he would forward all my paperwork to him. As I left his office for the last time, he waived any further legal fees he had coming, put his arm around my shoulder, and sincerely wished me, Kathleen, and the kids the best of luck. We then agreed that as soon as one of us got a hold of Jeff, we would let the other know, because time was of the essence.

As soon as I got into my car, I picked up my cell phone and left a message for Jeff. I actually felt that if I could get Jeff to represent me, I'd have a fighting chance in whatever I had decided to do. Later that afternoon, Jeff called back. Jeff had a soft-spoken tone to his voice, but was always very direct. Of course, we first exchanged pleasantries, and then we got down to business. He told me he had already spoken to Tony, who had brought him up to speed, but said he needed to sit down with me ASAP. Jeff asked me if I would have a problem meeting him in Rockford, Illinois, which is approximately two hours away from Chicago. I said no (I'd have driven to Alaska if necessary!). We agreed to meet on Friday morning, February 3, 2006, around 11:00 p.m.

I got one of my guys, Joe, to drive me to Rockford. We left around 9:00 a.m., and drove to a restaurant where I was to meet Jeff at exactly 11:00 a.m. I looked inside the restaurant and was relieved that I had arrived first, so I just waited outside, and had a cigarette. Around 11:15 a.m., my cell phone rang. It was Jeff's secretary, Kathy, who told me Jeff was running a little behind, but would be there in about a half hour. This gave me a few more minutes to talk to Joe and have another Marlboro.

Finally, around 11:30 a.m., while Joe and I were talking, I saw Jeff getting out of his car. Even though I hadn't seen him in over twenty years, I recognized him right away. Jeff was shorter than I was, around five-foot-eight with a medium build, receding hairline with thin, black hair, and round, black glasses. Kathleen told me to dress up for the meeting, so I wore a sport coat, khakis, and a crew neck shirt, even though I was over-dressed for a Friday meeting with Jeff, who was wearing jeans, a flannel shirt, and gym shoes. As we greeted each other, he gave me a big hug.

As we headed into the restaurant, I told Joe to give me a couple of hours, and I would call him on his cell phone to have him pick me up. Jeff and I grabbed a booth towards the back of the restaurant, against a wall. Jeff ordered a salad, whereas all I wanted was a Coke, with some ice. As we sat there, Jeff told me to relax, as he pulled out his pen and a yellow legal pad from his attaché. He wanted to go over quite a few things with me, but asked me to first listen to how he envisioned the next week. Besides being a brilliant attorney and a compassionate human being, Jeff was also very frank and straightforward.

He came right out and said, "Jim, your political career is over. You've done a lot of good things in office and you probably could have been mayor some day, but it's done now."

I didn't know what to say; I felt as if I'd just gotten a cold shower. He continued, telling me what I feared all along—I was going to federal prison. However, he told me that if I followed his instructions and did exactly what he asked of me, he would be able to accomplish his goal—to get me the "shortest sentence humanly possible," so I could be back with my wife and children as early as I could. At that point, the reality finally hit home. No matter what, I was going to prison.

Jeff also made some other interesting comments that I think I'll always remember. He said there were people in my life whom I thought were my friends, but that most of them were users. He went on to say that they never really cared about me or my family; it was all about what I could do for them. He also told me that when everything was over, including prison, I would be able to count my true friends on one hand, and that the rest of them I'd probably never see again.

The next reality check was that I would have to resign, either Monday or Tuesday of next week. Jeff told me he wasn't sure which would be the exact resignation day, but he would let me know on Sunday night. He also said he would fax to my house a draft of the resignation letter he wanted me to use. My formal letter needed to be delivered to the mayor in order to make the action official. Once that happened, I would put into effect a plan I had put in place with my Deputy, Ed Kantor, only a few weeks ago. In the event of my sudden resignation, he would see that my personal belongings would be packed and delivered to me. We both knew that if I resigned, the media would swarm over city hall like a plague of locusts.

Just in that short amount of time, I already felt as if my life had changed. Jeff then told me that he talk to Manish Shah later that afternoon, to give him a heads-up on my resignation, and thus become my attorney of record in this matter. We also spoke at great length about my health, including my drinking problems. Jeff also asked me to give him specific details about my drinking habits. Jeff's compassion made it easier for me to be honest and upfront with him about such a sensitive matter.

Before we finished, Jeff and I needed to speak about his legal fees. Quite honestly, he gave me a figure, and I agreed to pay him everything all at once. Jeff's reputation had preceded him everywhere. He was not only a master of plea agreements, but also well-respected by the various Assistant U.S. Attorneys in the Federal building. If anyone could help me out of this horrible situation, it was Jeff Steinback. He also told me that from this point onward, he would be at my side, all the way to the time I would come home from prison. When we left, he again gave me a hug, to assure me of his commitment.

That weekend, I stayed at home, and really didn't talk to anybody. Of course, I told Kathleen everything about my meeting with Jeff, so she would be prepared for next week, but I have to admit that I spent the majority of those two days trying to put some closure to my political career. This was a difficult time for me, because I was giving up not only a job, but a career that I loved. I always thought I would leave politics on my own terms, and not in disgrace.

Some time around 8:00 p.m., on Sunday evening, Jeff called me at home. He told me he was faxing over the draft of my resignation letter, which he wanted me to look over, and then have someone else type up. I would sign it, and have a member of my staff personally deliver it to the mayor's office by 4:00 p.m. the next day. He said the U.S. Attorney's office was aware of my resignation plans. We ended our conversation with the understanding that I would contact him as soon as my resignation letter was sent to Daley.

After I got off the phone, I grabbed a beer, sat on my basement couch, and thought to myself that at this same time the next night, I would no longer be Chicago city clerk. My political future would be dead, and most importantly, for the first time in over twenty-seven years, I'd be unemployed. That, plus the reality of going to federal prison, made my immediate future look dismal at best.

I then picked up the phone to call Ed Kantor, to tell him to stop by my house before heading downtown, because we needed to go over some things that we'd been preparing for, specifically, my resignation. The rest of our conversation was both quiet and sad, but I cut the call short and said I'd see him in the morning. After the kids went to bed, Kathleen and I stayed up quite late, just trying to figure out where we would go from here. We both knew that by the end of the next day, all we could do was to hope we could weather the rest of the storm.

When I woke up the next day, I tried to pretend it was like any other day, by taking the kids to school. It was my way of hiding information from Jack and Bobby, who were only eight years old. Unfortunately, Nina, who was twelve, was more aware of my problems. Every time the phone rang, or someone came over, she picked up bits and pieces of information. She also heard various comments in school when something appeared about me in the newspapers, or on TV. So, Kathleen, for the most part, was very honest with her, but had not yet disclosed the fact that I would be going away to prison.

After dropping off the kids, Kathleen and I went back home to wait for Ed to stop by. At 8:30 a.m., he pulled up in front of the house. When he came in, we all looked at each other sadly. We talked for a short time, with most of the questions centering on my plea agreement, and more specifically, prison time. Unfortunately, these were questions I couldn't answer yet. I didn't want to waste time, so I handed Ed the draft of my resignation letter. My instructions were simple—have the letter typed up, and invite the rest of my executive staff (Joe R., or "J.R.," Martha, Toni, and Marion) to follow him back to my house, so I could tell them about my resignation face to face. It was then only around 9:00 a.m., and we figured everyone could come back with Ed around lunchtime.

During the next few hours, I just sat around thinking about how hard it would be to say goodbye to my staff. Around noontime, they arrived. When they came in, I had Toni, Marion, and Martha sit on the couch, and Ed, "J.R." and Kathleen stood to the side. I really wanted to avoid a lot of dramatic bullshit, so I told them I had reached a dramatic crossroad in my life, and that I needed to move forward. No matter which direction I now followed, either fighting the U.S. Attorney on the charges, or accepting a plea bargain, I realized I could no longer try to fight for my very survival and be the city clerk at the same time. I told them that the best thing for my family and my office was to resign at this time.

All I can remember was the eerie silence in the room, and how in a matter of seconds, that had changed to some deep emotion, as there wasn't a dry eye in the house. I tried to explain that this decision was really best for everybody, even though I knew I really did not have any other choice.

The only way I can describe the rest of that afternoon was to compare it to a somber wake at a funeral parlor. We all sat around and reminisced about the good times. Over the next hour or so, Kay, Don, and "J.R." joined us at the house. As we got closer to mid-afternoon, I realized what I had to do, so I asked Ed for the letter, which had been addressed to Mayor Daley.

Basically, the letter said, "It is with a profound sense of regret and humility that I resign my position as City Clerk of Chicago, effective at 5:00 p.m. today." I just stared at the letter for a minute or so, with Kathleen and everyone else standing around me in the dining room. I then picked up a pen, and with real sadness, emotion, and with tears rolling down my cheeks, signed my own resignation letter. Afterwards, there wasn't much more to say. Ed and my soon-to-be former staff had to get back to the office and take care of business. Ed would take the letter up to Daley's office. We all exchanged emotional goodbyes as I turned to Ed and wished him the best of luck—turning over to him a job that I had loved for close to twelve years.

After the staff left, Ray, Don, and "J.R." hung around the house with me and the family for moral support. When the 5:00 p.m. news came on, my resignation was the top story in Chicago. It was also the lead story at 6:00 p.m., 9:00 p.m., and 10:00 p.m. Kathleen and I closed all the blinds, stopped answering the phone, and bunkered down with the kids. Throughout that evening, TV crews camped out in front of the house, with reporters going door-to-door, and asking our neighbors for comments. It was, to say the least, a media circus that had only begun.

That night, like so many of the most recent ones, ended with Kathleen and I just sitting down together and trying to figure out our next move. All I knew was that tomorrow morning, everyone would be calling me the "former city clerk," and I would be referring to myself as "unemployed."

Besides all these legal problems, I again needed to take a hard look at my financial situation, which had dramatically changed since my resignation. Kathleen was now working as a substitute teacher three or four days a week at the school our boys attended. The money she was making would help with the incidentals and the groceries. I was lucky that I had a supportive family, especially my brother-in-law, Art, who really stepped up to help us with some major bills. Between Art, my sister, my mom and my in-laws' help, Kathleen and the kids could keep our heads above water for at least six months, which would probably be my time frame before heading off to prison.

Soon, February 13, 2006, the date of my arraignment, arrived. That morning I met with Jeff at his office for a good hour before our scheduled court appearance. For that hour or so, Jeff explained to me in detail the arraignment proceedings, along with an update on the progress of his negotiations with the U.S. Attorney. He told me it would be another month before any meaningful agreement would be reached.

On that same morning, I had the pleasure of meeting a couple of Jeff's assistants, Barbara and Ed, who were former probation and parole officers for the Bureau of Prisons. They were both retired, each with over twenty-five years of experience. Both of them were very personable and compassionate, with a wealth of knowledge about the prison system. It was going to be their job, over the next few months, to work with me, and to help me, from the time we reached our plea agreement, through the appeal sentencing, to the time I left for prison, and actually beyond, when I would return home.

At my arraignment, I sat down in the first row of an area designated as general seating. Again, there were two courtroom artists who were drawing my likeness as I nervously tried to avoid eye contact with them. Barbara and Ed were nice enough to sit alongside me. In fact, some reporters were wondering if Barbara was my wife. It seemed like an eternity before we got to our feet, and Judge Norgle entered the courtroom. All I can remember about the judge was his stern and no-nonsense expression as he sat down and glanced around the room.

When the bailiff called *"U.S. v. James J. Laski, Jr.,"* I quickly stepped up to the podium, with both Jeff Steinback and Tony Pinelli. The first order of business consisted of Tony's withdrawing as my attorney. After Tony submitted his motion, Judge Norgle immediately asked me if I was aware of the situation, and if I approved of the switch to Jeff.

I answered with a confident and firm, "Yes, your Honor."

With that, Tony exited the courtroom.

After Jeff discussed some basic housekeeping details regarding the change of attorneys with Assistant U.S. Attorney Manish Shah, the formal charges were read. As in January, I was charged with two counts of bribery and two counts of obstruction of justice. As soon as Judge Norgle was satisfied that I understood the charges, he asked Jeff and me for my plea.

Jeff responded with a confident "Not guilty."

Again, I confirmed with Norgle that I understood and agreed with the plea. Jeff, however, jumped in right after my response to inform the judge that he was working out an agreement with the U.S. Attorney's office, and that our plea would probably later be changed. Norgle then ordered a state update on Friday, March 17, in his courtroom, and reminded everyone that in the event an agreement was not reached, a trial date would be placed on the docket for April. After relaying that ominous message to both attorneys, he adjourned the proceedings.

Jeff then told me he would talk to the press downstairs. The courtroom cleared, and we all walked out. What I didn't know was that two FBI agents were waiting for me right outside the courtroom, to take me to their office for processing. Everything I did in January, including the photographs and fingerprinting for the U.S. Marshals, I had to do again, for the FBI's records. Ed and Barbara walked with me while two FBI agents escorted me to their office. When we arrived at the FBI office's front desk, one of the agents informed me that Ed and Barbara could go no further, and would have to sit in the waiting area until they had finished processing me. They then led me to through a big door, which was adjacent to the front desk. I followed them down a long corridor, which, believe it or not, still had posters of old FBI movies featuring such actors as James Stewart, Sidney Poitier, and Gene Hackman, hanging on the walls.

A couple of quick turns later, we were in the processing office. I identified myself at the front desk, and was immediately handed a specimen bottle, as another agent followed me to the men's room to preserve the integrity of the process. After that, I went through an identical fingerprinting and photo session as in January, and was escorted back to their front office, where Ed and Barbara were waiting. We then took the elevator down to the cafeteria, where we met Jeff, who informed me that once we were downstairs, we would meet with the press, but that, under no circumstances, was I to answer any questions.

On the first floor, the throng of press was roped off, and awaiting our arrival. Jeff and I walked over to them for an impromptu press conference. I positioned myself directly behind Jeff, as the reporters started asking a flurry of questions, most of which concerned my further cooperation with the U.S. Attorney. Jeff, of course, was vague, if not cryptic, about our future plans. Still, everyone there knew that somewhere down the road, I would be pleading guilty.

Over the next month, Jeff used his power of persuasion and his masterful negotiating skills to work an agreement with the government that would be as fair as possible, under the circumstances. According to Jeff, in return for my guilty plea, the government agreed to drop both obstruction of justice counts and one bribery count. So, at the end of the day, all I would be pleading guilty to was one count of bribery. In addition, the U.S. Attorney would stipulate to my "acceptance of responsibility," which would be very helpful, because it would lower my sentencing points under the federal guidelines. The bottom line was, the fewer points, the lower my sentence level, which, hopefully, would mean less time in prison.

The month between my arraignment and the next court appearance was fairly quiet for me. The kids were in school, and Kathleen was substituting every day. I spent my time at home cleaning, cooking, and shopping, because I felt so useless, and wanted to do my part in some way to help Kathleen.

As the days kept moving forward, I was getting more nervous and apprehensive. I knew that as soon as I entered that guilty plea, my fate would be in the hands of Judge Norgle, who would be under no obligation to follow any sentencing guidelines. He could, in fact, give me a higher sentence or a lower sentence, depending on his view of the evidence, and of any mitigating circumstances in my case. Needless to say, the future uncertainty was pushing me to the brink of a nervous breakdown.

The night before the hearing, I was extremely anxious, because I knew I would have to face Judge Norgle and answer questions he would ask me after I entered my guilty plea. Of course, I felt the only way to handle my anxiety was to drink. On that particular night, I only needed a six-pack of Coors Light to put me to sleep.

It just so happened that my next court appearance would occur on St. Patrick's Day. In Chicago, St. Patrick's Day is almost like a holiday, with the river dyed green, the bars packed from morning to night, corn beef and cabbage served for lunch and dinner across the city, and everyone celebrating, and believing, for one day, that they were Irish. For me, this would be my third appearance in Federal Court in three months. I told myself, sarcastically, it would be no big deal. To preserve my false sense of security, I took a couple of tranquilizers before I left.

That trip to court proved no different than the previous two, as far as my routine was concerned. I again met my attorney at his office. Camera crews then followed us into the Federal building, where the reporters and camera crews were waiting for us. Even many of the same artists and reporters were present in the courtroom.

The whispering and buzzing inside quickly ceased as Judge Norgle walked in and the bailiff called my case. Standing at the podium with me were Assistant U.S. Attorney Manish Shah, and Jeff Steinback. Norgle looked directly over and asked about our case's status. Jeff and Shah both informed him that they had reached an agreement, and that I was changing my plea from "not guilty" to "guilty." In addition, the guilty plea would be to only one count of bribery, due to the government's having dropped the other three charges.

After Jeff and I entered the guilty plea, Norgle asked me if I had made my decision freely, and without duress. He asked if I had discussed the matter with my attorney, and if I understood that I had just pled guilty to one count of bribery. He also asked me if within the last twenty-four hours, I had taken any alcohol or drugs. I answered yes. He then wanted to know what I had taken, and how much. I answered, about four beers up until 11:00 p.m., and one Lorezopan and Lexapro that morning, for my anxiety. He then asked me one more time if I clearly understood my decision to plead guilty.

Again, looking directly at the judge, I answered with a firm, "Yes, your Honor, I do."

Before the proceedings ended, Judge Norgle asked me when I had resigned as Chicago clerk. I told him February 6, 2006. He then asked me if I thought I had done a good job as city clerk. I quickly answered that I thought I had.

Then, Norgle asked, "Until now?"

I answered, "Yes, your Honor, until now."

The last order of business was the sentencing date, which the judge tentatively set for May 23. However, after I had gotten back home and spoken to Kathleen about her teaching schedule, I learned that she was taking over a class until the end of the academic year, due to a full-time teacher's illness. Also, because of the kids' emotional well-being, we thought it best to move the sentencing date later, to a date after the school year had ended, which would be June 4 for Nina, and June 8 for Kathleen, Jack, and Bobby. I asked Jeff on Monday morning about pushing back the sentencing date until after everyone was out of school for the summer. By the following day, Jeff had spoken to Manish Shah and Norgle's office, and had my sentencing hearing rescheduled for Tuesday, June 13, 2006. Unfortunately, that would be one day after Nina's thirteenth birthday, but that new date would be final and non-negotiable. I had a little less than three months before Judge Norgle would sentence me, and nobody, not even Jeff, knew how many years I would be spending in federal prison.

During the first few weeks following my guilty plea, I was almost relieved that this whole agonizing experience would soon be over. Although I had only one more hurdle to jump over, it was the most difficult one, probably because of all the uncertainty surrounding the sentencing. Nobody had a clue as to how Judge Norgle would react to the media attention, the government's evidence, and his perception of me as a person.

In the meantime, I would have to be interviewed for my PSI (Pre-Sentencing Investigation) report, which would be a critical factor in Norgle's final decision. The PSI would not only consist of evidentiary material from the indictment, but also opinions and observations from the PSI officer, who would conduct a lengthy interview with me, and later, with my wife. Other information in the report would be a biography, and news clippings from my political career, as well as a detailed medical profile of me, and my entire family. A complete and detailed financial history, including a credit report and five years of tax returns, would also be included. In addition, all of my bills and monthly expenses had to be itemized. At the end of the day, all information regarding my life would be turned over to the PSI officer for review. I assumed that the more information I could provide, the more accurate a picture the judge would have of what kind of person I had been in the past, and of how my personality and character had evolved over time. There were hours and hours of work ahead for me to provide copies of all the necessary documents. I learned that my PSI officer would be a woman named Shelia. From all the reports from Barbara, Ed, and Jeff, she had a compassionate side when it came to caring about families with children. All I was hoping for was someone who would be fair, and who would look at the whole picture, including my public service accomplishments, and my love for, and commitment to, my wife and children.

Two weeks later, I was in her office at the Federal building for our scheduled meeting. Shelia, who was in her late forties, and very professional, was dressed that day in a gray business suit. She had known Jeff, Ed, and Barbara for some time, so all three of them met with us initially, to break the ice. We all met in a conference room outside the waiting area. Jeff started by breaking down the circumstances surrounding my case, and provided her with a working knowledge of the Hired Truck Program, and of my responsibilities as city clerk. He also laid out the criminal charges from the indictment, along with the names of those connected to me and also charged. Shelia then invited us back to her office for a one-on-one meeting. As I sat in a chair across from her, I couldn't help but notice how serious she was about this interview, but also how compassionate she appeared, which made me feel more comfortable.

We spent the next two hours going over my life, from my childhood to the present. We talked in great detail about my father, who was a drinker, and quite honestly, abusive at times. I admitted my fear and anxiety while growing up, and regrettably noted my son Jack's recent struggle with the same disorder. I was never abusive, but like my father, I was drinking heavily. I described my own drinking patterns, and brought every prescription drug I was currently taking.

We also spent time talking about my relationship with Kathleen and the kids, along with the rest of my immediate family, and my first marriage. When I finished discussing my life, I felt that Shelia, who had been taking notes the whole time, now had a fairly accurate profile of me. Before we finished the meeting, she handed me what I would call a worksheet or checklist of documents, bills, financial statements, and tax returns she would need to complete her report. Shelia also informed me that she would need to stop at the house to meet with Kathleen privately. Fortunately for me, they would arrange that meeting on their own, since I would be somewhere else with the kids. After our meeting finally ended, I felt emotionally drained.

A short time later, in May, the Illinois Supreme Court, with my voluntary consent (in order to avoid further disciplinary action) disbarred me. My misjudgments cost me the law license I had worked so hard to earn.

Meanwhile, Kathleen was substituting on a full-time basis, so I needed to do something to keep myself from going crazy. I started doing volunteer work at the boys' school. When I wasn't at the school, I was at home, doing something constructive, like cleaning, or cooking. In addition, I spent a considerable amount of time just getting all the paperwork together that Shelia requested.

Shelia and Kathleen then had their meeting. All of the kids finished school for the year, and all their birthdays came and went. It was now the evening of June 12. I was nervously looking through the closet, trying to decide what suit I would wear at the sentencing hearing the next day, and praying that the whole ordeal would quickly be over with. That night, Kathleen and I spent hours talking about the different possible sentencing scenarios.

During those last few days, I spent a considerable amount of time on the cell phone with Jeff, just to hear some positive reassurances from him. All along, Jeff told me that his goal was to get me the shortest sentence possible. It was those thoughts, and a six-pack of beer, that allowed me to fall asleep around midnight that evening before the hearing.

The next morning, I knew that in a couple of hours I would finally be told how long I would have to spend in a federal prison.

As soon as I finished showering and getting dressed, I popped a tranquilizer and my anxiety medication into my mouth. Not only was I sweating and shaking, but I was also gagging to the point of near-vomiting.

This would be my fourth and final appearance in Federal Court, and Kathleen was coming with me. Like me, Kathleen was scared to death, because she didn't know what kind of sentence Judge Norgle would impose. What my wife did realize, however, was that somewhere down the road, she would have to be a single parent for awhile.

Our good friend Patsy came over to watch the kids, while Ray drove my mother, and Don and Joe took Kathleen and me downtown. The rest of the immediate family would drive there on their own. As soon as I got into the car with Kathleen, I asked Don and Joe to drive me to my church, which was only a block away. When we got to the church, I quickly ran in, said a prayer, and blessed myself with the holy water on the way out. When I got back into the car, Kathleen, Don, and Joe all wanted me to touch them with my hand, which was still wet from the holy water, as we headed downtown.

The guys then dropped Kathleen and me off at the law office building, but instead of going up to Jeff's office, Kathleen and I first met Jeff's assistants, Barbara and Ed, at the building's coffee shop. We all sat down, and just waited for Jeff. While we were waiting, I saw Robert Sorich walk into the building. I quickly got up, and ran out of the coffee shop to the hallway to see if I could catch him. Fortunately, he was standing by the elevator when I approached him. Sorich's trial in the Federal building had already started. He was charged with rigging employment hiring for political purposes. Because he was Daley's patronage chief, the case was getting enormous media coverage. When I went up to him, he looked like a deer caught in a car's headlights. He had probably lost twenty to thirty pounds over the past months, and looked very tired and emotionally drained. It was kind of an awkward moment as we shook hands, and, with half-hearted smiles, wished each other well. I couldn't help but feel that he was going to be in the same boat as I was.

After I returned to the coffee shop, I decided to step outside and have a cigarette, but as soon as I did, I saw a camera crew directly across the street. Needless to say, I ran back into the shop, and waited with everyone else for Jeff.

When Jeff finally arrived, we all immediately left for the courtroom. As soon as we crossed the street, the cameras were ready for us. Barbara and Ed walked in front of Jeff, who was on one side of me, with Kathleen on the other side. The cameras followed us the rest of the way down the block, until we got to the front door of the Federal building. The media area was again roped off, just past the metal detectors. As we quickly walked through, reporters started yelling out questions, and the camera lights flashed.

Upon entering the courtroom, I could see the media sitting to my right; to my left, in the general seating area, were my family and friends. My palms were sweating as I clenched my fists together. Kathleen sat down with the family while I stood with Jeff.

About a minute later, Manish Shah walked in, and said, in a cold, solemn tone, "Good morning, Mr. Laski."

He then approached Jeff, who spoke briefly with him.

More than a couple of minutes later, Judge Norgle walked into the courtroom. In those few minutes, I had seated myself in the back, with Barbara and Ed, as the bailiff called my case. I got up quickly and met Jeff and Shah at the podium, and faced Judge Norgle.

After a few preliminary remarks by Norgle, which included a gracious offer for me to sit down behind both attorneys instead of standing the whole time, Jeff began his presentation to the judge. Once he started, I could see why Jeff was regarded as one of the best attorneys around. He was both articulate and passionate as he went through my life, highlighting my political career and accomplishments. He also noted my love for my family, and referred to my son Jack's anxiety problems. He then painstakingly went through the bribery charges, admitting my wrongdoing, but trying to minimize the damage by emphasizing the long, twenty-six-year relationship between me and Mick Jones. At that point, Jeff tried to hammer home the fact that I had merely tried to assist a friend in need of help. Jeff wanted Norgle to look at the big picture of my life, and not just at my dealings with the Joneses. I slumped over in my chair, and had to use a handkerchief to wipe the tears from my eyes. I realized, at that moment, how I had hurt my family, and was just praying that the sentence wouldn't be too harsh.

Mr. Shah now had his chance to address the court. He spent the next twenty-to-thirty minutes going through the charges, and offered a detailed account of the facts surrounding the case. It was both heart-wrenching and infuriating to hear Shah portray me as a corrupt politician with no conscience. During his presentation, he actually fudged some facts, for example, misrepresenting the truth by claiming I used some of the bribe money to fix my summer home in Wisconsin. First of all, I never owned any other house but my home in Chicago; the Wisconsin house was owned by my in-laws, which Shah knew all along. I feel Shah changed those facts to make me look like a career-long crook. Even when he stated that I solicited the money from the Joneses, he, in my opinion, deliberately misrepresented our twenty-six-year friendship as a casual business partnership. As for my legislative accomplishments, Shah countered that those were merely part of my job. In reality, they were the direct results of my dedication to public service.

Norgle now allowed Jeff time for rebuttal, and a chance for the government to respond. Both attorneys took full advantage of round two, in which Jeff again tried to characterize my actions as misjudgments that were totally out of character for someone who was otherwise such a dedicated public servant and dedicated family man. Shah, on the other hand, closed out with the allegations that I was a corrupt politician who had not only taken money, but obstructed justice by encouraging someone to lie to the grand jury.

When both finished, Judge Norgle asked me if I had anything to say before my sentencing. I stood up and read a statement that for the most part had been prepared by Jeff's crew. As I stood at the podium, I could feel my body shaking and my voice cracking. I apologized to the court, my family, and the citizens of Chicago. I told the court that I knew I threw my life away for $48,000.00. With that, the judge abruptly interrupted me, and sternly reminded me that it was more than the $48,000.00, but a betrayal of public trust, and a complete disregard for my oath of office. Fortunately, his remaining remarks were more apologetic, with a hope that when I got out of prison, I could once again be a worthwhile member of society. At that point, I felt lightheaded, and totally exhausted.

As I sat down next to Jeff, Judge Norgle began his remarks. I'm not sure how long he spoke, but I can tell you the silence in the courtroom was deafening. It was amazing how Norgle dissected the information given to him, not only by Jeff, and Manish Shah, but also by Shelia's PSI report, which he referred to on more than one occasion. The judge noted that he did not have to follow any sentencing guidelines, which meant that my sentence could range from thirty-one to thirty-seven months, with the government seeking the high end at thirty-seven months. The longer Norgle talked, the more anxious I became. There were times when he seemed sympathetic, and at other times annoyed and frustrated by the corruption in Chicago politics.

After some time, it appeared he was winding down, as he addressed my personal life. He spoke with a great deal of compassion when he referred to my son Jack, and the rest of my family. I began to feel quite emotional again, and pulled the handkerchief once more from my pocket. While I was wiping my eyes, the judge stared directly at me, and stated that despite his sorrow for my family, he felt there had been no one else to blame for this terrible situation but me. Quite honestly, at that point, I had to agree with him.

Then, with almost a tone of reluctance in his voice, Judge Norgle announced that my sentence would be twenty-four months, and that my date to report to prison would be August 31, 2006. Before Norgle could even get up, Jeff jumped to the podium and asked about a judicial recommendation for a drug and alcohol rehabilitation program. Norgle agreed, stating that my drinking problem had been included in the PSI, and that he had signed the order. With that, the proceeding concluded, and court was adjourned.

I thanked everyone who had come to court that day, and told Jeff how much I appreciated everything he had done for my family and me. Throughout those long, agonizing months, he had advised, motivated, and consoled me. Jeff Steinback was more than my attorney; I considered him my friend. I also thanked Barbara and

Ed, both of whom over the months had become attached to the family. Despite the fact that this long ordeal had finally ended, I sadly realized that something even more difficult was ahead for me. I knew that in two-and-a-half months, I would have to say goodbye to Kathleen, Nina, Jack, and Bobby, and head off to a federal prison somewhere in the country.

Photos and Documentation

The Salvation Army
(Founded in 1865 by William Booth)
CORRECTIONAL SERVICES DEPARTMENT
105 South Ashland Avenue
Chicago, Illinois 60607
Telephone: (312) 421-2406 Fax 421-0447

Date: April 8, 2007

To: Federal Bureau of Prisons
            Community Corrections Office
            200 West Adams Street
            Suite 2915
            Chicago, IL 60606

From: Paul D. Hall, Program Supervisor

Re: **Acceptance of: Laski, James   Reg. # 18413-424**

The above-named individual has been accepted as a resident of our Community Corrections Center with a **Community Management Concern** status due to: **Broad publicity in Chicago.**

The resident's confirmed date of arrival is: 08/07/07.

As a **CMC**, this person is automatically placed in the Community Corrections Component. This component limits movement in the community to job search, employment, and a weekly religious service. Persons in this component are evaluated after **30** days and every **30** days thereafter to determine if they qualify for promotion to the Pre-Release Component, which offers an increased opportunity for passes. Promotion requires full-time employment, a clean disciplinary record, and approval of the Program Manager.

Please call, fax, or write me if you wish to communicate about this individual. My telephone extension is 3314.

cc: U.S. Probation Office
       Parent Institution, with House Rules, Acknowledgment and Agreement

112001:F0502Ac-3

My assignment to a Chicago halfway house.

**Federal Bureau of Prisons
Psychology Data System**

Date-Title: 02-05-2007 - 60 Day Review Residential
Reg Number-Name: 18413-424 - LASKI, JAMES J.   **Unit/Qtrs:** BATES, T03-008U
Author: SHIELA A. LAND, B.S., DRUG ABUSE TRTMNT SPECLST   S. Land
Institution: MRG - MORGANTOWN FCI

First Sixty Day Review

Categories of Performance:

	Rating		Rating
Openmindedness	2	Anger Management	2
Honesty	3	Goal Progress	3
Participation	3	Giving Feedback	3
Ownership ("I" Statements)	3	Receiving Feedback	2
Positive Attitude	3	Responsibility	3

Treatment Goal Progress (Be specific with each goal):

1. Anxiety and Excessive Worry: Inmate Laski is actively working to improve in this area. He is reading several self help books. He was nominated and accepted the opportunity to chair the Therapeutic Community meeting. He did a very good job keeping things running in an orderly manner. He has several papers due over the next couple months to help develop insight into this problem.

2. Sentimentality: Inmate Laski has a big problem with anger with he covers up with the "nice guy" image. He is encouraged to dig deeper into his anger to help identify how he compensates with the use of sentimentality. It is important for him to understand that until he works on his anger, it remains a vicious cycle (anger/sentimentality).

3. Fraudulent: Inmate Laski has begun to identify his pattern of fraudulent behavior. He has completed an assignment identifying things that he has "gotten away with". He is encouraged to discuss more of his fraudulence with his small group and ask for feedback.

Other Comments: Inmate Laski is an active member of the community. He is insightful and has demonstrated the ability to give good feedback. He struggles with anger, openmindedness, and sentimentality. Ask for feedback to help you work on these areas.

Rating System:

5- Excellent: working program with all 8 attitudes 4-Very Good: willing worker with some shortcomings 3-Average: satisfactory general knowledge 2-Below Average: just getting by, not applying self 1-Fail: need help, not working, in denial

*DTS Shelia Land's report on my progress in
Morgantown FCI's RDAP program.*

Federal Bureau of Prisons
Psychology Data System

Date-Title: 03-07-2007 - Eval/Rpt - Team Report
Reg Number-Name: 18413-424 - LASKI, JAMES J.   **Unit/Qtrs:** BATES, T03-008U
Author: SHIELA A. LAND, B.S., DRUG ABUSE TRTMNT SPECLST   *S. Land*
Institution: MRG - MORGANTOWN FCI

Participant Progress in the Residential Drug Abuse Program (RDAP)is evaluated continuously throughout your tenure in class. This report is reflective of your progress from your last evaluative period to the present. Individual evaluations are multi-determinative and include, but are not limited to:

Bio-psycho-social considerations; practicing the eight attitudes of treatment; consistency of behavior across all domains; and, most importantly, engaging in recovery rather than just complying.

At the present, your progress in treatment has been determined to be:

____ UNSATISFACTORY

XXX MARGINAL

____ SATISFACTORY

Comments/Recommendations for the Next 90 days: Inmate Laski is really starting to get involved in both TC as well as small group. He is insightful and has demonstrated the ability to ask and accept feedback from others as well. Continue to work on treatment goals. Attend one self help meeting each week.

https://genie3.bop.gov/pds/Document/Print.d=23...

My RDAP Participant Progress Report.

JAMES LASKI
18413-424
RDAP 112
MS. LAND.

PROBLEM: Anxiety and excessive worry.

GOAL: To verbalize and understand that
you are a fallible human being and you
will make mistakes.

Treatment Activity: Make two journal entries
per week dealing with this issue and how it
continues to set you up for failure.

A typical RDAP class assignment.

217

Comprehensive Drug Abuse Treatment Program

CERTIFICATE OF COMPLETION

This certifies that

James Laski
18413-424

has satisfactorily completed the
500 hour Comprehensive Drug Treatment Program
presented on the 3rd day of August, 2007.

Federal Correctional Institution
Morgantown, West Virginia

Dr. E. Baker, Ph.D.
Drug Abuse Program Coordinator

Drug Treatment Specialist

My RDAP Certificate of Completion.

To James Laski
With best wishes,

Here I am, at O' Hare Airport, welcoming then-Vice President Al Gore to Chicago. The smiling woman in the foreground is my good friend Miriam Santos. To my left is the late Alderwoman Lorraine Dixon.

*August, 2007: Here I am, on the right, with
two friends from Morgantown.*

*St. Patrick's Day in Chicago: From left to right, Cook County Assessor
Jim Houlihan, Kathleen, me, and U.S. Senator Dick Durbin.*

I'm in the middlle between Governor Rod Blagojevich on the right, and, on my left, my former chief of staff, and now Circuit Court Judge, Joe Panarese.

Here I am posing with Illinois Secretary of State Jesse White, promoting my office's Organ Donor Cards program.

Laski Presents Organ Donor Cards to Secretary of State Jesse White

Chicagoans Sign Up to Give the "Gift of Life"

City Clerk Jim Laski recognizes the vital importance of the organ and tissue donation program in Illinois. In an unprecedented move, City Clerk Laski's office included organ donation registration inserts in the Chicago vehicle sticker mailing sent earlier this year. Chicagoans responded to the mailer en masse– 13,000 city residents signed up to be organ donors as a result, increasing the total number of donors in Illinois dramatically.

"There is a critical need for organ and tissue donors nationwide," said Laski. "As such, I am proud of the enormous response to the donor registration inserts by Chicagoans."

The decision to include donor registration inserts coincided with the theme of last year's City of Chicago Vehicle Sticker Design Contest, which was "Life Goes On, Be An Organ Donor."

The design contest enabled Chicago high school students to learn about the shortage of available organs for those in need of life-saving transplants. The winning sticker, which features Chicago Bears great Walter Payton walking into the sunset, is currently being displayed on all vehicles registered in Chicago until June 31, 2001.

City Clerk Jim Laski believes that last year's vehicle sticker competition highlighted the need for increased organ donor ship in Illinois, especially in the wake of Payton's untimely death last November. The contest "gave my office the unique opportunity to pay tribute and raise public awareness of the important work that Secretary of State Jesse White's office is accomplishing by managing the Donor Registry," says Laski. "In addition, the theme of the contest contributed to the overwhelming response to the organ donor registry inserts mailed citywide."

Due to the huge success of the donor registry insert program in terms of sheer numbers, Laski said the Office of City Clerk plans on including registry cards with vehicle sticker registration applications every year. For additional information about organ donation, call the Regional Organ Bank of Illinois at 800-545-GIFT.

Secretary of State Jesse White, City Clerk James Laski and Connie Payton with the new sticker. City Clerk Laski turned over the 13,000 cards to Secretary White for entry into the Donor Registry, shown on the table next to them and in Mrs. Payton's hands.

An advertisement for the Organ Donor Cards program.

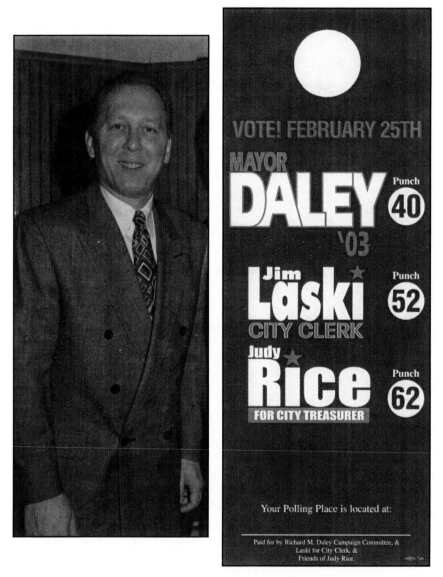

Left: A publicity photo taken of me as city clerk.
Right: A door knob-style Democratic ballot for my 2003
campaign for my third term as city clerk.

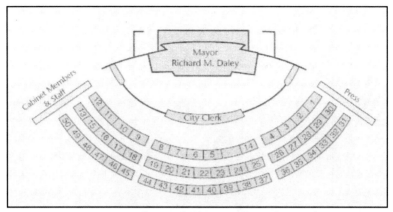

A seating chart of Chicago City Council.

*A 1993 Chicago Sun-Times political cartoon
satirizing the Laski-Lipinski split.*

My poltical brochure publicizing my 1990 re-election campaign as 23rd Ward Alderman. (Outside cover)

Values. Family-hard work-respect for God and country. These are the values Jim Laski was raised with and these are the values that will guide him as Alderman. With Jim Laski as Alderman, we'll have someone who will use the office to help us - not himself.

As a taxpayer, you deserve to get what you pay for-good services. Jim Laski will make sure that city services are first rate. He'll listen when something's wrong, and he'll fight to correct it. He'll maintain a full-time service office just to handle problems.

Reynolds Aluminum Recycling Pays

While other wards are still planning recycling efforts. Alderman Laski has already put a plan into place. His agreement with Reynolds Aluminum allows you to earn money while helping the environment. Call Jim at 582-7323 to find out how.

"The 23rd Ward has become one of the most attractive areas in the entire city to buy a house, to open a business, to send children to school. With Jim Laski as Alderman, it will get even better."

- Congressman Bill Lipinski

KEEP ☆ OUR ☆ C

My political brochure publicizing my 1990 re-election campaign as 23rd Ward Alderman. (Inside)

Who can get the job done? Jim Laski has built the relationships needed to get things done for our community. Because of that, when a problem arises, Jim will know who to call. And he'll get through because he knows the person. That's the difference!

As far as Jim Laski is concerned, our community can never have enough police protection. He'll fight for more police to be assigned to our community and our schools. He'll increase neighborhood watch programs.

Jim, seen here with his mom and dad, believes seniors deserve what they have and that government shouldn't take it away, especially through higher and higher property taxes. He also plans to increase programs for our local seniors.

"Jim Laski is my friend. I can think of no one more qualified to succeed me as Alderman. He loves this community - he knows how to work hard - he knows how to get things done. He'll be a great Alderman."

- former Alderman Bill Krystyniak

OMMUNITY ☆ STRONG!

STICKER SHOCK

City hunts down 1,007 garage-parking scofflaws in ticketing blitz

City Clerk James Laski's handful of investigators search just 40 city-licensed garages and issue more than $166,000 in violations, at $165 a pop. Laski says the first wave of ticketing "is just the tip of the iceberg," given that there are 496 sites they can search. STORY BY FRAN SPIELMAN, PAGE 3

Sticker sweep in garages nets wealth of scofflaws

City issues 1,007 tickets in 5 days – and it's just getting started

"They should drive up and down the street and run the plate. Like the old days."

TED DALLAS
Harbor Drive resident

A car with an expired city sticker in the garage at 180 N. Dearborn sports a ticket. It'll cost the owner a total of $165. — *SUN-TIMES/SUN-TIMES*

BY FRAN SPIELMAN AND ANNIE SWEENEY
Staff Reporters

City Clerk James Laski always said snooping for city sticker scofflaws in parking garages would be like shooting fish in a barrel.

Little did he know how much of an understatement that would be.

After only five days on the prowl at just 40 of 496 city-licensed garages, 8 to 19 of Laski's investigators have issued 1,007 tickets that are expected to generate $166,155 in sorely needed revenue.

The biggest single target was 188 N. Harbor Dr., where investigators wrote 103 tickets. That was followed by 311 W. Adams (78 tickets); 180 N. Dearborn (42); 233 N. Michigan (37) and 151 E. Wacker (29). One of the tickets at the 180 Dearborn building still sat under the windshield of a car on the 12th floor Thursday — nine days after it was issued.

It's not like the motorists couldn't afford the $75 sticker fee. In many cases, they're paying $25 a day to park.

If the ticketing blitz continues at the same frenzied pace, the sticker crackdown could rake in $4.1 million next year. The take would go even higher once Revenue Department investigators and Chicago police officers join the hunt.

"We still have a lot of garages to check out yet. What I believe this is is just the tip of the iceberg. If in five working days we can write a thousand tickets and generate $166,000 for the city, just imagine what we can do in a year's time," Laski said.

"This has been done by design with most people. People go from a parking garage where they live to a parking garage where they work, and they've hidden their cars. They've kept them off the street."

The crackdown got mixed reviews.

Some thought using the garages to track down scofflaws was fair. But some people, even those who had not been ticketed, thought it a bit extreme.

"They should be able to catch them out on the street," said Ted Dallas, 57, who lives on Harbor Drive. "They should drive up and down the street and run the plate. Like the old days."

"This is the last frontier," said Sabrina Balthazar, 33, who lives in Edgewater and parks in the Dearborn garage. "It's ridiculous. It's really getting outthroat.... Our city is getting more beautiful. Obviously there is a price to pay."

Some motorists are even being ratted out by angry neighbors.

"We're getting phone calls from people whose neighbors park in these garages to turn them in," Laski said. "We're getting 30 to 40 phone calls a day. The phone calls are coming in saying, 'Come to our garage. Check this car out.' If you want to use those words, 'ratting each other out,' you can use them," Laski said.

The $166,155 in penalties so far amount to $165 for every motorist nailed without a valid city sticker. The payments include a $75 sticker fee, a $30 late fee and a $60 citation.

In a recent survey of city-licensed parking garages, Laski's office found that 30 percent to 40 percent of all departing motorists did not have city stickers. Based on those results, he predicted the city would rake in as much as $10 million over the next two years.

The sweeping crackdown he proposed was watered down at the request of aldermen whose wards include a preponderance of residential high-rises. It now authorizes city sticker snooping only at those garages that offer a majority of their parking spaces to outsiders. Condominiums that reserve some parking spaces for visitors, but not more than 30 percent, are exempt.

The crackdown will also include garages and surface parking lots surrounding Soldier Field, the United Center, U.S. Cellular Field and Wrigley Field.

Chicago Sun-Times article by Fran Spielman and Annie Sweeney on my "City Scofflaws" program.

228

I'm being sworn in as 23rd Ward Alderman in 1990 by former City Clerk Walter Kozubowski. Mayor Daley is in standing in the background.

Proudly taking part in Chicago's Polish Constitution Day Parade.

Here I am greeting Lech Walesa, former Solidarity leader and President of Poland, to Chicago. Standing behind Mr. Walesa is Mayor Daley.

Greeting then-First Lady Hillary Clinton to Chicago.

EWCITY

Mayor
3?
achine
but city
im Laski
aying
he law.

A photo of me taken for the front cover of Chicago's New City
magazine, shortly after beginning my third term as city clerk.

Congressman William Lipinski raises my hand in victory following my February 1991 election as 23rd Ward Alderman.

Scott Fornek's January 15, 2006 Chicago Sun-Times article on my indictment in the city's Hired Truck Program scandal. The indictment was such big news that it sparked more interest than a Sun-Times article that same day about Chicago mobster Joseph "Joey the Clown" Lombardo's capture.

James Laski: White knight or opportunist?

January 15, 2006

BY SCOTT FORNEK Political Reporter

When Jim Laski was deputy Democratic committeeman of the Southwest Side's 23rd Ward in the early 1990s, Joe Novak remembers the advice Laski gave precinct captains going out to sell tickets for fund-raisers and advertisements for the ward's ad book.

"He encouraged bringing in cash," said Novak, who was then an aide to U.S. Rep. William Lipinski, the ward committeeman. "It was, 'Wink, wink. That way we can pay it out [for campaign expenses] on Election Day.' "

Novak said he never saw Laski pocket a dime of the money, but the advice always raised his suspicions.

"I personally thought he had sticky fingers when I was around him," Novak said.

But community leader Mary Ann Dybala, who has worked with Laski on everything from keeping Midway Airport open to improving neighborhood postal service, said she never saw any hint of corruption or evidence that Laski was on the take.

"No. Never," said Dybala, president of the Garfield Ridge Chamber of Commerce. "That would be the last person on my list -- the last person. I had true confidence in him."

Unfortunately for Laski, he just rose to the top of another list.

'He has blown a good gig'

City clerk for 10 years and 23rd Ward alderman for five before that, Laski is now the highest ranking city official -- and the first elected official -- caught up in the federal government's Hired Truck probe.

Beyond the bribery and obstruction of justice charges revealed Friday, Jim Laski is indeed a man of contradictions.

He craved the spotlight, but he held one of the most obscure city offices. He came from a political stronghold of Mayor Daley, but he made his name bucking the mayor. He constantly flirted with running for higher offices, but he never took the plunge.

And perhaps strangest of all, he styled himself a white knight who came in and cleaned up an office disgraced by one of his predecessors, Walter Kozubowski, only to find his own armor tarnished by scandals that could drive him out of office as well.

"He has blown a good gig," said state Rep. Daniel J. Burke (D-Chicago), a former deputy clerk under Laski and Kozubowski.

"How many people have four police officers assigned to drive them and their families around?" Burke said. "Very unfortunate. It's just like Kozubowski in terms of someone who did not appreciate the privilege that they were offered in that office. To think they would abuse their authority is very unfortunate."

Laski, 52, is a creature of the bungalow belt.

He lives in a simple ranch-style home with a second-floor addition -- a common improvement in the Clearing neighborhood, a haven for firefighters, police officers and other city workers on the southwest edge of the city.

A statue of the Virgin Mary sits out front, and a half dozen Marlboros are stubbed out in an empty flower box hanging from a porch railing.

'A political animal'

Neighbors say he is the typical neighborhood guy, occasionally borrowing an extension ladder to clean out his gutters, regularly attending mass at St. Symphorosa Roman Catholic Church and always stoping to chat when shopping on 63rd Street.

"He was just plain Jim," said Ann Miller, 75, his next-door neighbor. "We always called him Jimmy."

But politics was always part of his life.

Laski met his wife of 14 years, Kathy, working on a political campaign. They named two of their children, twin boys, Bobby and Jack.

"They are named after the Kennedys," said state Rep. Robert S. Molaro (D-Chicago). "He is a political animal. That is how much he enjoyed politics."

Laski grew up in the adjacent Garfield Ridge neighborhood, graduating from St. Laurence High School in suburban Burbank in 1971 and Lewis University in Lockport four years later.

Shortly after he received his law degree from Northern Illinois University in 1978, Laski got a job with Lipinski, who was then 23rd Ward alderman.

"He was a young kid," said William Krystyniak, 55, who took over as alderman in 1983 when Lipinski went to Congress. "He just came out of law school, was studying for the bar. He was upfront, honest. . . . He was there every day, never goofed off, came to work every day."

Sources say it took Laski a few times to pass the bar exam. But that did not hurt him politically.

'The guy you could call'

He started as Lipinski's press secretary, rose to chief of staff to Lipinski and Krystyniak and was appointed alderman in late 1990 when Krystyniak took a job with Cook County.

Laski made early headlines by championing an ordinance to require carbon monoxide detectors in homes, schools, nursing homes and hospitals.

Burke, the state representative and brother of Ald. Edward M. Burke (14th), insisted Laski did little to distinguish himself from the other 49 aldermen, only latching on to the ideas of others.

"I couldn't even suggest there was anything remarkable or important about him," Burke said. "One of the 50. . . . He's not a remarkable character in energy or commitment or force or whatever. Leave it at that."

But others disagree.

"Responsive, sincere, conscientious -- those are the three things that come to my mind," said Anita M. Cummings, 62, chairwoman of the Southwest Home Equity Assurance Commission and executive director of the United Business Association of Midway.

"From the very beginning of the ward office, he was the guy you could call, and he would give you the answers that were available to him."

Split with Lipinski 'gut-wrenching'

Few disagree that Laski showed a willingness to buck the mayor, fighting Daley's 1992 threat to close Midway Airport and leading a 1993 City Council rebellion against the mayor's proposed property tax increase.

"That was a very, very courageous thing back in the '90s," Molaro said. "No one did that.

"And the people responded to that. . . . There are people who think even though they like Daley and think he does a great job, there should be someone there who stands up and tells it like it is. And Jim did that."

The property tax battle cost him with Lipinski.

Laski left the Archer Avenue office they shared Feb. 8, 1993, saying the ward committeeman ordered him out when he refused to support Daley's proposal. Lipinski insists Laski went on his own.

Either way, it was a tense time. Political soldiers in the 23rd Ward still remember the date.

"That split was like gut-wrenching to these guys," said Eric Adelstein, a political consultant who has worked for Laski. "It was definitely an old-style system where the committeeman was king, and you never questioned him. . . . It was definitely like being kicked out of a family."

Novak disputes the portrayal of Laski as a champion of the taxpayers. He said Laski had other motives when he went on the old radio talk show of former Ald. Edward R. Vrdolyak (10th) to talk about the property tax fight.

"He became an opportunity that Vrdolyak was able to use," said Novak, a former political operative who earlier worked for Vrdolyak. "Laski was using Vrdolyak to promote himself. Vrdolyak was using Laski to jab the mayor. But it was not a 'white knight' thing."

Opportunist or white knight, Laski made the most of the situation.

Rather than face certain defeat against Lipinski's aldermanic candidate, Michael Zalewski, in 1995, he ran for city clerk. The office was vacant because Kozubowski went off to prison for a ghost-payrolling scheme, and his appointed successor, Ernest Wish, declined to seek a full term.

'Knew how to make it work'

And in a move typical of the strange world of Southwest Side politics, Lipinski supported Laski for the higher office and Laski won easily.

The clerk's office is charged with a variety of ministerial functions, including selling city vehicle stickers and dog licenses and publishing a record of City Council proceedings.

Despite that mundane job description, Laski still managed to remain a thorn in Daley's side. In 1997, he embarrassed the mayor by revealing that city employees owed $2.36 million in unpaid parking tickets and water bills, much to the delight of Laski's supporters.

"We were happy when he nailed those city workers," said Rich Zilka, 77, president of the Clearing Civic League. "You and I were paying, but they weren't. And he got them to do it."

Along the way, Laski has earned the reputation as a microphone chaser.

"That was Jim Laski," said one member of the 23rd Ward organization who spoke on condition of anonymity. "But he was good at it. He knew how to make it work for him."

Lipinski on Laski

Lipinski, 68, declined to discuss Laski for this article other than to insist Laski left the organization on his own and to dispute the contention of Lipinski's former chief of staff, Novak, that Laski told precinct captains to bring in cash.

"I certainly never heard anything about that," Lipinski said. "I don't know why Joe would say that. Jim had nothing to do with raising money or collecting money. Joe never did like Jim, but no, I never saw that as a problem."

Lipinski said Laski left the fold because "he was having problems with others in the organization."

"He wanted to leave and go on his own, and he used the property tax as a vehicle to say that I threw him out of the office," Lipinski said. "But he left because he wanted to leave."

Laski has not responded to requests for interviews, but his lawyer also questioned Novak's remarks.

"That's the first time I ever heard anything like that," said Anthony Pinelli, Laski's defense lawyer. "I talked to a lot of people recently, and I never heard that allegation from anybody else."

Laski has made his missteps along the way.

As alderman in 1994, he proposed mandatory annual HIV testing of police officers, firefighters, health and welfare employees and hundreds of thousands of restaurant, hospital and other private sector workers -- an idea gay rights activists blasted as "homophobic."

But leaders in the community say Laski has long since mended fences, supporting their issues in the Council and marching in the annual Pride Parade.

'He genuinely changed'

"He got on board, and he never looked back," said Rick Garcia, political director of Equality Illinois.

Garcia remembers about six or eight years ago when Laski noticed a guy in drag at an event before the parade stepped off and told Garcia he wanted someone like that for his own float.

"He said, 'We should really have one of those.' " Garcia said. "We found a 7-foot-tall drag queen dressed as the Statue of Liberty [to ride on Laski's float]."

Garcia believes Laski's change of position was prompted by his desire to move beyond his socially conservative Southwest Side base and run statewide.

"I think there was also a genuine change of heart, because then he started to know gay folk, and he changed," Garcia said. "He genuinely changed."

Despite the Mr. Clean image he has cultivated, Laski has not been scandal-free.

Five years ago, a television news crew filmed some of his employees golfing with Laski, shooting pool and running personal errands on paid sick days, forcing Laski to accept his chief of staff's resignation, fire two high-ranking employees and demote or suspend several others.

Still, Molaro said he was surprised at Laski's current troubles.

"There was no tinge of impropriety ever," Molaro said. "All right, he went out golfing with one of his guys that did not sign out. These allegations are night and day from that."

Laski was indicted Friday on charges he took bribes from his close friend and employee, Michael "Mick" Jones, in return for helping steer city business to Jones' trucking firm, Get Plowed, Inc., and then obstructed the federal investigation.

'It's just a nightmare'

If convicted, Laski could face 10 years in prison and up to $250,000 in fines.

"I just think he is overwhelmingly embarrassed," Molaro said. "He fought Daley. It was like, 'I did it because I'm a man of integrity.'

"And when this happens, it's doubly embarrassing. . . . It's just so devastating. It rocks you to the core. It's emotional. It's physical."

Perhaps the final irony is that rather than a political enemy, it is some of Laski's closest friends who are now cooperating with the feds -- Jones and Randy Aderman, a clerk employee who was fired last year in a scandal over having friends swipe workers in when they weren't on the job.

Laski, Jones and Aderman all played softball together on the Bulldogs, a local team that played at Hale Park and other area diamonds.

"That was his best friends," Krystyniak said. "It is hard to believe."

His next-door neighbors were shocked by the week's developments. "I could just cry," Ann Miller said. "It's just a nightmare, a shame."

"A nightmare," added her husband Bob, 76, a retired milkman and usher at St. Symphorosa. "Like they said about 'Shoeless' Joe Jackson, 'Say it ain't so.'

"But if they have wires on him, and he incriminated himself, so be it."

sfornek@suntimes.com

236

Sentencing Documents

My Federal indictment for bribery in Chicago's
"Hired Truck Program Scandal."

UNITED STATES DISTRICT COURT
NORTHERN DISTRICT OF ILLINOIS
EASTERN DIVISION

UNITED STATES OF AMERICA	)	No. 05 CR 96 **JUDGE NORGLE**
	)	
v.	)	**MAGISTRATE JUDGE SCHENKIER**
	)	
JAMES J. LASKI, JR.,	)	Violations: Title 18, United States Code,
SAM GAMMICCHIA,	)	Sections 2, 666, 1503 and 1512.
aka Salvatore Gammicchia,	)	
JOHN BRJATTA,	)	
RANDY ADERMAN, and	)	
MICHAEL JONES	)	

FILED

J.N

JAN 2 6 2006

MICHAEL W. DOBBINS
CLERK, U.S. DISTRICT COURT

COUNT ONE

The SPECIAL FEBRUARY 2005-2 GRAND JURY charges:

1.   At times material to this indictment:

City of Chicago

A.   The City of Chicago ("the City") was a unit of local government known as a municipal corporation, and a political subdivision of the State of Illinois. The functions and services provided by the City on behalf of its residents were coordinated through various agencies and departments. Several of the largest City operational departments included the Department of Water, the Department of Streets and Sanitation, the Department of Transportation and the Department of Sewers. Each of the departments was headed by a Commissioner, who was nominated by the Mayor of the City and confirmed by the City Council, the legislative body for the City.

The Clerk of the City of Chicago

B.   Beginning in or about 1995, JAMES J. LASKI, JR., was the elected Clerk of the City of Chicago. As City Clerk, LASKI presided over an office of approximately 120 City employees.

1

The Department of Water

C.   The Department of Water employed approximately 2000 employees, and was divided into seven bureaus, with separate and distinct functions. The largest of the bureaus was the Bureau of Operations and Distribution (hereinafter "Distribution"), which employed approximately 900 individuals. Generally, each bureau was headed by a Deputy Commissioner. With regard to Distribution, the First Deputy Commissioner effectively served as the overall manager of Distribution. The principal function of Distribution was the installation, repair and monitoring of water delivery systems within the City. The headquarters for Distribution was the Jardine Filtration Plant, located in Chicago, where the First Deputy Commissioner had his principal office.

D.   On or about January 1, 2003, the Department of Water merged with the Department of Sewers and the newly-formed entity was entitled the Department of Water Management. (Hereinafter, the pre-merger Department of Water and the post-merger Department of Water Management will be referred to as the "Department").

E.   Donald Tomczak began working for the City in or about 1958. Beginning no later than 1989 and continuing through approximately January 2004, Tomczak was a full-time salaried employee of the City. Beginning in approximately December 1989 and continuing through in or about January 2004, Tomczak was the First Deputy Commissioner of the Department and held that title until his retirement effective January 2004.

The City's Hired Truck Program

F.   The City's Hired Truck Program ("HTP") provided certain City operating departments with a mechanism to use trucking services on an as-needed basis to complete construction and operating obligations. Participating HTP trucking companies were hired by the City

2

and provided equipment and operators to the respective City operating departments to perform specific tasks. The principal operating departments using HTP services were the Department, the Department of Streets and Sanitation, the Department of Transportation and the Department of Sewers.

        G.   In conjunction with the HTP, the operating departments hired some trucks on a year-round basis for particular City operations; other trucks were hired on a seasonal basis for departmental projects, and still other trucks were hired for short periods of time on an as-needed basis for particular tasks of the respective departments.

        H.   Beginning in or about 1997, HTP participating companies and their individual trucks had to be approved for entry into the HTP by the program Office (the "HTP Office"), after an application and review process was conducted by the HTP Office staff. Once approved, an HTP participating company went on an approved list maintained by the HTP Office. The HTP Office staff was further responsible for ongoing monitoring and regulation of the participating HTP companies and their trucks regarding insurance, inspection, safety and other related issues. The HTP Office had the authority to suspend or discipline HTP participating companies for violations of the HTP rules.

        I.   There was no bid process and no formal, written contract for any particular job within the operating departments. Rather, certain City employees within the respective operating departments with HTP responsibilities participated in the process of "calling out" or hiring trucks for a particular HTP assignment within the department ("HTP supervisors"). The HTP supervisors also decided when trucks were to be laid off for a particular assignment and the order in which trucks were to be laid off. Generally, the decisions were made at the discretion of the HTP supervisors within the respective departments, though there was occasional input provided by the HTP Office.

3

J.   As to each department using the HTP, the City compensated HTP trucking company participants at a fixed hourly rate based on the size of the truck. Typically, on a monthly basis, participating HTP trucking companies would submit invoices for their monthly work for each City department. Thereafter, the City would process the invoices and typically would remit payments by negotiable instruments known as "warrants."

Get Plowed, Inc.

K.   Get Plowed, Inc., was a trucking company that participated in the HTP from in or about 1998 through 2003. For each year from 2001 through 2003, Get Plowed received over $100,000 in revenues from HTP business. Beginning in or about 1982 and continuing through 2003, Michael Jones participated in the operation of Get Plowed, Inc.

2.   From in or about February 2001 to in or about December 2001, at Chicago, in the Northern District of Illinois, Eastern Division,

JAMES J. LASKI, JR.,

defendant herein, being an agent of the City, corruptly solicited and demanded, and accepted and agreed to accept, things of value, namely cash payments from Michael Jones, intending to be influenced and rewarded in connection with Hired Truck Program business, including from the Department, in a series of transactions having a value of $5,000 or more, involving the City, being an agency that received in excess of $10,000 in federal funding in a period from February 1, 2001, to December 31, 2001;

In violation of Title 18, United States Code, Section 666(a)(1)(B).

4

COUNT TWO

The SPECIAL FEBRUARY 2005-2 GRAND JURY further charges:

1.   The allegations in Paragraph 1 of Count One of this indictment are hereby realleged and incorporated as if fully set forth herein.

2.   From in or about January 2002 to in or about December 2002, at Chicago, in the Northern District of Illinois, Eastern Division,

JAMES J. LASKI, JR.,

defendant herein, being an agent of the City, corruptly solicited and demanded, and accepted and agreed to accept, things of value, namely cash payments from Michael Jones, intending to be influenced and rewarded in connection with Hired Truck Program business, including from the Department, in a series of transactions having a value of $5,000 or more, involving the City, being an agency that received in excess of $10,000 in federal funding in a twelve-month period from January 1, 2002, to December 31, 2002;

In violation of Title 18, United States Code, Section 666(a)(1)(B).

5

COUNT THREE

The SPECIAL FEBRUARY 2005-2 GRAND JURY further charges:

1.   The allegations in Paragraph 1 of Count One of this indictment are hereby realleged and incorporated as if fully set forth herein.

2.   From in or about January 2003 to in or about December 2003, at Chicago, in the Northern District of Illinois, Eastern Division,

JAMES J. LASKI, JR.,

defendant herein, being an agent of the City, corruptly solicited and demanded, and accepted and agreed to accept, things of value, namely cash payments from Michael Jones, intending to be influenced and rewarded in connection with Hired Truck Program business, including from the Department, in a series of transactions having a value of $5,000 or more, involving the City, being an agency that received in excess of $10,000 in federal funding in a twelve-month period from January 1, 2003, to December 31, 2003;

In violation of Title 18, United States Code, Section 666(a)(1)(B).

6

COUNT FOUR

The SPECIAL FEBRUARY 2005-2 GRAND JURY further charges:

1. The allegations in Paragraph 1(A), and Paragraphs 1(C) through 1(K) of Count One of this indictment are hereby realleged and incorporated as if fully set forth herein.

2. At times material to this Count:

    A. JOHN BRIATTA was employed as a Chief Equipment Dispatcher by the Department within the Distribution division at the Jardine Filtration Plant.

    B. Randy Aderman was employed as a Projects Administrator by the Department within the Distribution division at the Jardine Filtration Plant.

3. From in or about January 2003 to in or about December 2003, at Chicago, in the Northern District of Illinois, Eastern Division,

JOHN BRIATTA,

defendant herein, being an agent of the City, corruptly solicited and demanded, and accepted and agreed to accept, things of value, namely cash payments from Randy Aderman and Michael Jones, intending to be influenced and rewarded in connection with Hired Truck Program business from the Department, in a series of transactions having a value of $5,000 or more, involving the City, being an agency that received in excess of $10,000 in federal funding in a twelve-month period from January 1, 2003, to December 31, 2003;

In violation of Title 18, United States Code, Section 666(a)(1)(B).

7

COUNT FIVE

The SPECIAL FEBRUARY 2005-2 GRAND JURY further charges:

1.   The allegations in Paragraph 1(A), and Paragraphs 1(C) through 1(K) of Count One and Paragraph 2 of Count Four of this indictment are hereby realleged and incorporated as if fully set forth herein.

2.   From in or about January 2003 to in or about December 2003, at Chicago, in the Northern District of Illinois, Eastern Division,

RANDY ADERMAN,

defendant herein, did corruptly give, offer and agree to give things of value, namely cash payments, with the intent to influence and reward John Briatta, being an agent of the City, in connection with Hired Truck Program business from the Department in a series of transactions having a value of $5,000 or more, with the City being an agency that received in excess of $10,000 in federal funding in a twelve-month period from January 1, 2003, to December 31, 2003;

In violation of Title 18, United States Code, Section 666(a)(2).

8

COUNT SIX

The SPECIAL FEBRUARY 2005-2 GRAND JURY further charges:

1.   The allegations in Paragraph 1 of Count One and Paragraph 2 of Count Four of this indictment are hereby realleged and incorporated as if fully set forth herein.

2.   From in or about January 2003 to in or about December 2003, at Chicago, in the Northern District of Illinois, Eastern Division,

MICHAEL JONES,

defendant herein, did corruptly give, offer and agree to give things of value, namely cash payments, with the intent to influence and reward James J. Laski, Jr., Randy Aderman and John Briatta, being agents of the City, in connection with Hired Truck Program business, including from the Department, in a series of transactions having a value of $5,000 or more, with the City being an agency that received in excess of $10,000 in federal funding in a twelve-month period from January 1, 2003, to December 31, 2003;

In violation of Title 18, United States Code, Section 666(a)(2).

9

245

COUNT SEVEN

The SPECIAL FEBRUARY 2005-2 GRAND JURY further charges:

1.   The allegations in Paragraph 1 of Count One and Paragraph 2(B) of Count Four of this indictment are hereby realleged and incorporated as if fully set forth herein.

2.   The SPECIAL FEBRUARY 2005-2 GRAND JURY, in connection with Grand Jury Investigation No. 02 GJ 1348, was conducting an investigation into possible violations of Title 18, United States Code, Sections 666, 1503, and 1512, among other violations of federal law, including an investigation of whether or not JAMES J. LASKI, JR. accepted cash payments or other things of value from Michael Jones, Randy Aderman or any individual associated with Get Plowed, Inc.

3.   In or about September 2005, defendants JAMES J. LASKI, JR., and SAM GAMMICCHIA, aka Salvatore Gammicchia, understood that an individual associated with Get Plowed, Inc., Individual A, was likely to be compelled to testify before a federal grand jury investigating Get Plowed, Inc.

4.   From on or about September 13, 2005, through on or about October 22, 2005, at Chicago, in the Northern District of Illinois, Eastern Division, and elsewhere,

> JAMES J. LASKI, JR., and
> SAM GAMMICCHIA,
> aka Salvatore Gammicchia,

defendants herein, corruptly endeavored to influence, obstruct, and impede the due administration of justice; namely, knowing the grand jury was investigating cash payments made to LASKI by Michael Jones and Individual A, defendants LASKI and GAMMICCHIA directed and advised Individual A to mislead the grand jury by: (1) falsely testifying that Individual A did not recall making cash

10

payments and did not know the purpose of cash payments to LASKI; and (2) falsely testifying that

the payments given to LASKI by Individual A were political contributions;

In violation of Title 18, United States Code, Sections 1503(a) and 2.

11

COUNT EIGHT

The SPECIAL FEBRUARY 2005-2 GRAND JURY further charges:

1.   The allegations in Paragraphs 1 through 3 of Count Seven of this indictment are hereby realleged and incorporated as if fully set forth herein.

2.   On or about October 22, 2005, at Chicago, Illinois, Northern District of Illinois, Eastern Division,

SAM GAMMICCHIA,
aka Salvatore Gammicchia,

defendant herein, knowingly used intimidation, threatened and corruptly persuaded Michael Jones, and attempted to do so, with intent to hinder, delay and prevent the communication to a law enforcement officer of information relating to the commission and possible commission of a federal offense;

In violation of Title 18, United States Code, Sections 1512(b)(3).

12

FORFEITURE ALLEGATION ONE

The SPECIAL FEBRUARY 2005-2 GRAND JURY further alleges:

1.   The allegations contained in Counts One through Three of this indictment are realleged and incorporated herein by reference for the purpose of alleging forfeiture pursuant to Title 18, United States Code, Section 981(a)(1)(C) and Title 28, United States Code, Section 2461(c).

2.   As a result of his violations of Title 18, United States Code, Section 666, as alleged in the foregoing indictment,

JAMES J. LASKI, JR.,

defendant herein, shall forfeit to the United States, pursuant to Title 18, United States Code, Section, 981(a)(1)(C) and Title 28, United States Code, Section 2461(c), any and all right, title and interest in property, real and personal, which constitutes and is derived from proceeds traceable to the charged offenses.

3.   The interests of the defendant subject to forfeiture pursuant to Title 18, United States Code, Section 981(a)(1)(C) and Title 28, United States Code, Section 2461(c) include but are not limited to all financial benefits and proceeds defendant LASKI received related to Get Plowed, Inc., including, without limitation, $50,000;

4.   If any of the property subject to forfeiture and described above, as a result of any act or omission of the defendant:

    (a)   Cannot be located upon the exercise of due diligence;

    (b)   Has been transferred or sold to, or deposited with, a third party;

    (c)   Has been placed beyond the jurisdiction of the Court;

    (d)   Has been substantially diminished in value; or

13

FORFEITURE ALLEGATION TWO

The SPECIAL FEBRUARY 2005-2 GRAND JURY further alleges:

1.   The allegations contained in Count Four of this indictment are realleged and incorporated herein by reference for the purpose of alleging forfeiture pursuant to Title 18, United States Code, Section 981(a)(1)(C) and Title 28, United States Code, Section 2461(c).

2.   As a result of his violation of Title 18, United States Code, Section 666, as alleged in the foregoing indictment,

JOHN BRIATTA,

defendant herein, shall forfeit to the United States, pursuant to Title 18, United States Code, Section, 981(a)(1)(C) and Title 28, United States Code, Section 2461(c), any and all right, title and interest in property, real and personal, which constitutes and is derived from proceeds traceable to the charged offense.

3.   The interests of the defendant subject to forfeiture pursuant to Title 18, United States Code, Section 981(a)(1)(C) and Title 28, United States Code, Section 2461(c) include but are not limited to all financial benefits and proceeds defendant BRIATTA received related to Get Plowed, Inc., including, without limitation, $8,000;

4.   If any of the property subject to forfeiture and described above, as a result of any act or omission of the defendant:

      (a)   Cannot be located upon the exercise of due diligence;

      (b)   Has been transferred or sold to, or deposited with, a third party;

      (c)   Has been placed beyond the jurisdiction of the Court;

      (d)   Has been substantially diminished in value; or

15

(e)   Has been commingled with other property which cannot
be divided without difficulty;

the United States of America shall be entitled to forfeiture of substitute property under the provisions

of Title 21, United States Code, Section 853(p), as incorporated by Title 28, United States Code,

Section 2461(c).

    All pursuant to Title 18, United States Code, Section 981(a)(1)(C) and Title 28, United States

Code, Section 2461(c).

A TRUE BILL:

_____

FOREPERSON

_____
UNITED STATES ATTORNEY

16

My sentencing on bribery charges in the
"Hired Truck Program Scandal."

(Rev. 03/05)

United States District Court
Northern District of Illinois

UNITED STATES OF AMERICA   )
)
       v.   )   **Case Number: 05-CR-964-1**
)   **Judge: Charles R. Norgle**
JAMES J. LASKI, JR.   )

Jeffrey B. Steinback, Defendant's Attorney
Manish S. Shah, AUSA

JUDGMENT IN A CRIMINAL CASE
(For Offenses Committed On or After November 1, 1987)

THE DEFENDANT ENTERED A PLEA OF:

guilty to Count(s) Three of the Indictment, which was accepted by the court.

Count(s) any remaining is/are dismissed on the motion of the United States.

THE DEFENDANT IS CONVICTED OF THE OFFENSES(S) OF:

Title & Section	Description of Offense	Date Offense Concluded	Count Number(s)
18 U.S.C. §666(a)(1)(B)	Bribery	12/01/2003	Three

The defendant is sentenced as provided in the following pages of this judgment.

IMPRISONMENT

IT IS THE JUDGMENT OF THIS COURT THAT:

the defendant is hereby committed to the custody of the United States Bureau of Prisons to be imprisoned for a total uninterrupted term of **twenty four (24) months**.

The Court recommends to the Bureau of Prisons:

Participation in Comprehensive Substance Abuse (alcohol) Treatment Program.

SUPERVISED RELEASE

Upon release from imprisonment, the defendant shall be on supervised release for the periods specified for each count of conviction.

The defendant is sentenced on all count(s) of conviction, namely, Count(s) Three to a period of two years of Supervised Release, said periods to run concurrent.

The defendant shall report immediately to the probation office in the district in which the defendant is to be supervised, but no later than seventy-two hours after sentencing. In addition, see the attached page(s) defining the mandatory, standard and discretionary conditions of probation that apply in this case.

MANDATORY CONDITIONS OF SUPERVISED RELEASE
(As set forth in 18 U.S.C. § 3583 and U.S.S.G. § 5D1.3)

1)   For any offense, the defendant shall not commit another federal, state or local crime;

2)   for any offense, the defendant shall not unlawfully possess a controlled substance;

3)   for offenses committed on or after September 13, 1994, the defendant shall refrain from any unlawful use of a controlled substance and submit to one drug test within fifteen days of release from imprisonment and at least two periodic drug tests thereafter for use of a controlled substance as determined by the court:

   Not to exceed 104 tests per year.

4)   for a domestic violence crime committed on or after September 13, 1994, as defined in 18 U.S.C. § 3561(b) by a defendant convicted of such an offense for the first time, the defendant shall attend a rehabilitation program in accordance with 18 U.S.C. § 3583(d);

5)   for a defendant classified as a sex offender pursuant to 18 U.S.C. § 4042(c)(4), the defendant shall comply with the reporting and registration requirements set forth in 18 U.S.C. § 3583(d);

6)   the defendant shall cooperate in the collection of a DNA sample from the defendant if the collection of such a sample is authorized pursuant to section 3 of the DNA Analysis Backlog Elimination Act of 2000 and the Justice for All Act of 2004; and

7)   The defendant shall pay any balance on the special assessment, restitution and/or fine imposed against the defendant.

STANDARD CONDITIONS OF SUPERVISED RELEASE

1)   For any felony or other offense, the defendant shall not possess a firearm, ammunition, or destructive device as defined in 18 U.S.C. § 921;

2)   the defendant shall not leave the judicial district without the permission of the court or probation officer (travel outside the continental United States requires court authorization);

3)   the defendant shall report to the probation officer as directed by the court or the probation officer and shall submit a truthful and complete written report within the first five days of each month;

4)   the defendant shall answer truthfully all inquiries by the probation officer and follow the instructions of the probation officer;

5)   the defendant shall provide to the probation officer access to any requested financial information including, but not limited to, tax returns, bank statements, credit card statements, credit applications, etc.;

6)   the defendant shall support his or her dependents and meet other family responsibilities;

7)   the defendant shall work regularly at a lawful occupation, unless excused by the probation officer for schooling, training, or other acceptable reasons;

8)   the defendant shall notify the probation officer ten (10) days prior to any change in residence or employment;

9)   the defendant shall refrain from excessive use of alcohol;

10) the defendant shall not purchase, possess, use, distribute, or administer any narcotic or other controlled substance, or any paraphernalia related to such substances, except as prescribed by a physician, and shall submit to periodic urinalysis tests as requested by the probation officer to determine the use of any controlled substance;

11) the defendant shall not frequent places where controlled substances are illegally sold, used, distributed, or administered;

12) the defendant shall not associate with any persons engaged in criminal activity and shall not associate with any person convicted of a felony unless granted permission to do so by the probation officer;

13) the defendant shall permit a probation officer to visit him or her at any time at home or elsewhere and shall permit confiscation of any contraband observed in plain view by the probation officer;

14) the defendant shall notify the probation officer within seventy-two (72) hours of being arrested or questioned by a law enforcement officer;

15) the defendant shall not enter into any agreement to act as an informer or a special agent of a law enforcement agency without the permission of the court;

16) as directed by the probation officer, the defendant shall notify third parties of risks that may be occasioned by the defendant's criminal record or personal history or characteristics, and shall permit the probation officer to make such notifications and to confirm the defendant's compliance with such notification requirement; and

17) if this judgment imposes a special assessment, restitution or a fine, it shall be a condition of probation or supervised release that the defendant pay any such special assessment, restitution or fine in accordance with the court's order set forth in the Criminal Monetary Penalties sheet of this judgment.

CRIMINAL MONETARY PENALTIES

The defendant shall pay the following total criminal monetary penalties in accordance with the "Schedule of Payments." Unless waived, the defendant shall pay interest on any restitution and/or fine of more than $2,500, unless the restitution and/or fine is paid in full before the fifteenth day after the date of judgment, pursuant to 18 U.S.C. § 3612(f). The payment options may be subject to penalties for default and delinquency pursuant to 18 U.S.C. § 3612(g).

Total Assessment(s)	Total Fine	Restitution	Mandatory Costs of Prosecution
$100.00	Fine Waived	$	$

The defendant shall notify the United States Attorney's Office having jurisdiction over the defendant within thirty days of any change of name, residence or mailing address until all special assessments, restitution, fines, and costs imposed by this judgment are fully paid.

SCHEDULE OF PAYMENTS

- Payments shall be applied in the following order: (1) assessment, (2) restitution principal, (3) restitution interest, (4) fine principal, (5) community restitution, (6) fine interest, (7) penalties, and (8) costs, including cost of prosecution and court costs. If this judgment imposes a period of imprisonment, payment of criminal monetary penalties shall be due during the period of imprisonment.

- All criminal monetary penalty payments, except those payments made through the Bureau of Prisons' Inmate financial Responsibility Program, are to be by money order or certified check payable to the Clerk of the Court, U.S. District Court, unless otherwise directed by the Court.

- Unless waived, the defendant shall pay interest on any fine and/or restitution of more than $2,500, unless the same is paid in full before the fifteenth day after the date of judgment, pursuant to 18 U.S.C. § 3612(f). Payment options included herein may be subject to penalties of default and delinquency pursuant to 18 U.S.C. § 3612(g).

- Pursuant to 18 U.S.C. §§ 3613(b) and (c) and 3664(m), restitution and/or fine obligations extend for twenty years after release from imprisonment, or from the date of entry of judgment if not sentenced to a period of imprisonment.

Payment of the total criminal monetary penalties shall be due as follows:

In full:

Due immediately.

The costs of incarceration and supervision are waived.

Pursuant to 18 U.S.C. § 3664(k) the defendant must notify the court of any material changes in the defendant's economic circumstances. Upon such notice, the court may adjust the installment payment schedule.

Pursuant to 18 U.S.C. § 3664(n), if a person is obligated to provide restitution, or pay a fine, received substantial resources from any source, including inheritance, settlement, or other judgment, during a period of incarceration, such person shall be required to apply the value of such resources to any restitution or fine still owed.

FORFEITURE

Forfeiture is ordered as provided in the attached preliminary order of forfeiture.

LOT 31 IN BLOCK 1 IN CENTRAL ADDITION TO CLEARING, BEING
A SUBDIVISION OF THE SOUTH 3/4 OF THE EAST ½ OF THE
SOUTHWEST 1/4 OF SECTION 17, TOWNSHIP 38 NORTH, RANGE 13
EAST OF THE THIRD PRINCIPAL MERIDIAN, IN COOK COUNTY,
ILLINOIS.

Permanent Index Number: 19-17-316-010-0000.

4.   On March 17, 2006, defendant entered a plea of guilty to Count Three of the
indictment, thereby making certain property subject to forfeiture pursuant to the provisions of 18
U.S.C. § 981(a)(1)(C) and 28 U.S.C. § 2461(c).

5.   In the plea agreement, defendant agreed he subjected certain property to forfeiture,
namely $48,000, which funds represent financial benefits and proceeds the defendant obtained as
a result of the conduct to which the defendant pled guilty, in violation of 18 U.S.C. § 666.
Defendant further agreed to the entry of a forfeiture judgment in the amount of $48,000 and also to
the entry of preliminary order of forfeiture relinquishing any right, title or ownership interest that the
defendant has in funds in the amount of $48,000, pursuant to 18 U.S.C. § 981(a)(1)(C) and 28 U.S.C.
§ 2461(c) for disposition according to law.

6.   In addition, as part of the plea agreement, the defendant understands that
approximately $15,400 in United States currency provided by the defendant to the government on
December 13, 2005, shall be applied in partial satisfaction of the forfeiture judgment. The agreement
further provided that defendant shall provide funds not subject to claim by any other third party to
satisfy the remaining forfeiture judgment in the amount of $32,600. Defendant has agreed to tender
one cashier's check, made payable to the United States Marshal's Seized Assets Deposit Fund, in
the amount of $32,600 prior to sentencing. On or about April 24, 2006, defendant tendered a check
for $32,600 to the United States Marshal's Service.

2

HC.

UNITED STATES DISTRICT COURT
NORTHERN DISTRICT OF ILLINOIS
EASTERN DIVISION

UNITED STATES OF AMERICA	)	
	)	
v.	)	No. 05 CR 964-1
	)	Judge Charles R. Norgle
JAMES J. LASKI, JR., *et al.*	)	

PRELIMINARY ORDER OF FORFEITURE

This matter comes before the Court on the agreed motion of the United States for entry of

a preliminary order of forfeiture as to specific property pursuant to the provisions of Title 18, United

States Code, Section 981(a)(1)(C), Title 28, United States Code, Section 2461(c), and Fed. R. Crim.

P. 32.2, and the Court being fully informed hereby finds as follows:

1.   On January 26, 2006, an indictment was returned charging defendant JAMES J.

LASKI, JR., with three counts of bribery, in violation of 18 U.S.C. § 666 (Counts One, Two, and

Three), and one count of obstruction of justice (Count Seven).

2.   The indictment sought forfeiture to the United States of specific property, including

but not limited to, all financial benefits and proceeds defendant received related to Get Plowed, Inc.,

including, without limitation, $50,000, pursuant to the provisions of 18 U.S.C. § 981(a)(1)(C) and

28 U.S.C. § 2461(c).

3.   The indictment also sought forfeiture of the real property located at 6029 South

McVicker Avenue, Chicago, Illinois, ("McVicker Avenue property") as a substitute asset, in the

event that these funds could be located to satisfy the forfeiture judgment or were not available to

satisfy the judgment, pursuant to Title 18, United States Code, Section 853(p), as incorporated by

28 U.S.C. § 2461(c). The McVicker Avenue property is legally described as follows:

3.   That, as part of the defendant JAMES J. LASKI's plea agreement, approximately $15,400 in United States Currency provided by defendant to the government on December 13, 2005, shall be applied in partial satisfaction of the $48,000 forfeiture judgment. Defendant shall provide funds not subject to claim by any other third party to satisfy the remaining forfeiture judgment in the amount of $32,600. Specifically, defendant has agreed to tender one cashier's check, made payable to the United States Marshal's Seized Assets Deposit Fund, in the amount of $32,600 prior to sentencing. According to the government's agreed motion, on or about April 24, 2006, defendant tendered a check for $32,600 to the United States Marshal's Service.

4.   That, pursuant to the provisions of 21 U.S.C. § 853(g), as incorporated by 28 U.S.C. § 2461(c), following entry of this preliminary order of forfeiture, the United States Marshal shall seize and take custody of the foregoing funds in the amount of $15,400, and any future payments toward the remaining $32,600 judgment, for disposition as the Attorney General may direct.

5.   That pursuant to the provisions of 21 U.S.C. § 853(n)(1), as incorporated by 28 U.S.C. § 2461(c), following entry of a preliminary order of forfeiture, the United States shall publish notice of this order and of its intent to dispose of the foregoing funds according to law. The government may also, pursuant to statute, to the extent practicable, provide written notice to any person known to have alleged an interest in the property that is the subject of the preliminary order of forfeiture.

6.   That pursuant to the provisions of 21 U.S.C. § 853(n)(2), as incorporated by 28 U.S.C. § 2461(c), if following notice as directed by this Court and 21 U.S.C. § 853(n)(2), any person, other than the defendant, asserts a legal interest in the property that has been ordered forfeit to the United States, within thirty days of the final publication of notice or this receipt of notice, whichever

is earlier, and petitions the Court for a hearing to adjudicate the validity of this alleged interest in the property, the government shall request a hearing. The hearing shall be held before the Court alone, without a jury.

7.   That following the Court's disposition of all third party interests, upon the government's motion, the Court shall, if appropriate, enter a final order of forfeiture as to the foregoing funds, which is the subject of this preliminary order of forfeiture, which shall vest clear title in the United States of America.

8.   That upon satisfaction of the remaining forfeiture judgment by defendant, the United States will release the *Lis Pendens* notice it recorded against the McVicker Avenue property to secure its interest in the property.

9.   That the terms and conditions of this preliminary order of forfeiture entered by this Court shall be made part of the sentence imposed against defendant, and included in any judgment and commitment order entered in this case against the defendant.

10.   That this Court shall retain jurisdiction in this matter to take additional action and enter further orders as necessary to implement and enforce this forfeiture order.

CHARLES R. NORGLE
United States District Judge

Dated: 4-26-06

261

The defendant shall surrender for service of sentence at the institution designated by the Bureau of Prisons: before **2:00 P.M. on August 31, 2006.**

Date of Imposition of Judgment/Sentencing: June 13, 2006

CHARLES R. NORGLE
UNITED STATES DISTRICT JUDGE

Dated at Chicago, Illinois this __13__ day of June, 2006

CHAPTER 17

GOODBYE

I spent the next few months basically attached to the hip with my family. This was an extremely difficult time for me, simply because the thought of going to prison was constantly on my mind. No matter what I did, if I were watching a video with the kids, or jumping into the pool with them, my thoughts would eventually turn to prison.

As I mentioned earlier, as a family we would spend at least two weeks every year at my in-laws' summer home in Eagle River, Wisconsin. This year would be no exception. The only difference was that I had to get permission from my pre-trial officer, Tiffany Millard, who technically would have jurisdiction over me until my departure date on August 31. She very graciously gave me the go-ahead, in return for my in-laws' address and phone number, and the dates I would be leaving Chicago and returning home.

The visit to Wisconsin was quite enjoyable, and it was probably the first time in a long while that I could actually relax. The kids did their thing and had a blast, as usual—swimming, tubing, and fishing. Kathleen, too, enjoyed the water, and on a couple of occasions she was able to lie in a raft and get some sun. I, on the other hand, just hung around, and watched the family. My enjoyment came at dinner time, when I was able to grill. I thoroughly enjoyed grilling, and I would cook something different every day. During those two weeks, I cooked ribs, chicken, steaks, hot dogs, hamburgers, brats, and pork chops. It was real therapy for me.

My evenings were basically spent watching the kids fishing and running around. Later in the evening, I would sit on the deck with Kathleen and have a few beers, or go to a neighbor's house for a friendly poker game. I spent very little time thinking about anything back home. The hardest moment was saying goodbye. Many of the people out there were our friends. As a matter of fact, we'd gotten together with the same group of people there for the past seventeen years. I wondered when I would see them again.

We stayed just short of two weeks. The plan was for me to head home first, with Nina, while Kathleen and the boys would stay an extra day. It was a family tradition that before any of us would leave, we would take a picture together. I remember standing there with my family, fighting back the tears and faking a smile, while one of our friends took the picture.

After returning to Wisconsin, I had about four weeks until I had to leave. The boys had only three weeks before school started, while Nina wouldn't start until the day after Labor Day. Fortunately, the weather was very warm, so the kids and I spent a considerable amount of time in the swimming pool. Each day that went by, the kids wanted to know where I would be going at the end of the month.

Right after the sentencing, I told the kids I was going away. The boys already knew that I had quit my job, but all I told them was that I needed to go away for a little while to a school for job training. I never told them how long I would be gone. On the other hand, we recently told Nina where I was really going. It's hard to get a handle on how Nina feels, because she internalizes everything, and hides her emotions. As the departure date grew closer, she asked questions about where I would sleep, what kind of clothes I would wear, what kind of food I would eat, and if I could watch TV. I could tell she was very concerned, and I tried to answer her questions as honestly as I could. There were days when the kids would ask me if I would be home by Christmas, and I would have to literally run from the room and cry somewhere. It became harder and harder, as each day went by, to think about saying goodbye.

About two weeks before my departure date, I scheduled all of my doctor and dental appointments. I wanted to make sure that I didn't have any outstanding medical issues before I left. Everything went fine with the eye doctor and dentist, but when I went to see my physician, I needed to take a few blood tests. A few days after those tests, my doctor called to tell me he had found traces of blood in my urine. This happened once before, about five years ago, and I had to get a kidney x-ray, along with intrusive scope, and a procedure through the penis to check my bladder and prostate. My physician, Dr. Costas, recommended that I take the same tests again. Unfortunately, time was running out, and I only had about a week until I would leave. Fortunately, I was able to get Jeff to file a motion with Judge Norgle, requesting an extension on my departure date. Dr. Costas faxed Jeff a letter outlining the tests, and the U.S. Attorney's office had no objection to the extension. Less than forty-eight hours after he filed that motion, Jeff called me to tell me my new date would be September 11—9/11! When I heard that, I instantly thought, uneasily, about 9/11/2001, but I guess any date would have bothered me. (What was really ironic was that later, all the media would erroneously report that I left for Morgantown on August 31, to begin my sentence.)

With those extra twelve days, I was able to schedule both tests, which proved negative. The only explanation Dr. Costas had for the blood in my urine was that my prostate was slightly enlarged, a condition that for my age, was neither serious nor unusual. I just needed to have my prostate checked again during my yearly physical.

Even though the extension merely delayed the inevitable, I was still happy to spend those extra days, including Labor Day, at home with the family. My daughter asked me if I would take her to school the first week after the holiday, which would be my last full week at home. I could tell that she was starting to struggle with the idea of my leaving.

I spent the last week just hanging around the house. Everyone was back at school, so I took Nina in the morning, monitored the boys outside for recess around lunchtime, and then headed back to pick up my daughter after school. I pretty much followed that routine every day. I spent the evenings watching TV with the kids. After they went to bed, Kathleen and I would talk for a couple of hours. Each and every day that went by that week, I would say, "This is my last Monday," or, "This is my last Tuesday," etc. I had my own countdown going on in my head. I was also trying to cut back on my beer drinking, because I knew it would be tough when I got to prison. That last week, I probably drank only two or three beers a night. In addition, when I found out that the Bureau of Prisons had a smoking ban, I decided to try a nicotine-withdrawal procedure involving lasers. Since I was so addicted to nicotine, I had to attend the program two different days, the last being Friday, three days before I would report to prison.

It's really hard to describe that last weekend. Quite honestly, I was in a daze, and almost in denial. I needed to finally talk to my guys about what time we would leave for Morgantown, West Virginia, where I was sentenced. Don, "J.R.," and Ray all looked at Mapquest on the Internet, and found that Morgantown was about 540 miles from Chicago, and that the trip by car would be around nine-and-a-half hours. Although I would not have to report until noon on Monday, we still needed to leave late Sunday night, about 11:00 p.m., to make sure we had plenty of time to get there. I knew then I was down to the bitter end, and I tried to prepare myself mentally for my departure.

The last couple of days at home were quiet. We all tried to pretend as if it were any other weekend, which we knew it wasn't. I tried to hang out with the kids as much as possible. During the week, I said goodbye to most of the people in my world, including my sister and brother-in-law, on Friday. Saturday was my last full day and night at home, and I was just trying to keep myself together. I took my mom to church on Saturday evening, for a couple of reasons. Number one was to say goodbye the day before I would leave. Secondly, I didn't want to go to my own church, where too many people would try to talk to me at a time when I just wanted to be alone with my family. Before church, Mom and I stopped by the cemetery, so I could say goodbye to my dad, who had passed away the previous September. It was something I felt I needed to do before I left.

After church, I took my mom home. She then remembered she had forgotten to go to the bank for a money order for me to take to prison. I would need to purchase food out there from the prison commissary with an ID card, which would be used like a credit card. However, I had to bring a money order out there with which to start my account, so I needed to go back on Sunday to pick up the order from my mother.

On Saturday night, my last full night at home, I watched TV with the family, and talked to Kathleen. We reminisced about everything, from the time we had met, to our children, family vacations, politics, and the future. If anything, we tried to be upbeat, and to put whatever positive spin we could on a terribly tragic situation.

When I woke up Sunday morning, I knew it was hours now instead of days before I would report to prison. This, by far, would be the hardest day of my life. If any one day would define the pain of this nightmare, it was that day.

Quite honestly, I can't remember a lot from that Sunday, except the rest of my goodbyes. I finally said goodbye to Mom early in the day; which, to say the least, was quite emotional. To that day, my mom held out hope that her son would not have to go to prison. She prayed and prayed, but at the end, I told her God has a reason for everything.

When I returned home, I sat on the front porch and watched the boys play as some of the neighbors came over to wish me well. I remember my mother-in-law, Pat, coming over without her husband. My father-in-law, Wally, a wonderful guy, couldn't stop, because surprisingly, it was too hard for him to see me; he just wanted to say goodbye on the phone. Each and every goodbye became harder and harder. Everyone I saw had that painful look in their eyes. I think the last people I saw were my sister-in-law and brother-in-law, who stopped by in the early evening. They probably stayed about an hour or so, and left around 7:30 p.m. Afterwards, Kathleen closed the door and shut the blinds. Then, I called my father-in-law, who assured me that everything would be fine. He said he would take care of Kathleen and the kids. He also told me to get home as early as I could.

I now needed to get myself ready to leave. I showered and put on some fresh clothes—my dark blue nylon sweat pants, a gold T-shirt, a gold fleece sweatshirt, and gym shoes. The clothes I wore were the only ones I could bring. I could take a week's supply of all prescriptions, my contact lenses, and eyeglasses. When I finished dressing and putting my prescriptions in a bag, I had nothing else to do but sit with my family for the last two hours.

The hardest time was yet to come. Jack and Bobby were nervous, and they wanted to stay up and see me leave. I knew that would be much too hard on them, so I set up their sleeping bags and pillows on the floor in front of the TV, and told them to relax, while I prayed that they would fall asleep. As they lied down, Jack had tears in his eyes, and Bobby looked nervous. I told them everything would be fine, that the time would go fast, and to please listen to Mommy. Those were the last words I said to them. An hour later, they were fast asleep. The rest of the time, Kathleen, Nina, and I just sat with the TV on, and talked off and on. At times, I thought the silence would kill me, as I watched the clock downstairs getting closer to 11:00 p.m. While we sat there, Nina said very little about anything, but every so often she would look over at me, and just smile. Kathleen kept getting up to do something—putting clothes in the washer, folding clothes, and making lunches. She couldn't sit still. Finally, at the end, she sat down next to me, and all I could do was hold her hand as tightly as possible. In our sixteen years of marriage, we never did a lot of hand-holding, but that night, I did not want to let her hand go.

At just before 11:00 p.m., the phone rang. It was Ray telling me they were parked by the garage, waiting for me. The thought of saying goodbye tore my heart and soul apart. I cannot begin to describe how heart-wrenching and horrible the next few minutes were to me. I didn't wake up the boys; they were still sound asleep.

I gave each of them a couple of kisses and little hugs as I whispered to each of them, "I love you."

I already had tears in my eyes as I went up to Nina, who was quiet and scared, and sitting on the couch. We hugged, kissed, and told each other, "I love you." As Kathleen walked with me outside to the garage, I waved one last time to Nina, and blew kisses toward her and the boys. It was, to say the least, a very somber moment. Kathleen and I were both crying, and neither one of us wanted to say goodbye.

When Kathleen finally said to me it was time to go, I don't know how long we hugged outside the car. The guys were sitting in the car as Kathleen and I said our final goodbyes. During those moments, all I could think about was how sorry I was that I had hurt Kathleen and the kids, and how it felt to have my heart ripped out of my chest. The loss and ultimate despair I felt were beyond description. Finally, I forced myself to jump into the car's back seat. All I could do was watch as Kathleen stood by the garage while we pulled away. I cried as Kathleen waved, and when we reached the end of the alley, I gave one final wave. Then Kathleen turned, and walked into the garage.

It was probably a good thirty-to-forty minutes before my emotions subsided. Most of the time, I was fairly quiet, just thinking about the family, and how lonely and empty I felt. The trip was going to take anywhere between nine and ten hours, so I tried, as difficult as it was, to fall asleep. I dozed off quite a bit as we drove across Indiana and Ohio. I do remember pausing at a few rest stops along the way. I don't know if it was due to all of the soda we were drinking during the trip, or our nerves, but we did stop often.

We drove most of the night before hitting Pennsylvania. I remember thinking that I would try to fall asleep again before we got to Pittsburgh, because once there, I would only be about an hour away from my new home for the next year or more.

There is no way to accurately describe how I felt on my way to Morgantown, because you would have to experience that situation yourself in order to feel that same sense of loneliness and despair. If I live for another thirty or forty years, I will never forget the sorrow and pain I experienced when I left home that September 10 to go to prison.

CHAPTER 18

MORGANTOWN

The trip from Chicago to Morgantown was pretty much a blur. I slept off and on all night. Around 8:00 a.m., on 9/11, I awoke to the bright sun, while we sat in a traffic jam on the way to Pittsburgh. As I gazed outside the window, I wondered how the hell I had put myself in this situation. Don, "J.R.," and Ray were trying during the whole trip to keep me as upbeat as possible, but as we got closer to the West Virginia border, everyone in the car seemed to grow quieter.

As we crossed the border into West Virginia, the scene was quite picturesque, with mountains and trees everywhere. It was not long before we saw the hustle and bustle of a college campus, West Virginia University. Of course, being a sports nut, I wanted to catch a glimpse of the football stadium, which I did, along with the rest of a quickly moving and vibrant campus.

The guys, naturally, were starving from the all-night drive, and since it was only 9:30 a.m., they wanted to stop for breakfast. I reluctantly agreed, but only if we found the prison's location first. Then we could take our time in Morgantown, because I knew I wouldn't be late.

As we followed the directions, we turned up and down a number of winding roads and not surprisingly, got lost a few times. The streets were fairly narrow, and it seemed as if almost every house and apartment were occupied by college students. After about a half hour, we regained our bearings, and turned up a steep road. Don then said we were only a couple of minutes away. As we turned down the road, it seemed as if we were in the middle of a forest, with trees everywhere. We drove past a park and a couple of small manufacturing plants, when we came upon the prison. At first glance, it almost looked like a retirement home or a boys' camp. I could see a few buildings in a valley, surrounded by hills everywhere.

The first thing I saw was a decent-sized brick building, where a guard was stationed. Directly in front of the building was an automatic white gate that was currently in the downward position. We saw the sign "Morgantown Federal Correctional Institution," and we quickly turned into the parking lot. I told Don since it was only about 10:00 a.m., to park at the end of the lot, so I could get out and get a closer look. However, Ray, Don, and "J.R.," in unison, loudly objected, fearing that if we parked the car and the guard saw us, I would probably have to report right away, so we quickly exited the parking lot.

The guys were now on the verge of collapse, and their stomachs were growling. Don turned around and headed to downtown Morgantown. On our way back, we probably saw every fast food restaurant imaginable, but not one diner that served breakfast. While Don kept driving, I grew increasingly tense, with absolutely no appetite whatsoever. From the car's back seat, I looked at Ray, leaned forward to Don and "J.R.," and told all three that I needed to get this whole ordeal started, and that they should turn around and take me back to the prison. After I said that, you could have heard a pin drop all the way to about a block away from the prison. I then told Don to pull into a parking lot of a local business. When he parked the car, I just jumped out to get one last breath of fresh air and freedom. As we all stood outside the car, each one of my friends offered his support. My closest friend in both politics and life, Ray, just kept telling me to stay strong, and that the time would go fast. I knew that Ray was as nervous and as frightened of the unexpected as I was.

In the back of the car was a cooler Don had brought along for the trip. I opened it to see what was left inside. We still had some

Pepsi, Diet Pepsi, Mountain Dew, and water. I wanted one last Pepsi
before they would drop me off. I also needed to put my eye contacts
in, because I wore my glasses all night, and wanted to look, or at
least feel, confident.

The last few minutes outside the car were my private moments.
The car was parked at the end of the lot, overlooking a deep gulley.
There appeared to be about a thirty-foot drop to the bottom, where
a narrow creek ran as far as the eye could see. While I stood there, I
knew the guys who had all climbed out of the car, were talking, but
for a few minutes, I couldn't hear a word they said. I sipped my Pepsi,
and was craving a cigarette; it was already six days since either Ray
or I had one. Then, for the last time, I tried, as I had done for the
last ten months, to close my eyes, open them, and believe that I was
at home, in my bed and waking up, with a deep sigh of relief, to the
realization that this was all merely a bad nightmare. Unfortunately,
as in the recent past, I stood there in disbelief, knowing what now
faced me. I took the last couple of minutes to reflect on Kathleen,
Nina, Jack, and Bobby, and prayed fervently that they would all be
fine, and that we would be back together soon.

I then turned around and looked at my watch. It was10:25 a.m.
After a deep breath, I said to the guys, "Let's get this over with."

We all slowly got into the car; I was the last one in. I took one
last glance around, sat down, and looked out the window, while Don
drove up the short stretch of road. It was only about a minute before
we arrived at the prison. As soon as we pulled up to the building, the
gate rose upwards. I jumped out of the car and walked to the door at
the side of the building, where a guard, whose uniform patch read,
"Morgantown Bureau of Prisons," was stationed. He was probably
in his forties, with a medium build, short-cropped black hair, and a
somber expression on his face. I quickly told him that my name was
Jim Laski, and that I was here to report to prison.

He simply answered, "Empty out your pockets."

I had approximately eighteen dollars in cash, about six money
orders totaling about $700.00, my driver's license, a Swiss Army
watch, and about three holy cards—one to St. Jude, as a prayer for
strength, one to St. Francis, and one motivational card from my wife,

reading, "Don't quit." I also had a plastic bag with a list and supply of my medications. The guard quickly gathered up the cards and the watch and told me I could not keep them. I quickly motioned to the guys who were standing by the car, to wait. The guard gave me the okay to go back. I quickly gathered up the cards and the watch, and ran out to the car, as he followed. I don't remember whom I gave them to, because Ray, Don, and "J.R." were all standing nervously around.

I knew it was time to say goodbye, so each of the guys gave me a hug and a kiss, and wished me well. As my eyes welled up with tears, I told them to watch out for Kathleen and the kids, and to check on them periodically. With tears in their own eyes, they all promised they would. Our emotions were running high, so I looked at them and said it was time to go. I turned and walked back toward the door where the guard was standing, stepped around him, and entered the building. As I turned around, he pushed a button, and the gate went back down. I stood there and looked through the big viewing window as my friends drove off, straight down a long, narrow driveway to the road. As they made a right-hand turn, they could see me as I returned their last-second wave. Wiping the tears rolling down my cheeks, I watched for a split second as the car quickly traveled out of my line of sight.

I then turned to the guard. He first gave me a breathalyzer, to see if I had been drinking, and then he told me to sit down, as he pointed to a chair that was about three feet away from his desk. While I sat there waiting, he took a preliminary written inventory of what he had gathered. During the time it took him to record each item, he accepted a delivery from Fed Ex, and allowed a food delivery truck access to the compound. Meanwhile, feeling all alone, all I could think about was my family.

Probably fifteen minutes went by before a female officer, a young woman probably in her late twenties, about five-foot-five with medium-length brown hair, and a fair complexion, walked in. I don't recall much else about her, except her abrupt personality. She and the other guard exchanged pleasantries, and he gave her the items he had collected from me. She then told me to get up and follow her out the door.

As we walked out of the building, I noticed that the entrance to the complex and the guards' buildings were elevated, and actually on a hill. We walked downhill with a bird's-eye view of the entire complex.

The female guard then looked at me, pointed sharply to her left, out over the compound, and said, "Whatever you do here, you don't want to end up over there."

As I looked, I couldn't believe what I saw. It was a brick building, maybe 125 feet long, and 120 feet wide, with barbed wire, and I mean real barbed wire, in rolls over the entire foot of the building, with a fifteen-foot brick wall that provided the base of the razor wire, which extended another forty feet. She affectionately called this place the "SHU," which stood for "Special Housing Unit," another name for a maximum security isolation area where inmates who broke the rules were sent for punishment. When I saw that building, I thought, "Where the hell am I?" since I assumed this was a minimum security camp.

As she led me down the road to another brick building, I wondered what else was in store for me. She opened the door, and escorted me to what she told me was the Visiting Center. As we walked down the hall, we approached a tall gentleman in uniform behind a long counter. She then told me to sit down in a chair that was in front of the counter, and handed the guard all my money orders for deposit. He told her that paperwork needed to be filled out separately on each money order. After multiple frowns and sighs, she then told me to get up and follow her. She escorted me a few yards down to another building, which was the Processing Center.

She led me down a short hallway, an open area, where another guard, a man with short, salt-and-pepper hair, was sitting. He wore glasses that were too dark for his relatively red, patchy complexion. He also had a pudgy nose, and a round face. What I most remember about him, though, was his mean glare and arrogant smirk. He called me over to the back of the room, where he informed me that he was going take my fingerprints. My fingerprints were taken twice before, several months ago, so I was quite accustomed to the process by then. If I remember correctly, this time the computer only rejected one of my prints, which we had to do over again.

The guard then led me to another room, which appeared to be some type of changing room. The room wasn't very big, and it had about four or five large bins with various items of prison attire, including shirts, socks, pants, underwear, and shoes. As I stood in the corner, he told me to disrobe. He stood there and watched while I took every stitch of clothing off. When I was completely naked, he ordered me to lift my testicles up. Then, he had me turn around, bend over, and spread my buttocks cheeks. When he was satisfied I hadn't carried any contraband in, he started handing me clothes from the bins, but without any regard to size. He first handed me peach-colored boxer shorts that looked thin and worn, then khaki pants, which were two sizes too big, and a T-shirt that looked like a surgeon's faded olive scrub shirt. Like the pants, it was also two sizes too big; one side of the shirt, which I constantly kept pulling up, actually hung off my left shoulder. To complete my outfit, he handed me two socks, one dark green, and the other gray, along with a pair of canvas beach or deck slip-ons and two mismatched shoes, one blue and the other teal. After I put everything on, I couldn't help but think I must have looked like a clown. Everything was either too big or didn't match. In fact, I had about six different colors on. The guard just grinned, while I kept my head down, feeling totally humiliated.

Next, I was told to step over to another station, which was about ten feet from the changing room, to get my ID picture. I stood in front of what I would call a neutral-colored screen, behind which were lines and numbers to measure height. The guard flashed a couple of shots with a camera, and was finished. A couple of minutes later, he handed me my ID card—a sturdy, plastic card, with the texture of a credit card. The card stated, "U.S. Department of Justice, Federal Bureau of Prisons," then, in big, bold print, "18413-424," which was my ID number, and finally, "Laski, James J., DOB 10-38-1953. EYE: BL. HT. 5'10." From the lower left-hand corner, all the way to the middle of the card, was a scanning bar, next to which was the word, "INMATE." The guard handed me the card, and told me I should keep it in my possession at all times. It would be scanned at all meals, and used for all commissary, vending machine, and laundry purchases—basically, for everything.

The guard then informed me that he was going to process me into the system. However, before he finished, he glanced at the female guard who escorted me in, and they quickly whispered to each other. He then told me to follow him, and we walked about ten feet, where, to my shock, he unlocked a cell door, and ordered me to step in. The cell was maybe eight-by-eight, with just a toilet and a sink. There was also a gray metal bunk extending from the wall. After I was locked in, he told me, with a silly-ass smirk, he was going to lunch, but that he would be back. Before he left, he handed me a prison handbook through the cell bars, and told me to read it while he was gone. It was close to 11:30 a.m. when the two guards then left for lunch.

As I turned and looked at the cell I was in, I thought I was having either an anxiety attack or a heart attack. I was dizzy, sweating profusely, and had a difficult time breathing. I sat down on the metal cot to try to regain my composure, and started to read the prison handbook, but I couldn't even tell you what I'd read. I just paced back and forth, feeling a little claustrophobic, and hoped the time would pass quickly.

An hour later, I heard a door open from a distance, but from where the cell was located, I couldn't see anybody. However, it wasn't long before I heard the voices of the same two guards discussing how good their lunch had been. After they had exchanged a few more pleasantries, the male guard, whom I will call "Mr. Sunshine," opened the cell door and let me out.

Now he told me to sit down and wait for both the psychologist and the doctor. About ten minutes later, Dr. Roth, a man whose black, frizzy hair made him look like a mad scientist, walked in. He told me to step into his office. After sitting down and taking a deep breath, Dr. Roth asked me how I was feeling. For a split second, I wanted to say, "How do you think I feel?" But I just simply told him that I felt a little nervous.

He informed me that that was normal, but then he asked if I felt suicidal.

I emphatically answered, "No!"

He then asked about all the prescriptions I was taking, and I gave him the list I had brought with me. After looking it over briefly, he got off his chair and said he would talk to me again soon. As he was leaving, he told me to wait in the office, and to wait for the doctor. Within a few minutes, a short, thin man in a white smock with the name "Dr. Watson" clearly printed on it, walked in. I couldn't tell by his dark complexion whether he was Middle Eastern or Pakistani, but I knew he wasn't from this country. At any rate, he was a no-nonsense type of guy, as I soon realized when he sat down and began asking me about my medications. I then took out a plastic bag, which I had brought from Chicago. I figured I'd be safe, and bring a two-week supply with me. He quickly confiscated all my sedatives and anti-anxiety medications, as well as sinus spray and pills, cholesterol medicine, and eczema cream. He informed me that most of these the prison did not carry, but that he would get comparable substitutes. He then wrote down a few notes, told me to report to the clinic pill line at 7:00 p.m., and had me follow him out of the office, where he turned me back over to "Mr. Sunshine."

It was now 3:00 p.m. My favorite guard then handed me a neatly and tightly rolled blanket, which also included another blanket, two sheets, and a pillow case. Then he quickly led me out into the compound.

I was amazed by how big the complex appeared. The first thing I noticed was the beautiful pond, which was probably one-hundred feet long and maybe thirty feet wide, with about ten benches surrounding its perimeter. To the left was a chapel with beautiful, stained glass windows in front, its roof shaped just like the bow of a boat, which I later learned was patterned after Noah's Ark. There were a number of other structures that looked like education buildings, surrounded to the right by trees, and a narrow walkway, with grass everywhere. One of those buildings was a large cafeteria with windows that stretched along the entire front of the building, and which appeared to accommodate at least 500 people. As we continued to walk straight ahead, I saw two large hard-back courts, several tennis or racquetball courts, an outdoor weight room pit, two bocce ball courts, and two horseshoe pits. As we continued, I saw numerous hills and mountains, and what appeared to be housing units all over the grounds.

The guard then led me over a narrow bridge, maybe four-to-six-feet wide and thirty feet long. This bridge was built of metal railings, with a concrete base and floor over a beautiful, clear stream that continued through the heart of the complex. As I walked over the bridge, which had a noticeable incline, and up a steeper sidewalk to the front of a housing unit, I saw inmates walking in and out of that building. They all had khaki pants and either white T-shirts or short-sleeve khaki shirts. (I later found out T-shirts were allowed during the summer months instead of matching khaki shirts, if you chose to wear them.) When I reached the front of the building, I saw a lightly colored brick one-story structure with windows everywhere, but which had been designed with a center, and four wings. As I walked to the front door, I saw a fairly large brass or metal sign with a black base and gold trim, and lettering clearly spelling out the name, "Alexander Unit."

As I walked through the front doors, my first reaction was, "This is *not* a camp." The noise was unbearable, with inmates everywhere yelling up and down the corridors. I'd never been in a state facility, but what I'd seen from news updates looked very similar. I could also tell immediately that this was not a white collar camp. It did not service East Coast high rollers; in fact, the majority of the inmates were from Baltimore, Cleveland, Detroit, and various parts of North Carolina and Virginia.

I was immediately escorted into the Alexander guards' office, which was approximately twenty feet straight ahead from the front doors, and up two steps. The office was quite small, with only a computer, a coffeemaker, and what appeared to be mail slots with "2" printed on the wall. At this point, everything was a blur, and all I remember was a guard whom I couldn't even describe giving me my bunk assignment, which was "C 28, Upper." Since I had no idea where the C-wing was, the guard called an inmate who was standing outside his office, to escort me. He was a nice enough guy who was in prison for a parole violation, but who would be leaving in about a month. We exchanged pleasantries, and he offered his assistance if I had any questions. He gave me a quick tour and pointed out four different hallways that led to the A, B, C, and D wings. As we walked down the long hallway to the C-wing, I noticed five phones on the wall to my left that were next to what I assumed was the C-wing public bathroom; another fifteen feet down were two big metal doors that swung open. As we walked through the doors, the place looked, misleadingly, like a dormitory from a boys' camp to me.

The C-wing dorm was both wide and long, and was exactly the same dimensions as the other three wings in Alexander. There were four rows of bunk beds lined up and down the unit. My bunk was located down the middle, second from the end. This was a tiny space called a cubicle, or "cube," which consisted of the two bunk beds (with a little three-ring metal ladder built onto the bed frames) and a small wall unit desk, along with two chairs and two lockers. The bottom bunk was more spacious, and its adjacent locker actually included a second set of shelves.

As I looked around, the inmate told me that he had to do something else, and simply said, "Good luck," and then he told me not to forget to make the bed with those rolled-up linens I'd been carrying.

Before he left, I noticed I did not have a pillow on top of my mattress, which by the way, was quite old, with a couple of severe tears in the middle, exposing both the foam and feathers inside. He told me that it was 3:00 p.m., and that the laundry room was closed for the day, so I wouldn't be able to get a pillow until the next morning, which meant I had to improvise for the night. With that, I proceeded to make my bed, which turned into quite a job, since I had never made an upper bunk bed in my life. While making the bed, I noticed how quiet it was, but I also realized that it was eighty degrees and sunny outside, so my roommates were either outside enjoying the weather, or they were working at their daily jobs, with the exception of about five inmates, who were sleeping in their bunks.

It was 3:45 p.m. when the loud speaker went off, and the voice on the other end said, "Re-call! Re-call! All inmates report to your units for the 4:00 p.m. count! The compound is closed!"

Within a couple of minutes, there were inmates swinging doors open, and they were talking and laughing while heading for their respective bunks. As they walked by me, I would say about half stopped and said "hello," while the other half just walked by and stared. As the wing started to fill up, I began to get a little nervous again. This was a totally different experience for me, and more importantly, the most difficult environment I had ever known. No sooner did I finish making my bed, my roommate bunkie stepped into the cube. He was a middle-aged African-American man, about five-foot-nine, and probably about forty pounds overweight, as he was over 200 pounds. He had very short hair, almost in a crew cut, and his face was aged, with spot and pock marks from earlier in his life.

He introduced himself with a deep, guttural, bass voice, "Hello, I'm Norman."

I didn't know if that was his first or his last name, and I chose not to ask. There was no handshake involved, or a long exchange of pleasantries; all I learned was that Norman was from Ft. Wayne, Indiana, and that he had been at Morgantown for over four years, because of drugs. He did inform me that at 4:00 p.m., the guards would walk up and down the aisle to make sure all inmates had been accounted for on the complex. He also told me that during the count, I had to stand in my cube. As soon as Norman told me that, the loud speaker went off again.

The man on the other end sternly said, "4:00 p.m. count! Report to your cubes!"

While I stood in front of my bunk for my first 4:00 p.m. count, I actually said to myself, "You really *are* in prison now!" Then, I wondered how many more of these counts I would have to face during my stay.

Suddenly, an inmate yelled, "On your feet!"

Out of the corner of my eye, I saw a guard dressed in a white shirt and dark blue slacks, briskly walking down the far right aisle, looking both to his right and left, and counting each inmate. Going in the reverse direction, was another guard, who started down the left aisle and finished down our aisle, also conducting a count. So, at the end, both met at the wing's entrance to compare their counts.

I then heard, as I would in most cases, the words, "Count is good!"

That meant that we could start moving around again.

After the guards finished the 4:00 p.m. count, we had about forty-five minutes to kill before being called to dinner. Since I didn't really know anyone else there, I sat on my bed, just watching everyone else. The rest of the inmates either went to mail call, which was done every weekday, right after the afternoon count, or to one of the four TV rooms. Some just decided to lie down on their bunks.

At approximately 5:00 p.m., the loud speaker again went off, to announce which unit would be first for dinner rotation. Each week, various prison officials, who would inspect each of the seven units (Bates, Bennett, Byrd, Carlson, Randolph, Alexander, and Gerard) for cleanliness and sanitation, would determine the rotation each week. The unit with the highest score (the cleanest) would be the first in the meal rotation for lunch and dinner for the entire week, beginning Sunday and ending on Saturday. The order of the units called was quite important when you have 1,300 inmates, because in many cases, the earlier you are called to meals, the warmer the food usually is. Sometimes, bigger portions were given earlier, and you were never in jeopardy of getting a substitute for something if the kitchen ran out of an item by the time your unit had been called.

That week, Alexander was number three in the rotation, which made me think just by my quick observation of the bathroom and the living quarters, that if they had been third, I would have hated to have seen the bottom four units. It took about fifteen minutes between intervals for all the units to be called.

I think it was close to 5:30 p.m. when the loud speaker announced, "Alexander Unit to main line!"

The only comparison I can make to about 300 men pushing their way out of a front door would be to a herd of cattle racing out of a corral. I stayed in the middle of the pack, so I wouldn't get lost.

The distance between Alexander to the cafeteria was about one-and-a-half city blocks, which would be a pain in the ass in inclement weather. As we walked up, I saw a mass of humanity traveling in two rows through two brown double doors. As I walked in, the scene reminded me of my meals in high school, where there were hundreds of students who would just pile in, and sit at tables lined up everywhere. As I walked down one of the two rows, I saw an official or guard standing in front of a monitor; behind him was a picture screen. When each inmate had gotten to the front of the line, he would take his ID card and scan it below a device that seemed to shoot out red laser lines. When his card was hit, a beep would go off, and his picture would be flashed on both the screen and the monitor. After swiping my card through the device, I went down a line where fellow inmates behind a counter served the food. I can't remember clearly, but my first meal consisted of a sloppy Joe and French fries. After I was served my food on a tray, I went down another line, where there were various vegetables and salads, along with a soda machine and a water dispenser. I think I poured a Coke into my glass. All I can remember from that point on was finding an open table, and for the first few minutes, sitting by myself and trying to eat. Before I knew it, other inmates sat down. They politely said "hello," and ate their dinners without saying another word to me. As soon as they left the table, I immediately got up to leave. When leaving the cafeteria, all inmates must take their trays to either side, where there were open counters. Before handing the tray to the inmate who was working the dishwashing detail, we first had to place our plastic utensils down a shoot, where they were washed separately.

As I exited from one of the two doors on either side of the mess hall, I saw an open area that I would call a quad. As I mentioned earlier, there are buildings surrounding this area, with a pond, and benches and trees everywhere. All I could see were inmates walking or sitting on the benches, or just standing around. Then, right in front of the pond, I stopped, frozen, and just looked around, not knowing what to do next. I felt faint, with sweat pouring down my forehead.

I thought I was about ready to pass out, when, suddenly, I heard, "Jim Laski! Jim Laski!"

I turned around anxiously to see who could possibly know my name. When I looked, I saw a gentleman walking briskly toward me. He was in his mid-forties, about seven-feet tall and quite stocky, over 200 pounds, with grayish, short hair, and a matching mustache and goatee. He was dark-skinned, possibly Hispanic, and wore a smile from ear-to-ear.

When he came up to me, he asked, "Are you city clerk Jim Laski?"

I replied quickly, but apprehensively, "Yes. Who are you?"

He answered that he was Carlos Ayala from Chicago, and shook my hand. He told me that he had recognized me from my pictures in the newspaper, and from reports on TV. I was curious (or I should say, "skeptical") about his friendliness, but he immediately informed me that he, too, had been involved in Chicago politics. Before his incarceration, he had served under Alderman Danny Solis as a precinct worker. After having heard that, he became slightly more comfortable, and we sat down on one of the benches next to the pond.

Carlos spent the next hour giving me a synopsis of his life and family, and explained that he was in prison for cocaine use. I actually took an interest in his stories, and was quite relieved that I had met someone from Chicago. As we continued to talk, I found out that Carlos had already spent over fifteen months at Morgantown, and really seemed to know the place from top to bottom. This was my chance to ask a number of questions regarding prison life. One thing I quickly learned was that, with Carlos, it was difficult to get a word in edgewise, so I remained a patient, good listener, and waited for my opportunity to jump in, which at that time, felt like an eternity. Carlos offered his assistance to take me the following morning to the laundry room to be fitted for, and to pick up my khaki uniform, which was a mandatory dress item for most individuals on the compound. Before he ran off, we had agreed to meet in front of the Alexander Unit, around 6:30 a.m. We exchanged a few basic pleasantries while we walked together to our respective units.

I forgot to ask Carlos which housing unit he lived in, hoping against hope that maybe, just maybe, he also lived at Alexander. Those hopes were quickly laid to rest when Carlos stopped walking as I approached Alexander's doors. I reluctantly turned to him with a half-hearted smile, and asked where he lived. He quickly replied by pointing to the building about fifty yards to his right, and said he resided over there, in the Bates Unit. At least Carlos lived next door to me. Before he left, Carlos shared one more piece of information that would be very important to my future. He informed me that he was enrolled in the drug and alcohol rehab program, for which inmates received time off their sentences if they successfully completed the class, and everyone in that program resided at Bates.

I felt an even closer attachment to Carlos now, because my twenty-four month sentence had included Judge Norgle's recommendation for a rehab program at this facility. My goal was simple—get into the program, complete it, and get as much time off my sentence as possible (which, in my case, would be about ten-to-twelve months). As I wished Carlos a good evening, I thought about how to go about enrolling in the next class as soon as possible.

When I returned to Alexander, I couldn't wait to fall asleep, and put this day behind me. When I looked at the clock, though, and saw it was only 8:30 p.m., I knew I had some time to kill. As I looked around, I saw inmates watching TV, playing cards and chess, reading, or just standing around, talking to each other. I again felt desperate and alone, and wondered what it would take on my part to make it through this ordeal.

The next couple of hours for me consisted of just checking out everything there was in the unit, from the various TV rooms, each of which had designated programming, to the card room, and even a quiet room. At the same time, I kept one eye on the clock, and anxiously waited for the 10:00 p.m. count. It seemed like an eternity, but I finally heard the announcement on the loudspeaker to return to our cubes for the day's final count.

The 10:00 p.m. count was different from the 4:00 p.m. one, simply because we could be sleeping or sitting in chairs when the guards came in. The afternoon count was the only one we actually had to stand up for during the week.

After the guards completed the count, I quickly removed my pants and shoes, and jumped into bed. The main lights were turned off around 10:15 p.m. I lay in my bunk and did the same thing I had done at home when I went to bed; I said my prayers. I asked God to protect Kathleen and the kids. I also called on Him to watch over my mom, and my in-laws, Pat and Wally, along with the rest of my immediate family. Lastly, I asked God to please walk with me and guide me during my stay in prison. I told him that I was scared, and heeded His help. With that, I finished by asking for forgiveness, and by simply thanking Him for everything I had accomplished in my life.

September 11, 2006, finally came to an end. As I lay there in the dark, trying to close my eyes, for the next thirty minutes or so, I thought about my family, and tears rolled down my cheeks. Sometime after that, the stress of the day finally forced me to fall asleep, at least for a few hours.

The morning actually came quickly, with inmates getting up around 6:00 a.m. to prepare for their daily jobs. As the lights came on about 6:15 a.m., I carefully climbed down from my bunk. I quickly dressed and brushed my teeth, so I wouldn't be late for my meeting with Carlos. About 6:25 a.m., I stepped outside of Alexander, and proceeded down the sidewalk, where Carlos had been waiting for me at the foot of the bridge.

The sun was just coming up over the mountains as we headed over to the laundry room, which was located next to the cafeteria on the compound. Carlos was proving to be a crafty individual. Instead of going to the front door and waiting in line, he directed me to the back of the building, and to the loading docks and a back door, which Carlos now led me through. When he entered, half of the employees came up to greet him. It was obvious that Carlos had connections. We then walked over to a room that appeared to be locked. Carlos knocked on the door and waited about ten seconds, when another inmate opened the door. Carlos introduced himself, and asked for Doc; the inmate, in turn, asked him to wait, as he closed the door. About two minutes later, the door again opened, and out walked another inmate. This man was older, in his late fifties; he was short, only about five-foot-two, with gray hair, and a Hispanic complexion. When he saw Carlos, they embraced. Although he was an inmate, Doc, through his maneuvering and hard work over the years, had become the foreman of this operation—a position that entitled him to not only some perks, but also a lot of respect, which in a place like this was important.

As soon as Carlos introduced me to Doc and told him who I was, Doc called over three other inmates to assist me. Before I knew it, I had been fitted for a pair of black, ankle-high work boots. I also received five pairs of white briefs, and five white T-shirts. I was then taken into another room, where I was measured for my uniform. Soon, I was wearing a khaki shirt with a white label ironed on the garment's left side, with my last name, my registration number, and my laundry number, "1069" printed on the label. I also received two extra pairs of pants and two extra dress shirts. I thought I actually now looked like a Morgantown inmate. Before I left, I was given one more item that each new inmate receives—two rolls of toilet paper. In this facility, not all bathroom stalls in the residential units (and in some of the public areas) have toilet paper, so each inmate must bring his own when nature calls, and to never forget to lock the roll back up in his locker, or it will be stolen! Before I left, I thanked Carlos, who informed me that he now had to attend class that morning, so I headed back to the Alexander Unit by myself.

The first month of being in prison was difficult enough, let alone being housed at Alexander, which many considered the loudest, dirtiest unit in Morgantown. Alexander's reputation, as far as I knew, had always been bad—so much so that the guards called it "Thunderdome." The unit housed over 320 inmates, while it could realistically only accommodate half that amount. Eighty-five percent of Alexander's inmates were either African-American or Hispanic, many of whom were from the Washington, D.C., Baltimore, Cleveland, or Detroit areas. The real problem, however, was the age factor. Many of the inner-city kids from D.C. and Baltimore, for example, were in their early twenties, while the majority of Alexander's population were in their forties and fifties. Of course, there was also an education gap between most of the older criminals and the rest of the prison population. It was no exaggeration or misinterpretation to state that most of the conversations in Alexander either began or ended with the words "motherfucker," "fucker," or some derivative of "fuck." When you house older, more mature inmates, both white and of color, with gang-bangers who have a difficult time behaving responsibly, there are going to be problems. Most of the younger inmates came from state prisons that were closed. Due to overcrowding in other state prisons, they were moved to Morgantown. Many of them were drug dealers and violent criminals, who were now being housed with a good many non-violent "white collar" criminals. Many of us in Alexander routinely urged the prison to more closely consider age, type of crime committed, and even education before placing him in a particular unit. Even Warden Gutierrez agreed with this proposal, when later addressing our unit following a shakedown.

As I pointed out earlier, the meal rotation for each housing unit at Morgantown was based upon its sanitary conditions every week. It was no surprise that the Alexander unit was either last, or close to the bottom of the list. One of the reasons was Alexander's bathrooms. Inmates routinely left food in the sinks and the water fountains after cleaning off their dishes. Toilets and urinals were left, many times, un-flushed. In addition, many of the toilet seats were either dirty, or wet with urine. Shower stalls were caked with soap scum, or littered with hair on the floor from haircuts or shaving. Shower shoes, in any of the units, were an absolute necessity, in order to avoid any type of fungus or disease.

In addition, many of the inmates, from time to time, cooked their own meals in the unit's microwaves. The only problem with that was they would often leave their dirty bowls and dishes in their cubes for days on end, which left a nasty odor and created unsanitary conditions in the sleeping areas.

Before arriving at Morgantown, I was a very heavy smoker. I smoked a pack-a-day for over thirty years, although I recently underwent a fairly new treatment involving laser. Basically, the lasers target certain nerve endings in the ears, nose, and hands, and supposedly decrease a smoker's nicotine cravings. Needless to say, after two treatments, and consuming gallons of water, I felt pretty confident that I would be okay in prison. However, to my surprise, there was still plenty of smoking going on in this complex. When I first arrived, I saw big, red signs reading, "Smoking for Employees Only," and, as I walked by, I could smell the smoke. I thought no smoking meant just that, and for both inmates and employees, but as time went on, I actually smelled smoke on certain guards, and witnessed other guards chewing tobacco and spitting it in the wastebaskets. When it comes to inmates smoking, guards will usually look the other way, as long as the behavior isn't blatant. The most popular smoking spot in Alexander was the C-wing bathroom. For someone who had just quit smoking, it was difficult walking into that bathroom with its clouds of smoke. When I would walk out, my clothes would actually smell of cigarettes. The biggest joke about smoking at Alexander was that the inmates knew the times when the guards would walk out of the building for their own smoke break, and that's when they themselves would light up. So, in order to avoid the temptation, I quickly started using the D-wing bathroom, both day and night.

There were also times when I saw marijuana and alcohol in the bathrooms. Now remember, Morgantown FCI is noted for its drug and alcohol rehab center. The saddest testimony is that there are inmates who actually drink and smoke, and then brag about getting into the rehab program, just to get the time off, and when they get out, it will be back to business as usual for them.

All of this was very depressing to me during my first month of incarceration. I used to call my wife every day, just to tell her I couldn't take much more. Even making phone calls proved difficult. The phone area, which is located in the middle of the hallway right next to the bathrooms, is a popular congregating point for Alexander's inmates, many of whom know only one way of conversing with each other, and that is to yell. I had never been in a place, except for my kids' former day care center, where there was that much noise and commotion. Many of the younger inmates were the biggest culprits, often showing absolutely no respect for anyone else. Late evenings were a perfect example. Many of us actually wanted to go to sleep around 10:00 or 10:30 p.m., but were usually awakened at all different hours by yelling, loud music or conversations at 2:00, 3:00, or 4:00 a.m. I was hoping each and every day, that could I get into the rehab program, just so I could move out of Alexander.

My wife once told me, "The fish stinks from the head down," and that's exactly how I felt about Alexander's administrators—its two counselors, two case managers, and one unit manager. Those individuals were supposed to help counsel inmates, but in reality, they were insensitive, arrogant, mean-spirited, and rude. Many of the inmates I knew at Alexander were reluctant to ask the staff for help, because when they did, they would strongly imply that they were bothering them. In fact, numerous times I saw signs on their doors reading, "Don't Bother Me Unless It's an Absolute Emergency!" Once, when I asked one of the counselors about moving from Alexander because of the loud noise and the smoking, his response was a simple, cold and direct, "No. That will not happen." Those individuals looked down on, and had no respect for the inmates as human beings.

If there was one bright note during my first few weeks at Alexander, it was meeting a really nice guy by the name of John Tokosh, from Pennsylvania. He and I became good friends. John and I met at the beginning of my second week in prison. I was anxious to meet someone from the unit that I could talk with on a regular basis, and it just so happened that we started talking to each other while standing in the foyer of Alexander, just waiting to be called to lunch. As soon as we began conversing, we discovered many things we had in common. John had six children, and I had four. We were both earlier divorced, we were sports maniacs, and, most importantly, we were both romanticists who deeply loved and missed our families. John was in his mid-forties, but still with jet black hair and a mustache; he was around five-foot-ten and a little over 200 pounds, with a little bit of a stomach that hung over his pants. We had instantly become friends.

Over the next six weeks, while we were both waiting for job assignments, John and I began to walk around the cinder running track that circled the baseball diamond, which was located in the back complex, adjacent to the Alexander Unit. The track was also located at one corner of the prison, where we could clearly see the mountains, the stream at the bottom of the hill, the trees, and the hundreds of deer and geese that populated the area. Our routine further consisted of walking the one-fourth mile oval track from approximately 8:00 a.m. to 10:00 a.m., and in the afternoon from 1:00 p.m. to 3:00 p.m. We averaged between seven-to-ten miles a day, and during the first week, we each had lost about ten pounds. The most important part of our walks was not the exercise, but the release of tension, and the actual mental and emotional support we gave each other by just talking about our families, our beliefs, and our feelings about prison. We spoke often about our wives—how they had handled everything with such courage and determination; how much we loved and missed them; and how lonely we both were without our children. We also commiserated about how stupid we had both been in having made decisions that had put us in prison. We vowed that when we got out, any future decisions we would make would have to be in black and white, and that we would stay away from those gray areas that had gotten us into such trouble. One other topic John and I would frequently address was the importance of appreciating the little things in life, avoiding petty arguments with our loved ones, and spending less time in front of the TV watching sports, and spending more "quality time" with our families. I even went so far as to say that I would take accompanying Kathleen shopping over watching a sporting event on a big-screen TV. It was amazing how we analyzed ourselves, and spoke so openly about our faults and weaknesses. We often spoke with tremendous gratitude about our second chance in life, and the opportunity to make things right again with our loved ones.

As the weeks slowly moved by, I knew that another class would be starting soon at Bates, and that if I wanted to get home as soon as possible, I needed to be in that class.

Morgantown's drug and alcohol program was supposedly one of the premier programs in the entire country. To enroll in the class, an inmate not only needed a recommendation from his judge, but also supporting documentation in his PSI, as well as a favorable interview with a member of the DAPP (Drug and Alcohol Prevention Program) staff. In fact, on my second day at Morgantown, I submitted a cop-out, or request form for an interview to determine my status for the next class. Only two weeks later, their office called me in for my interview, which had basically consisted of questions from my PSI regarding what and how much I drank, as well as the different kinds of prescription drugs I was still taking. There were questions about my dad, who had also had a drinking problem, and how that experience affected me. Unfortunately, he only passed away last September, and I still found it hard to talk about his drinking.

I was taking Lorazepam (a form of Valium) and Lexapro, an anti-anxiety drug. In addition, like my father, I abused alcohol. Between the prescription drugs and the alcohol, I was on a downward spiral. After my indictment, I drank more and slept less. On most evenings, I would stay up until about 2:00 a.m. and consume approximately twelve beers a night. I would get up in the morning, around 6:30 a.m. to take my medications, and take either my daughter or my sons to school. I could not make it through each day unless I took my medications, and drank enough beer at night to put me to sleep. Kathleen, on many occasions, told me that I needed to chew gum or brush my teeth again before leaving the house, because I still had beer on my breath. There were times when I didn't want Kathleen to know how many beers I was drinking, so I would take some of the beer cans and put them in a separate bag, which I would throw in the trash can outside before going to bed. The young lady who interviewed me at Morgantown actually seemed quite concerned about my situation, since she was taking down many notes while I spoke to her. They told me I would be informed of my status in about two weeks. She must have sensed how anxious and nervous I had been about being in the program, because she told me not to worry, and that everything would be fine. I left her office feeling relaxed, and cautiously optimistic about being in the next class on November 6.

As each day went by in October, I was becoming more of a nervous wreck. I was hoping every morning that I would hear my name over the compound P.A. speaker to report to the J Complex Building to sign my contract. In the meantime, conditions were getting crazier at Alexander. The staff, including the unit manager, Mr. Adams, was getting stricter, and even petty, about certain rules. For example, one day a memo came out stating that between the hours of 7:30 a.m. and 4:00 p.m., we could not lie in our beds, use the microwaves, washing machine and dryer, or watch TV. After that memo, I thought there was going to be a riot in the unit. Many of the inmates believed that this was punishment for Alexander's having always either been last or next-to-last for the weekly sanitary inspection.

The memo had only been out less than twenty-four hours when some of Alexander's inmates retaliated. The following morning, none of the staff could get into their offices because there had been some type of material, wood, or cardboard strategically placed and pushed deeply into the door locks. Some of the locks could be easily fixed, but others had to be either taken apart or broken. Mr. Adams went crazy, and ordered all the TVs shut off for a month. He also ordered a shakedown. Each inmate was taken out of his wing, searched as he left, and placed in rooms as holding areas. Then, the correctional officers from all over the compound were summoned to tear apart each bed and bunk, in order to find any type of contraband—cigarettes, food taken from the kitchen, liquor, pills, and anything not on the commissary list. The whole process took about five hours, while our wing waited in the holding room. I asked one of the younger Correctional Officers, or COs, who was guarding the door, if I could use the bathroom. He simply stared at me, leaned over, and spat tobacco juice into a nearby wastebasket.

Before I could ask someone else about the bathroom, I was ordered out of the holding room, and into one of the counselors' offices, where a Mr. Schuman was waiting. Mr. Schuman was a counselor over at the Bates Unit, but at Morgantown, every one of the staff members, including case workers, counselors, drug treatment specialists, and pharmacists—even the priest and chaplain—is a Correctional Officer first, then his or her other position second. I spent about five minutes with Schuman, who asked me what I knew about the tampering of the locks and the ongoing smoking problems at Alexander. I told him I had no knowledge of either issue. He then told me to step out of the office, where two other individuals were standing. One happened to be Counselor Turner, from my unit, and the other was Dr. Baker, who was in charge of the DAPP. Baker was a chubby individual of medium height, fair-skinned, with short, blondish hair, and some noticeably feminine mannerisms. He was probably in his last thirties or early forties. As I walked out into the hallway, Baker called me over, and told me to take off my gym shoes, which he then examined. I also had to lift up my sweatshirt, so he could see if I was carrying anything. After Baker had cleared me, he instructed me to go to the front door. When I reiterated my request to use the bathroom, he told me to walk down to the recreation building, which was approximately one city block in distance, and use its restroom, and to wait for further instructions. By 11:00 a.m. I had rejoined my fellow inmates from C-wing. When we were allowed back into Alexander, it was close to 3:00 p.m. Each of us then had to straighten our bed and locker, all of which of which had been torn apart and gone through with a fine-tooth comb. At the end of the day, twelve inmates were removed from Alexander, and taken to the SHU.

At that point, morale seemed to be at an all-time low. My continued hope was that I would be moving out of Alexander to begin my rehab program. Unfortunately, I began to realize that the prison bureaucracy moved at its own pace, and that I had better get used to that fact.

Apart from the bureaucracy, one of the biggest issues we inmates had at Morgantown was the quality of medical attention and care. I was told that whatever happens, don't get sick. I first took that advice with a grain of salt, but as more and more people spoke to me, I began to have some grave concerns. Tom Mortimer, who still resides at Alexander, works in the medical building. Tom reminded me, both in his mannerisms and his physical appearance, of Oliver North. He's also a former Marine, and very adamant about the lack of medical care at the prison. According to Tom, there were over 200 inmates with AIDS or HIV, and another 300 with hepatitis. The problem was that Morgantown's medical care was severely limited. The institution had approximately 1,300 inmates, with only one acting physician. The rest of the staff consisted of physician assistants. There was no sick bay or infirmary on the compound. So if an inmate had a contagious illness, or a condition that needed to be monitored, or if he required specialized treatment including rest and isolation, none of those services were available. One inmate arrived here in a relatively normal condition, but according to a number of different inmates, he soon suffered numerous debilitating mini-strokes that impaired his speech. He was diagnosed with Lou Gehrig disease, and was given a two-year life expectancy. With less than six months left on his sentence, instead of being sent home, and because his wife had left him, he was instead sent to a women's medical facility in Kentucky to finish those remaining months.

Another inmate recently fell in the gymnasium and split his head wide open. He was taken to a nearby hospital for emergency surgery to close up the gash in his head. However, instead of keeping him in the hospital for a few days, the staff sent him back to prison the next morning with his head stitched up, and with no dressing on his wound. He was given a walker, and according to Tom, was in severe pain, and on the verge of collapsing. He was then sent back to the hospital to recuperate.

If an inmate is ill, he must report to sick call, which is held between 6:45 a.m. and 7:15 a.m. each day, except Thursday. Therefore, if you are an inmate, just don't get sick on a Thursday. At sick call, inmates must bring their ID cards, because they will be charged $2.00 off their commissary accounts to see the doctor or his or her assistants. If medical personnel decide that an inmate's situation is not an emergency, he or she may have to schedule another appointment. For example, an inmate named "Charlotte Rob" Stamper (because of his home town) long suffered from severe knee pain, even though he had been given a job that required him to walk outside and perform various maintenance duties! Unfortunately, when he reported for sick call, the medical staff told Rob to come back the following week, because they needed advance notice for x-rays and a knee scan. He was eventually told to get a knee brace, which he had to purchase on his own, from the commissary.

Another amazing—or shocking—fact about medical treatment is that there is no dentist or eye doctor on the compound. Many inmates who cracked a tooth, lost a cap, or had a toothache had to fill out request forms to see a dentist in town. Recently, one inmate had to take Ibuprofen for a toothache that he had been putting up with for over six months. John, who recently put in a request to have his teeth cleaned, was informed that since he had less than a year to go on his sentence, he was not eligible for any type of cleaning. If an inmate needed any type of eye exam, or if he required a prescription change in his eyeglasses, I don't know what he would do. As far as I know, Morgantown would have an eye doctor come in if necessary, but only once every six months.

Adjusting to life in federal prison is hard enough, without having to be literally frightened to death about getting sick there. I can't tell you how many inmates, especially those who have been here for an extended period, felt they had to devise their own preventive measures, just to fight off the common cold. At the very least, inmates needed to wash their hands as much as possible, and to buy every vitamin pill available at the commissary. A closer look definitely needed to be taken at federal camps and prison health care, not only in this institution, but also across the country.

As I quickly approached the end of October, I was still somewhat optimistic about entering the rehab program at Bates, and also anxiously anticipated my departure from Alexander, which for the most part was a nightmare. One particular story that sums up life here occurred at the end of my first week at the unit. It was somewhere around 3:00 a.m. that night. I got out of my top bunk to use the bathroom. While trying to climb down the three-rung ladder, I slipped, and literally tumbled downwards. I hit my metal locker and a plastic chair, and landed on the tile floor. I checked to see if I was bleeding, because I had used both my arms and legs to brace myself. When I realized there was no blood, I picked myself up slowly, and hobbled to the bathroom, with multiple bruises. About six weeks later, my bunk or cubemate, Shawn Norman, admitted to me that he actually heard me fall off the ladder. I immediately asked him why he didn't check on me after the fall. He said he really didn't know me very well at the time, and wasn't sure he even liked me. When he saw I wasn't seriously hurt, he simply rolled over and went back to sleep. That kind of attitude epitomizes the mindset here at Alexander. Shawn turned out to be a nice guy, but in prison, there would always be that emotional distance and suspicion, at least initially, between some inmates.

In my opinion, Alexander's unit manager, Mr. Adams, had never helped the inmates' cause. To my surprise, I found out that Adams was also Bates' unit manager. An African-American man, he was probably in his early forties, and with a stocky, football-type build (maybe around six feet, and about 250 pounds). In a way, he reminded me of a young Jim Brown. In addition, he had a very clear complexion and shortly cropped hair, and was an impeccable dresser. He always wore nice suits and sports coats, and when he dressed casually, lots of leather jackets, coats, and expensive sweaters. Unfortunately, that's where the compliments must end. He came across to many as very aloof and arrogant. A few weeks ago, when his office floor was being waxed, he took his rolling executive chair and sat in the middle of the hallway, watching everyone trying to work around him. Moreover, in the opinions of many of Morgantown's white inmates, he was a racist. John Bowman, an inmate from Pittsburgh, and a former, prominent attorney, told me that Adams seemed to have very little time for white inmates. I can say truthfully that not once in my first two months at Morgantown, did he ever call me into his office, even for a minute, in his role as unit manager, to introduce himself to me, or offer any type of concern or assistance, even if it wasn't sincere.

The only real conversation I ever had with him was on a Saturday morning, in late September. It was cold and rainy, and he was standing in the hallway talking football with two black inmates when I walked by. I said "hello" to him. He replied by mumbling back a faint "hello" of his own. I stopped and commented on the early fall-like weather in West Virginia. In response, he asked me where I was from, but with a smug look that clearly told me, "I don't really give a shit about you and what you have to say."

I answered, "Chicago."

He shrugged and said, "You should be accustomed to this type of weather."

Then, after hesitating, I asked him where he was from.

He quickly raised his hands, stared directly at me, and curtly replied, in a loud voice, "I can't answer that. It's against BOP (Bureau of Prisons) policy."

I then walked away. That was the last time I tried to interact with him. To many inmates, Adams was a pompous asshole who did absolutely nothing to help morale or improve conditions at his two units, especially Alexander. I can't remember one—not one—time when he offered any type of compassion or sensitivity to an inmate. What I will instead always remember is his arrogant scowl and demeaning remarks about most of the inmates at Morgantown.

If someone were to tell me that prison was supposed to rehabilitate inmates, I could state, unequivocally, that it certainly didn't begin at the Alexander Unit, because the only help or recourse to counseling that John Tokosh, Rob Stamper, and I had was our daily walks around the track. While walking, we would not only analyze our behavior, both inside and outside of prison, but we would also discuss our families, our faults, and most importantly, the meaningful changes each of us would make when returning home. As we learned every day, none of those discussions were possible with the Alexander staff. In fact, we started to realize that we needed to encourage as much self-help as possible on the compound, in order to maintain our well-being—physically, mentally, and emotionally.

I couldn't wait to say goodbye to the "Thunderdome."

CHAPTER 19

GOODBYE TO THUNDERDOME

It was October 27, around 8:00 a.m., and John, Rob, and I were taking our daily therapeutic walk. The morning was cloudy and cool, in the low fifties, with just a little drizzle. While we were walking, all I could think about was November 6, the starting date for the new RDAP class (the rehab program of the DAPP). It was only ten days away, and I hadn't yet heard a word. I knew I was driving my two walking buddies crazy over the past few weeks with my constant talk about the program, and my chances of getting in it. During the first few minutes of the walk, I wished John a happy forty-fifth birthday. When we first met, we commented on how our birthdays were only one day apart. Since the next day would be my birthday, the only present I wanted was to get into the program.

No sooner had I mentioned that wish, and then the compound loudspeaker went off.

The woman's soft voice on the other end announced, "Inmate Laski, report to J Complex."

That was the call I'd been waiting for over the past month and a half. I clenched my fist and jumped about a foot off the track. John and Rob couldn't have been nicer, as they congratulated me, and told me to hurry up and get over there.

Since I was in my sweatshirt and pants, I had to go back to Alexander and put on my khakis. When I returned to Alexander, other inmates had been informed that they, too, had heard my name called over the loudspeaker. There was no time for a shower, and I started throwing on my uniform.

Before I finished, the loudspeaker again went off, "Inmate Laski, report to J Complex."

I felt panic set in, as I tied my boots and ran out the door. Absolutely no running is allowed in the complex, so I walked as fast as I could without drawing attention to myself. The walk from Alexander to the J Complex was only from one end of the compound to the other, but instead of five minutes, it felt like five hours. When I reached Dr. Baker's office, his door was already open. As I walked in, Dr. Baker was sitting at the front desk, and the woman who had interviewed me for the program was standing directly to his right.

He quickly said, "Good morning," and I, in turn, apologized for my tardiness, explaining that because I was on the track, I needed to change clothes before coming over to the office. They both smiled, and Dr. Baker told me they had a contract for me to sign, enrolling me in the RDAP. I exhaled an enormous sigh of relief as I thanked both of them for my early birthday present. I was to go to the classroom on my left, read the contract, and sign my name on the four or five lines designated for my signature.

I quickly took the contract down to the classroom and signed my name before I had even read it. I noted, however, a litany of rules regarding basic behavior, some of which seemed a little petty, such as no holding spots for microwaves or TVs, no sunglasses, no untied boots or shoes, no hats in the treatment unit, etc. I then returned the contract to Dr. Baker. I thanked him again, and asked if the contract I had signed was for the November 6 class. He informed that the list of the forty individuals for the class would be posted on Monday, so I had the whole weekend to think about my decision.

That weekend was like most here at Morgantown, uneventful. The only highlight was Friday evening, when I called Kathleen to let her know I had signed the contract, and felt optimistic about my chances for the November class. On Saturday, which was my fifty-third birthday, I called home again, to talk to Nina, Jack, and Bobby. Whenever I talked to the boys, they always asked (at least Jack did) when I was coming home. It broke my heart whenever I had to tell them, "Maybe next year."

The only other significant change or news in my life occurred when the call-out sheet came out on Friday night. A call-out sheet was simply a collection of five or six sheets with the names of various inmates who had appointments, interviews, job placements, changes, education classes, or those who had been transferred to other units. By that time, I had been at Morgantown for seven weeks, and John, eight. Neither of us had found, or had even applied for a job. Most inmates were given two-to-three weeks upon arrival to find a job or the prison would find one for him. After all that time, we felt we had done a good job of staying under the radar. So, when I looked at the call-out sheet, I was hoping to see my name under the "Transfer" section, to the Bates Unit, which would mean that I had gotten into the November class.

Unfortunately, I found my name under "Job Placement" instead. To my disappointment, I was assigned to the morning kitchen duty. Since misery loves company, John found his name under the same heading. He would be working for the Communications Division, in the Facilities Department. My placement was a total surprise, but John's job had actually been pre-arranged through a couple of inmates I had met who lived in Bates, and who worked in Facilities.

I spent the rest of the weekend talking to the kitchen timekeeper, who happened to live in Alexander, about my new job. My hours would be from 6:00 a.m. to 12:30 p.m. Tuesday through Saturday, and my days off would be Sunday and Monday. He basically told me that I would be doing a little bit of everything, from serving food, to cleaning up. In addition, I could not only change my days off, but when I had started my rehab program, I would only have to work half-days, as all RDAP students did on the compound. When I had received that news, I felt better, and looked forward to Monday. I wanted to find out one way or another if I would be starting class within a week.

I could hardly sleep Sunday night. I tossed and turned just waiting for Monday. It was still dark out when I had gotten out of bed. I also realized that it would be my last day off for awhile, because kitchen duty would start tomorrow. As soon as all the offices and education buildings opened at 9:00 a.m., I scurried out of Alexander to the J Complex, to look for that all-important list. To my frustration, nothing was posted, so I headed back to Alexander to check and see if anything had been posted there. The rest of the morning and afternoon was simply an exercise in futility. I went from building to building, trying to find that secret list. I even had a hot tip that the kitchen might have posted it, but, again, no such luck.

My big break finally came around 5:00 p.m., when I saw Dr. Baker walking up to the Bates Unit. He carried what appeared to be one or two sheets of paper. If in fact that were the list, I knew it would now be available on the compound computer system. I then went back to Alexander, and straight to the computer system's CO's office, where he was working the 4:00 p.m. to 12:00 p.m. shift. Since arriving at Morgantown, I had never been a big fan of COs, but he was an exception to the rule. He was in his later forties, with a stocky build, about five-foot-nine. His hair was black with noticeable silver highlights filtering through his crew cut, and with a matching four o'clock shadow. There was no doubt that had we met on the street, we would have become friends, because he never looked down at us inmates. In fact, he was one of the few COs who treated us like human beings.

As soon as I stepped into his office, I wasted no time asking him for a favor. I asked him if I could check on the office computer to see if the list had been posted. With his usual smile and upbeat personality, he turned his chair completely around, and faced the computer. Within a couple of seconds, the list had flashed on the screen.

When I told him the spelling of my last name, he turned around and said, "You're on it."

Being my usual confident self, I asked, "Are you sure? Can I see for myself?"

He was laughing when he invited me up to the computer, where I saw, with my own two eyes, my name, listed alphabetically, alongside the number twenty-one. I probably thanked him about twenty times by the time I ran out of his office and the unit. As I got outside and looked toward the sky, I enthusiastically pumped my fist in the air while thanking God. No sooner after I did that, I saw Carlos walking out of Bates. He immediately ran up to me, threw his arms around me, and yelled congratulations. He told me the list had just been posted, and that he wanted to be the first to welcome me aboard.

It was the first time since coming to Morgantown that I felt as if I was finally turning the corner in my life. That day, though, would not have been complete without calling Kathleen on her cell phone, to tell her. After all we had been through, I needed to give her some positive news, and to thank her again for her love and support.

That night, it was quite easy to fall asleep, because I knew I would soon be moving to Bates. In exactly one week, I would not only be starting the drug and rehabilitation program, but I would begin my countdown toward returning home.

It was Halloween morning when I jumped out of bed at 5:15 a.m. to get ready for my first day in the kitchen. I quickly got dressed, headed to the front door of Alexander, and patiently waited for the PA announcement, which came around 5:55 a.m., for me to report to the kitchen. I reported directly to a Mr. McDougal, whom everyone called "Mac." He was in his mid-fifties, about six-feet tall, with a thin build, silver-and-black hair that seemed fuller and longer than that of other COs, and a neatly trimmed beard and mustache, both of which had some silver aging streaks. When I introduced myself, he marked me off the list and told me to get some breakfast and relax until lunch, when I would be serving my first meal. The only problem was that lunch was about five hours away, and I needed to find something to do, or be bored out of my mind. So, after I ate a cinnamon roll and had a glass of milk, I looked around for something to do. I found a couple of inmates folding napkins around plastic silverware. It seemed like tedious work, but I needed to kill some time, so I jumped in. I had been about two hours into my new job, when Mac told me to stop by the Bates Unit immediately and see the counselor, Mr. Gribble. I took off my red smock, which all kitchen employees were issued, and headed over to Bates.

The only way I could describe my first impression of Bates would be to say that it reminded me of an Illinois state prison I once saw pictures of on TV. When you first walk in, you see a room called the "Bubble," which is located in the center of the building, and which is also the congregating or atrium area. Next to the Bubble, which is surrounded by glass, were small TV rooms and classrooms. Extending like tentacles from both the Bubble and the TV rooms were the building's four wings—A, B, C, and D. Because of the skylights and all the glass, you could see someone entering a wing from either a classroom, TV room, or the Bubble. I have to admit that my first impression was that of a highly regimented military, or sterile, atmosphere.

Instead of walking around aimlessly looking for Mr. Gribble's office, I asked one of the inmates, whom I assumed lived there. He patiently led me down one of the hallways, and pointed to one of the offices, which had the nameplate "Gribble" on the wall. I knocked on the door, which was only partially open, but enough to see that someone was sitting at the desk.

I heard a deep, guttural, "Come in," and entered.

Gribble was a wiry individual, probably about five-foot-ten, and maybe 150 pounds. He wore a BOP baseball cap, white shirt, and dark blue slacks. I could tell he had short black hair under the cap, along with a well-trimmed, full black mustache. His most noticeable feature was his wide-open, bug eyes. He had a stare that was kind of spooky, almost as if he should have been an inmate himself. All in all, he looked tough, like a Clint Eastwood type, or maybe even a drill sergeant. In any event, he fit right in at Morgantown.

He asked me who I was, and I introduced myself. I informed him that I would be moving to Bates later in the day. He then looked over a number of sheets of paper to find my cube assignment. At first, he gave me a cube in the A Wing (A08, Upper). However, when I reported there, the bed had been made, and the locker had been locked. As I turned to go back to Gribble's office, I heard him bark out my name. He had walked over to the A-wing to tell me he had made a mistake, and that my assignment was actually C08, Upper. When I walked over to the C-wing, I was pleasantly surprised to find that my bunk was second from the end of the wing. It appeared to be nice and quiet, and I even had a window overlooking the mountain side, where I could see a number of deer grazing. The bottom bunk had already been made. I wondered where my new bunkmate was from, and what kind of person he was. I then left Bates, and hurried back to the kitchen.

When I returned to the kitchen, I finished folding napkins until lunch, when I was put on the A serving line. My job was to hand out apples to each inmate. I was situated at the end of the line, so the last item to be given out was the apple. I would say that over 1,000 inmates from the compound go to lunch, and with two lines, A and B, I was looking at serving at least 500 people. During lunch, the lines were unofficially divided along race. Blacks and Hispanics, for the most part, used the B line, and sat on that side of the cafeteria, while most of the whites used the A line, and that side. The A line probably gave out less food, because of the prison's dominant racial breakdown.

Out of a seven-hour cafeteria shift, I probably would only really work about one hour of that time, since after everyone came in for lunch, the rest was pretty much down time. As soon as the last inmate was given his lunch, the servers were allowed to leave. That was fine with me on that first day, since I wanted to use that time to get all of my belongings together at Alexander, and be ready to move by 6:00 p.m.

When I retuned to my unit after work, I immediately changed into my sweats, and started picking up my clothes and toiletries. Quite honestly, inmates don't have many belongings—probably about six T-shirts, six underpants, six pair of socks, three uniforms, two sweatshirts and sweatpants, one pair of work boots, and one pair of shower shoes. The only other items that took up room were all the snacks and soda we could buy at the commissary. Even though there wasn't much to move, I still needed a little cart, so I could make it in just one trip. I went to the front of the unit, right by the door, and grabbed a metal cart. I brought it back to my cube, and started to load up. Soon, I was finished, and ready to go. I said goodbye to a few people in the wing, including my bunkie, Shawn, and headed out of Thunderdome. It was pouring rain as I pushed my cart one-hundred yards or so down the sidewalk, and hurried through the front door of Bates. It was time to begin another change in my life that would hopefully lead me home sooner.

I was a little wet from the rain as I moved my belongings down the C-wing of Bates. The first real difference I noticed was its army barracks look. The beds were neatly made, and the cement floors shined as if someone had just waxed them. As I walked down the wing, I noticed how everything looked the same—each cube had beige lockers and matching metal bunk beds. Also, in contrast to Alexander, there wasn't much junk. In fact, everything seemed to be pretty barren. Right away, I met my new bunkie. His name was Cletus Warren, an African-American man, bald, and in his early forties. Cletus was a stocky guy, about five-foot-eight, around 200 pounds, and he appeared to be in excellent shape. He looked as if he may have played some football. He was from North Carolina, and had been sent to Morgantown on a drug charge. I could tell he was basically a quiet person, and that it would take some time for him to warm up to me. The rest of the evening was uneventful. I spent a little time with Carlos, but because it had been a long day, I went to bed early.

I had six days before class would start, so I took that time to get accustomed to my new environment, and to just get used to the new rules at Bates. There were some noticeable differences between the two units. The most striking was the actual peace and quiet after 10:00 p.m.. One of the rules was no noise or loud talking in the sleeping areas after the 10:00 p.m. count. I actually slept very well my first night there. The other noticeable difference was how clean the sleeping areas were. Each inmate and his bunkie were responsible for keeping their respective cubes clean on a daily basis, which meant regular mopping and cleaning. That was one of the many reason why Bates had always been rated highly during the weekly inspections for meal rotations.

In addition, the bathrooms were cleaner than those at Alexander (which isn't saying much). Still, there was much room for improvement. It still amazes me that there are grown men, many of whom are enrolled in a program that emphasizes personal responsibility, who can't even clean up after themselves. Many sinks and floors, as at Alexander, were filled with hair after some of the guys had shaved their heads. Moreover, guys at Bates were just as lazy about leaving empty shampoo bottles, little pieces of soap or soap boxes, and old razor blades in the shower stalls. Probably the most disgusting behavior was from those inmates who forgot to flush toilets or urinals, which not only is unsanitary, but leaves a terrible odor. There were also individuals who didn't have the first clue about sanitation or hygiene—or they did, but would rather live like animals, or just be plain lazy.

Overall, Bates was much better than most of the other units, but again, I believe overcrowding still played a negative role. Bates currently holds about 320 inmates, with only about 200 actually enrolled in classes. Therefore, there are around one hundred or so inmates who don't have the same vested interest in the rules.

During my first few days at Bates, I had the opportunity to develop relationships or associations with both students who would be graduating, and those who were just starting, like me. One person I met, named Joe, was from Oak Brook, Illinois, an affluent suburb outside of Chicago. Joe, who was of Italian descent, was fifty-five years old, stood over six-feet tall and weighed around 200 pounds. He had aged gracefully, with his silver hair down the sides, although he was pretty much bald around the middle of his head. Joe, who was the CEO of his own insurance company, had made a financial killing in Chicago, Las Vegas, California, and Florida by insuring everything from restaurants and night clubs to taxi cabs. However, when you sat down with him, you never felt that he was arrogant because of his wealth. Joe was a down-to-earth guy who just wanted to do his time and go home. In addition, his dedication to completing the program made him a model to others. I, personally, was delighted to learn that we had some mutual political friends in State Representative

Bob Molaro and Alderman Mike Zalewski, both of whom Joe had occasionally taken golfing.

All in all, there was much to learn in Bates, one of which was that there were many different types of people in this unit—from doctors, dentists, pharmacists, and lawyers, to an ex-Congressman and a former rock and roll star, as well as drug users and dealers, gamblers, and gang bangers. Some guys were unselfish, and would try to help their fellow unit mates move forward; others were jealous and petty. As I talked to a number of people at Bates, the one advice that came up in every conversation was, "Watch whom you associate with here, because that person could come back to haunt you." Those were the words that should be engraved on the walls of this building.

Before I could start class, I needed to clear up one piece of unfinished business, which was switching my working hours in the kitchen from a.m. to p.m. I went to see Mac, who already had the necessary information from Bates regarding my enrollment in the program. He immediately told me that my hours would now be switched to the p.m. shift, from 3:30 p.m. to 6:30 p.m. He was also gracious enough to move my days off from Sunday and Monday to a more flexible Saturday and Sunday. I definitely liked the prospect of having the mornings off, not only for doing homework and writing letters, but to relax and shower before my afternoon class. The new kitchen schedule would take effect on Monday, which would also be my first day in RDAP class. That pivotal day would mark a major turning point for me at Morgantown.

CHAPTER 20

THE PROGRAM BEGINS

It was around 6:30 a.m. on Monday morning, when the lights went on throughout the unit. The sun was just starting to peek over the mountains, as everyone began to move around. The RDAP offers both morning and afternoon classes, each consisting of one-hundred students each. The morning session begins promptly at 8:00 a.m., so those inmates were up early, taking a shower, or having a cup of coffee. Those who attended the afternoon session had until 12:30 p.m., but the rules at Bates called for everyone living in the unit (from Monday through Friday) to be full dressed in their khaki uniforms by 7:30 a.m. Also, everyone had to be out of bed and dressed every morning during the week. Before I knew it, the morning group, which included Joe and Carlos, were out the door, heading for class.

I took time that morning to read over some notes and basic definitions that Joe had given me, as a kind of jump start to the program. On our first day, an orientation was scheduled from 10:00 a.m. to 11:00 a.m., to introduce all the new students to the program. The RDAP is a nine-month session divided into three, three-month phases. A student had to pass each phase before moving on to the next. In our orientation were two, phase-two students and two, phase-three students, all of whom were quite informative. They explained the program's format, what was expected of us, and most importantly, its rules. Two of the inmates conducting the orientation were down-to-earth, really nice guys who I had soon become friends with. One was a pathologist from New York, a Dr. Falitico, who was in his third phase; the other, Dave Barry, a motorcycle shop owner from a Detroit suburb, was in his second phase. They took the program seriously, and offered their assistance to me. The more I heard about this program, the more I knew this was going to be a challenge I had never before experienced.

About 12:15 p.m., a few of us first-phasers headed from the unit dorm to the Union Building, which was located next to the Education Building, about two minutes from Bates. The Union Building was the future site for Morgantown's Information Center, which would be run by the prison, with inmates as trained PC operators. That program would be similar to the 311 system back in Chicago, which would provide city service information upon request. The Union Building, which was quite large, had originally been designed as a warehouse. When I walked through its metal doors, I immediately felt its sheer size. The ceilings had to be over forty feet high, and the length close to that of a football field. It already held more than one-hundred PC stations, which took over half the building's middle space. What really struck my eye, though, was the set-up in the front of the building. There was a long aisle or path that ran parallel to the other side. It contained a desk, an erasable board, and a podium. On the wall were a number of posters listing different key terms and phrases used in the program. Then, on both sides of that aisle, were three rows of twenty chairs, each chair neatly placed next to the other.

At approximately 12:25 a.m., the doors opened. We first-phase participants were quickly told to sit in every third seat, so as to allow second and third-phasers to sit between us. I was fortunate to have been one of the first through the door, so I took my seat near the front (or the speaking area), in the first row on my left. Within a matter of two or three minutes, the chairs had been filled. Out of the corner of my eye, I saw two DTSs (Drug Treatment Specialists), Mr. Sowden and Ms. Land, who were the moderators for the TC

(Treatment, or Therapeutic Community) portion of the orientation. As I quickly learned, the TC meetings were run for an entire week at a time, by two inmates who were called "facilitators," and who were chosen each prior week by fellow inmates.

During my first week, the two facilitators were two New Yorkers named Daville and Rodogo. Before this first meeting began, Mr. Sowden took attendance, and then asked all first-phasers to stand up, one by one, and identify themselves by state, and their drug of choice, which could be marijuana, cocaine, crack, ecstasy, alcohol, heroine, etc.

When it was my turn, I quickly stated, "My name is Jim Laski, from Chicago, and my drugs of choice are alcohol and prescription medications."

As soon as I had finished, I returned to my seat, kept my head down, and exhaled a deep breath. Before I had known it, the introductions were over, and the facilitators were in charge. Mr. Daville asked all the participants to stand up, and to recite the RDAP philosophy Morgantown FCI:

I will embrace the challenge of change for myself, my family, and my community.

I will expose who I was, learn who I am, and decide who I will become.

I will give help and receive help from others, with honesty, caring, and humility.

I will strive for a better future, a new beginning, step by step, one day at a time.

After the philosophy statement, the facilitators called upon various inmates who had been selected over the weekend to give the following reports:

News/Weather—a brief description.

> *Sports*—a brief report on the previous evening's sporting events.
>
> *Community Business*—any schedule changes for the week, current activities, staff announcements, and minutes from the morning meeting.
>
> *Thought or Word of the Day*—the inmate reads a thought or word, and explains how it applies to his recovery process. Four other inmates would then stand up, and each one would explain how that concept related to his own recovery.

We then came to *Personal Issues.* This, by far, was the program's most controversial provision. The facilitators would ask for any new or tabled issues that needed discussion. At that time, inmates that the community was concerned about, and who would like to help, could also be identified. The facilitators would then select six inmates who would speak on an issue of their choice pertaining to a fellow participant; this activity was called offering "feedback." Right after that, the facilitators would then consult with the staff to determine if additional feedback was needed. Inmates receiving feedback must thank the individuals who had brought the issue up, and summarize those individuals' concerns. For example, participants in a Community Treatment meeting might express their views regarding another participant's problematic behavior (i.e., he had received an incident report for having stolen food from the kitchen, or is believed to have sold commissary items to another inmate). During any part of the meeting, any participant could suggest clarification of a particular issue. If either a majority vote or a staff's direction determined that such clarification was needed, the facilitators would call on individuals in sets of three to determine if appropriate clarification had been provided, or if another activity should be ordered. The facilitators would assist the community in clarifying issues by asking questions (i.e., "Where were you? What did you say to him? Did you steal food from the kitchen?"). Participants were to ask such questions in a non-judgmental manner; the individual being questioned should answer in a similarly appropriate and respectful manner, using "I" statements, so they could focus on speaking for themselves. Participants may then provide their own clarification (i.e., "I heard you tried to sell the chicken to your roommate. You told me if I didn't get out of your face, I'd be sorry.") The staff was always in control of treatment activities, so they would give the community direction at any time.

The RDAP booklet on policy, as we were told that first day, states, "[. . .] Snitching refers to a behavior that is inappropriate in the treatment program." Snitching, according to the booklet, occurs when an inmate tells on someone else for the express purpose of getting back at that person, or to get himself out of trouble. On the other hand, the booklet does encourage the practice of holding someone "accountable" as a means of helping that person with his behavior by pointing out issues with which he is struggling. This action, however, should be motivated by genuine concern for that individual's progress and well-being. As we shall see later, that was seldom the reason for most of the accountability activities I observed in this program.

The handbook goes on to state:

> Community discussions are viewed as crucial to successful treatment. These meetings can be positive, intense, confrontational, and challenging. Peers may, at times, provide support and encouragement to each other and at other times intense confrontation. In short, we believe that just as addicts get other people addicted to drugs, recovery addicts can help other addicts off drugs into recovery. We also believe that people do not change because they see the light, but because they feel the heat.

I really believe it is important to detail the community/personal issue format, because it plays such an integral role in the lives of program participants, which I would quickly learn. According to the handbook, the format for the remaining portion of any community meeting consists of the following:

Community Positive Issues/Praise:

[. . .] This is an opportunity for inmates to thank one another

313

for positive actions and as an opportunity for inmates to share positive things they are learning from one another. [. . .]

Upbeat Ritual:

An inmate is selected each class day to participate in an uplifting activity [. . .]. This can be a game, song, comedy routine or skit [. . .].

Closing the Meeting/Philosophy Statement:

Minutes are read to assure clarity on the issues discussed [. . .] and then all inmates will stand and recite the philosophy statement to end the meeting.

The afternoon class runs from 12:30 p.m. to 3:30 p.m., and the TC takes up at least half of that time. After that first meeting, I soon wondered if I could handle this program, let alone benefit from it.

For the first two weeks of the class, following the community meetings, all the first-phasers participated in an orientation process, in which DTSs Land, Sowden, and Livengood discussed rules and regulations during the first week, and during the second week, graduates and third-phasers covered key program terms and philosophy with all us beginners.

It quickly became apparent that not only was this program *not* going to be a cake walk, but that it would also encourage tension, insecurity, and open hostility. Just in that first week alone, I saw many individuals either bringing themselves up, or being brought up by others for feedback. For example, a second-phase student, a participant named Tony Blair, an African-American man in his late thirties, was talking with his mother over the phone about what he believed was some type of racial intimidation he encountered during an earlier conversation with three white classmates. Unfortunately, Tony forgot that all phone calls are monitored, and that, in fact, DTSs monitor calls from students on a daily basis. Within a couple of days, Tony was summoned to Dr. Baker's office, where he was confronted with the issue; Tony decided he simply misinterpreted his classmates' remarks. This should have resolved the issue, but in the program, nothing is sacred, and everything needs to be brought up before the community. So, that day, Mr. Blair not only brought himself up for his apparent misinterpretation of those earlier comments, but had to go into detail about his conversation with his mom. Following his presentation, Tony was subjected to feedback from a number of classmates, including the three white gentlemen whom he had presumably misunderstood. What took place next could be compared to a mob action. Tony was verbally attacked and abused, and his motives and character questioned. In addition, past behavioral problems were brought up as reasons for "learning experiences."

Learning experiences are tools used (my choice of words would be "punishments dealt out") for those individuals showing a pattern of unacceptable behavior over and over again. Fellow participants can be vindictive in assigning learning experiences if they have personality conflicts with that person. Once learning experiences are listed before the community, the class would then vote on each and every one, to determine which experiences would be assigned. In Tony's case, he was assigned approximately ten learning experiences, one of which included writing a two-page letter to his mother, apologizing for misleading her with false information about the alleged racial intimidation. Before sending the letter, however, he had to first read it to the entire community. Because one of his earlier crimes was fraud, the community also required him to write a letter to each of his alleged fraud victims, and a five-page paper on racism. He also had to spend one hour with each of the three white classmates he claimed had intimidated him, and was prohibited from shooting billiards, one of his favorite leisure activities, for one week.

There were other learning experiences given out during my first three weeks to other classmates. One student was given twelve learning experiences, because the community had determined he was not honest about why he was moved from one wing to another; he didn't want to admit it was because of a falling out with his former bunkmate. He had to write a two-to-ten-page paper on manipulation and blaming others, and a three-page paper on how diversion may stop him from going home. In addition, he had to devise a report card listing various personality traits on which he would be graded by fellow classmates, and he had to share those grades with the community. He was also required to read one self-help book, and give one of his classmates an oral report on that book. Finally, he was not allowed to play racquetball, or to exercise, for one week. I later learned that a student in the morning session was brought up before the community for farting in someone else's cube, and for that he was given fourteen learning experiences, including apologizing to his entire wing—that's about seventy people!

During those first few weeks, the punishments were dished out with not only pleasure, but total disregard for others' self-esteem. Some of those learning experiences were no better than being required to write 500 times on the blackboard, after school, "I am a jerk," while others seemed as psychologically cruel as a public flogging.

Attending TC sessions always includes one or more DTSs, who monitor the day's activities. During Thanksgiving week in class, three different incidents brought the wrath of the DTSs and Dr. Baker down on the community. During that past week, two students in the A-wing had a physical altercation in which one of them ended up being placed in the SHU. There was also an increase in smoking incidents in the Bates bathrooms (a smoking offense will land an inmate in the SHU, and very likely kick him out of the program). Lastly, someone who used one of the C-wing showers crapped in the shower stall and kicked some of the feces around in the corner, spreading it all over the walls. Mr. Gribble immediately padlocked the bathroom door, and as part of our punishment, shut it down for a week. Needless to say, all of the DTSs heard about these recent developments. One DTS, Mr. Livengood, the so-called "bad ass" of the group, was particularly upset.

Mr. Livengood was in his thirties, with a slender build, short, jet black hair, and a complexion marred by marks and red blotches. He always reminded RDAP students that he is a Correctional Officer first, and then a DTS. It was after the community meeting, the day before Thanksgiving, that he went completely crazy on our group. Livengood's tirade included his own dissertation on the issue of accountability. He pointed out that holding a fellow inmate accountable actually helps that person correct his behavior. He then reminded all of us that we were in this program on a voluntary basis, and that rules are rules, and we must hold both ourselves and others accountable to them. If we did, he emphatically said we could "get the fuck out the door!" Let me point out that Livengood, as a DTS, is supposed to lead by example, and that one of the program's rules is no swearing.

Next, Mr. Sowden and Ms. Land weighed in on the situation, and basically gave everyone a speech on being responsible, and that unless behaviors were corrected, there would be severe consequences, including but not limited to the loss of TV privileges in the unit. Dr. Baker closed the lecture by reminding people that graduating from the program was not automatic, and that everyone needed to step up to the plate and be responsible, not for himself, but for everyone else in the unit. He sternly reminded us that by not coming forward, an inmate was just as guilty as the offender.

After Baker finished, he, along with the three other DTSs on duty that day, left the room so that we could hold a private meeting, and possibly deliver some of our classmates up for punishment. The ensuing conversation was, to say the least, frank and direct. Some of my classmates who were close to graduating were particularly adamant about everyone's monitoring proper behavior, along with bringing ourselves up if we had done something wrong. That comment fell on deaf ears. There were other participants who spoke quite eloquently about the fact that they would never snitch, and that this was a prison first, in which there are unwritten and unspoken rules, or etiquette, one of which prevents one inmate from telling or snitching on another. The conversations started getting louder, and we could feel both the tension and frustration in the room when the DTSs returned to see if we had made any "progress." Livengood, Land, and Sowden stepped up to the front of the room and waited for our responses. Instead, at first, five minutes of total silence greeted them.

I have to admit that was quite unnerving, with everyone either staring at one another, or keeping their heads down, because of fear or guilt. The DTSs, on the other hand, seemed quite comfortable watching us squirm. It almost felt as if a bomb were going to go off, when one of our facilitators stood up and gave us a little speech that I'm sure pleased some of the DTSs. A third-phaser (we'll call him "Mr. D.") stood up, and said that he was tired of watching everyone else's back, and that he was going to watch out for himself from now on, putting his classmates on notice that he would start turning in anyone who had broken a program rule. As some of the DTSs' eyes lit up, another three or four classmates stood up to echo "Mr. D.'s" sentiments, indicating they, too, would be watching everyone else very closely, and that holding them accountable would be no problem for them. At that point, I believe that some of the DTSs were satisfied, because they had put the fear of God in a few of the RDAP participants, and although they had not gotten anyone to snitch, they had put additional eyes and ears out there in the Bates Unit.

Livengood then dismissed all of us about an hour early, and told us to go back to our unit and think about our futures. He also gave the second and third-phasers an early holiday gift—a five-page paper for each to write over the Thanksgiving weekend—Happy Holidays!

Even though I had only been in the program about three weeks, I was already acutely aware of its cold, hard policies. When I first met Carlos in September, he was bubbly, funny, and free-spirited, but as time went on, I started noticing subtle changes in his personality. Since I was in the afternoon class, I had no firsthand knowledge of what was happening in the morning session, except what I read from the brief submitted to the afternoon class. I did realize, even from those brief notes, that Carlos was experiencing some real difficulties in the a.m. TC. According to what I heard and was told, he was recently grilled by a number of his classmates for a variety of reasons. Unfortunately, Carlos had held himself up as a politician and a big-time mover and shaker from Chicago. I learned that over the past month or so, he had some confrontations for which he was brought up, and received learning experiences that included no commissary, weight-lifting, or pool-shooting privileges. He was also assigned papers to write, and required to attend weekend meeting with fellow classmates, in which to discuss behavioral problems.

For these reasons, I believe, Carlos was growing more and more irritable—distant, and, if given the opportunity, confrontational. With each passing day, I learned more little tidbits about Carlos, and I didn't like what I heard. I found out that he had about twenty different confrontations with various individuals over the past eight months. Each time I would try to talk to Carlos, he would either give me a bullshit excuse that he had to go somewhere, or would tell me not to worry about him. In any event, he started to develop a mean-spirited, defensive personality that was, honestly, no fun to be around.

About two weeks before Thanksgiving, a major blowup took place in the a.m. class. I was told later that Carlos was not only placed on the hot seat for his confrontational issues, but also for forgetting his notebook before class, for leaving a book and papers under his mattress (an action that was against both program rules and the fire code), and for losing focus on his everyday class preparation.

These issues continued to mount for Carlos, as his scheduled December 1 graduation day approached. Then Carlos made racist remarks during a recent confrontation, and actually referred to some people as "blue-eyed white devils" and "fags." Not only did some of his classmates who had been head-hunting for him during the last few months jump all over him, but even some of his friends and supporters shook their heads in disbelief, and turned their backs on him. That was such a volatile issue that it was on the Therapeutic Community's schedule on back-to-back days. Consequently, Carlos not only received harsh and brutal feedback, but his designated advisors basically gave up and quit on him. Ms. Lindsley, a DTS who was particularly offended by his remarks, told Carlos he had wasted enough of the community's time.

Even through all of this turmoil, Carlos remained upbeat, thinking that he only had a couple of weeks to graduate. My advice was that he remain quiet, stay out of everybody else's way, and, most importantly, fly under the radar.

In the RDAP, there is absolutely one word that no participant every wants to hear, and that's "recycled." As mentioned earlier, the program consists of three, three-month phases, and certain tests and written assignments must be completed in order to move from one phase to the next. Unfortunately, some individuals are kept in the same phase for an additional three months, or in some cases, demoted or set back one or two phases. In the most extreme cases, a participant may even be required to take the entire program over again.

It was now Thanksgiving week, and the talk in Bates was that Carlos had survived the axe. When I spoke to him Tuesday morning, he was excited about graduating in ten days, and actually leaving Morgantown in exactly two weeks. His wife and children were coming to pick him up, and his halfway house papers had been signed, and final fingerprints taken. So, basically, everything had seemed to be in order for Carlos to leave as planned.

Our TC meeting ended that afternoon around 2:00 p.m., and all first-phasers reported back to Bates and to the A-wing classroom to begin our first "Rational Thinking" class with DTS Ms. Ratay. A third-phase student had been called in to deliver the first day's lecture on rational thinking skills, because Ms. Ratay would be attending an emergency meeting in the DTS conference room. At about 2:30 p.m., the compound loudspeaker went off, instructing Carlos Ayala to report to Dr. Baker's office immediately. At that moment, I had an empty, nauseating feeling that something was going to be bad; I just wasn't sure how bad. I had been told that any time Dr. Baker or one of the other DTSs gathered in the conference room and brought a student in, it was either for recycling or dismissal. While trying to concentrate on my own work, I couldn't help but look out the windows, and out into the hallway, because our classroom was directly across from Dr. Baker's office and the conference room.

I should have stopped looking at Baker's office, because the more I looked, the more DTSs (including Ms. Ratay) I saw marching, one by one, into the conference room. Carlos walked in, and looked petrified. He nervously knocked on the secretary's office door, whereupon she told him to wait to be called to the conference room.

Veteran RDAP students sarcastically calls the conference room "the round table" (which I had never really understood, because the table is actually rectangular). However, one thing that everyone agrees on is that nothing good for a program participant ever comes from that room, and this day was no exception. Before I knew it, Carlos disappeared into the conference room. I now couldn't resist keeping my eyes glued to that room. I could see the front door, and a couple of the DTSs sitting around the table.

About thirty minutes or so went by before Carlos left the conference room. I knew he would not be graduating in two weeks. He actually looked dazed; his eyes were glassy, and his skin tone was chalky. Out of the corner of my eye, I saw Carlos talking to a fellow student, Joe Nicosia, before rushing out the front door. It seemed like an eternity waiting for class to end, but I knew I had to see Joe and find out what had happened. It was now exactly 3:20 p.m., and not a second later, when I hurried back to the C-wing to talk to Joe.

Before I could say one word, Joe told me, "Carlos was recycled all the way back to the beginning."

I couldn't believe it. After eight-and-a-half months, and only ten days to graduation, and fourteen days until his wife would drive him home, Dr. Baker told him he must start the program over, from day one. The previous months were now meaningless for any type of credit or time served, because he failed to graduate.

As I headed off to work, and toward the kitchen, I saw Carlos walking very quickly past the pond, about ten feet from me. He shouted out in a choked-up voice that he needed to be alone to figure things out. I certainly respected his wishes, and I walked off to the kitchen.

Sixteen days later, Carlos' fellow classmates would leave for their halfway houses. Before any of their beds were even cold in the B-wing where Carlos slept, a whole new batch of inmates were brought in to begin future classes. Meanwhile, Carlos tearfully called his family, who were, and continue to be, supportive about the bad news. As far as he was now concerned, his future was still up in the air. His attorney is working on a number of options, including filing a lawsuit against the RDAP for their allegedly untimely and unwarranted recycling. At this point, no one is sure what course of action Carlos will take, but what I can tell you is that he will be emotionally scarred by this experience for the rest of his life. Not only had he not been given any type of warning or written notification prior to his recycling, but he had regulary had better-than-average scores from the DTSs on his six-month evaluation, with three's and four's out of a possible five in the reports. He also had regularly had a clear record for his eighteen months in Morgantown, without one incident report, and an impeccable work record, with over sixty hours in community service outside prison. No matter what the future holds for Carlos Ayala, I believe he was treated unfairly. If, in fact, he had made racial remarks, or had shown some inappropriate anger, the proper punishment should have been a three-month recycling. Anything more was not justifiable, based upon his record.

One problem that definitely needs to be addressed is the DTSs' responsibilities. An inmate's future should not be determined by other inmates under the guise of a community therapy session. Students are ripped apart by their classmates, while DTSs look on with smug satisfaction. If a student like Carlos has a problem along the way, the DTSs should give him some special assistance, or at the very least, prior written notification about behavioral problems. I honestly believe that a TC environment is not only a venue for confrontation and head-hunting between classmates, but it can also be emotionally damaging to some recipients. Many of the third-phasers in particular, are extremely skeptical of the exercise's benefits. It appears that those individuals who may be a little more reserved or passive not only do not fare well in the TCs, but in fact, actually feel more isolated and self-conscious in such a setting. Only time will tell how much I will benefit from this experience.

After about thirty days of classes, each student receives his treatment plan, which identifies particular psychological issues and criminal behaviors. This plan then sets specific treatment goals with accompanying activities. Each DTS is assigned a certain number of students in each new class, and is responsible for determining their individual treatments. My primary DTS is Ms. Land, a nice enough woman who is in her thirties. I've been told she admires family men and honesty, and no inmate can just bullshit his way through her class and expect to graduate. Ms. Land called me into her office about a week after class started, and basically went over my PSI, and asked me the same questions asked earlier—about my childhood, my parents, and my drinking, etc. She then used that information, along with other details listed in my PSI, to draft my treatment plans.

In the meantime, Thanksgiving arrived. When I woke up, it was around 8:30 a.m. I looked outside my window hoping to see sunshine. Instead, it was cloudy again. I quickly got dressed, and ran outside to meet John, and to report to the pill line. We were both surprised that for late November, the weather was not really that cold, probably around the upper forties. As we walked over to the pill line, John and I both agreed that we were happy that Thanksgiving was here, because by the end of the day, one more holiday would be in the books.

After we had gone through the pill line, John and I continued to walk around the compound until the 10:00 a.m. count. John's fiancée was coming over for a visit around 11:00 a.m.. He said she would then leave around 2:45 p.m., and that I could meet him back by the pond at that time to continue our walk. The announcement then came over the compound loudspeaker for the 10:00 a.m. recall, and John went back to Alexander, and I to Bates.

Our big turkey lunch would be around 11:30 a.m., and later in the day we would get a bag lunch of microwaveable cheeseburgers, chips, cookies, and lemonade. Joe Nicosia met me there, and we ate together. The turkey lunch, in my opinion, was not that bad; maybe I was now used to prison food. Everybody received one big turkey leg that was a little tough and dry, but edible. There were also mashed potatoes and gravy, cornbread dressing, salad, and a slice of sage pie. Afterwards, there was so much grumbling in the cafeteria about the meal that Joe and I couldn't wait to hurry out of there.

Joe then went over to the auditorium to see what movie was playing, and I returned to Bates, where I ran into Carlos. He had been very despondent ever since the news two days earlier that he was being recycled all the way back nine months in the drug and alcohol program. It was depressing seeing him now. At one time he was a confident, happy, and secure individual but he now appeared to be a broken and tired man who didn't know which way to turn. We talked around for an hour or so and talked about his situation.

I couldn't help but feel a little depressed myself. After all, it was Thanksgiving, I missed my family, and I felt sorry for Carlos.

After an hour or so, there was another recall, to pick up our bagged meals. I then went back to Bates, and waited for our unit to be called. After I had picked up my meal, I put it in my locker, and headed towards the pond to meet John. I was about ten minutes early, so I sat down on one of the fourteen benches surrounding the thirty-foot wide and one-hundred-foot long pond. After about fifteen minutes, John came walking over from the Visiting Center. He had a smile on his face, but he also looked sad, if that makes sense. I guess it's always nice to see your loved ones, but I can't imagine saying goodbye at the end of the day.

The rest of the day was uneventful. I walked in the evening again with John and Rob. We all agreed how much this first major holiday away from home had made us realize how important the little things in life are, and the true significance of family and friends. We all felt incredibly empty. I knew that another friend I had made, Bruce Drennan, a Cleveland sportscaster who had been here for about a month, was feeling particularly lonely. He said that Thanksgiving was his toughest day here since he first arrived. He had already called his wife of twenty-six years a total of four times that day, just so he could feel better.

The rest of the evening I spent walking around the unit. Some of the guys were watching sports; others were watching a movie in the prison auditorium. For some reason, I no longer had any interest in TV or sports, so I wound up going to bed around 11:30 p.m. As I lay in bed, I was just happy to have gotten through the day.

The day after Thanksgiving was sunny, and in the mid-sixties. John and I walked most of the day. In the evening, I called home, and spoke to Kathleen, Nina, Jack, and Bobby. What I will always remember was telling the kids to each come up with a list of five things that we could do together when I got home. They were so excited that they said they were going to start that night. As my eyes swelled with tears, I told Bobby to ask Mommy to put her own list together, so that she and Dad could do five things together, too. Bobby yelled over the phone, telling Kathleen to create her list. What amazed me the next day when I had called again, was for Jack and Bobby to tell me some of the things they wanted to do with me—go to a White Sox game, have me buy a video game for each of them and watch them play their games together, or watch wrestling on TV with them. These were the moments where I felt so lucky to have my family supporting me. I was so anxious to know what I would do when I got back home and could see all of them. Those are the times when I actually feel blessed.

On Wednesday, December 5, I received my treatment goals, and had my first small group class with Ms. Land. About five of the eight DTSs received eight or nine students from my class to be in their small group classes, and to provide each of them with his own individual plan. During the first phase of the program, our class would start with TC, from 12:30 p.m. to about 2:00 p.m. After TC on Mondays, students would return to Bates and clean their respective cubes and wings from 2:00 p.m. to 3:30 p.m. On Tuesdays, all first-phasers would have a "Rational Thinking" class with Ms. Ratay. On Wednesdays, we would gather into small groups of eight or nine to meet with our primary DTS to work on our individual goals in a smaller, more comfortable environment. Finally, on Thursdays and Fridays, our entire first-phase class would have an orientation class with Mr. Satterfield. This would be my schedule for the first three months of the program.

After TC that Wednesday, I, along with eight other classmates, waited for Ms. Land back at Bates, to receive our treatment goals, and for her to actually move us full-speed-ahead into the recovery process. When she walked in, she informed us that we would first receive our treatment plans, and that our first group session would be the following week.

She then handed out each of the treatment plans, and we walked over to her desk to receive not only our individual plan, but also a notebook and any additional reading materials, which were based on each person's problems and activities. I was the first person called, and I anxiously gathered all my materials from her. I returned to my seat, and began reading about what my treatment would entail.

My treatment plan was approximately two pages long, and Ms. Land identified three problems I needed to address through a number of treatment activities she had recommended. It will be interesting to see how this plan will ultimately work out for me. There was no scheduled one-on-one therapy; this was basically a group therapy program. My treatment plan read as follows:

Type of Treatment: Residential DAP Five Session/WK: 3 Hrs. Daily

Goals to be Accomplished:

Goals established on Dec. 06, 2006. These are ongoing and will be reviewed every sixty (60) days as needed during the RDAP. The final sixty (60) day review will be incorporated into a Drug Treatment Summary and Referral. The projected graduation date is for August 03, 2007.

Problem: Anxiety and excessive worry.

Goal: To verbalize and understand that you are a fallible human being and you will make mistakes.

Treatment Activity: Discuss this issue with the group on a regular basis and receive feedback on progress.

Treatment Activity: Make two journal entries per week dealing with this issue and how it continues to set you up for failure.

Treatment Activity: Explore this issue and its origin to better understand why you feel a need to be perfect and how it relates to your feelings of inadequacies.

Treatment Activity: Read "Managing My Anxiety" and write a five-page paper. Due February 06, 2007.

Treatment Activity: Read "Adult Children of Alcoholics" and write a five-page paper on what you learned from this book. Due March 06, 2007.

Problem: I have a problem with Sentimentality. I use the

"nice guy" façade to manipulate and commit crime.

Goal: To identify and eliminate Sentimentality issues.

Treatment Activity: Write a five-page paper detailing how I have used Sentimentality. Due by April 02, 2007.

Treatment Activity: When I find myself in a situation using Sentimentality tactics,

Treatment Activity: Report to group episodes of Sentimentality. Be open to feedback.

Sentimentality tactics, I will stop and make immediate corrections.

Treatment Activity: Write a five-page paper detailing how my use of Sentimentality as a manipulation tactic has impacted my family. What have they learned from me? Due April 23, 2007.

Problem: Fraudulent. Have used deceit to perpetuate need for power and money.

Goal: Address fraudulent behavior, analyze it, apply it presently, and learn how it relates to my relapse process or sobriety retention (minimize, play to my advantage, manipulate situations for self-serving motives, greedy, superficial, on own agenda).

Treatment Activity: List 50 things that I have "gotten away with." Due January 06, 2007.

Treatment Activity: Identify errors in thinking used throughout the "things I have gotten away with." Due January 06, 2007.

Treatment Activity: Using recovery resources, write a five-page paper addressing my fraudulence, specifically, how it was, is, and will be in my growth/recovery. Due June 04, 2007.

Consent to Treatment: The purpose, goals, and methods to be used during these treatment sessions have all been explained to me. I understand that I can end these sessions at any

327

time without negative consequences. I also understand that materials discussed in these sessions are confidential, except where otherwise agreed, or in cases where potential harm to self/others, major security issues, or court requests are involved. My signature indicates that I agree with this treatment plan.

Treatment Began: November 06, 2006.

Total Hours of Treatment Under this Program: 500 (Res. DAP)

Now the program would step into high gear. Besides my treatment plan, I would have weekly assignments, both in orientation and in the "Rational Thinking" program. However, one of my ongoing concerns continued to be the TC, which some were using as a form for grandstanding, and others, an arena for verbal flogging or execution of their classmates. Over the weekend, I had actually overheard a third-phaser telling a fellow inmate in the compound that the TC does not actually help inmates, but does, in fact, hurt, and even destroy, self-esteem.

Time would now be moving at a quicker pace, as I would begin my seventh week in the program, only two weeks away from Christmas Day. At this time, Dr. Baker offered Carlos an opportunity to start taking the entire class over in January, 2007. Carlos respectfully declined, and signed out of the program on Tuesday, December 12. He then moved from Bates to Carlson that same evening. Besides Carlos, another recycled RDAP student also chose to sign out.

On December 18, at around 5:30 a.m., I was awakened by a light tapping on my leg. It was my friend, Joe Nicosia, who wanted me take a short walk with him. Joe was leaving Morgantown that day, and heading to a halfway house in Chicago to complete his sentence.

As we walked through the compound down toward the chapel, Joe and I could not help but comment on such warm temperatures for mid-December. It had to be in the mid-fifties. He was extremely nervous. All he wanted to do was to get out of Morgantown, where he had spent the last nineteen months of his life. Joe and a number of other inmates were going by shuttle bus from Morgantown to Pittsburgh, where they would be given vouchers for the Greyhound bus rides to their respective cities.

As we were waiting outside for his name to be announced over the P.A. to report to the R&D (Receiving and Departure) building for his final processing, he assured me that I would be fine, and that time would pass quickly for me. He also promised me that his wife Lee would call Kathleen, to let her know that everything was okay, and that Kathleen should stay in touch with her and Joe, especially if she had any concerns.

It's hard to explain, but Joe provided me with a real sense of stability and comfort. During the past six weeks, we had spent almost every evening together, talking about everything. Probably the reason why we got along so well was because we were so much alike. It had taken me fifty-three years to find someone who was just as anxiety-ridden and as nervous as I. He was now worrying about what he was going to eat, where he was going to sit on the bus, and whether the clothes his wife had sent him were going to fit. Undoubtedly, he was my kind of guy.

It was about 6:50 a.m., and Joe had just turned in his bedding to the laundry, one of those housekeeping requirements each inmate must attend to before he leaves.

Then, the P.A. went off, "Joseph Nicosia, please report to the back of R&D."

As the quiet and pleasant female voice continued to call more names, Joe turned to me, shook my hand, gave me a hug, and said he wished we could have been in class together.

As he turned and walked briskly to the R&D's back door, I said, "Good luck."

Although I could no longer see him, I waved anyway, and whispered to myself, "Take care, my good friend. Hopefully, we'll see each other again sometime toward the end of next year."

I then turned and walked over to the medical building, to stand in line for my pills.

By Wednesday, December 20, Christmas was only five days away. That day in TC, the community ripped apart one third-phaser (Mr.

Solomon) and one first-phaser (Mr. Carter). The DTSs particularly ripped into Mr. Solomon for what they claimed was his dishonesty, and basically told him they didn't know what to do with him. In fact, Ms. Land told him to sit down during his feedback, because she didn't want to waste any more time on him. In Carter's case, he received nine learning experiences, which included the usual papers on irresponsibility, as well as a letter to his family on why he might not come home on time, which, of course, he would have to read to the class. Some of those assignments were due on Tuesday, December 26—Merry Christmas!

In this, my seventh week into the program, we were two-thirds done with the first phase, which would end during the last week of January. It seemed that most of our recent instruction had taken place in TC. Although I'd made an effort to speak in the community sessions, I didn't believe I had made any strides in addressing my drinking or anxiety issues. Still, I completed week number seven of the RDAP. All we had on Friday, December 22, was TC, in which I spoke on the word of the day, "pride." Mr. Nelson, a first-phaser, then brought himself up for having overslept and missing a smoking cessation class. Six of his classmates gave him feedback regarding lack of personal responsibility. In addition, Ms. Land said because this was the second time he had missed the class, he should be assigned learning experiences. He then received nine such experiences, including writing papers on irresponsibility, open-mindedness, smoking, and a letter to his family on why his coming home may be delayed, which was to be read before the class, along with a 10:00 p.m. curfew for one month. I guess my problem that day was with the punishment's timing—only three days before Christmas. Ms. Land defended the assignments, even this close to a holiday, on the grounds that when we had been out on the streets, there had been no holiday exemptions for abusing alcohol or drugs. So, why should Mr. Nelson be exempt on Christmas weekend from learning experiences? After hearing that, I was convinced that old Scrooge would have felt right at home here as a DTS.

CHAPTER 21

CHRISTMAS AND NEW YEAR'S
AT MORGANTOWN

Christmas weekend started in a typical Morgantown fashion. Two out of the four urinals in the C-wing's bathroom were not working. In fact, one had been broken for at least a month. That night, the second one had partially flooded the bathroom, and a number of us refused to walk in there because of the wet floor, and also the smell from the urinal's overflow. I know this is a prison, but I don't think broken urinals are luxury items whose repair should be put off indefinitely.

Before going to bed that night, I called Kathleen. It was so nice to hear her voice on the phone again, especially when she said she had been waiting for my call, as if it were a date night. We talked twice in the evening, and we both agreed we couldn't wait to get the holidays over with for 2006. She told me that the boys reminded her that my time away was now 30 percent over, and that each new month that went by would be another 10 percent. She then asked me to do everything in my power to get home by August 2007. I had received her Christmas card and the boys' but not Nina's. Kathleen had also sent me a bunch of pictures of herself and the kids, but unfortunately, I'd have to wait until Tuesday for the mail. I love Kathleen and the kids so much, and I can't wait to be with all of them again.

Because the weather on Saturday, December 23 was partly sunny and breezy, in the upper forties, that was a day to get outside. For the most part, the weather had been great for this time of year. After lunch, John and I got together and walked, which was something we had done lately during the day. We walked about three yards in the afternoon, and as usual, discussed a number of issues. John informed me earlier that week, that twelve of his co-workers were talking about the Alexander Unit and its problems when Mr. Adams' name came up again. Those inmates, too, all told him that Adams was a racist, and treated black inmates in a much more professional manner than white inmates. In addition, a number of those same inmates focused on the lack of counseling and help from Alexander's staff. John and I then discussed the unfairness of different types of inmates, based on age and crime, together. We agreed that white collar inmates should be separated from drug dealers. John also told me that there were actually inmates who had been in prison for over two years, and that after a period of time, had been transferred from another institution to Morgantown. He also had been told that some of those individuals had been sentenced for violent crimes, including sexual assault and rape.

In addition to these negative aspects, we also talked about some positive alternatives we both would recommend for the future, such as providing time served incentives to those inmates who had, in prison, earned their GEDs, or who had completed x-number of hours of college accredited courses with a C average or better. Why shouldn't inmates be rewarded for completing such classes successfully in the same way the prison rewards alcoholics and drug addicts for having completed the RDAP? Also, Morgantown should work with local corporations to hire paroled or released inmates, in return for federal, state, and/or local tax breaks. I do hope that when I am released and get home, I can provide some input about this institution that will actually help some inmates and their families.

Meanwhile, the holiday weekend wore on. I slept until about 9:30 a.m. on Sunday, December 24. It was cloudy outside, and very quiet in the C-wing. In fact, half of the inmates in my wing were still sleeping. I felt a little depressed that morning, since I had stopped taking one anti-anxiety medication a couple of days ago. I hoped I could still get out that day and walk around the track, because walking always helped to relieve my anxiety.

As I walked around the unit that morning, the compound seemed quieter than usual, probably because it was the day before Christmas. While walking that afternoon, I ran into Carlos. He seemed happier that he was no longer in the RDAP, but still a little bitter. In fact, he compared his situation to a political assassination, claiming he had been set up by the TC. He also said that being in the Carlson Unit was like being on vacation. That unit was so close to the hills and a thriving local black market, with all types of contraband, including liquor, cigarettes, marijuana, and cocaine available. It was obvious that the program didn't help Carlos, but I believe that this was due to the program letting him down.

During the evening, I watched the movie *Twin Towers* in the auditorium. It was a good movie, but because it dealt with the 9/11 terrorist attacks on New York, a bit depressing. When the movie was over, I took a walk by myself, and met up with John. Together, we had a chance to look at the prison's Christmas tree on top of the highest mountain in Morgantown. Right above it was a quarter moon. The sky was so clear that the moon provided a spotlight effect for the lighted tree, which looked so tiny in the distance. John and I walked about a half hour. It was now a bit chilly, maybe in the low thirties, but we took the opportunity to reminisce about our first few months at Morgantown, and reiterated our determination that this would be our only Christmas in prison. We were trying to make the best out of a bad situation.

Later, around 9:30 p.m., I talked to Kathleen and Nina, and learned that Jack was running a fever around 103. All in all, it was a difficult weekend for everybody.

Finally, Christmas morning arrived. I again woke up around 9:30 a.m., and to a cloudy and drizzly morning. We ate our Christmas dinner at 11:30 a.m. We each had a Cornish hen, stuffing, biscuits and gravy, corn, sweet potatoes, and a cinnamon cake. Bates was fifth out of the seven units for the meal rotation, and it was very difficult just to get a seat. I ate lunch with Dave Brady, whose cube was right next to mine. It was so noisy that we ate quickly, and walked back to the unit, even in a pouring rain.

Later, I went to Christmas Mass. I arrived at the chapel at 2:00 p.m., a whole half hour before Mass would actually begin, because I was the altar server, and had to help with the preparations. With some assistance, I set up the altar, and then brought out the chalice and the water (because I was in rehab, I couldn't touch the wine normally used), as well as the pitcher and the bowl for the priest to wash his hands in. Well, I used one of the washrooms, as I had usually had, to fill up the pitcher. When I finished, I decided to use the washroom myself. When Father Alex, who was standing in another room across from the washroom, saw me opening the door and walking out, he abruptly and curtly told he I was not allowed to use that facility. I had not noticed, the sign reading "Staff Washroom Only" on the nearby wall. I apologized, but was annoyed by his rude and authoritative attitude. Like Chaplain Price, Father Alex evidently considered himself a CO first, and a man of the cloth second. Even at Christmas, we inmates were treated as if we had no rights or feelings, and by the prison clergy as well. I was ready to walk out, but continued my duties by helping set up the appropriate readings in the mass book. The only bright side to the day was that after Mass ended, the clouds and rain were gone, and the sun was shining brightly. As I looked up, I thought maybe God was telling me to hang in there, that better days were coming.

I then called Kathleen to wish her a Merry Christmas and a Happy New Year. We both agreed that we just wanted to get this year behind us. She had been home all day, because Bobby was now sick. Whatever virus Jack had, he had given it to his brother. The only salvation for Kathleen was that everybody in the house was on break until January 8. I told Kathleen that when I got home next year, I wanted to start a new tradition around Christmas. I didn't care if it would be going to the zoo, or driving downtown to see the holiday lights the weekend before Christmas. Whatever the activity would be, Kathleen, I, and the kids would all celebrate the holiday together. I was explaining the whole concept to her when my maximum fifteen minutes remaining on my monthly phone calls home allowed by the prison expired, and we were cut off. It figured!

Two days later, my friend John had a terrible attack of kidney stones. He was in so much pain that he actually went to Ms. Little, one of the case managers, to tell her he was ready to faint from the pain. She immediately called the medical building, and the staff there told her to inform him to come down. There, they checked his vitals, and took an x-ray. The doctor told him that something had shown up, but he wasn't sure what, so he sent it out to another federal prison to examine. He also told him he might have to go into town for another x-ray. John then told him that when he had similar attacks before, his primary care physician back home had put him in the hospital for observation. The Morgantown doctor said that, unfortunately, would not be possible here. In the meantime, the doctor gave him morphine and an IV for about two hours. When he awakened from the IV, he was given a script for Ibuprofen, about 800 mg. per pill, and the doctor told him to take the rest of the day off. John later told me he was frightened because of the lack of medical care here, and prayed he would be okay. He also reminded me that he heard that two people had died at Morgantown over the years, due to health-related reasons. I tried to not let that fact bother me, but it couldn't help but prey on my mind. Still, I tried to hope and pray for the best, and to look forward, as much as I could, to the New Year.

Four days later, on December 31, the last day of 2006 arrived. As my wife so eloquently remarked over the phone that evening, "Good riddance!" I completed week eight of the RDAP, and could honestly state that much of what I learned was self-taught. During those first eight weeks, the first-phasers had one Rational Thinking class out of a possible eight, and one small group class out of a possible eight. I felt the whole program needed to be examined, from the TC all the way to down. One first-phaser told me privately that TC was the worst part of his day. Something that is supposed to be uplifting and helpful is more often than not, degrading and self-defeating. I could only hope that conditions would improve over the next seven months.

Meanwhile, even though I'd been out of the Alexander Unit ("Thunderdome") for quite some time, the stories about that place just kept on coming. Just two nights before, John told me about Inmate Hoffler, who, by all accounts, is a peaceful man who pretty much keeps to himself. In fact, he can usually be found in one of the quiet rooms, reading the Bible. Well, the usual 10:00 p.m. count is never quite exactly at that time. It could be as early as 9:55 p.m., or as late as 11:00 p.m. On one particular night when the count was late, Mr. Hoffler decided around 10:15 p.m., to jump into the shower. As soon as he had done so, the P.A. system finally announced the count, and the COs arrived to begin their rounds. They yelled into the D-wing bathroom and Hoffler told him he would be right out. Before he was able to, however, the count was finished. Two minutes after, they had to announce a recount. Hoffler then made his way back, but after the recount, one CO, whom I can only describe as a total asshole, handcuffed Hoffler and took him to the SHU, where he had to spend four days, even New Year's Eve. This had been typical behavior for that CO. In fact, you couldn't find a nastier, meaner person if you'd tried. He has a stocky build, is totally bald, and walks around all day with a scowl on his face. He doesn't *talk* to inmates; he *growls* at them. One time, at Alexander, when I was talking to another CO, this idiot rudely interrupted our conversation, and kicked me out of the office. Once, when inmates were peering through the glass Bubble at Bates, to see if the mail had arrived, he took his clenched fist and forearm and banged it against the window, not only shaking the entire glass, but scaring them half to death! Sometimes I think I'm in the old movie *Cool Hand Luke*, which is about the terrible treatment of prisoners on a Georgia chain gang. Like the guards in that movie, this CO takes great pleasure in humiliating inmates. If I have one goal when I get out of here, it would be to help make life in this institution a little better for those inmates who suffer such degradation daily.

One more point about degradation—each individual, after a pre-approved visit from friends and family members, must undergo a strip search behind closed doors to check for any hidden contraband that may have been passed on during that visit. That New Year's weekend, John, "Charlotte Rob," and another inmate I knew, "Detroit Joe," all received visits from their families. According to John, he had to drop his pants and underwear, and take off his shoes and socks. He was then required to lift his feet, one at a time, and afterwards, he had to lift his ball sac. Lastly, he had to bend over, spread his cheeks, and cough. Unfortunately, the CO then made him start the whole process all over again from the start, because he claimed John had been facing him in the wrong direction. Why this place is designated as a "minimum security prison" is beyond me. If the COs are that worried about contraband, all they need to do is station themselves along the hills near the prison, where black market trafficking is frequent, because any alcohol, drugs, or other illegal items are certainly not coming from visitors.

As 2006 was quickly ending, all I could hope for was that the time would go fast, and that my faith would remain strong. Hopefully, this entire situation would change me for the better as a person, and someday I could take a step back and start enjoying the simple things in life again. There is no doubt that when I do look back on 2006, it will be with a sigh of relief. All I now hoped for was that life for me would start all over, beginning with the first day of 2007.

CHAPTER 22

MORGANTOWN, 2007

I didn't have much time to bask in the promise of a new year, as RDAP class soon resumed on January 3. In TC, I gave feedback to my classmate, Mr. Jackson, who was a very nice man whom I also worked with in the kitchen. Again, in order to give feedback to a particular person, that individual must have an issue that either he or someone from the community has brought up. In Mr. Jackson's case, it was the anxiety of going home soon, and being back with his family for the first time in five years. Well, for me, that scenario was perfect for the feedback I could provide, because I suffer from anxiety, and could relate to Mr. Jackson's trepidation. I think feedback should be caring and supportive, and not vindictive. I described to Mr. Jackson my own struggles with anxiety, but also told him that much of our mutual problem stemmed from our negative thinking, and how we perceive future events. Generally, an anticipated fear that never happens causes our anxiety. Our challenge is to face our fears head on, which is really half the battle. Everyone in this world has some anxiety, but people like me and Mr. Jackson often let fear and uncertainty consume us, to the point where we have trouble functioning on a daily basis. That was the kind of feedback I thought this program would be all about. If someone has an anxiety problem or is worried about a sick parent at home, these are important issues.

Neither is juicy or confrontational enough for the DTSs who want participants to hold their classmates responsible for engaging in such RDAP violations, such as swearing, sneaking in pornographic materials, swiping food from the kitchen, or visiting a fellow inmate in a different wing after 10:00 p.m.

Every Wednesday after our TC meeting, all first-phasers have a small group meeting. When we had started our class on November 6, our class, RDAP 112, had consisted of forty individuals. That number was now divided into four groups of ten, with each group assigned to one DTS instructor. My group fell under Ms. Land's auspices.

Our first small group meting of 2007 started with Ms. Land asking one of my classmates, Bob, how he was feeling. He expressed concern over the TCs emphasis on accountability, and the type of confrontational feedback given. She then basically turned on Bob, referring to his alleged anger issues and criminal thinking errors. Before long, a couple of my classmates, who had the same concerns, but instead sold out and became ass kissers, openly agreed with Ms. Land.

That particular day, Mr. Livengood was absent, so all of his small groups were divided up among the three other groups. Mr. Warren, my bunkie, and Mr. Powers, joined our small group for the day. Over the past couple of weeks, Warren and I had expressed our concerns to each other over what we felt was the TCs chief fundamental flaw. We agreed that there were days when TC became a blood sport. We concurred that the activity was not about therapy, but about mercilessly attacking the behavior of individuals to the point where they became passive or submissive, gave up, and quit the program. We both harbored deep reservations about the TCs ultimate benefits. As the attack on Bob's behavior continued, it became obvious that we needed someone in that group to either side with him, or change the direction of the discussion's focus. Fortunately, my bunkie Cletus Warren jumped into the fire, and said that he had similar concerns as Bob. After a brief discussion with Cletus, Ms. Land heard a noticeable and vocal sigh from me, and asked me what I was thinking about.

This was the first time in awhile that I felt as if I had something important to say, not only for myself, but for those who were afraid to speak up. I began my response with some fire in my belly, telling Ms. Land that I felt there were some problems with TC. I told her that if everyone were honest, they would agree with Bob and Cletus. I complained about some individuals' use of TC as a forum for their own personal agenda, and about those in class with a "holier-than-thou" attitude in acting one way in TC, and entire differently in the unit. There also, I explained, appeared to be some difficulty in holding people accountable for certain rule infractions while ignoring other violations by their friends. This double standard was apparent, but the overriding question, I contended, was the false premise behind accountability as a whole, and that there were those of us who wanted a different approach than simply snitching on one another. After I had finished, there was a sense of relief in Bob's face that someone had finally had the balls to speak up. Cletus looked at me with pride, and maybe for the first time, was glad to be my bunkie.

I don't know how to describe Ms. Land's reaction. I think she was surprised that I came out of my shell so vocally. More importantly, though, I believe she thought there were some legitimate concerns after all that she had not acknowledged. Although she said she didn't believe in discussing the issue in TC, she did feel there would be merit in looking into the question of accountability, albeit in a different forum. I really can't say for sure if I accomplished anything productive that day, but I did feel better in just getting some things out in the open. If I could only persuade more of my classmates to be more honest and open about their own feelings, then I would truly believe that some real headway in the program would be made.

I don't mean to be entirely negative about the program, but the people who can make the difference (the DTSs) seem to believe that addiction comes down to criminal thinking. In fact, Mr. Livengood told us many times that most of us will probably be back in prison some day, due to nothing else but our own refusal to accept responsibility. For Mr. Livengood and similarly minded DTSs, the problem comes down to nothing else but our own innate character flaws. I don't entirely agree. I think some issues like environment and education also play a role. Besides, the Morgantown DTSs are by no means experts in their fields; a fact that could be proven by a background check on their education and training. How many, for example, have Ph.D.s, or have been state-certified as substance abuse counselors? Despite their licenses, how much of their training had been spent in actual, hands-on clinical counseling, and in what settings? How, often, too, are DTSs evaluated, and according to what standards? These are questions that needed to be asked.

Meanwhile, day-to-day life at merry Morgantown continued steadily on. January 5, 2007 was an unbelievable warm day, around seventy degrees. Since it was nice that day, a number of COs stood outside both cafeteria exit doors, randomly and arbitrarily stopping inmates to pat them down and search them for contraband. It amazes me that the prison worries abut an inmate walking out with an extra piece of fruit or bread, while, after dinner, COs and inmates working in the kitchen often leave with half the store. Just two nights before, I saw a CO walking out with at least one dozen bananas after the kitchen closed. In addition, inmates working the dinner shift sometimes take extra food back to their units. I've seen some inmates stop cleaning up in the kitchen, just so they could take food and hide it in their jackets. But a female CO actually stopped an elderly inmate, maybe in his early sixties, who was being pushed in a wheelchair by another inmate. She actually made this man lean forward in the wheelchair so she could see if he had tried to hide something near his backside. She also made him empty out his jacket pockets, and patted him down by his upper torso. If I didn't know better, I would think I was in a maximum security prison, and that she was searching for weapons, not apples. Since, by that time, I had worked in the kitchen for over a month, I could speak with reasonable clarity regarding the conditions of Morgantown's kitchen and dining room.

Many inmates don't like the kitchen, because they would have to work a little bit, but most people don't like it because of the dirt they'd experience from just cleaning the place up, or from mopping the floors. Plus, most think there's something psychologically demeaning about wearing a red smock and serving food to our fellow inmates. Clearly, some of us do feel we have been placed in a highly subordinate position in the prison hierarchy.

On the other hand, some inmates actually cherish their jobs in the kitchen and dining room, and wouldn't give them up for any other position. They can either steal food, or some of the COs will give them extras after dinner. In some cases, having extra food, especially fried chicken or fruit, is just like having cold, hard cash to trade with someone else.

Both the kitchen and the dining room, however, leave much to be desired when it comes to sanitation. There are some inmates who take pride in doing their jobs and keeping their own areas clean, but the majority working in either place couldn't give a shit about cleanliness.

Between every meal, the floors are mopped and the tables cleaned—at least in theory. One afternoon, before dinner, and right after the 4:00 p.m. count, CO Bartz, who was in charge that evening, pulled one inmate off to the side and asked him to show everyone else how he wipes a table. Unfortunately, that inmate left half the table dirty, because he never really used any elbow grease, and the water was dirty from lunch time. I've seen dirty water used not only to clean the tables, but also to mop the floors. I am sure this happens quite a bit on all the shifts. In fact, the COs constantly remind the inmates to change the water. I've also seen some dirty rags used to clean the stainless steel tops and sides of the main line where hot food is served. The plastic utensils used day in and day out are put through an industrialized dishwasher, but after cleaning, staff workers still need to check them for lingering food residue.

Now, every dining room and kitchen employee who either handles or serves food must wear a cap or hairnet and disposable plastic gloves. Despite these regulations, the kitchen, in particular, is often very unsanitary. For example, when chicken is served on Thursday nights, I've seen the trays or cooking sheets with baked or fried chicken routinely being laid across greasy cardboard on the floor, because of lack or room on the tables. On one such Thursday, a CO and one of the cooks saw a big, brown bug walk right across the floor, next to the trays.

342

The inmate tried to step on it, but missed, while the CO laughed and said, "I think you wounded it, though."

Still, the chicken was left on the floor. Moreover, very recently, cookies seventeen months over their expiration dates were served, as well as cheese whose green tops had been thrown away. "Waste not, want not," apparently is Morgantown's philosophy!

In the kitchen area is a water fountain that is occasionally filled with filthy utensils. In addition, I've often seen dirty food trays laying next to equally dirty buckets of water and mops. The employees' restroom, which is off the kitchen hallway, is one of the most disgusting places imaginable. Disposable gloves and hairnets are routinely strewn across the restroom floor. There are also eating utensils frequently lying in the sinks and on the floor next to the door, as well as cardboard on the floor around the toilet, and sheets of toilet paper and plastic gloves lying about. The one urinal looks as if it hadn't been cleaned in weeks. In fact, I've seen gas station restrooms that would put this one to shame. I must also sadly add that many inmates leave the restroom without washing their hands. If most of the inmates knew about these conditions, they would refuse to eat in the dining room.

I would be remiss if I didn't also talk about the quality and quantity of the food served. The CO in charge will tell the server ahead of time how much food to give out. One night, I was serving pepper steak out of a ladle, and putting it in the circular dish in the tray.

Since I was serving grown men, I filled the dish to the top, until CO Hartzel yelled out, "Laski, only one ladle per inmate!"

I'm sure everyone I served that night wanted to do their best Oliver Twist imitation and say to me, with big, soulful eyes, "Please, sir, I want more!" It's ridiculous the portions given out—one tablespoon of eggs, one portion of chicken, one piece of sausage, etc. It all comes down to prison over-crowding. When you have too many inmates for one facility, instead of transferring people to similar facilities, you simply cut back on the food. Many times, however, following dinner, the COs and staff would enjoy a double or triple portion of food on their trays, while inmates were still sitting there!

Having said that, there are items on the menu that are absolutely horrible. Some of the worst include: (1) Salisbury steak, which smells as bad as it tastes. It's so bad that on the days it's served, I'll either have just a salad, or just not go to the cafeteria at all to eat. (2) Hungarian goulash, which looks as bad as it tastes. (3) Ranchers steak—90 percent fat. (4) Beef and corn pot pie (more corn than beef). (5) Baked salmon, which smells and tastes as if the fish had been caught about ten years ago, and with more bones than actual meat.

That's why the microwave rooms are so busy, because many inmates would rather make their own food than eat in the cafeteria.

One of the worst things, however, about working in the kitchen are some of the COs who run the operation. The real asshole of the group is a CO named Hartzel, whom I mentioned earlier. He's about five feet tall, and one of the meanest, most uneducated people you'd ever had the displeasure to meet. First of all, he plays up to younger, blue-collar crime African-American inmates, because he's afraid of them, and wants them to think he's from the hood. Now, on the other hand, he treats white-collar crime inmates, both white and of color, with a noticeable dislike or cruelty. If a worker needs to leave early for class, or for any other reason, he'll give him all kinds of grief before letting him go. I hate just asking him a question about anything; he usually just stares, and grumbles some profanity. He's the same CO who once told me, in front of seventy or so inmates, that I could be his bitch any time, and clean anything he needed to be cleaned. Mr. Hartzel would certainly be in my top five of least favorite people at Morgantown.

Although COs Green and Bartz have generally treated us in a civil manner, they've also played the hard-ass role. I guess most employees at Morgantown are home-grown, born and raised in West Virginia. Many of them, for whatever reason, resent the inmates. This attitude may stem from the fact that most of us come from big cities, and at one point had power, money, prestige, or all three. So, unfortunately, most of the COs and prison staff feel that we had chances in life, but blew them, and that they're going to show us they're in charge here. Their arrogance and mean-spiritedness bother

344

us the most. If I possessed one good trait as a politician, it was never having to think I was better than anyone else. That goes back to the old adage that you should treat people the way you would want to be treated, even in a federal prison.

In the meantime, the first month of 2007 continued to drag on. January 7, 2007, was another warm day, probably in the mid-fifties, though a little cloudy. John and I had decided to walk for a short time that afternoon. When I first saw John at lunch, he seemed worried, and I wasn't even sure he wanted to walk, but we took a stroll around the pond anyway.

As we started to walk, John reminded me of a conversation we had back in September. I had mentioned then that I hoped I wouldn't change much from this experience, and that I was prepared to seek professional help if I did. Well, John believed that he had already changed a bit, and would change even more by June, when he would be returning home. He then proceeded to describe in detail his reactions to the noise and utter chaos that took place in Alexander the night before, when he was trying to play cards with a couple of guys in the big game room. I'd been there, and I knew that when the D.C. boys were in there playing, you couldn't hear yourself think. I don't know if it's a culturally-encouraged behavior or not, but those young urban gang-bangers couldn't seem to carry on a normal conversation without yelling. They could be right next to someone else, or across the table from that person, but still shout at the tops of their lungs. Apparently, this is what happened last night. In addition, some domino players couldn't just play the game and place a domino down on the table. No, they had to slam it as hard as they could. I don't know if it's for dramatic effect or not, but I find it very annoying. Even the counselors here at the Bates Unit request that anyone playing dominoes no longer slam them down, out of courtesy for those around them. At Bates, we have a classroom across from where the guys play dominoes; just imagine trying to read or study when someone continuously slams dominoes down on a table.

John and I again agreed that day that there were individuals here who absolutely didn't care about anyone else except themselves, and that many of them were both morally and educationally bankrupt. So, to top off that evening John was talking about, he said he had been asleep for about two hours, when a group of inmates from his wing waited until the curfew before heading off to bed. They were talking loudly and laughing, showing total disregard for other inmates' right to sleep. Needless to say, John was utterly fed up with these recent disturbances. I myself had to cut my phone conversation with Kathleen short that same night, because of the unbearable noise from the foyer area where the phones are located. Between the football game on TV, and the card and dominoes games, there was no way I could have carried on a normal phone conversation with my wife, so I had to hang up early.

This conversation led both John and me to the conclusion that we were indeed changing, by virtue of the fact that we were becoming annoyed by situations that probably would not have bothered us before coming to Morgantown. Thus, we were both worried about how we would react to other situations when we returned home. I'm worried because it's difficult for Kathleen (or anyone else who has not experienced prison life) to understand what's happening to me here. She hopes I can jump right into the normal swing of things when I get home and just pick up where I had left off, but I may, in fact, need at least a couple of weeks, like a returning combat solider, to first readjust to life back home. John and I both realized there would be financial and family problems to address, and I know both of us would give 110 percent back to our families, and try all we could to make our wives' lives easier. Still, we would first definitely need an opportunity to catch our breaths, and be shown just a little patience or understanding while going through a decompression period.

It's scary to think how a place like this plays on my psyche. Recently, I talked to a nice, twenty-five-year-old man from Pittsburgh who had explained to me how his older brother had been shot and killed right in front of him about six years ago by some gang-banger. Not only had his brother's murderer gotten off on the murder charge, he allegedly still brags about his crime back in the neighborhood. The young man I spoke to is not sure he wants to go back home when he is released later this year, because of the fear of what he might do if he runs into his brother's killer again. Another inmate, who is about twenty-eight-years-old, and who was once a member of a major Chicago street gang, told me about how, when he was sixteen years old, he had once been shot by a rival gang member, and ended up in the hospital for about three weeks. Then, I met a thirty-six-year-old man from Detroit who confessed to me that when he had been younger, he had been a sex addict, and had fathered thirteen children with thirteen different women. To his credit, he is now trying to either find or contact all of his children—a task that will cover several different states. These are just a few of the people I have met in prison who come from totally different environments than mine. The often tremendous void between our backgrounds, interests, cultural values, and ages can be staggering.

Just as staggering are the prison clergy's continued coldness and arrogance toward the inmates. One day, just before my tenth week in the program, I was serving Mass as usual for Father Alex. When Mass was over, I began helping anther inmate put the altar items, such as the chalice and consecrated hosts, lines, candles, etc., away. All of these items are stored in the Chaplain Rev. Price's office. Well, as I and another volunteer were bringing them in, my hands were so full that I had to push the door open with my shoulder. The chaplain indignantly rose from his desk and stood by the door as we started putting the articles away. At that point, I informed him calmly and respectfully, that all that were left were a couple of other items to run to the next room. He then curtly said he had to leave and locked the door, so either we could wait for Father Alex to return, or store the remaining items in the hallway, by the door. I guess the rudeness and arrogance towards the inmates know no boundaries here, because even Morgantown's clergy follow the same cold, disrespectful behavior toward us as the other COs.

By January 12, 2007, I was completing the tenth week of the RDAP class. It was a lively TC that day, with the issue of saving chairs in the TV room taking center stage. The day before, Mr. Koger, a second-phaser, had brought up the issue, even though he never watches TV. Then, two third-phasers, Mr. Washington and Mr. Stit, had taken Koger to task for grandstanding, and for totally ignoring the real issue-at-hand—rule-breaking. DTS Sowden criticized the whole third-phase class for not showing the leadership to stand up and defend Mr. Koger. So, in the January 12 TC, Mr. Washington and Mr. Stit both held themselves accountable for unwarranted criticism of Koger, and the rest of the third-phasers stood up to provide their feedback. The feedback was intense, as their classmates ripped Washington and Stit apart for not being responsible, open-minded, caring, and anything else they threw at them, including having not addressed the unfairness of chair saving in violation of basic "first come, first served" courtesy.

I hadn't planned on speaking up at that day's TC on this issue of seat saving, but a recent story I heard from John about a new arrival changed my mind. This inmate, Don, was a big college football fan who wanted to watch the National Championship game between the University of Florida and Ohio State. Since Don had lived in Florida for a period of time, he was an especially big fan of their football team. Unfortunately for Don, he was living in the Alexander Unit, where watching football and basketball was as important to some other inmates as eating and breathing. The night of the game, veteran Alexander inmates set squatter rights on designated spots in the TV rooms that they called their own. These particular inmates believed that by virtue of their self-proclaimed seniority, they were entitled to their own pre-designated areas, even if it meant putting their chairs down there only five minutes before a game, and moving other inmates out. Well, after poor Don heard about how things were done at Alexander, he went to one of the inmates who had a front row seat in front of the TV. Again, since inmates don't have money to bargain with, food, instead, is used from the commissary, such as bags of tuna, salmon, and mackerel, all of which are especially popular with many of the African-American inmates. Even though it actually comes in bags, the inmates barter with the word "cans." So, in order to borrow a more senior inmate's seat for the big game, Don had to pay for that seat, before the game, with three "cans" of tuna, which he, despite the risk of being placed in the SHU, stole from the kitchen.

Now I believed I had something worthwhile to say on the issue, so I decided to provide my own feedback to Mr. Washington. I gave what many of my classmates later told me had been an emotional and passionate speech that had really hit home with them. I related Don's story, and how the whole saving of seats is nothing more than bullying, extortion, and criminal behavior. I spoke about how no one is entitled to own a spot for himself, and how, more importantly, this issue was about how we should treat one another with respect and basic fairness. As I kept speaking, I became more emotional, and louder, but I held everyone else's attention. When I finished, I thought about more that I could have said, but was, overall, happy with my remarks. Later, a number of classmates came to me, including Mr. Koger, who not only said, "Good job," and "Thanks," but that he was also looking forward to being my classmate over the next three months, until he had graduated. That meant a great deal to me personally.

However, by the end of that TC, Mr. Livengood and Mr. Sowden were both convinced of the third-phasers' insincerity. So, each member of the third-phase class had to write one, two-page paper-a-day for the next five days on how their lack of leadership hurts the community. In addition, Mr. Livengood informed all the potential graduates that next week's ceremony would be put on hold until all third-phasers had been re-evaluated, so the staff could determine who would graduate and who would be recycled.

On a side note, one of the third-phase students, whom I had become friends with, had earlier expressed to me his concern about going back to his hometown. He is fearful that because some of his old friends might try to influence him to return to a life of drugs and crime, he may have to move to another state, where his parents are living. By contrast, another third-phaser who was scheduled to graduate the following week, was openly looking forward to selling drugs when he got out of prison. So much for rehabilitation! That particular inmate has an older brother who is on the front end of a twenty-one-year-old drug sentence. He is only twenty-two years old, became a father for the first time when he was only thirteen, and fathered three children from two different mothers. Now, an in-depth interview would have identified some flaws in his personality that would have required more than the RDAP's help. I've met this person, and unless something truly dramatic or life-changing happens to him, I'm sure he will be back in prison. He has a number of issues, including anger, extreme immaturity, irresponsibility, and most disturbingly, lack of desire to change his life when he returns home. Still, the RDAP continues to graduate such inmates, without really helping them change their lives at all.

As January 19, 2007 approached, it marked graduation day for the afternoon third-phasers. However, many found, to their disappointment, that their graduation plans would be put on hold. The day before the graduation, Dr. Baker addressed the group of nineteen. Their class started with thirty-one men, and because of recycling, or students signing out of the program, they lost a dozen people. Dr. Baker told the remaining group that they should really not be graduating, because they were viruses that had infected the entire therapeutic community. Even though they were leaving, he told them he believed some of them would be back. Some of the graduates later told me that Dr. Baker's report to the various halfway houses regarding each of them indicated they were high-risk candidates, and that if there were even the slightest problem out there, his recommendation would be to send them back to prison. According to what I heard, Dr. Baker told these agencies that this had been the worst class he had ever seen at Morgantown, and that it would be best for the rest of the students that this group was leaving.

At the actual ceremony, DTS Livengood read the names of the graduates. Dr. Baker was a no-show, and we were told he was under the weather that day. Mr. Adams, Alexander, and Bates' Unit Manager, gave some brief remarks, and of course in his own, arrogant way, felt he had to publicly mention that his own unit team had not been listed in the program. Warden Gutierrez, who, in my opinion, is not the most compassionate or caring individual one would care to meet, then gave a short speech. He said that as graduates, these men would be leaving prison shortly, and would go out and become people again. So, I guess my classmates and I are not truly considered people until we graduate. As soon as the warden opened his mouth, we could sense his abrasiveness and arrogance. Every time I've heard him speak, which has been on at least four separate occasions, he's made every effort to remind us that we are here because of our mistakes and bad choices. I certainly understand why I am in prison, and accept my share of responsibility. I hope to be a better person when I've gotten out, but it won't be because of the treatment here, or because of the warden's help. If I've learned one thing about this place, it's that it destroys inmates' self-esteem, and turns us into guilt-ridden, passive people when we leave this institution.

By January 22, I'd just gutted out the usual mind games in TC, and had completed the twelfth week of the RDAP. I would be remiss if I didn't comment on the frightening disparity between the program's morning and afternoon sections.

When I get up every morning, I thank my lucky stars that I'm in the p.m. class. It all starts with the Peer Counselors, who are graduates of the program, and who are assistants to the DTSs. The DTSs don't run the TC meetings per se. They are more like advisors, while the inmates (students), under the Peer Counselors' direction, set the agenda for each meeting. The p.m. Peer Counselor, Mr. Murphy, is also the Head Counselor of the six or so other Peer Counselors on the compound. Murphy is well-respected by the DTSs, and Dr. Baker occasionally confers with him on upcoming policies. Murphy knows about things that happen in the classes before they happen, but the great thing about Murphy is he is, just simply, a nice guy. He spends much of his time with the p.m. class, and offers input that is both fair and honest.

On the other hand, the a.m. class is nothing more than a head-bashing, brainwashing, and demoralizing experience for some of the students. Mr. Tschida, the Head a.m. Peer Counselor, could be classified as the Head Attack Dog for the class. Many of the a.m.. students had probably come in there with an open mind, but Tschida and others view the TC as a blood sport to psychologically break down other inmates. Mr. Tschida's cube is right next to mine, and his bunkie, Mr. Brady, is a second-phaser in the a.m. session, and one of Tschida's enforcers.

Tschida is somewhere in his late twenties, tall, with a medium build, and short, black hair and glasses. He's from Louisville, Kentucky, and has been here on drug charges. He had supposedly been a very good student in the RDAP class, and one known for vicious feedback. Certainly that kind of behavior played well with the DTSs, who later wanted him to be a Peer Counselor. Tschida comes across as a young, arrogant kid. His claim to fame now is being a Peer Counselor, but he's immature, and cannot take any type of criticism. He also laughs at night with his bunkie about how he destroyed someone with his feedback earlier that day, and frequently snickers about future attacks.

The a.m. TC hit an all-time low the morning of January 24 for the sake of what some in the TC sadly call "treatment." Mr. Nastasi brought up an issue before his group, and mistakenly asked some of his classmates to give him some less-than-critical feedback. Unfortunately for Nastasi, someone had already brought him up for a different issue, so he received twice the feedback, and potentially twice the number of possible learning experiences.

As I said before, some situations and circumstances naturally demand some type of treatment. However, treatment should never be given as punishment. In the a.m. community especially, the DTSs stand by and let some of the RDAP students, under the direction of Peer Counselor Tschida, run wild with their assigning of learning experiences.

In Nastasi's case, he received over fifteen learning experiences that included writing over fifty pages on various topics, as well as wearing a sign reading, "I am a manipulator, and I will try to manipulate you!" Another so-called treatment experience prohibited him from talking to anyone outside his cube. If Nastasi wanted to speak to someone, he had to begin the conversation by telling the person that he was a manipulator. He had to make the same statement in class each and every time before giving feedback, or participating in any other class activity.

When I later saw Nastasi, who was only in his fifties, he seemed a much older, broken man, the victim of egregious public humiliation, and with the approval of licensed DTSs.

Afterwards, Nastasi was in his cube working on his papers, while Mr. Tschida was twenty feet or so outside his own cube, playfully wrestling and roughhousing with another inmate, instead of working with and helping Mr. Nastasi. I personally have heard Tschida and his bunkie laugh about how they planned to figuratively split someone's head open in an upcoming TC session. Just that morning, I overheard Brady tell Tschida that he was going to give "special treatment" to someone, but Tschida stopped him with, "Don't *tell* me; *surprise* me!" Brady was known for telling people that he was very good at giving out vicious feedback, and for reminding everyone that his bunkie was the great Mr. Tschida.

I became very concerned that the whole RDAP class, at least the a.m. session, was taking a very negative direction. It was disconcerting and frightening that some DTSs could actually sit back and tacitly authorize that type of behavior. Over the past week, the a.m. class had unmercifully crucified three of their classmates with over 150 pages of writing assignments, bedtime curfews, wearing of signs similar to Hester Prynne's scarlet "A," and standing by the front door of the Bates Unit to tell residents on the way in or out, that among other things, they were crooks.

It is regrettable that the BOP gives its stamp of approval to this type of program. A drug/rehab program should be simply that— a drug/alcohol rehabilitation program. I would have envisioned a treatment method that is frank and open about a patient's addiction, but that also provides uplifting lessons and tools to help inmates raise their own self-esteem. We have all made mistakes in our lives, and the worst thing someone can do is to ridicule us in front of our peers. This program should be about challenges and changes, along with the importance of positive thinking as a means of encouraging individuals to take a good, honest look at themselves. I know that any significant changes that come in my life will be the result of positive reinforcement, not public humiliation.

In the meantime, every time I thought I'd seen or heard it all, something else would shock me. One of my classmates, Mr. Aronowitz, had to be taken to the hospital because of internal bleeding. He had spent one week there earlier, and according to him, had needed a transfusion of at least four pints of blood, plus a couple of scopes, resulting in a diagnosis of diverticulitis. What is so disturbing about this story is that when he politely asked one of the female administrators in the medical building to notify his wife about having to return to the hospital, she came right out and said that was not her job. He supposedly made one more request before the ambulance pulled away, but again she refused.

Mrs. Aronowitz did not hear from her husband for two days. As things would have it, she needed to sign consent forms for her husband's procedures, and the nurse on duty asked if he had a Living Will or a Power of Attorney, both of which he told her his wife had back at home. Luckily, the nurse called his home and spoke to his wife, whom I can only imagine was very upset at the prison's lack of communication with her.

The next day, Aronowitz's wife called the prison to speak to someone at the Bates unit. She, in fact, reached her husband's counselor, Mr. Shuman, and complained that no one had contacted her about her husband's condition. Shuman answered that it had not been *his* responsibility to call her, and that while the BOP needed to know his whereabouts at all times due to his inmate status, she, on the other hand, didn't. Nevertheless, she became very upset with Mr. Shuman's indifference. In turn, he became very belligerent, and hung up the phone on her. One of the senior inmates later told Aronowitz that the BOP only has to contact family members in the event of an inmate's death, or impending death. If that is true, we really should question our prison system's moral and ethical policies.

Fortunately for Ms. Aronowitz, one of the nurses kept her up to speed on his condition, and she was able to visit him on the weekend. I can imagine, however, how nervous he must have been in a strange hospital, and with an uncertain prognosis. Also, his stay was less than pleasant, because some of the nurses openly remarked that because he was a federal prisoner, he wasn't entitled to the same attention as other patients.

Meanwhile, I, along with third-phaser Mr. Graves, were selected by our peers to serve as facilitators for an upcoming week. One of the issues the community had recently discussed was Tony Blair's inability to be on time for TC, because he had recently overslept more than once. As mentioned earlier, Mr. Blair had been under the DTSs' microscopes ever since one of his telephone conversations to his mom, in which he had accused two of his classmates of racist treatment toward him. Now, the community questioned Tony's motivation, and called him "lazy." After the feedback, the community assigned him approximately twelve learning experiences, including beginning every class conversation with, "I'm Tony Blair, and I'm lazy," for the next month. As facilitator, I now became quite vocal about how I felt about the difference between treatment and humiliation, and moved us to vote on the fairness of Tony's punishment. Then, DTS Sowden jumped in and defended the leaning experiences by comparing them to an alcoholic's admitting his or her problem at an AA meeting. I didn't agree at all with that false analogy, and announced that I was ready to take the vote. Then, Peer Counselor Murphy shot me down, and said there would be no vote. He later told me privately that sometimes the TC operates as a democracy, but at other times, because of the DTSs, as a dictatorship. If I had been allowed to proceed with such a vote, the DTS s would no doubt have used their powers to make things worse on the TC, so he had actually done me a favor. Be that as it may, there was a verbal confrontation between two inmates, and it became so intense that they had to be separated. That issue then took up most of the subsequent class time, with both individuals receiving ten learning experiences apiece.

When the session finished, I thought that Graves and I had done a decent job running the meeting. However, it's hard for a facilitator to do his job, be fair and unbiased when a DTS spouts off his or her philosophy about how things in TC should be handled. As a facilitator, as Murphy told me, a student is locked in by the power imbalance, and he had better do things the STSs' way, for the safety of himself and his fellow TC participants.

Two days later, on February 1, Dr. Baker, along with DTSs Land, Sowden, Livengood, Lindsley, and Ratay, brought in Tony Blair to their conference room, and recycled him back three months, or the equivalent of one phase. They basically told him that he was not ready to graduate in April, and that he needed additional treatment.

Tony was so distraught that he considered signing out of the program the next morning. Two other RDAP students, Mr. Nastasi, and Dr. Falitico, both third-phasers in the a.m. class, were up for re-evaluation by Dr. Baker and his crew. Natasi was supposed to have graduated in February, and Falitico in April, but both had been subjected to relentless attacks by some of their community members and the Peer Counselors, including Mr. Tschida. They both had been assigned punitive papers to write, and as pointed out earlier, Nastasi had to wear a sign around his neck telling everyone he was a manipulator. Although both were supposed to have their fates decided that day, Dr. Baker postponed those final decisions for an undetermined amount of time. In the meantime, they both looked as if they were on the verge of nervous breakdowns. In fact, the two admitted to me that the entire way of life here at Bates was intolerable, and that signing out of the program might be an option.

Honestly, I was happy I was no longer a facilitator. Mr. Murphy, surprisingly, was quite critical of me for my performance during the past couple of days. He told me that I had been unprepared, nervous, and power-oriented. Frankly, I didn't give a shit, because I believe I had done the best I could have done under the circumstances.

Later, when I went back to Bates, Mr. Carol, one of the a.m. Peer Counselors, told me that he thought our p.m. class seemed much more relaxed than the morning session. When I told him that being relaxed was a positive sign, he quickly replied that it wasn't, because TC treatment is *supposed* to be uncomfortable, and that we should not be so relaxed. Instead of arguing with him, I just shrugged my shoulders and walked away, thinking that the more comfortable one is, the more willing one may be to openly discuss his problems with others. These philosophical differences make it very difficult for me to identify anything of value in this program.

The next day in TC, a friend of mine, Mr. T., from Pittsburgh, disclosed some shocking information about the a.m. meeting. The topic that day involved a classmate's outrage over his brother's physical abuse of his wife in front of their children. She had called the police and had her husband arrested. According to Mr. T., the ensuing class conversation was truly disturbing. Almost all members in the group incredibly blamed her for aggravating the situation, and in their opinion, it forced her husband to strike her. Then, one of Mr. T.'s classmates asked him if he had ever hit a woman. When he unequivocally answered "No," the classmate then asked the group of eighteen men, by a show of hands, if they had ever hit their spouses or girlfriends. Out of those eighteen, sixteen raised their hands affirmatively. Some subsequently proceeded to lecture Mr. T. about their own domestic relationships, which included comments like, "She deserved it," "I was tired after work and she aggravated me," and "After she cooled down in a day or so, she let me back in the house." One inmate actually said that the woman who had called the police should be worried about her man now understandably coming after her and killing her.

These are inmates who obviously may need more than just drug and alcohol rehabilitation. This type of thinking is not only morally deficient, but borders on criminal. Even the Peer Counselor who sat in on the session remarked to these guys that they needed some serious treatment if they really believed what they had just said. In two days, the next first-phase class would start in the p.m. session, and my class's second-phasers would be stepping up to lead as an example. I can't even imagine some of my classmates who condone domestic violence providing any positive role modeling to the program's new students.

A few days later, I would experience day number two of our full Therapeutic Community. When I woke up that morning, the heat wasn't on. It was below zero outside, and it couldn't have been more than fifty degrees inside the unit. I now sleep every night in my sweatshirt and sweatpants, along with a pair of socks. I've actually seen people sleep with their stocking caps on, and also use their jackets as extra blankets. We were told that it was so cold the night before that it might have screwed up the computer system that controls the heat in the building. I don't know if I buy that one, but at least it sounds plausible. At any rate, it was so cold that even the running stream outside froze over.

The most important component of class that day was the orientation portion for the forty students in the new first-phase group, which brought our TC to one-hundred inmates strong.

Later in the week, Mr. Livengood introduced himself to the first–phasers, and then immediately asked, "Who in the new class has heard I was a prick?"

Of course, most of my class and the third-phasers wanted to raise their hands. What an unprofessional way for a drug treatment specialist to greet new students!

One new RDAP student I met this week was a Mr. James Keating, from Charlotte, North Carolina. Just a few weeks back, my friend, "Charlotte Rob" Stamper told me that Keating had been a wheeler dealer who had made millions with his car dealerships, one of which Rob himself had managed. There were approximately forty defendants in Keating's case. After all was said and done, Keating received a thirty-month sentence, and Rob, a twenty-four month sentence. As you can well imagine, Rob still harbored a lot of bitterness for his former boss.

Well, I kept an open mind when I first met Mr. Keating, who was around fifty, with grayish hair, and a facial appearance that seemed as if stress had played a major role in his life. As soon as I met him in class, I instantly knew what Rob was talking about. He sat in the front of the class, and spoke to anyone he saw. When one of the DTSs asked for first-phasers to comment on the program, he was the first to raise his hand, and tried to deceive everyone with his comments about how important the program was to him. Trust me, I know a bullshitter when I hear one.

My suspicions were confirmed that evening when I talked to Rob, who told me that he had just seen Keating leaving Alexander's ever-popular C-wing smoking bathroom. In fact, Rob also told me that Keating had been seen on Super Bowl Sunday smoking at Alexander.

The next day at orientation for the new first-phasers, we divided our TC into small groups, so that the third-phasers and the second-phasers could go over the basic rules and the program's philosophy. Well, as fate would have it, Keating was in my small group that afternoon when I spoke on the issue of accountability. Basically, I told the group there were consequences for their actions, including smoking violations, and they should try to do the right thing. Keating then got up in the class and spoke on the importance of honesty and accountability. At the end of the day, I was in the Recreation Center, and ran into Rob, who told me that he had just seen Keating again leaving the infamous C-wing Alexander smoking bathroom. Rob had been on the phone talking to his wife, when Keating, who evidently knew he had been spotted, stopped by the phones to interrupt their conversation with a request.

"Whatever you do, don't tell Laski, because I could get kicked out of the program."

As much as I disliked Keating, I could never bring myself to turn him into the DTSs. My only hope is that he will get caught smoking due to his own carelessness, or just self-destruct when people start seeing how phony and insincere he really is.

Around this same time, I also received my first sixty-day review, which was really my ninety-day review. My DTS, Shelia Land, wrote the following report:

(1) *Anxiety and Excessive Worry*: Inmate Laski is actively working to improve in this area. He is reading several self-help books. He was nominated, and has accepted the opportunity to chair the Therapeutic Community meeting. He did a very good job keeping things running in an orderly manner. He has several papers due over the next couple months to help develop insight into this problem.

(2) *Sentimentality*: Inmate Laski has a big problem with anger which he covers up with the "nice guy" image. He is encouraged to dig deeper into his anger to help identify how he compensates with the use of sentimentality. It is important for him to understand that until he works on his anger, it remains a vicious cycle (anger/sentimentality).

(3) *Fraudulent*: Inmate Laski has begun to identify his pattern of fraudulent behavior. He has completed an assignment

identifying things that he has "gotten away with." He is encouraged to discuss more of his fraudulence with his small group and ask for feedback.

Other Comments: Inmate Laski is an active member of the community. He is insightful and has demonstrated the ability to give good feedback. He struggles with anger, open-mindedness, and sentimentality. Ask for feedback to help your work in these areas.

That report was based on what she had periodically observed in TC. I believe she attended over four small group sessions during the first three months. In one of those sessions, I had expressed concern over how the TCs were run. That probably accounted for the first reference to my anger issue, because it was never mentioned among my initial treatment goals. This portion of the report, then, was unfairly based on very little one-on-one communication between the inmate and the DTS, and more on her casual observation of the TC and small group sessions. It is very difficult to treat someone for an addiction and alleged behavioral problems if all conclusions are based on a PSI report and two short interviews at Morgantown. If an inmate is really going to get help here, besides doing it on his own, he needs substantial one-on-one interaction with a DTS or a psychologist. The program's current format is not getting to the heart of anyone's problems.

Meanwhile, John gave me his weekly update from the Alexander Unit. First, "Charlotte Rob" Stamper requested a transfer out of Alexander to the Bennett Unit, which is not only a quieter unit, but also holds only one-hundred inmates as compared to the over 300 at "Thunderdome." According to Rob, the noise and the continued criminal behavior over there had taken its toll on him.

Another inmate over at Alexander, Frank Carducci, just had knee surgery. John told me that Mr. Carducci had slipped in the A-wing bathroom almost a year ago, and had hurt his knee. He had immediately gone to the medical building for an x-ray, which had not shown any broken bones. He then had been sent back to the unit. Now, according to Rob, who had spoken to Frank, he had been in pain for almost a year, and had requested that the medical staff send him out for an MRI, for a fuller evaluation. Each request had been denied until Frank had filed a lawsuit against the prison. Finally, he had been sent out for the MRI, which revealed that he had actually had some ligament damage that required surgery. This is just another example of how insensitive and cold the medical staff here is. They are clearly reluctant to take that extra step to make sure their diagnoses are correct. I'm sure Mr. Carducci would agree with me.

Even I had to report to the medical building on February 13 for my three-month blood test. While sitting in the waiting room, I overheard some inmates talking about the poor medical conditions here. One particular inmate said that he had recently had a terrible toothache, and had tried to describe his condition to a female staff member whose language he could not understand. She left the room for a minute and came back with a package of hemorrhoid pads. He had then frantically pointed to his mouth, and to his rear, shaking his head negatively, to try to point out that his problem was not there. Ultimately, he had left in the same condition in which he had walked in—with a toothache. Unfortunately, as mentioned earlier, this institution has no dentist on staff.

I also saw Dr. Falitico and Mr. Nastasi, both of whom had graduated from the a.m. class the past week. They seemed very happy, but physically worn out. After a short conversation, I heard the emotional exhaustion in their voices as well. These are two well-educated men who had been beaten down by their classmates, and with the DTSs' approval. All three of us joked that we would need treatment at home for our treatment here, but I realized there was nothing humorous about that.

By February 17, another week of RDAP was in the books; the first phase for the beginning students had been completed, and we were ready to become fully engaged again in TC. Speaking of TC, its location had moved from a roomy warehouse-type building on the compound back to the unit in our regular classrooms. Since we were now in a small area, both the a.m. and the p.m. classes were divided into two TCs each. Previously, both TCs had consisted of approximately one-hundred-or-so students, but now each TC was about fifty strong. This new classroom setting, although more intimate, put greater pressure on each student to participate. For example, that week alone, in the smaller TC, I spoke ten times; in a bigger group, I would have been lucky to have done half of that in one week.

Despite these changes, one thing remained the same—the Peer Counselors' constant encouragement of confrontation. Mr. Tschida and some of the a.m. Peer Counselors were now sitting in on the p.m. classes, and raising all types of havoc. Again, these were young, immature guys in their mid-twenties who thought they were professional psychologists, but acted like South American dictators. They continued to try to impose their will on the community by criticizing and embarrassing us. The time wasted in the TC on vindictive accountability could be better spent on such issues as those currently facing a classmate of mine from West Virginia, who had recently been informed that his brother had been shot and murdered that week. Another classmate had been shot approximately eight times in his life, and yet another student had been shot four times, and run over by a car. These people have real issues, but they will have real problems bringing anything of that magnitude up within a class dominated by Peer Counselors who have an entirely different agenda.

On top of everything else, that night I spoke with Kathleen, who informed me that our daughter Nina was not accepted to St. Ignatius High School. Nina, who had made high honors that entire year at Morgan P.R. Academy, was extremely disappointed. The frustration and the helplessness I feel when my family struggles back at home makes the time here seem even harder to deal with than usual. This kind of day I would just as soon remove permanently from my memory banks.

Several days later, on February 20, Dr. Falitico and I sat down for one hour, just to talk, because early that morning after close to four years at Morgantown, he was heading home, to a halfway house in Syracuse, New York. The following month he would appear before the New York Medical Board to get his license back. From the first time I met him, he was always a gentleman, but I could see the pain and exhaustion in his eyes from this program's damage to his psyche. The mental torture his classmates and Peer Counselors had inflicted on him had been inexcusable. He had actually set up an appointment back at home to see a therapist to correct the effects of the therapy he had received here at Morgantown. When we were saying goodbye, he said one of the nicest things I'd ever heard from anybody else.

After we shook hands and wished each other well, he said, "Jim, just get through this program. You're a good man who doesn't deserve to be here."

I'll always appreciate those words, with the hope that he will once again be happy and successful back home.

Afterwards, John and I took a walk, something we hadn't done much of recently, because of the bitterly cold weather that had settled in this area in the last couple of weeks. He told me he had a visit earlier in the day from his fiancée. After every visit, John always had a story about the Visiting Center. One of the more strictly enforced rules involves physical contact between an inmate and his significant other. The rules allow one embrace at the beginning and one when one's mate leaves. Some inmates, however, have actually been put in the SHU for various physical contact violations (in fact, an inmate was recently placed in the SHU for groping his girlfriend). According to John, Richard Hatch, the former *Survivor* star, who is serving time for tax evasion, received a visit from his same-sex partner, and during the course of their visit, they were hugging, holding hands, and laying their heads on each other's shoulders constantly, all of which the COs on duty that day simply ignored. That was clearly a double standard. The physical contact rules should apply equally to both gay and heterosexual couples, but there seems to be different rules for different people at different times.

I have seen greater tolerance by prison officials of unauthorized touching in general by the gay population. One inmate, who is trying to look more like a woman than a man, has been taking medication that has given him larger breasts and a smooth, puffy facial complexion. He was allegedly engaged in sexual activity with other inmates—a situation that the prison authorities never show the slightest interest in investigating, even though it is a blatant physical contact violation. In fact, sexual behavior between inmates in any prison would normally warrant a transfer to another institution, but apparently not here. I have also seen gay inmates openly holding hands, romantically caressing each other's faces, and erotically massaging each other's bodies, which are all physical contact violations that again, the COs simply overlook. I guess, though, such a double standard is a fact of life in a federal prison like Morgantown.

Two days later, on February 22, I chaired my self-help group, which meets every Wednesday night. We usually have a pre-set topic, but that evening I decided to wing it by discussing the RDAPs pros and cons, taking the opportunity to criticize what I considered another recent humiliating learning experience.

That student had been held accountable for both his sarcasm and a verbal confrontation he had recently had with a Peer Counselor. One of his learning experiences, which had been assigned by the aforementioned Peer Counselor, had been before giving feedback or speaking on any issues at any meetings, to first state, "I have a tendency to use sarcasm to cover up my low self-esteem." Of course, I questioned the purpose and quality of that type of learning experience, and several of the students that night agreed with me. They pointed out the exercise's potentially harmful effects on the participant's self-image. Unfortunately, the majority seemed scared of criticizing any part of the RDAP. It is becoming increasingly apparent that the only way for me to survive this program is to keep to myself as much as possible, The less I discuss my personal issues with others here, the better off I will be. Each day I keep learning to stay under the radar, and to avoid controversial subjects that could be used against me down the road.

Despite my determination to keep a low profile, Mr. Murphy recently informed me that the time had come for me to step forward and bring up another issue in the TC. Most of my personal issues regarding my wife and kids I never shared (and would never) with my classmates, because they were just too sensitive and personal. Therefore, I restricted myself to simply offering feedback to others. Even that practice, according to Murphy, left something to be desired. Murphy claimed that my so-called "sentimentality" caused me to sugarcoat some of my feedback. He claimed I wanted to maintain my "nice guy" image, and that I was afraid to be totally honest with people. He had a point. My struggle with that image probably stemmed from my political career, which was all about maintaining a favorable image for the purpose of convincing people to vote for me. In fact, I practiced that philosophy every day in the political arena.

My present concern, though, was that Murphy, like some of the other DTSs, was putting too much importance on how many issues an inmate brings forward to the TC, whether they are helpful or not—in other words, on *quantity*, and not *quality*. This philosophy is based on the faulty premise that if an inmate is in this program, then he must be screwed up in the head, and thus have a host of personal issues to bring before the community. So, even if a participant does all the assignments, obeys the rules, participates in class with feedback, and stays focused, he still might not graduate if he fails to bring up enough personal issues about himself.

There are three major weaknesses underlying this policy. First, RDAP students all sign a contract requiring them to obey the rules at Bates, yet, in order to receive treatment, they must first bring up an issue about themselves, and that issue almost invariably requires breaking a rule in order to have an issue to present! Secondly, the program's so-called "treatment" comes from fellow inmates who have known each other only for a few months, on the average, and yet they are expected to respond to complex, deep-seated personal issues and problems that would surely require professional and clinical expertise to be truly effective. Thirdly, as pointed out before, the feedback offered is often insincere, vindictive, and destructive. Finally, this philosophy does nothing more than encourage some students to expose self-faults that may not be genuine, just for the sake of passing the program. Trust me, some RDAP students do make up issues just to show the DTSs they're engaged in treatment. Unfortunately, some inmates even use their family members as ploys to create phony issues to further their treatment goals.

Despite my reservations about having to bring up another issue about myself, I realized I had no other choice. I had to be careful, though, to not bring up an issue I had brought up before. Otherwise, the community could claim that my behavior had fallen into a pattern, which would make me eligible for learning experience assignments. I decided then on something I truly had not addressed before about myself, and which Mr. Murphy had recently mentioned to me—my reliance on sentimentality as a behavioral disorder. When I stood up before the TC, I explained my struggle with sentimentality, and how it had affected my earlier feedback in class. I expressed my concern about how much I wanted to be regarded as a "nice guy," an obsession that sometimes caused me not to be totally honest with my classmates. I said I had sugar-coated my remarks in the hope that they would like me, and help me in the future.

In return, I received feedback from seven of my classmates, who told me to "keep it real," and to be honest in my feedback, so I could help others. I was also told to take a close look at my motives, and to make sure I wasn't on a hidden agenda. Each time I received this feedback, I had to repeat it to the community, and to the person who had given me the treatment.

Following the meeting, I saw Ms. Land in the hallway, and she gave me some positive reactions to my issue. However, she informed me that I lied about my past lack of honest feedback, and it was one more problem to add to my "anxiety," "anger," "sentimentality," "fraud," and "deceit." The next five-page paper she required me to write would be on how sentimentality impacted my family. Ms. Land also told me she wanted me to dig deep to the core of the matter, and to talk about how both manipulative behavior and "nice guy" image negatively affected my children's thinking. I already knew, only too well, what I had done to my family. This type of treatment exercise would do nothing more than compound my guilt.

That evening I talked to my TC Peer Counselor, Mr. Williams, a recent graduate of the program, who unfortunately had become brainwashed. He had gone from fair, friendly, and compassionate, to arrogant, rude, and cold. When I asked him how I had done that day with my issue, he looked at me and laughed. When I asked him what was so funny, he told me that when *I* became serious about my *treatment, he* would be more serious about his *reactions*, and would try not to laugh. He actually accused me of using sentimentality when bringing up that very same issue. This was the same guy who, following his graduation, told me he wasn't sure he really wanted to become a Peer Counselor, but I encouraged him to try, because I thought he'd be a real asset to this program. His subsequent ego and closed-mindedness, however, have hindered his abilities as a role model for the community.

Later that day, as a welcome respite from self-aggrandizing Peer Counselors, I sat down and talked again with my buddy, Bruce Drennan, the Cleveland sportscaster who would be leaving the following day, after a five-month sentence. Before he said goodbye, he told me a couple of intriguing stories about his Morgantown stay. The first one involved former Congressman Bob Ney from Ohio, who had recently been sentenced to thirty months for his part in a corruption scandal involving Washington lobbyists. He arrived that very same day at Morgantown to begin his sentence. After he was processed, one of the inmates named Mark Gee, who is the compound driver, showed him around the prison, and helped him get his uniform and other clothing. Gee had then taken Ney to the cafeteria, and used his own ID card to buy lunch for the ex-Congressman. Just to be nice, he even sat with Ney, just to keep him company. Then, Warden Gutierrez came by, and asked Gee what he was doing. Gee told him that he was just showing the new inmate around, and answering some of his questions. Before Gee even finished his explanation, the Warden abruptly interrupted him, and told him to leave the cafeteria and let the new guy figure things out for himself. Welcome to Morgantown, Mr. Ney!

The second story involved one of Bruce's roommates over at the Carlson Unit, who had needed gallbladder surgery that past week, and had been sent to a Morgantown hospital. Following successful surgery, and while he had been recovering from the anesthesia, the hospital staff had decided that since there had been no more available beds at their facility, he would have to be sent back to the prison. According to Bruce, he returned with some very strong painkillers, and strict instructions not to bend over for a day. Well, the prison staff took away all of his painkillers, and replaced them with Tylenol. The poor guy then spent most of the night in agonizing pain. To make matters worse, the next day, this lost soul walked from his unit to the cafeteria, and since he couldn't bend down to tie his shoes, he had left them undone. As fate would have it, he ran into a CO who told him to tie his shoes. He tried to explain his situation, but the more he tried, the more adamant the CO became, until he had no other choice but to bend over to tie his shoes. The pain then became so intense that he went straight to the medical building instead of to lunch, where he was prescribed similar pain medications to the ones they had taken away from him the night before! Fortunately, after a couple of days, he was able to get back on his feet, but again, Morgantown FCI is *not* the place to become ill.

While we're on the subject of medical care, regrettably, I cannot exempt the prison pharmacists from their fair share of criticism either, as I myself discovered two days later, on March 2. I went to the pharmacy for my weekly refill of Zoloft. Back at Bates, when I opened the bottle to take my daily dose of one-and-a-half pills, or 75 mg., I noticed how different their color and size were from my usual refills. Around the same time, my classmate, John Marshall, who lives in the same wing, and who takes 50 mg. of Zoloft daily, had just picked up his prescription. So I went over to John's bunk and asked him if I could look at his pills. I was amazed to see that he had the same colored and sized pills in a bottle labeled "Zoloft, 100 mg." We found out that we both had received the right medication, but the wrong dosage. In fact, for John, that was double his prescribed dosage, and for me, 25 mg. more than I had been prescribed. Needless to say, we both went back to the pharmacist and gave him our bottles. When he looked inside, and at the labels on the bottles, he admitted he had made a mistake. He said that because he had filled both prescriptions at the same time, he had inadvertently grabbed the 100 mg. bottle of the bigger yellow pills, instead of the 50 mg. bottle of the smaller, blue pills.

When he corrected his mistake, he looked at us, shrugged his shoulders, and simply said, "Sorry about that."

The scary thing was that particular individual was the Senior Pharmacist for the entire compound.

On that same day, our first class in "Criminal Thinking Errors" met together. The DTS for the class was Mr. Turner, who just happened to be the twin brother of Counselor Turner over at the Alexander Unit. When DTS Turner began class, he spoke on what the program identifies as "the eight thinking errors" —MOLLIFICATION, ENTITLEMENT, POWER ORIENTATION, CUT-OFFS, SENTIMENTALITY, SUPER-OPTIMISM, COGNITVE INDOLENCE (LAZY THINKING), and DISCONTINUITY. Turner went through each error, and gave examples of how they applied to our lives.

When he got to SENTIMENTALITY, he immediately remarked, "This thinking error is for you white collar guys." He went on to say, "You fraud guys are the worst, stealing millions of dollars out of insurance funds and pensions. You're nothing more than criminals dressed up, wearing ties!"

During that whole time, I had been slumped over at my desk, while some others had been staring at me. He then talked more about "fraud guys" using their "nice guy" image to steal money from people, both young and old, and ruin their lives. By the time he had finished with his dissertation about white-collar criminals, I felt like hiding under my desk.

The other interesting news for the day concerned my friend, Cyrus Bland, who happened to be in the other afternoon TC with some of the more intense inmates, including Mr. Carrol, the a.m. Peer Counselor. Cyrus forgot to carry his focus card (the card that carries information about his treatment goals and solutions) to class. This meant that he had to bring himself up in front of the community. Since this was the second incident of so-called irresponsibility for him (about three months prior, Cyrus had too many books on his cube shelf; the limit according to the unit rules is ten per inmate), the community determined such behavior was a recurring pattern, and subject to learning experiences. By the end of the class, Cyrus had earned eight such experiences, including one by Peer Counselor Carrol, which required him to stand by the front door of Bates at least one night after dinner that week, greeting people, and reading each one a rule out of the Handbook. Yet Mr. Carrol would later break a unit rule himself that night by taking a shortcut through the

Recreation Building after dinner to go back to the Bates Unit; RDAP students are not allowed to cut through the Recreation/Education Building to get to the other end of the compound. An inmate must walk *around* the building, and not *through* it. This would be just one more example of that old adage, "Don't do as I do, do as I say."

I also learned that "Charlotte Rob" Stamper had finally gotten his wish, and been transferred from "Thunderdome," or Alexander Unit, to Bennett. That unit holds only about eighty people, and has some private rooms for two people, besides dorm-style accommodations. Also, the beds there have spring mattresses, not like the military-style ones that lay flat on metal bunks, as at Alexander and Bates. Rob noticed immediately how quiet Bennett was as compared to Alexander. Moreover, the unit had some extra perks, such as three different vending machines—one for sodas, one for snacks, and another for coffee and hot chocolate. The only thing left for Rob was to somehow convince our friend John to leave Alexander, too, and follow him to Bennett.

No matter where an inmate lives on the compound, however, medical concerns, as I've explained before, continue to be the number one issue for many here. Recently, I cut my finger, and was having a difficult time just finding a bandage. One of the inmates who had been here a few years reminded me to be careful of any open wounds, because of the rampant HIV and Hepatitis on the compound. So even a little cut on the finger could turn into a major deal here.

My biggest medical concern recently, though, was my toothache. One of my back molars was giving me some problems. I was taking 800 mg. of Ibuprofen to kill the pain, along with some aspirin, which I put on top of my tooth. It didn't taste very good when it dissolved, but it seemed to help relieve the discomfort.

As stated several times before, Morgantown, FCI is the worst possible place for an inmate who has any type of dental problem. I was here for over four months before an outside dentist was brought in for some simple exams. Some individuals have had to wait even longer before seeing an outside dentist. When the visiting dentist examined me, he did nothing more than look in my mouth and describe to his assistant the condition of each tooth. When he examined my back teeth, he asked me when I was scheduled to return home. When I told him I'd be leaving for home in August, he recommended seeing my dentist about getting some crowns placed on my back molars. In fact, about a week before I had arrived at Morgantown, my dentist had cleaned my teeth and applied a desensitizer on my molars. I can understand now why some of my back teeth have been starting to bother me.

I have spoken to some other inmates who have told me horror stories about their dental experiences. One of classmates, Mr. Hussing, recently told me a classic story about the time he had a terrible toothache. Supposedly, he was put on a waiting list to see a dentist for a tooth extraction. Unfortunately, about two months went by, and Mr. Hussing was unable to take the pain any longer, and kept probing and prying at his tooth in order to loosen it. When he thought it had been loosened enough, he took a ballpoint pen, wedged it against the bad tooth, and asked one of the other inmates to take a book and swing it like a hammer on a nail to the back of the pen. With one full swing of that book on the pen, his tooth was dislodged! Not all Morgantown FCI stories are that extreme, but when an outside dentist is brought in, often the only remedy recommended is extraction. Nine times out of ten, procedures involving root canals and crowns are not even suggested. For a federal prison that houses over 1,300 inmates, such a situation is unacceptable.

Dental concerns aside, it was now March 15, the Ides of March, and I had reached the halfway point in the RDAP class. I continued to hope and pray that I could make it through the program. Just in the past two weeks alone, I saw a third-phaser expelled from the program, and another, who was also in his third phase, recycled all the way back to the first phase. As hard as I tried to stay under the radar, I knew I'd eventually have to come out of my shell and participate in the TC again. Still, I was as skeptical of the program's merits as when I had started in November, because the DTSs simply do not require students to address the chief causes of their addiction as core issues. Until that happens, its success in helping inmates change their lives for the better will be negligible at best.

Around this same time, the prison was rocked by the news that Warden Gutierrez was relieved of his duties. There were many rumors flying around the compound regarding his departure. I heard that he was forced to resign, or that he was fired due to the numerous complaints filed against him by inmates and staff. I don't know the real reason, but he was a terrible administrator who had absolutely no respect for the inmates, and exhibited an arrogance that aggravated anyone he came into contact with. As the rumors subsequently circulated around the compound about the ex-warden's potential legal problems, I couldn't help but remember the first week I was here, when he reminded all of us that we were in prison because we hadn't obeyed society's rules or laws. Only time will tell, but let's see if the former warden practiced what he preached.

As I close the book on the first half of this program, it is fitting and appropriate to relate a recent class experience that highlights the deficiencies of the RDAP and the DTSs.

After class, the entire second phase normally has a class once a week called "Living with Others," taught by DTS Ratay. She had given an assignment a few weeks back to write a three-page paper on what was wrong with our thinking, and what we could do to correct it. Well, every week, two or three students read their papers, and the rest of the class, along with Ratay, critiqued the students' observations. It had just so happened that a student named John, who had read his paper, had not been as forthcoming as Ratay and the rest of the class would have liked. In fact, some people believed that he had been holding back some of his true feelings. As John was being questioned about his alleged lack of openness, one of our classmates disclosed the fact that when he was younger, he had been sexually molested. His eyes swelled from the tears while he told us how his own wife and mother didn't even know this, but that he had wanted to share that story with us, so as to convince John of the importance of getting things off his chest. When he finished his story, you could have heard a pin drop in that classroom. Ms. Ratay praised the student for his honesty, and offered her own sympathy for what he had endured. She then turned to the rest of the class and told us not only to support our classmates, but to openly share any information about ourselves that we might consider terrible or shameful, so that we and others might learn from such disclosures. Then, a couple of hands went up, one regarding parental abuse, and another, molestation. Before that class ended, Ratay reminded us again to support each other, and for the rest of us who hadn't spoken up that day, to similarly open up during future classes.

As class was disbanding, many of us went up to our classmates and shook their hands, or patted them on their backs, offering our support. However, the individuals who had disclosed such private, painful secrets about themselves, and with such genuine pain in their eyes and horror in their voices, would have no available professional follow-up help. In short, these students had exposed their souls, but they were ultimately left to wallow in their own miseries. People in this program, including me, need and deserve truly professional counseling, especially if we are expected to reveal such sordid details about our pasts.

Over the past four-and-a-half months, I'd seen many RDAP students come and go. Some had graduated, others had been recycled, or even expelled, and still others had quit. The common denominator was that all of them had changed, but not for the better. Many had been psychologically beaten down into passivity, with their self-esteems destroyed. I know I will someday need to share my experiences with a therapist to recover from the emotional rollercoaster I'd been riding for months.

CHAPTER 23

REFLECTION

At this point, I would like to reflect on the past few years, and try to answer the question posed at the beginning of this book—how did my life, which was going so well, fall apart at the end?

First and foremost, I let my ego/power orientation, and trust in so-called "friends," cloud my judgment. If there is one thing I've learned from being in prison, it is that my decisions in life do have consequences, and that I am ultimately responsible for being where I am today. But let me be clear in saying that there were many people in my political world who impacted my thinking and behavior over the years.

My earlier political environment taught me about shortcuts, and about doing what I felt had to be done to accomplish my goals. My early days with Lipinski taught me Basic Chicago Politics 101, in which I learned about the importance of delivering garbage cans and cutting down trees to get votes. I also learned about intimidation, fraud, and deceit. Eventually I would learn about the even darker side of politics, which would prepare me for my own career in public office. At that point, I surrounded myself with many people I thought were my friends, but who would later abandon both me and my family. I believe they were, in reality, nothing but leeches. Once I resigned as city clerk, they threw me out of their lives quicker than yesterday's newspaper. I don't need to mention their names, except to remind all of them, especially two individuals, who in particular, made my wife and children suffer for their own misdeeds, that life has its strange twists and turns, and that what usually goes around comes around.

I have now spent almost seven months in federal prison, and I have certainly come to appreciate the little things in life that I took for granted—first and foremost, my wife and children, none of whom I've seen since that fateful September evening, when I said goodbye to them. I missed my children's school year, including my daughter's confirmation, school play, and June graduation. I missed the boys' soccer season, and the many sporting events that we would have watched together. Of course, I struggle every day without my wife, who's my best friend in life. I can't even begin to describe the emotional void I've felt over these past months.

While in prison, I don't see people going in and out of stores and restaurants, or cars or buses traveling down the street, or children walking to and from school. I miss sitting on my deck and grilling hamburgers, or renting a movie, and watching it downstairs with my family. I miss driving my car and listening to my CDs. I miss jumping in the pool with Nina, Jack, and Bobby, kissing them all goodnight, and laughing with Kathleen.

My hopes are to be a better father and husband who has more patience, and who doesn't sweat the small stuff. I hope to put less value on material things and more emphasis on life's simple pleasures. I also hope that my family will forgive me for what I have done, and have put them through. Moreover, I hope the people of Chicago who had supported and trusted me will view my career in its entirety, and not just my mistakes. Finally, I pray for a new beginning, and an opportunity to have fresh goals and dreams, and for my family to continue on a road of good health and happiness. At the end of each day now, I ask God to hear me, as I pray, "God, grant me the *Serenity* to accept the things I cannot change…the *Courage* to change the things I can…and the *Wisdom* to know the difference.

CHAPTER 24

THE CULTURE OF CHICAGO POLITICS

As an appropriate coda to my story, let's take one final, hard look at the world of Chicago politics. When looking at the Chicago political arena, the question immediately arises—how much is real, and how much is power and ego under the guise of public service? The culture of Chicago politics over the years has not been about *what* you know or how *hard* you *work*, but *who* you *know* and how much *money* you can *make*. Now, don't get me wrong. I'm a product of Chicago politics, and had taken full advantage of its perks and benefits, but what I'd never done was insult the public's intelligence. There are political leaders in Chicago today who still believe, but deny their feelings that elected offices are not *earned*, but *inherited* or *passed on*, as under the old English monarchy, by lineage.

There is no clearer example of that policy than that of Todd Stroger, who is president of the County Board of Cook County, the second-largest county in the nation. His father, John Stroger, had served as board president for a number of years with distinction, until health issues forced him to step aside. Now, before he would announce his decision not to seek re-election, he had one more important task, and that was to cut one more backroom deal, by which he would call in all his favors and line up all the support he could for his son to replace him as president. Suggesting that his son start small and run for a commissioner's seat on the board instead of immediately seeking the presidency would have been insulting. Even though there were several higher-ranking county officials, including elected members of the County Board, who were more than qualified to run for the seat, it was decided that blood was thicker than experience, and that Todd Stroger was entitled to the job. This was a young man whom his father had hand-picked to be the area's State Representative, and then alderman of the 8th Ward. The few years Todd did spend in those offices were relatively quiet, with no real effort on his part to pursue any type of meaningful legislative agenda for his community. The most disturbing aspect of Todd's ascension to the County Board presidency was his total lack of seasoning and experience, although one could argue those could have been gained by just being on the job. My concern was his total lack of motivation and work ethic. I can state unequivocally that he had never been a pillar of ambition. In fact, the standing joke was who would be the latest to arrive at a city council meeting, Todd Stroger or Dorothy Tillman? When Todd arrived, invariably he would be either sitting in the chambers with his eyes on the verge of closing, or just gazing out into space, with a look of sheer boredom. He was so totally oblivious to what was going on during a meeting that he would usually have to ask either me or one of his colleagues what issue we had just discussed before he could vote.

Historically, Mayor Daley would not endorse a candidate ahead of time in the Democratic Primary, and would wait until the outcome to support the winner in the General Election. However, in Todd's case, Daley came right out and endorsed the young Stroger, touting his skills as a public servant. Of course, an agreement had earlier been reached between the elder Stroger and Daley for the mayor's endorsement. If anyone could understand the Stroger situation, it would be Daley, because he wouldn't be mayor today if this hadn't moved him, too, up the political ladder. He was blessed with the Daley name, which carries both respect and a Kennedy-like image in Chicago.

The most blatant example of nepotism in Chicago politics, however, certainly was Bill Lipinski's anointing his son Dan as successor to his Congressional seat. At the time of the coronation, his son was a professor at the University of Tennessee, and had not spent much time of late in Illinois. In fact, during my thirteen-or-so years with Lipinski, I never saw the slightest interest on Dan's part to follow in his father's footsteps. Despite that fact, after winning the Democratic Primary and stepping aside, Lipinski, along with his fellow Democratic committeemen, then appointed Dan to replace him on the November General Election ballot. Since that Congressional seat was primarily Democratic, and there was no significant Republican opponent even on the ballot, it was a foregone conclusion that young Dan would succeed his father as the next Congressman of the Third District of Illinois.

This, unfortunately, is the mindset of many of Chicago's political leaders, including Daley. It's all about entitlement, which generally carries a strong political name, powerful support, and tons of money. Just ask Congressman Jesse Jackson, Jr., whose wife just won a seat on the Chicago City Council. She defeated a candidate put up by former alderman and now County Commissioner Bill Beavers. By the way, that hand-picked candidate was Beavers' own daughter. So, in that particular election, Jackson carried more clout than the Beavers name.

When discussing Chicago politics, one must invariably return again to Mayor Richard M. Daley. About three years ago, Daley's friend and former alderman and floor leader, Pat Huels, and I spent the entire morning sharing stories while struggling through eighteen rounds of golf. One thing I learned that day was how involved in, and committed to, Daley is to his political/power agenda. When Lipinski first ran for congress back in 1982 against incumbent John Fary, Daley, according to Huels, gathered his inner circle together to discuss the race. That group included Huels' brothers Bill and John, Huels himself, and Tim Degnan. Surprisingly, Daley was concerned about Lipinski's chances, and supposedly told everyone at the meeting to make sure that Lipinski would win before advising him to stick his neck out for him. Daley did not want to burn bridges until he was reasonably assured of Lipinski's chances, and then, and only then, would he move forward to insure victory for Lipinski.

When Daley became mayor, he established the Inspector General's office, which would help him on two fronts. First, it would create the public perception that he would not tolerate any type of corruption or misconduct on his employees' part. Secondly, since this department would be totally under his control, he could direct any investigation at city hall and get valuable information before anyone else.

In my opinion, he used the Inspector General's office to harass me over the years. There were at least three direct investigations of my office, and a litany of individual inquiries involving alleged no-work vouchers, ghost-payrolling, and misappropriation of administrative days off. The main investigations were as follows: (1) 1999: an investigation into my staff's alleged political work during regular business hours; (2) 2001-2002: an investigation into alleged time sheet fraud, with a recommendation from the Inspector General's office to terminate at least six people, including my chief of staff; (3) 2005: an investigation into the "Hired Truck Program Scandal," including police officers assigned to my office. Since the Inspector General publicly admitted that the only person he answers to or communicates with is the mayor, it would be logical to assume that Daley has substantial input into that office's investigations.

Was it coincidental, for example, that each time either the Inspector General or the FBI was probing around my office, one of Daley's people (usually Victor Reyes, Robert Sorich, or John Doerrer) would always call me to see how things were going? I remember back in 2001 telling Doerrer about how unethical I thought it was for the Inspector General and TV reporter Pam Zekman to work together. In fact, the Inspector General once appeared on TV with Zekman to express concern regarding certain aspects of my office. Zekman's expose ran five straight nights on the evening news, and resulted in at least eight suspensions or terminations of my employees. When I asked Doerrer about either he or Daley's having talked to the Inspector General, he basically told me that neither one of them had anything to do with those investigations. However, time and time again, the Inspector General, as I pointed out earlier, admitted to always communicating directly with Daley.

Even more disturbing about the Inspector General's tactics was that office's secrecy, and total disrespect for me as an elected official. Not once did the Inspector General call to either give me a heads-up, or ask me to work directly with him on the investigations. It was very clear that the Inspector General's office never trusted me, and that I would never be given the respect, or even the presumption of innocence, that I believe I was entitled to as an elected official. Would the Inspector General have followed the same protocol for an investigation into the mayor's Intergovernmental Affairs office? I think not! Other elected officials, members of the press, and numerous city employees have all told me privately that the Inspector General's office is just another weapon in Daley's political arsenal, a weapon that, in my opinion, he can use at any time against his enemies.

Following my indictment, *The Chicago Sun-Times* reported that officials in the police department were called off my police detail because of my alleged absenteeism during December 2005. The paper inferred that I had been absent from work for over one month, during the Christmas and New Year's holidays, and that I was delinquent in fulfilling my responsibilities. This was another maneuver, in my opinion, both orchestrated by the mayor's people and by Daley himself. Whenever I needed to see the police superintendent or his deputies, there was no confusion about the chain of command.

I was told, "If the mayor doesn't have a problem, we don't, either."

The superintendent never called my office, or even talked with any of the officers assigned to my detail. If the paper had checked, it would have found that I, in fact, had been at the office during the first two weeks of December. Furthermore, it would have been discovered that for the past ten years or so, I had consistently taken at least two weeks of that month to spend the holiday break with my children, who were off from school. It was no secret where I was during that time. This had been just another opportunity for the mayor's people to try to stick another nail in my coffin.

To add insult to injury, the Inspector General's office, which was basically incompetent and nonexistent during the Hired Truck Program scandal, began in the aftermath of the *Sun-Times* article. They questioned everyone in my executive office about my whereabouts during the past couple of months, including the amount of time I'd spent downtown, and how often I would check in when I was at home. Those investigations continued even after my resignation. I'm sure the Inspector General was looking for something else to hang on me, and to send to the Feds. I do know that, over time, either some or all of the police officers on my detail spoke with either the investigators in their department, the Inspector General, or the FBI. Those were totally unfounded rumors that the officers knew of, or were involved in, some type of criminal activity with me.

Finally, after my investigation, individuals made inquiries to the Inspector General regarding Traci Jones and possible ethics violations. Clearly, Traci was granted immunity before her grand jury testimony. In my opinion, then, she is immune from future prosecution in the Hired Truck Program scandal, despite writing out checks from the company checkbook. In fact, one of those checks was to my political campaign fund after she started working for the city of Chicago, and after the Joneses divested themselves of all interest in their former company. Even after joining the city clerk's office, she continued to write "Get Plowed" checks.

With that information readily available, why didn't the Inspector General's office take action against Ms. Jones? That same agency, with some of the same investigators, in 1995, sent me a letter during my first six months as city clerk. They recommended that I terminate the employment of a worker in my personnel division, because this individual made a personal loan to the former city clerk, Walter Kozubowski, who, like me, later ended up in federal prison on corruption charges. Because of that relationship, the Inspector General didn't believe it was appropriate for this person's employment with the city to continue. After I read the letter, I ripped it half-a-dozen times into little pieces, and threw it in my wastebasket, because I suspected it was just another attempt by the mayor's people to harass me. But if someone back in 1995 objected to my employee's behavior, what would that same person say now about Traci Jones and her conduct before, during, and after, the Hired Truck Program scandal? Of course, if you would ask Daley about this issue, his standard answer would be that he has nothing to do with the Inspector General's office, and no knowledge about any of its investigations.

About one month before my sentencing, I ran into a former city employee who was, at one time, connected with the Daley family, both personally and politically. He was quite gracious toward me, and wished my entire family the best in the future.

He did, however, make one telling comment about the Hired Truck Program and future investigations, "You'd be surprised by how much power and influence Daley has beyond city business at a higher level, and I do mean at a *higher* level."

One could surmise many things from that remark, but he might have been referring to possible access to information concerning outside investigations.

Perhaps an example of that influence was revealed at a downtown award luncheon for police officers I attended after the Hired Truck Program scandal had broken. When I arrived, I met Ed Kantor, who at that time, was still working for the police department. He immediately took me to the head table to pay my respects to the mayor. After exchanging greetings with Daley, I went around the table to say "hello," and had gone full circle, when I thought my heart would stop. Sitting next to the mayor was U.S. Attorney Patrick Fitzgerald.

I had never met the man before, but I remember his ice-cold glare, along with a firm handshake, but a quiet "Hello, I'm Patrick Fitzgerald."

Later, following my indictment, when I picked up *The Chicago Sun-Times*, I noticed a little blurb about Daley's trip to China with the then-current U.S. Attorney for the Northern District of Illinois, Scott Lasser. I'm sure the two of them flying together after my investigation and indictment was no coincidence.

Having said all of that, though, there is no question that Rich Daley has done a good job as mayor. He has changed this city's landscape and uplifted neighborhoods. We have seen new police stations, firehouses, and libraries, along with some improvements in our schools. The city is basically clean and thriving, with a beautiful skyline and lakefront. The man on top certainly has an eye for detail. In fact, he could point out a pothole in the street or a slightly faded stop sign in a second, call Streets and Sanitation, and have those problems taken care of immediately, so that they could be repaired or replaced by the end of the day. This is a man who is so meticulous and observant about the little things that he has police officers assigned to his detail and while driving him home calls the Bureau of Electricity right away, from the car, because of a streetlight that had gone out. However, this same man, who has such a hands-on approach to most issues, both big and small in this city, claims he never knew anything about the Hired Truck Program's abuses, nor about unethical hiring practices by other municipal agencies, or his own Inspector General's investigations. I'm not convinced.

Let's look again at the Hired Truck Program, and Daley's people who granted my requests—Pat Huels, Victor Reyes, and Robert Sorich. During an eleven-year period, each of them helped me, in one way or another, to put my friends' trucks on with the city. These same people talked to Daley on a regular basis, and not one of them ever told him they were doing favors for me, the city clerk, by giving out city business contracts to my friends?

How about hiring practices? Whenever anyone needed additional positions for his or her office, each and every city budget director would tell me the person to talk to was someone from the mayor's office. Pat, Victor, or Robert would then say he said he would first have to talk to the guy "on the fifth floor."

During city council meetings, I would be seated directly below the elevated rostrum where the mayor would sit, and I can't tell you how many times aldermen would come up to him, asking for jobs for somebody. Depending on the alderman, Daley would write the information down and give it to someone in his office. While working for Lipinski, on a couple of occasions I sat in the congressman's office when he would call Daley at city hall. Each phone conversation was short and to the point—usually a request to hire or transfer someone, or to grant that person a raise.

At the end of each conversation, Lipinski would say, "Thanks, Rich."

I also spoke with at least one union official over the years who told me that whenever he needed a job for a family member or friend, he always went to Reyes or Sorich. I personally find it difficult to believe that Daley knew nothing about those appointments.

Over the years, I attended a number of functions across Chicago, from groundbreaking ceremonies and political fundraising parties, to senior citizens' picnics and library or police station openings. At each of those events, I was always impressed by Daley's awareness of his surroundings, and especially of his key employees. Again, his eye for detail, and his working knowledge of those people who could either help or hurt him were certainly qualities of any good mayor. That's why I question his selective amnesia regarding persons, places, or things that could harm him. For example, when the media turned up the heat about Angelo Torres, the Hired Truck Program's coordinator, the mayor pleaded ignorance. Mr. Torres would later wind up in federal prison after pleading guilty to accepting kickbacks from various people in the program. Now, when I had to help Mr. Jones with his trucks early on, we would, before even notifying Tomczak, first go through Sorich or Reyes.

Torres and employees of Jones's "Get Plowed" never saw eye-to-eye, often resulting a couple of times in Jones's trucks getting knocked off the city payroll. There were also times when Torres' people did inspections, and found that certain paperwork, such as insurance certificates for Mick's trucks, were not in place, and suspended his trucks. When these shutdowns would occur, I would ask Daley's people to call Torres, and to order him to put the trucks back on the payroll. Sooner or later, they would be back on, because of my earlier call to either Victor Reyes or Robert Sorich. So, my question is, how could the mayor have *not* known about Torres when first asked by the media?

At this point, there remains many troubling questions that are left unanswered. These are the questions that I still find particularly troubling:

(1) Did the U.S. Attorney's office and Daley give Traci Jones immunity, even though she may have violated city ethics and personnel codes?

(2) What happened to John Novak, Mick Jones's mysterious partner whom the FBI supposedly interviewed, and who according to Jones, gave Hired Truck Program employees cash gifts, and who allegedly destroyed evidence (trucks) during the investigation?

(3) Did the FBI and the U.S. Attorney follow up on agent Phil, who is now retired, but according to their investigation, had a social relationship with the Joneses and Novak? This would seem to raise important ethical issues, since discussions between Jones and Phil involved confidential information about undercover agents' surveillance of Sears Tower, as well as of other downtown areas at risk of terrorist attacks.

(4) What did Mayor Daley know about:

(a) Hiring practices?

(b) The Hired Truck Program, including relationships between Reyes, Sorich, Torres, and Tomczak, not to mention that same program's fundraising and political campaign work for the mayor's re-election?

(c) Past and current information regarding investigations conducted by the Inspector General's office regarding the Hired Truck Program scandal, and about city hiring practices? In particular, did the Inspector General ever receive or investigate any complaints about Ms. Jones's conduct?

(d) The U.S. Attorney or FBI's possibly leaking inside information to his office that he then could have in turn leaked, in order to embarrass other elected officials?

Again, I am not trying to minimize my own mistakes, or make excuses for my past misconduct. Nor, on the other hand, am I minimizing accomplishments of mine that I am proud of, such as introducing initiatives in Chicago that helped save lives and taxpayer dollars. I am particularly proud of my work on behalf of the senior citizens, children, and working men and women of this city. However, I would be less than honest if I did not concede that these were overshadowed by my own greed, and by my relationship with the Joneses. During my sentencing, Judge Norgle expressed his sympathy for my wife and children, but placed their pain and suffering at my doorstep, where it truly belongs.

The business of Chicago politics has always had a unique reputation for its own style of power and corruption, at times resembling a pool of sharks attacking its prey. It's a game that can leave its players morally, ethically, and even spiritually bankrupt. I have lived, accepted, and thrived off a system that tempted me, betrayed me, and ultimately cost me my freedom. In the final analysis, I have only myself to blame for this nightmare, but this brand of politics was in place long before I came on the scene, and will continue to thrive.

Over the years, increased FBI investigations and media scrutiny have forced the business of "old-time politics" to become much more sophisticated and covert. The Daleys and Lipinskis of the last couple of decades have orchestrated and manipulated this system for their own benefits, and to satisfy their own thirst for power and financial reward. In short, they have become the new architects of POLITICS, CHICAGO STYLE.

SUPPLEMENT

JOURNAL ENTRIES

The following is a collection of my RDAP journal entries, from January to August, 2007. This required class assignment incorporating my spontaneous, unstructured reflections on my prison experience, ending with my graduation from the program. Thus, readers should excuse the entries' free-style appearance, grammar, and punctuation. I have tried to provide as accurate and representative an account of daily life at Morgantown FCI as possible.

12/7/2006: This is my first entry regarding my problems of anxiety and excessive worry. I just came back from the auditorium where they had a Christmas concert. There were a number of beautiful songs performed and I couldn't help but feel sad and lonely for my family, just thinking about sitting at home with them and just watching a Christmas movie. Last year at this time I was just indicted, so this makes the second Christmas in a row that I feel sad and depressed, but I kept telling myself next Christmas will be terrific!

I also received a letter from Nina today and although she is only thirteen, I felt like she was writing me from college and she was eighteen years old. She starts the letter, "Dear Daddy: Everything is going great with me. I just wanted to say I miss you very much." She ends the letter, "I love you very much. I can't wait until you come home." After the letter, I had tears in my eyes.

This is going to be a very difficult holiday season, but I keep telling myself that the changes I am making will have a positive impact on the entire family and I believe we will all be happier.

12/10/06: I spoke with Kathleen this evening, and she told me that a woman a block away from our house was murdered. No other detail, except everyone in the area is quite concerned. It's one of those situations again where I feel helpless. Kathleen also told me that Nina is having problems with some of her classmates, some personality conflicts and Kath may have to stop at the school. These are situations that come up that I'm not sure I want to know about because there is nothing I can do except listen and try to offer my support. Sometimes I think if I don't know about it, I wouldn't worry as much, but then again I need to provide input. I'm not a really big fan of the weekends. They drag too much, and I think way too much. Another week in the books.

12/13/06: Today, I heard four guys were recycled from both the a.m. and p.m. class. I believe two of them were within days of graduating and leaving here. Certainly, these developments can make you nervous. Joe Nicosia is leaving on Monday, and he is out of his mind with worry just thinking about those other people. Sometimes I think Joe and I worry about other people more than we do about ourselves. I can't help but think about him leaving in five days, and the following week being Christmas. I continue to write and try to keep myself busy.

12/14/06: I wanted to write an entry today because I gave the word of the day and also my first feedback. The thought of the day was, "All things are possible to them who believe." I believe it went better than expected. Dr. Baker and the regional director attended. I was very calm and spoke very slowly, directly, and I think coherently. The feedback, on the other hand, I was very nervous about, and in fact, I tried to give feedback when clarity was still being given. I was embarrassed when I was told to sit down until clarity was finished. I believe when I finally gave feedback it went well. I had some of my colleagues tell me I did a good job, which certainly made my day. I think it hit me that I am officially part of the TC.

12/18/06: Joe Nicosia left this morning! He woke me up at 5:30 a.m. and I walked with him down to R & D (Receiving and Departure). He and I are so much alike. Joe worried about what kind of seat he would have on the bus. He worried about the type of food he should eat in Pittsburgh. The only thing I do know is I will miss him. Every night for the past two months I would sit in his cube and we would talk. He helped me tremendously with the class, and he gave me some good advice. Maybe Joe didn't help me with excessive worry, but he sure helped me in so many ways—including building up my self-confidence. The one thing I struggle with is change and just walking past Joe's empty cube this morning I felt sad. I am happy for Joe and I look forward to the day we can get together again.

12/23/06: Yesterday, I completed week number seven of the program. I also decided, along with the doctor here, to get off one of the anti-depressants I was taking. Hopefully that won't be a problem over the holidays. I'm reading one of my books on anxiety. The bottom line is that I have to learn that I'm in control of my life. I spoke with Kathleen last night and we just talked about everything. It was very casual conversation. I'm just trying to take one day at a time and treat this weekend like any other weekend. Kathleen did send me a bunch of pictures of her and the kids for Christmas, but I didn't get them yesterday. Oh well! Hopefully I'll get them Tuesday. I just keep telling myself one day at a time.

12/26/06: Christmas is over, and I'm so happy! I talked to Kathleen last night, and we're both looking towards 2007. She told me no more sadness, just be positive and get home this summer. She told me that she wants me to find a job that will fit my personality. I'm starting to believe that I can actually control how I feel. My anxiety comes and goes, but since I just went off the one anti-depressant, I'm still adjusting. All that I'm taking now is Zoloft once a day—75 mg. My ultimate goal would be to go home pill-free, with a greater control of my anxiety. I think I'll always worry, but hopefully I'll be a little less anxious.

12/30/06: I just finished reading the book *From Panic to Power: Managing Your Anxiety.* I really enjoyed it. If I can just learn that I'm in control of how I feel—I need to take responsibility for my feelings, because if I want to be truly happy again in my life, it's entirely up to me. I'm the only one who can make it happen. I spoke with Kathleen tonight and we both agreed that it's about time that 2006 is ending. We are both anxiously awaiting 2007. Nina is still not sure which high school she wants to attend, however she needs to start filling out the necessary paperwork for some school. I am going to speak to her on New Year's Day. These are the kind of things I get frustrated over because I'm not home to take a hands-on approach. I am so happy I received my pictures from Kathleen of her and the kids.

1/2/07: The first entry of the new year. I'm so happy 2006 is over. I finished my first project in my treatment goals—the fifty things I've gotten away with. When I get something off my plate, I feel better, like finishing that project. I spoke with Nina last night and tried to encourage her about her high school selection. I basically told her to relax, and pick a school that she feels the most comfortable with. Nothing is forever. If it doesn't work out she could transfer the following year. I'm still feeling bad about Jack not wanting to talk to me on the phone. When I get home he and I will work on our anxiety problems together.

1/5/07: I was kind of down in the dumps yesterday. Ms. Land tells me I have an anger issue. It's my sentimentality that fuels my anger. I'm just confused about the whole accountability issue and when do you hold someone accountable? It bothers me because there are people in TC who act one way down there, and back at the unit they act another way. I try to stay to myself because I'm afraid to tell people too much and have them use it against me down the road. I guess I'm very suspicious of people now and afraid to trust people again. It's almost two weeks since I've gotten off the anti-depressant, and for the most part, I feel okay, but my anxiety, of course, makes me feel nervous, and I still need that medication. I'm also trying to learn that I control my feelings, and I need to keep positive feelings and thoughts going.

1/7/07: Another warm day today. I walked a bit around the pond with John. We were talking today about how we are changing from this whole experience. I'm wondering if I will have more or less patience when I get home. I certainly hope more with the program I'm in now. My main objective right now is to keep up my positive self-talk and help alleviate more of my anxiety. I can't always wait for something to go wrong. I have so many anticipatory results in my head, and 99 percent of them will never happen! I need to build up my self-confidence in TC, because there are days I feel like I can conquer the world, and there are other days when everything I do is a struggle.

1/10/07: I had a very good day today. I spoke at TC on the word of the day, but most importantly, in class later, I brought up my anxiety issue. It was amazing how people in my class either had an issue themselves with anxiety or they had a question about it. It just felt good talking about it. Tonight was my first night chairing the Wednesday night self-help meeting. Our topic tonight was, "What have you lost because you went to prison?" I thought the meeting went well. Lastly, I spoke with Kathleen; the Christmas break is over and everyone is back at school. She does not tell me everything but I know that Jack's emotional problems are very hard on Kathleen. I'm really trying to get my life together, and the hardest issue I have is my son Jack's anxiety and my guilt and helplessness over the entire situation. I just need Kathleen and the kids to hang in there. I'll never forget how important my family is, along with my freedom when making decisions in the future.

1/14/07: It's been a rainy weekend, and it's been hard to get out and work. I did, however, have a good TC on Friday where I actually gave some emotional but well thought-out feedback regarding saving chairs in the TV rooms. I spoke about bullying tactics, extortion, and entitlement, but most importantly, I talked about inmates respecting one another. I did receive a lot of compliments for the feedback, but I'm also worried that more will be expected of me in the future. I'm also concerned about my job in the kitchen. I'm really not comfortable being in a situation such as that. There are too many things going on there, especially the way people treat each other. My anxiety level seems to increase when I go to work. I talked to Kathleen tonight. She told me she needs to see Dr. D'Asta, Jack's therapist, tomorrow. He's having issues that Kathleen needs advice on to handle. She also told me that my brother-in-law, Art, has lost his job as VP at Navistar. I think he's around twenty-five years of service, and hopefully he will get a decent retirement package. I feel very bad for him, because he has been so helpful to Kathleen and the kids, and I'm very thankful for everything he has done.

1/20/07: Yesterday, I attended RDAP 108 graduation. The whole ceremony was a bittersweet experience. I was happy for most of the guys; however, Dr. Baker said the class had problems, and some of them were like a virus that infected the community. It seems like most people become complacent or just lose focus, but I've seen the problems occur during the last four to six weeks. We had a short week and used the work community where I talked about honesty, caring, and respect. I gave John Marshall some feedback on emotional control which I struggle with on a regular basis. I think I still have a hard time adjusting to being on just one medication but maybe I'm just nervous because of all the medications I was on in the past. I'm also thinking of getting out of the kitchen. I've been there almost three months, and I'm sick of all the bullshit. That includes the way the people working there are treated by the COs. Also, the stealing of food and just the attitude of those inmates working there. It's an uncomfortable situation for me, and I think I'll try to find something a little quieter. It's the dead of winter now, and with the clouds and cold temps, I'm a little down in the dumps, so I need to kick it up a notch and snap out of it.

1/21/07: It's Sunday morning. I'm looking out of the window, and it's snowing. I'm calling my mom today. It's her eighty-fifth birthday. The last time I spoke with her was on Christmas. I don't know what's gotten into me lately, but I'm just down in the dumps. I'm trying to get back on track. I'm lonely, and miss Kathleen and the kids. I just got off the phone with my mom and she was very happy to hear from me. She wants to know what I'm doing. I told her, going to classes, working and writing. There's not much to do here in a federal prison. It's now about 12:30 p.m., and the snow is heavy now.

I spoke with Kathleen tonight, and she's struggling with some issues about the kids. She seems both physically and emotionally exhausted! Jack's anxiety and where Nina is going to high school are on her plate. All I can do is listen.

1/26/07: Today, I'm completing week number two of the program. It's amazing how the time is moving along. I am getting more comfortable each and every day in the program. I try to speak four to five times a week in the TC. In another week a new class will be starting and my class will move into the second phase. Hopefully, today will be my last day in the kitchen. I spoke to Mr. Gribble, who is supposed to transfer me to compound 2. The kitchen is getting a little crazy, and last night was chicken night. Of course, everyone goes crazy with chicken. I was serving last night, and wouldn't you know it, the CO had me serve the chicken. The inmates were yelling at me, "I want this piece," "That piece is too small"—it was a little crazy, and definitely high anxiety for me. Over the next six months I just want to be in a less stressful situation.

1/29/07: I am the first person from my class to be selected or elected facilitator for the TC. I was both happy and honored that a majority of my classmates elected me and Mr. Graves. I was a little nervous today, especially when I jumped from news and weather to community business and forgot all about sports. Overall, I thought it went pretty well and it certainly can't hurt me or my participation points. Today is my first day on compound 2, because I am now out of food service. What a load off my mind. I needed a change in jobs just to feel better about myself.

1/31/07: It was my third day of facilitating, and I think I'm calming down. Mr. Powers had an issue about feeling guilty regarding feedback. A number of people gave him feedback including myself. However, my feedback was more like an editorial telling him that it's difficult to decide what rules are really important and those that may be more obscure. I have a lot of opinions, but I need to be careful and not get carried away. A number of people in my class who are stepping up now. Sometimes I feel a little insecure when some of my classmates shine, but that's my low self-esteem and anxiety. I strive to be someone who I'm not. I was so used to being a leader that I struggle now just because I positioned myself at times to be in the middle of the pack.

2/5/07: I'm ready to officially begin phase two of RDAP. The new class begins this afternoon. and we will be going through another two weeks of orientation. I had a tough weekend; it was very cold outside, and so I couldn't walk. It was also the Super Bowl and quite frankly, even though I'm a sports nut, I just didn't have it in me to watch it. Maybe because it's the dead of winter, and I feel more trapped by the weather is the main reason I felt depressed. When I talk to Kathleen, I can tell from her voice that she struggles every day with all of her problems. I know I can't change the past, but I sure wish I could. It's months away, and I'm starting to think abut Nina's graduation and not being there. I'm glad that I'm done with facilitating; it was a lot harder than I thought it would be. Also, I have to start all over again, learning to take criticism, because although I received many compliments for the way the meeting went, Murphy did have some criticism, which I took personally. I'm realizing there are many things in my life that are different now.

2/8/07: I talked to Kathleen last night, and we had a nice conversation, except for the fact that it still amazes me how people I've helped and actually thought were my friends have abandoned my family. She's waiting for a simple W2 from downtown, left messages with people a week ago and still hasn't had a return call. It's just hard to figure out people, and I guess no one owes me and my family anything, but it certainly adds to my resolve to eventually move sometime after I get out of here.

Class is going okay! I got back in the groove yesterday after a week of facilitating. I commented on the word of the day, and also gave some feedback. The class is much larger now with the addition of forty new students. I'm starting to realize that every time I experience some sort of change in my life, there's always a short period of adjustment for me to get my feet wet again. I'm also getting together with a couple of guys every night as kind of a support group to help each other. John Marshall and Walt Tymoczko are both really good guys who have issues like I do, and all of us have a common goal to get out of here in August. It's important to have a few friends around here for support and feedback.

2/12/07: The past weekend was quite boring and uneventful. The weather has been very cold, which prevents me from getting outside to walk. Murphy told me it's best if I stay to myself and avoid any types of cliques. I've been helping out in the classrooms every night with Marshall and Tymoczko, and sometimes McClellan. I guess when people see you together all the time, it sends the wrong message. Ms. Tyner, assistant psychologist, has picked me and five other RDAP students to participate in an anger/anxiety workshop—me, Koger, Marshall, Majors, Bland, and McCaloney. We're supposed to meet every Thursday for one hour or so for the next eight weeks. I really believe this workshop could be beneficial.

2/17/07: We completed another two-week orientation, and I think some of the new first-phasers are ready to engage in TC. The smaller TCs do not allow anyone to hide anymore. For example, this past week I think I spoke at least twice at every meeting. I also had my first meeting of the special anger/anxiety group. Honestly, I enjoyed it. Ms. Tyner seemed a little nervous, but she did a good job. Our first session was kind of, "Let's set a format," however, we did talk about Mac's current anxiety issue, and everyone gave feedback. What I like is that this group has a confidentiality agreement, so hopefully we can all open up and get some help with the anxiety. I also spoke to Kathleen, who was very upset because Nina didn't get accepted to St. Ignatius. I know Nina is very bright (high honors), but when it comes to standardized tests, she's not as strong. My problem continues to be this constant frustration and helplessness I have when I get unpleasant news from back home. I can also tell Kathleen is very depressed. She is overwhelmed at home with everything and many so-called friends don't even call. I can't even begin to explain how hard it is to listen to Kathleen's voice with emotional pain and depression. Obviously, I wish I could help. The other problem continues to be the terrible weather, both here and Chicago. Neither one of us likes to be stuck inside, and the last few weeks have been frigid and snowy. March is around the corner, so maybe some warmer weather may help.

2/22/07: We had our first "Living with Others" class, and everyone had to stand up and basically tell the class their personality flaws. Well, I stood up and said I had a power-orientation issue with a need to always be right. Although this is true, one of my biggest problems is my anxiety, which I believe fuels other behaviors in me. Also, Ms. Ratay and Mr. Major had a confrontation that really brought about his anger issue.

Speaking of anger, sometimes I feel as if I'm getting both

frustrated and angry over the way some of the peer counselors treat people. I've talked about it in my anger group, and McCaloney thinks I should bring it up to TC. I also believe that some of my classmates would have me throw it out there and put my neck on the line.

2/28/07: I'm struggling with my anxiety and frustration regarding my situation at home. I spoke to Kathleen last night, and she told me how bad the boys are behaving. I just don't know how to address it. The boys are struggling at school, and then swearing at home. I don't know how to help Kathleen, and also help myself. Yesterday was also Election Day in Chicago; the first election in the city that I've missed in twenty-eight years. No matter how bad politics got for me, I still miss it. Murphy also brought to my attention my struggles with sentimentality, and the need for me to bring it to the attention of TC. He believes that I sugarcoat my feedback because I still want to be perceived as a nice guy and I don't want to make enemies. I think avoiding conflict with others is still an issue for me, along with holding my feelings in on accession.

3/4/07: I found out that tonight, on the phone, Jack is really struggling. I knew there were still problems, but for Kathleen to put in an emergency call to Dr. D'Asta on a Sunday, I know it's bad. There are times I'm laying in bed here with tears in my eyes. I just don't know what to do, as far as support. I struggle myself everyday here just trying to get through the program. Trust me, if I could do something for Kathleen to help her, I would. The prison experience is bad enough, but now I'm worried about each and every day at home. All I can do is pray that they hang in there. The weather here is still cold and cloudy, and just very depressing. I'm hoping I can turn the corner and start feeling better about myself. This entire situation for me continues to be like an emotional roller coaster, when one day I'm feeling good and positive, and the next day down and depressed.

3/7/07: Exactly five months from today, if everything goes right, I'll be heading to the halfway house in Chicago. Everything seems to be progressing well in class. I'm participating everyday with feedback, and getting my arguments in on time. I'm still trying to deal with on-and-off blues. Some days I feel great, and other days I'm ready to scream. I think, or at least I hope, the weather has a lot to do with my moods. Today for example, it's snowing like crazy outside. I just feel like I'm trapped inside the building much of the time. I'm also having some discomfort with a bad tooth; I hope it's just temporary, because there's no dentist here.

3/10/07: My tooth has been really bothering me. I'm taking Ibuprofen and aspirin. I actually take the aspirin and put it on top of my tooth and let it dissolve. It doesn't taste well, but it seems to help. I'm very nervous about having any medical problems here; I'm just trying to keep the pain at a lower level until I can get back to Chicago. I'm down to 150 days. If everything goes right, I can leave and head back to the halfway house. The class is going okay; I'm trying to really stay involved. The weather is starting to warm up to the fifties, which means I'll be walking much more. It seems as the weather goes, so do my moods. By the way, one of my classmates, Tony Blair, was expelled from the program. He just wasn't motivated enough to stay engaged in the process.

3/13/07: I spoke to my mom on the phone for the first time since Christmas; she seems to be doing fine. The one thing that hasn't changed is she's still trying to tell me what to do even when I'm in prison. She's telling me to write letters to certain people. One of the things I have a hard time with is just writing letters to people. What do you say? I guess I just have to be motivated. My mom also told me that all the people in my old world don't contact her anymore, which doesn't surprise me. They are the same people who were supposed to stop and check on Kathleen and the kids. Besides that, the classes are moving along and that small group with Ms. Tyner seems to be a good opportunity for me to talk about more sensitive issues regarding my family and myself. I probably should talk about my dad and some of the things from the past.

3/18/07: I held a smoking cessation class to help Mr. Kirk and Mr. Keating last night. Smoking has become a hot issue again, and Kirk and Keating struggle with it. I know if I can quit, they can quit. It's all about willingness to do it. Every time I think about smoking again, I remind myself what Kathleen told me months ago, that the kids were proud of me that I quit. There is no question that not drinking is easier than not smoking.

The time is moving fairly quickly, I'm at 140+ days to go, and I just want to focus on the task at hand with the class work and keep participating in TC. The small group with Ms. Tyner is productive and interesting. At least in that group, you can talk about more sensitive issues and hopefully it will bring down my anxiety levels.

I talked to Kathleen Friday and Saturday evening as I usually do, and I find the fifteen minutes on the phone going so quick. I'm really missing the family; I love them all very much.

3/23/07: I gave feedback on Wednesday to a student, and it was controversial. He refused learning experiences when asked, but the DTSs were out of the room. He lied about a confrontation with our counselor, Williams. I gave him feedback about his honesty, power orientation, entitlement, ego, and about bringing bullshit issues to TC. At the end of the day, some people supported him, and others supported the community. DTS Sowden gave me positive praise for having the guts to say what I did. McCaloney thought I was grandstanding because Baker, Land, Lowden, and Livengood were all in the room. I was giving feedback prior to going to TC. I told Duncan to look for me for feedback when I saw him in the morning. Unfortunately, Murphy told me I made enemies, and to watch my back. Ms. Tyner told me one of my goals should be not to worry what other people think. I'm always afraid that I'm being judged in TC about what I say. Today, I gave Mr. Carrol feedback about going home and his nervousness, and no DTS was in the room. It goes back to my sentimentality and being worried about what other people think of me.

3/25/07: A friend came to visit me on Friday. It was nice to see someone from Chicago. We had a good time. Kathleen's dad (Wally) is up and down with his health. He's in the hospital, but was doing better. I just hope he hangs in there. I know that each day that goes by, Kathleen gets a little more tired. I can't imagine the strain on him with trying to keep the household afloat. Ms. Tyner wants me to work on my treatment goals and not worry about what people think about me.

3/29/07: It was a rough couple of days in TC. I've been front and center with my feedback. I'm trying to be honest and lead with some solid feedback. In addition, I brought up an issue in TC, regarding my frustration and helplessness when I call home and I can't do anything to help. The DTSs are putting the pressure on certain people in TC to lead and really embrace treatment. They're tired of the bullshit issues. I haven't made a lot of friends, but my new treatment goal with Ms. Tyner is to engage in treatment and not to worry what others think of me. I'm getting tired of feeling guilty all the time and I need to step it up and be happier.

4/2/07: The beginning of another week, and who knows how it will go. There are only three weeks to go for the third-phasers. I don't know how to describe it, but the whole atmosphere here has changed. I feel like our TC is under so much pressure, and there are very few people who want to step it up. All I want to do is stay out of controversy, which isn't easy. I continue to worry about what people think about me and all I should do is work through the program and worry about my family. I'm happy it's April, and the weather is getting so much nicer. You know it's really hard to believe that I've been here since September 11. The time does seem to move a little faster if you keep yourself busy. I try to stay outside more now than ever. The more I stay out of this building, the better off I am. I'm really trying to stay upbeat, but it's hard.

4/8/07: This was a very eventful week. I brought up my dad in the small group and it got very emotional. The following day, I brought up an issue in the big TC, regarding my arrogance and power orientation. I received feedback from thirteen different people. I also brought up my dad in the victim impact class, and again, got emotional. I never really talked about my dad before, regarding his drinking and mental and physical abuse. Sometimes I really wonder if a lot of my anxiety stemmed from my childhood. I also gave some direct feedback to Mr. Ayers in Ratay's class. Everyone sat back and was afraid to give feedback about his laziness and lack of involvement in class. I told him he needs to be more self-critical, and disclose something to the community.

On a brighter note, Kathleen got her contract renewed this past week at school, and Nina was accepted to the high school she really wanted. It was so nice to receive some good news from the home front.

4/13/07: Seven days till the third-phase graduation! I can't wait! The TC is going well, and I'm giving feedback everyday. I'd like to think that the DTSs believe I'm one of the leaders of the group.

The weather here is terrible. Last week, we were close to eighty degrees, and now we're in the forties with rain and a chance of snow for the weekend.

My small group with Ms. Tyner is going well. I had to write a self-evaluation paper, which helped me immensely. I talked about my childhood and anxiety. Sometimes I believe that much of my anxiety and emotional make-up stems back to my childhood when so much happened.

I can't help but think about the small group last week, when I brought up my dad, and talked about his drinking and the emotional, mental and physical abuse that occurred. I was even more embarrassed to disclose that when I was a child, I had a bed wetting problem, which I was never treated for; I just grew out of it. I remember so many things from my childhood, and someday I'll need to get rid of those thoughts.

4/15/07: The weather this weekend was horrible. It rained the entire day and most of yesterday. I've never seen the water level of the stream so high. It's one of those days where I'm depressed about everything. I'm worried about graduating from the program, because anything could happen here. I'm afraid, since I've made some enemies here, that I could be a target for someone to set me up. I'm also worried when I get home what I'll do as far as a job. I also think I'll need treatment, and will need counseling. There is so much that goes on around here. A couple of weeks ago, after my friend left following a visit on Friday night, I was strip-searched by a CO who makes you lift your shirt up, but also makes you drop your pants and underwear, bend towards him and cough. It's so humiliating and unnecessary, but it proves that this place is not a camp, but a lower-level security prison. There are also stories about women bringing their babies to the visiting room, and being told they can have only one rattle and one milk bottle, and they have to go back to their cars with the extra rattle and bottle. There were young kids who were sent back to their cars because they wore hooded sweatshirts, which are not allowed. Thank God they had extra clothes in the car, or they would not have been permitted back in, because hoods are not permissible. I try to associate with as few people as possible, just to avoid any conflicts in the program.

I'm also worried about Kathleen and the kids, and wonder how they will react when I get home. I have only a little more than three months to go.

4/20/07: It's graduation day for the third phase. Hopefully next week I will be considered for the new third phase. It stinks that we have class today, because we're breaking tradition of holding class on graduation day. The weather is fantastic, around seventy degrees and sunny. The forecast for the next five days is great. Nina is in Washington, D.C. on her eighth grade trip; she will back tonight. I brought up an issue on Wednesday about being angry when I found out Kathleen was splitting up the boys next year in school. I received feedback from about thirteen people regarding my lack of gratitude, power orientation, and arrogance, etc. The bottom line is Kathleen is doing a wonderful job under extremely tough circumstances. I need to be more positive and grateful. I need to focus on the task at hand.

4/25/07: It's a little different now without the third phase—with less people in the TC, we all have to step it up a notch. I'm giving at least one to two feedbacks a day. I'll need to bring up another issue in the next couple of weeks. I'm thinking about taking shortcuts and my feelings of guilt. I finished my last paper for Ms. Land. It's not due until June, but I have it done.

The weather has been great. I get out as much as I can, especially at night, walking. John T. from Alex. is leaving June 19. By this weekend, I'll be under one-hundred days. I'm starting to get a little anxious. Everything seems to be going well at home. Nina just got back from her Washington trip; another thing I missed.

4/27/07: One inmate today had his leg amputated at the ankle because of a severe staph infection, and another has contracted the same infection. Supposedly, the infection had stemmed from bacteria from the Randolph Unit shower stall. Visitors tonight were informed of the infection before they had checked out this evening.

Meanwhile, Rob Stamper's roommate told me tonight that last year someone here had been complaining about back pain, and had been sent to the medical building. The medical staff had diagnosed his condition as arthritis, and had advised him after he had returned home to see his doctor. In the meantime, they had prescribed 800 mg. of Ibuprofen. When he had returned home a few months later, his doctor had instead diagnosed his true ailment—bone cancer, which because of the delay in treatment, is now terminal.

4/28/07: I woke this morning to find out that a fifty-six year-old inmate from Bates died last night after he had collapsed at 11:20 p.m., in the B-wing TV room. Since there had been no CO in the unit at the time, inmates there had run to Alexander to find someone. According to eyewitness Jim Keating, it had taken almost twenty minutes before any CO arrived. When they did, they found they had forgotten their CPR paddles, and had to go back to get them. The COs and inmate Williams then worked on him extensively. The ambulance arrived sometime around 12:30 a.m. Numerous resuscitation attempts had then been tried, but had failed. Finally, the ambulance, without flashing lights, drove away with the body.

This is appalling! An institution of this size is supposed to have 24/7 medical care. Tom Mortimer, who works in the medical building, told me that this unfortunate inmate had been scheduled the upcoming week for a stress test.

Tragically, you have inmates getting limbs amputated because of diabetes, or staph infections, and now someone dies of an apparent heart attack. This is what happens when you don't have around-the-clock medical care in an emergency where minutes are all you have to save a life.

In TC, Mr. Williams mentioned my name in front of the entire TC that I need to bring up more personal issues. I've brought up four issues; I participate in class, one of the top ones in my class. I've headed a self-help group. I'm in two small groups—one I volunteered for. All my assignments are done ahead of time, and quite honestly, I'm tired of the bullshit, and I'm tired mentally and emotionally. I honestly believe if it wasn't for Kathleen and the kids, I would drop out of the program. It comes to a point where you begin to question what is therapy and what is psychological bullying. I feel like I'm really invested, and trying to do my best, and now I feel like that's not good enough. Right now in Ms. Tyner's group, we're working on anger and keeping track of the situation on a daily basis. I've done paper charts and graphs on anger, anxiety, moods in general, and I've exposed my soul and childhood, regarding my father in my small groups. I'm tired!

5/1/07: Tom Mortimer informed me today that the individual who had passed away, Percy Smith, had been at medical all morning the day he had died. He had been complaining of chest pains and vomiting, but had been sent back to his unit without a definite diagnosis.

5/4/07: This has been a brutal week!! I was held accountable by McCaloney. I still don't agree that I was guilty of that entirely, but it is what it is. I tried to argue my point with Williams, who shot me down. I received feedback from over a dozen classmates who verbally assaulted me. I received over ten learning experiences, including one where I have to say, "I'm a master manipulator" before I begin to speak in TC. In addition, I got teamed on by my class after TC, where everyone discusses your faults and weaknesses. This all happened on Monday, and I felt horrible. I also spoke to Dr. Baker, and told him that I thought I was being set up by other people. I was quite emotional, but I needed to vent. The following day, I missed most of TC, because I had to go to medical to give my DNA sample. Before you leave prison, they take your DNA and ship it off to the FBI headquarters in Virginia for their permanent record. On Wednesday, in our "Victim Impact" class, we watched a video called "The Reflections from the Heart of a Child," which depicted a family who happened to have an abusive and addicted father, and husband. The movie tore me apart because it reminded me so much of my own childhood and my dad. After the video, DTS Turner had us write a one-page paper on how we can relate to the movie. I sat down with tears in my eyes, discussing my childhood and father, and how I was terrified as a child and what I experienced. In any event, the following day I stood up before the entire TC and discussed my situation. I felt so alone and weak as I stood there and talked about my dad. It was very emotional, but I actually felt relieved when others in my class got up and related to my situation. This whole class is so stressful and difficult at times. I feel emotionally and mentally drained today. This has been a week that will stay with me for a long time.

5/7/07: It was a very nice weekend, or at least Sunday. I heard they turned away fifty people on Saturday, and thirty-one on Sunday for not complying with the dress code for visitors. I called Kathleen last night to tell her to let our friends, Chris and Bob, know before they visit next Friday. Speaking of Kathleen, she seemed so stressed out. I can't imagine, between her job, Nina, and the behavioral problem of the boys, how she's keeping it together. It seems lately that everything is closing in on her, and she seems much more negative. I feel the pressure of being in the last phase and I'm becoming more and more anxious about things, especially about trying to graduate from the program. There are more times that I feel guilty about so many things that I will need therapy for my therapy.

I also found out that Percy Smith, the gentleman who passed away here at Bates, was at medical the day he died, complaining of chest pains, and also vomiting, but seemed to get slightly better before day's end, when he had an apparent heart attack. It's ironic also that Mr. Smith was supposed to start the RDAP program this afternoon.

5/11/07: Today is the end of the first week for orientation and my third phase. I'm still struggling with standing up and saying I'm a master manipulator, but OH, WELL! I'm teaching the two-step recovery program to the new first phase this afternoon. That should be interesting. The ex-Congressman Bob Ney is in my class. I've had an opportunity to speak with him on a number of occasions and found him to be very personable. Of course, we do have a lot in common. In addition, we both feel the pressure from the program and the expectations to do the right things. As time goes on, I feel more and more pressure with this program, and the anxiety level keeps rising.

I'm excited that my friends Chris and Bob are stopping tonight to visit me. Their son, Don, is graduating over the weekend.

5/13/07: It's been a beautiful weekend, close to ninety degrees on both days. However, my visit on Friday night was horrible. When the COs called me up to the visiting room around 6:15, I found that they had terminated Chris's visit! The reason why was that she walked into the visiting room with sunglasses on her head! She offered to throw them in the garbage, but they said no, her visit was terminated. I actually saw Chris through the glass window, leaving the building with tears in her eyes. I felt terrible as I sat there. One of the COs came up to Bob, and asked what time he wanted his wife to come back and pick him up. Since Chris doesn't drive much, and especially since she didn't know the area well, Bob and I visited for only an hour, because he was worried about her. It was nice seeing Bob, but it was very uncomfortable under the circumstances. The visiting room policy has become suspect lately. Last weekend alone, over eighty-one people were turned away for various reasons. Children with shorts and hooded sweatshirts have been forced to leave, or change clothes. How about extra rattles and formula bottles sent back to the car, because the COs said so, and these items were for a baby who was under one year old.

I don't know what's up lately, but I feel very depressed and anxious. The program puts so much pressure on people, and you struggle emotionally each and every day.

I went to a self-help meeting on Saturday night, and the theme was "Coping Strategies for Urges," and one of my classmates said, for him, it was going to simply be, "Remember the Nightmare"—I think that will be very applicable for me in the future.

5/16/07: On Monday, I received feedback on my issue regarding my lying to them about being in prison. I received fifteen hands for feedback, and some of them thought I was mean-spirited and malicious. Some people spoke about my manipulation and power orientation. It seemed to go to my character, and not to my behavior. It seems unbelievable at times in TC, where I believe the inmates run the asylum. There are moments where some of them go to another level of bullying and get away with it.

One of the female COs came up to me on Monday and basically told me that the person responsible for terminating the visit of my friend Chris on Friday was Dr. Roth, our compound psychologist. He was the officer in charge for the weekend. The CO told me that Roth was so inconsistent the entire weekend that it was nothing more than chaos the whole time. Roth is the same guy who John T. said he didn't have time to answer a question when he asked him if his mother had arrived for a visit on Mother's Day.

One of the guys in my TC, Mr. Zaccadelli, supposedly contracted a terrible bacterial infection at Randolph Unit. He ended up in the hospital with a temperature of 104 degrees, and the possibility of losing his leg or his life. The infection was actually eating away at his skin on his leg. In fact, he still hobbles around this unit, and his leg is still bandaged up. Allegedly, a couple of other inmates caught the infection over at Randolph Unit. The medical care and sanitation conditions are quite honestly very suspect here.

5/18/07: On Wednesday evening, I called home. It was a disaster. I needed to wait until this morning to even write about the situation. Kathleen sounds like she's ready to explode. All of the kids are acting terribly. Our friend Patsy keeps helping us, despite the kids' misbehavior. I try to listen to Kathleen vent, but I'm starting to feel that she's beginning to feel resentful and very angry at me for this entire situation. The boys wouldn't even get on the phone with me. For the first time since I've been here, Kathleen and I didn't say goodbye to each other on the phone. Nina said goodbye as she told me how everyone is picking on her. The stress of being in prison and the guilt over not being home becomes increasingly more difficult. However, I try to keep it together because there is light at the end of the tunnel. I can't begin to tell people the emotional and psychological strain a family goes through when you go through an ordeal like this. The whole incarceration thing takes a toll on everyone.

5/21/07: I was elected facilitator for the second time in the program. It's a nice change of pace for me. Today, I have exactly eleven weeks or seventy-seven days to the door or to the bus. I spoke to Kathleen last night; she told me that Mr. Jones will be getting out of prison in July. Traci's been talking about getting out of work to pick him up. She still has the job I got her. I still have to wonder with her involvement in the Hired Truck Program, how she was able to hold on to her job. She must have been given super, super immunity from the Feds and the city to keep her job in the city clerk's office.

Yesterday, at lunch, John T. and I were going to the salad bar, when we saw a cockroach running across one end to the other. One inmate who was cleaning the salad bar, took his rag that he wipes the table with, knocked the roach to the floor, and stepped on it. He then proceeded to use the same rag to continue to wipe off the salad bar.

5/25/07: I'm completing week three of phase three today, and hopefully only have ten weeks to go. It's another holiday weekend; fortunately, Memorial Day should be nothing like Thanksgiving or Christmas. The weather forecast is in the nineties all weekend. Quite honestly, it gets harder to concentrate as the weather gets nicer.

Yesterday, we had a recall in the morning, which meant the entire compound was closed. The compound remained closed all day. We went down to the main line to pick up bag lunches, which was the only time we were allowed out of the building. Even though we did not have class, it was quite boring being stuck in the building all day. The closer I get to finish this program, the more anxious I become, simply because things change so rapidly in the RDAP program. There are inmates who continue to get recycled quite frequently. I've been helping out a first-time phaser, Bob Ney, the former Congressman. We both have Ms. Land as our primary DTS and since we had similar careers, there were similar treatment goals, including sentimentality, fraud and deceit, power orientation, and manipulation.. In the past, the DTSs would actually look at your PSI, interview you, and then write up your plan. Now, they want the first-phasers to diagnose themselves and basically put their own plan together. In any event, I helped Ney, who was very appreciative. He is actually a very personable man who loves to talk about his career. In fact, last night he told me how the former Speaker of the House, Newt Gingrich, asked him to run for Congress back in the early 90s, when he was state senator from Ohio.

I've also helped another first-phaser, Mr. Abrahamimi, a former Afghan freedom fighter who fought the former Soviet Union back in the eighties. The interesting point about him is his language barrier, which amazingly Bob Ney helps with. Ney actually learned some of the Afghan dialect when he was in Congress. He has become friends with Abrahamimi, and helps translate various issues for him in class. They first met when Ney arrived on March 1, when he was initially sent to the Gerard Unit. They became friends and moved over to Bates together approximately three weeks ago.

5/26/07: It's Saturday (Memorial Day weekend), and I don't have to think about TC. Last night I walked with John up until about 9:00 p.m. He has only twenty-five days to go. It will be a little rough for me when he goes home.

I spoke to Kathleen last night. She told me she's hit that proverbial brick wall. Only two weeks to go before the school year is done. She still has all her grading to do yet, besides helping our kids with their final exams. I made the mistake of asking her if anyone has called or stopped by to check on her and the kids. She went off on the fact that since I went to prison, only a couple of people checked on her. Out of the hundreds of people in my former organization, or that I have helped over the years, basically nobody stops, for all intents and purposes. I feel like I've been abandoned, along with my family. All my so-called friends used me for what they could get. Once I couldn't help them anymore, I was no longer of any use to them. For Kathleen and me, it's hard not to feel bitter. Hopefully, when I get home, not only will the family be closer, but I think I'll find a whole new circle of real friends. As I have said over and over, Chicago politics has been a life-altering experience for the entire Laski family.

5/28/07: I'm down to seventy days, and it's Memorial Day! It's around ninety degrees and humid. For lunch or brunch, we'll get one scoop of eggs or one hamburger, or two slices of bacon—basically very small portions of anything. Today, we received two grilled hamburgers, two grilled hot dogs, four buns, potato salad, and beans. I couldn't eat four buns to save my life. For a bag dinner, we were given one piece of microwave pizza, one bag of cookies, one bag of Bugles, with an apple, and two packets of fruit punch. The bag of Bugles (corn chips) on the back side said, "Fresher if used by February 12/07—I guess three months later is not bad. Last week, Thursday, we had a bag lunch with the same Bugles and the same expiration date. Sometimes I wonder where they get the food from around here.

This afternoon they have a horseshoe tournament, and a bocce ball tournament. Tonight, they have a concert, along with a couple of softball games. At least with the warm weather, I'm able to get outside and at least pretend that I'm enjoying myself. I'll call Kathleen and the kids later this evening to see how their day went. I know they have a week-and-a- half of school left, so I'm sure it's still a little hectic at home.

I'm not a big fan of the holidays around here, and I'm really down in the dumps. Unless you've actually experienced this type of situation, it's really hard to explain the mental and emotional strain you go through with the RDAP and Morgantown FCI. Hopefully, someday I can actually tell my story, and along the way, provide some support and help for people who may be struggling in a similar situation.

6/1/07: (Class 111) graduation this morning, and the goods news is that class 112 (my class) is the next to graduate on August 3. I'm so happy we're in the month of June, so if everything goes right, I'll only have two months to go!

The next couple of weeks are going to be a little rough on me. This Sunday is Jack and Bobby's tenth birthday. Next Friday is Nina's graduation, and four days later is her fourteenth birthday. Although I'm missing all this, I guess I should be thankful that this whole situation could have been worse. I can't help but think of Judge Norgle last June 13 when he told me at my sentencing that this is a terrible situation for the family, but at the end of the day I had no one to blame but myself. I'm just hopeful that someday down the road a lot of that guilt and self-pity will leave.

6/5/07: I just received my final paperwork for the halfway house. My travel plans are confirmed. I leave here on August 6 around 8:00 a.m. to go to Pittsburgh. There's a layover there for quite a few hours. I don't know exactly when I leave Pittsburgh, but I'm scheduled to be at the halfway house in Chicago at 5:40 a.m. on August 7. It's nice to get the paperwork out of the way.

A bunch of the a.m. guys who graduated last week left today, including Brady from Detroit and Alvarez from Chicago. We exchanged info for the future, but we'll see what happens down the road.

I called the boys on Sunday and wished them a Happy Birthday. Nina's graduation is this Friday, and a friend of mine from home is coming to visit me that evening.

Everything seems to be getting closer and closer, and the less I talk to people here, the better off I am. Everyone starts getting paranoid about graduating, and quite honestly, I don't trust most people in this program.

6/9/07: I just completed a very relaxing and relatively stress-free week, because there was no TC or any other classes. All the DTSs were at a seminar, so I had the entire week off. I spent much of my time walking and even jogging around the track. I also took the time to complete my last workbook of the program, which was entitled *Recovery Maintenance*. I began my "Victim Impact" project where I and another inmate do a role play, and he portrays my victim, and in my case, it's Kathleen. He will tell me all the things that I did to victimize her, and at the end, I need to offer up an apology. This is a very difficult assignment.

It's amazing when I speak to my fellow classmates how we all felt so stress-free this past week. Unless you're in this program, you have no clue how tense and emotionally draining it is.

My friend from Chicago flew in yesterday and visited with me last night. Of course, what would be a visit for me, unless there was an incident? During the visit, there was a bad storm, so the COs closed the compound. When they close the compound, special counts take place to make sure everyone is accounted for. In the visiting room, there were a number of inmates with their guests. There were children, moms and dads, wives and girlfriends, and it was a little noisy, so if someone was going to make an announcement, he or she would have to speak up. In this case, one of the COs was calling for a special count that no one could hear. In any event, probably the meanest, most unprofessional of the COs, Hopkins, stood up and at the top of his lungs, screamed for all the inmates to go outside and be counted. He was actually red in the face, and his veins were protruding from his neck when he screamed. Children who were there jumped in their parents' arms, and other guests jumped out of their chairs in fear. I actually had strangers (guests for other inmates) come up to me, and asked me if everything was okay. This CO has a history of this type of behavior, including strip searching of inmates, which I have gone through personally. I can only say that this particular CO should find a new job, because he should be fired. Overall, we had a nice visit, besides the one incident. I hope that he will be able to help me with a temporary job when I get home and until I get my feet back on the ground again.

Yesterday was Nina's graduation, and quite honestly, I thought about it numerous times yesterday. I hope everything went well. I tried calling home last night on three different occasions, but I'm sure they were out celebrating. Kathleen told me on Thursday that the family was going to take Nina out for dinner. I can't help but feel guilty about missing her graduation, but through it all, Nina has always been positive and upbeat with me. Even on Thursday when I spoke with her, I apologized, and told her I would be home soon. Nina told me she loves me, and understands. On Tuesday, Nina will turn fourteen, and she asked me if I could call her on her birthday. These are things that go on when you're in prison that people don't really understand.

6/10/07: I've been an altar server at Catholic Mass every Sunday now since November, and quite honestly, it's been a refreshing change for me. Today, Father Alex, during his homily, said if you do anything in prison, try to reconcile with God. That's an interesting concept by Father Alex, who is both a CO and a Catholic priest, which I believe would put into jeopardy any type of confidentiality agreement you may have with him. I do, however, like serving at Mass, and will continue to do so as long as I'm here.

Tomorrow, class starts up again, and I just dread going back after that week of being off. The time has been moving along, and word has it that we will have another week off in July, which will just about wrap things up for my class.

My friend John T. is now down to nine days before he leaves this place. He and I met back in September, and have logged many hours together walking the track and entire compound. When he leaves, it will be a big adjustment for me. We've spent the last nine months talking about everything and supporting each other mentally and emotionally. I feel like I've known him and his family for years. Once John leaves, I'll only have forty-eight days to go—God willing!!

6/13/07: I talked to Nina last night on her fourteenth birthday. She went shopping and out to dinner; it seemed like she had a very good time. It's always hard to miss days like this, but, hopefully, this will be the last.

I'm back in class, and my issue regarding Jones came up, and nine different people gave me feedback. The most important feedback I received was not to let Jones get control over what I do and feel—I need to move forward, learn from the past, and move ahead. Lately, I feel depressed and anxious—I'm starting to think about what I'm going to do when I get home, and I'm nervous about our financial situation.

Last night I got called down to the compound office for a random drug test. They take a urine sample and within a matter of minutes, a color strip in the cup indicates a positive or negative result. Needless to say, I had a negative result, but this was my second test in three months—just a coincidence?

6/17/07: It was Father's Day today—hopefully the last of the tough holidays before I go home. Rob and I had a little going away celebration for John. We had someone make a homemade pizza, and we all sat outside and talked about John's time here. I also took John to Mass with me. At the end of the Mass, Father Alex always asks if anyone is leaving, and since John was, he went to the altar to get a blessing from the Father and the congregation. It's nice to get that spiritual uplifting before you leave.

I went to the baseball game in the evening. There were two

games played—and they were between the best teams on the compound. One of the most disturbing things happened during the game. It sounds crazy, but when male ducks go after a female duck, it's a brutal scene—it's nothing more than a gang-rape. The male ducks actually hold her down—one will actually hold her down by stepping on her neck, or just grabbing her neck, while the other male ducks take their turn with her. There had to have been five male ducks attacking the one female. I've seen this happen before, and if I could have, I would have run over to break it up. What was so disturbing tonight was that it happened behind the grandstands during the game, and inmates actually surrounded the ducks—while watching and cheering. I never realized how sick some of these inmates are here. If they take enjoyment out of something like that, what kind of attitude and behavior could we expect when they get home? For a so-called minimum security facility, there are some real hardened, morally bankrupt, sick people here.

I spoke with my mother-in-law this afternoon. I was supposed to talk to Wally (my father-in-law), but he still has a hard time talking to me. He wants to wait until I actually get home. He wants to see me after I get out. I understand this whole ordeal has been hard on him and Pat. It seems that she is really disappointed in my former friends.

I also spoke to Kathleen tonight—nothing new. The kids were swimming in the pool when I called. Nina picked up the phone and wished me Happy Father's Day dripping wet, while the boys yelled it out from the pool. I'm all out of school and can enjoy the summer.

6/19/07: This morning I said goodbye to John Tokosh. He and I met last September—he arrived on the 4th (Labor Day), and I arrived one week later, on 9/11. We actually met about two days after going to Alexander. It didn't take long before we became instant friends. Even after I moved over to Bates on Oct. 31, there wasn't a day that went by when we didn't talk and walk around the compound. There were times that we would walk for hours. In fact, last September, there was one day when we walked around the track for about ten miles. We spent much of our time talking about our respective families and how we missed them.

I met him about 6:30 a.m. in front of Alexander, and walked with him to the laundry as he turned in his bedding, his khakis, and his boots. We walked to the chapel and sat outside and waited. About 7:20, the call came over the P.A., "John Tokosh, report to the back of R & D!" I walked him as far as I could, and then watched and waved as he walked inside R & D. He's a good guy, and we certainly helped each other, especially the first couple of months, when we walked so much and actually talked to a point where it seemed like therapy. He made life for me here at least tolerable. I'll miss him, but am hopeful someday we can see each other again.

After I arrived at the unit this morning, I saw my name on the bulletin board instructing me to see caseworker Schuman. In the past, when my name was on the board, it was a good thing because it involved paperwork for my halfway house and my departure date. However, I'd filled out all my paperwork, and received my confirmation from the halfway house; I was leaving on Aug. 6, traveling from Pittsburgh to Chicago, arriving back in Chicago on August 7 at 4:40 a.m. I've done my fingerprints, and for all intents and purposes, I'm done, so seeing my name on the board concerned me. When I walked in to see Mr. Schuman, my concerns were confirmed. He told me that my date had changed, and that I would be leaving a week later, which meant I wouldn't be in Chicago until August 14. I remember when I first arrived here in September, and caseworker Little, over at Alexander, had me sign paperwork that stipulated I would not spend any time with my co-defendants in prison or a halfway house. I know Jones is getting out in July, and I'm afraid they moved my date back because of him. So I signed new paperwork and took a new thumbprint for my new date at the halfway house on August 14. I also called Kathleen to tell her, and to ask her to call my attorney to make sure of the new date. I'm very aggravated!!—and feel haunted by my past!

6/20/07: When I think I'd heard or seen it all here, something new comes up. Today, in TC, a first-phaser brought up an issue about his self-centeredness. Specifically, he'd been dating—or, I should say, having sex with the woman who was involved in his criminality a few years back. He hadn't seen the woman now for a few years, and she is now forty-three years old. He told the class that he's thirty-six years old, and she is over forty. He no longer wants to have sex with her because of her age. However, the woman's daughter is only twenty-seven years old, and he wants to have sex with her as soon as he gets out of prison. I asked him in class if he wanted to have a relationship with the daughter, or just sex. He told the class and me that he hadn't decided yet. My feedback to him was that he's morally bankrupt, and his overall recovery will be in jeopardy if he involves himself in an unhealthy relationship with the daughter.

What makes this situation even worse is that this individual has four kids (two daughters). Besides being a convicted drug dealer, he has been allowed to teach both a parenting class, and a relationship class at this institution—how sick and twisted is that for this guy to teach others about being a good parent or building a healthy relationship with others?

When he was receiving feedback, he had an arrogant attitude, and actually believed he wasn't doing anything wrong. I heard him say after class that men in his class would like to be in his situation with the mother and daughter. I can't believe that this guy is even in this program with that attitude. He believes that men should be able to have as many women as they want, and his preference limits women to thirty or younger for a sexual relationship. DTS Sowden asked him how he would feel if one of his daughters came home and told him that she'd been dumped by her husband or boyfriend because she turned a certain age.

His reply was it wouldn't bother him.

This guy is sick, and needs more than this RDAP program in his life. How could he ever be allowed to teach here?

6/25/07: The last few days have been uneventful. The weather has been beautiful, so I've been outside quite a bit. Yesterday was Nina's dance recital, and this is the first one I've missed since she started approximately nine years ago. Hopefully, this is the last event I'll miss now. I feel that this past year I've missed so many things in Nina's life, from her graduation on. When you're in prison, I think there are times you wallow in self-pity, because of all the positive self-talk in the world, and it still won't help make you feel any better.

6/26/07: Yesterday, I did my "Victim Impact" project. Needless to say, my victim was Kathleen. One of my classmates did a role play as my wife. He basically told me, as Kathleen, what I did wrong, and how poorly I treated her and the kids. The rest of the class then jumped in and gave feedback about my past and the errors I'd made. At the end, I gave an off-the-cuff apology to my wife. When I was finished, I certainly felt emotionally drained.

6/30/07: Today is the last day in June—all I have left is the month of July, and twelve days in August. One more full month here, and some change, hopefully. Yesterday, in class, I gave feedback a couple of times, but I'm starting to get burnt out by the whole class and treatment experience. You can only give so much honest and genuine feedback, as far as bringing up issues that becomes problematic, because you start making up issues to meet a so-called quota.

This is also a big day at home. It's Nina's graduation party! Kathleen said there's about four or five people coming for a sleepover. I know she's excited about her sleepover at our house.

I keep looking for John on the weekends. It's only been two weeks, and I'm trying to stay to myself as much as possible. I really don't have much confidence in confiding or talking to very many people in my class.

7/3/07: Today brings back some bitter memories. A couple of years ago, my family, along with the Jones family, went to a mutual friend's house that was a couple of hours outside of Chicago, to celebrate July 4. I still can't forget our families' spending quality time together, and then to see what transpired later. I really am trying to forget those memories.

The TC class is starting to wear on the third-phasers. We are in our ninth and final month. Quite honestly, it's becoming increasingly more difficult to stay focused and engaged. Some of the issues are very difficult to address and give feedback to the class. One inmate described how his eighteen-year-old son beat up his mother and his sister, while another classmate related how one of his nephews (he has *twenty-three* brothers and sisters, and over *400* nieces and nephews!) was arrested for shooting and *killing* an off-duty policeman. I wouldn't even know where to begin giving these guys feedback.

It's exactly thirty days today until the completion of the class on August 3. I can't begin to describe the stress and anxiety, along with many of my classmates who have experienced the same feelings over the months. As I have said repeatedly, I will need treatment for my treatment. Unfortunately, there are some memories from this institution that I will never forget, especially from this RDAP experience.

7/4/07: The last of the holidays is here. Yesterday, we had a memorial service for another inmate (John Lewis) who died here. I heard he was in his upper sixties and had diabetes. Supposedly, he got some type of sore or blister on his foot that led to eventual amputation of one or both of his legs. However, his demise was brought about by a heart attack. This gentleman, I was told, came in on a one-year sentence (was to leave in September). With all his medical problems, why would he be kept here? This is the *second* inmate to die here in *less than* five *months*!

Honestly, with less than thirty days to go before graduation, I'm concerned and nervous about going home, and I wonder what I'll be doing and how to start my life over again. I'll tell you that this whole prison experience definitely affects your mental and emotional well-being.

7/9/07: I'm down to the last four weeks of class. I'm done with all of my papers, and workbooks, etc. Quite honestly, I'm not sure I will bring up another issue in TC. I've had eight, and for the most part, they've been very good issues. It is so difficult now to get motivated. After eight months, I feel tired and disengaged. In any event, I try to muddle along. As I get close to the door, I become more anxious about home and how I will readjust and start over. I'm very anxious about the entire starting-from-scratch theory. Lately, I've been somewhat depressed, and very tired all day long. When I get home, I need to re-evaluate my meds that I'm taking here.

7/12/07: The last few days I've been giving some serious attention to what the future will hold! Quite honestly, I'm very nervous about the future. I suspect I will lose my pension, and that will have a tremendous negative impact on my financial security. I need to do some real soul-searching about a new career.

I feel like the TC is starting to wind down a bit, however. I still feel the stress and anxiety of being in class and I wonder what can possibly still go wrong.

7/9/07: This past week has been unbelievable! On Friday, one of my classmates, Zaccadelli, asked to have a private conversation with me in one of the classrooms. He asked me my thoughts on having someone write a paper for him and pay that individual. I basically told him he was crazy, and don't do it. I informed him that, as a 1st phaser, he could lose out on the whole program if he got caught. I suggested that he at least sleep on it and talk to me the next day. I also showed him some of my notes, and offered them to him to read, with the hope that it would re-kindle some ideas in his head. He really showed no interest in doing that. Before we ended our conversation, he told me that another first-phaser, Haas, was the one who was trying to talk to someone to pay him to write the paper. He told Zac that he might know someone. The next day everything fell apart. Zac did not listen to me, and went to someone to have his paper written. In the meantime, second-phaser Singleton went to my buddy, third-phaser Duncan, to tell him that Zac was getting a paper written by Ramsey for a price (one to two cans per page). When Duncan and I found this out, we confronted everyone we both knew, and told them that unless these people came forward and held themselves accountable, Duncan and I would be in violation of the criminal code. As third-phasers, we could be in deep trouble. As we found out through Singleton, there were other instances in which papers had been written by him and another third-phaser, Doran, for a first-phaser, Simon. Duncan and I tried to sort out the whole mess with the people involved, but as we got deeper into it, everyone there seemed reluctant to hold themselves accountable. Duncan and I had no other choice but to go to Peer Counselor Williams, and inform him of the situation. Following his investigation with all of us, there were six people who needed to hold themselves accountable.

On Monday and Tuesday in TC, six people—Zaccadelli, Haas, Singleton, Simon, Doran, and Ramsey were grilled and given feedback. During clarity, McCaloney tried to come after me and Duncan about waiting too long to hold Zac accountable, but Williams put a stop to that. I found out through another inmate in Bates, that a second-phaser and a third-phaser who both work in the laundry department were plotting before TC to get Duncan and me. They, by coincidence, were good friends with McCaloney. I also found out through other inmates (Short, C. Smith), that McCaloney was out to get Duncan and me. McCaloney would pretend to be my friend when I'd confront him, but after I'd left, he'd go to Short and tell him that Duncan and I should be expelled.

The bottom line at the end of the day was that all six people would be expelled from the program. Doran was three weeks from graduation; Mr. Haas (from Illinois) had made a mistake, and along with Simon, didn't deserve expulsion. Singleton, Ramsey, and, especially Zac, all got what they deserved. The only other problem was that Duncan and I, in some people's eyes, were considered traitors. There are some people who will have nothing to do with us because of this situation. We did the right thing, but it's still uncomfortable. With only a couple of weeks to graduation, I feel like I really have to watch my back now.

7/25/07: Yesterday I was outside when Dr. Baker and Ms. Land were walking by, and they waved me over to talk. As I walked with them over the bridge, Dr. Baker asked me how my book was going. I was surprised, but said it was going fine. Ms. Land asked me what I was writing about, and I said a little bit of everything, but that most of it was about politics. Later that day, I received a letter from Fox TV, and they mentioned the book, so I knew since all mail is opened, why Baker and Land had asked me.

This morning, Singleton, Zaccadelli, Ramsey, and Simon moved out of Bates. Fortunately, Doran was allowed to stay after being recycled back to third phase, along with Haas, who will start his first phase over again. I'm happy they will be allowed to stay in the program.

It was uncomfortable for Duncan and me over the past week with Singleton stalking us and staring at us wherever we went. A couple of days ago, I walked past Singleton and Ramsey on the bridge where they were standing, and as soon as I was behind Singleton, he farted and laughed at me. He's such an asshole! This is the same guy who borrowed mayo from another inmate and put it all over his crotch because he said that mayo helps with rashes, and that he had some type of jock itch. He's a sick individual whose hygiene is suspect. Singleton is one of those inmates who still has that "gangster mentality" as a drug leader.

The TC classes are moving along quickly—only seven days to go. I've been laying back the last few days, and hope to limit my participation over the next week. Again, I'm that tired and burnt out!

7/28/07: One more week to go! Yesterday, Ms. Lindsley told us we're going to have a test on Tuesday. Out of a possible twenty-four classes, she's probably been there six times. When she was there, we talked about the movies we watched on intervention, and about some other basic info. We have a workbook called *Recovery Maintenance,* which she never talked about. So she's going to keep us guessing on what this is going to be on, when, in fact, she's given us very little direction on anything. When she is in our class, she comes across as this bad ass who knows everything, while talking down to us. She has described in great detail on a couple of occasions, the different foods we're missing, such as McDonalds, Burger King, Subway (sandwiches, fries, and shakes). Yesterday, she talked about Dunkin' Donuts. I believe she can be downright cruel and mean at times. Every man in that class comes from a different environment and set of circumstances, yet she talks to us like we are all degenerates who have only a 50/50 chance of staying out of prison. She might impress some of the younger guys, but the others and me think she's full of shit!

Unfortunately, I feel more bitter now, and have a lower self-esteem than before I'd started the class. So many of the third-phasers are walking on pins and needles. The stress and anxiety are killers, but those in control love that stuff.

When Ms. Land went over my final treatment goals, she recommended that I see a psychologist for my continued anxiety. I told her I have that set up already. Remember, treatment for my treatment! She also asked me if I said nice things about her in my book. She wasn't concerned about anyone else, except what I said about her.

I can't begin to describe how emotionally drained I am. I just want to get out of here and try to rebuild my life.

There are also a number of people who give me and Duncan the evil eye and avoid us like the plague, because of the plagiarism incident where six people got expelled. There are a number of people in the program, including third-phasers, who will never lose their "gangster mentality." Let me repeat that there are people in the program, including third-phasers, who still have, and probably always will have that "gangster mentality." I was told by Ms. Land that over the last couple of weeks, she and Dr. Baker have received anonymous notes about me, accusing me of different things and basically trying to sabotage my graduation. It's like Chicago politics all over again.

7/31/07: Today was my last test for the program! Ms. Land had each of us in class write three questions that we thought were insightful and important. Then, we turned in those papers, and she shuffled them up and passed them out again. Whatever paper you received, you needed to answer those three questions that your fellow classmate had made up. We turned the papers in again; she reshuffled them, and passed them out again. Now we had to grade the new paper for both the questions written and the answers given. Fortunately, I received two "Supers" ("Superiors") for my questions and my answers. It's such a relief that the test is over. All I have left is three days of TC.

One of my biggest concerns when I leave here is smoking. I really don't want to start up again and make matters worse. Between the medical building and the psych. building, smoking cessation classes are held near designated smoking areas for prison employees. The areas have one of those long-nose ashtrays, and a bench for people to sit and smoke, in plain view of the inmates—another double standard here at Morgantown FCI.

Someone would remind the new warden that next time, just maybe, his staff could lead by example, and comply with federal law to make the compound a *true* non-smoking facility.

8/2/07: Two classes left—of course, they're making us go to class on the last day. Historically, the other classes had the last day off, and just went to graduation.

On another note, I'm getting a little tired of some of the *real* criminals here! John Singleton, who got expelled from the program, continues to harass Duncan and me when he sees us. Today, he came up to me in Rec., and asked me in front of another inmate, if I've had anyone lately. A real first-class asshole! *He's* the criminal here, and yet he tries to portray himself as the victim. All I try to do is avoid people like that.

There are criminals here from my class, who will graduate tomorrow—Aronowitz and Tymoczko, from Pittsburgh, and McCaloney, from Ohio. These so-called "leaders," who, for the most part, bullshit the DTSs, have the *real* criminal thinking and vindictiveness embedded in their minds and souls. One of these guys who had allegedly bragged about owning a strip club and screwing half the strippers while his wife was at home, pretends like he's a reformed person in TC, but when he's outside, every other sentence begins and ends with the "F" word, as he glorifies his past. In fact, one of his classmates has a lawyer in Pittsburgh, and this seedy individual (who is one of the class speakers at the graduation) gave his buddy the name of a place his lawyer could go to for a tan. He told him he should ask for "Norma," and to tell her Walt had sent him for some *"special"* treatment—wink, wink! Another one of those individuals, Mr. McCaloney, has an additional ten months on his sentence, so the DTSs have asked him to become a Peer Counselor. Now, for starters, this individual's best friend is the guy from Pittsburgh who owned the strip club. Mr. McCaloney is probably the most vindictive guy in the class. It was he and Tymoczko (who I thought was such a nice guy at first) who set me up in class for manipulation.

McCaloney was actually telling people that Duncan I should have been recycled. His bunkie is Murphy (another guy whose character had deceived me), and they have tried everything to sabotage me. Yet the DTSs, in their infinite wisdom, see McCaloney as a role model for future RDAP students—it's a joke!

8/3/07: It's finally over!!—Graduation Day! We had TC from 12:30 to 1:30 p.m., and at 2:00 p.m., DTSs Sowden and Land, along with Dr. Baker, presented Class 112 with our certificates. We had two speakers from our class (John Marshall and Walt Tymoczko), and the DTSs and Baker spoke, too. We were presented with our certificates in alphabetical order, and when my name came up, Land said, jokingly, that my name was not printed on the certificate, and Baker asked me if I needed a XANAX. I politely went to Land as she presented me with my certificate, and I shook Sowden's and Baker's hands as I thanked them. The entire RDAP class was 500+ hours, and I can't begin to tell you how difficult this whole experience was. There were times I really thought I wouldn't make it. As soon as the graduation ceremony was over, I asked for permission to leave the building, and ran over to the chapel, just to thank God for His help. It is really hard to believe that this journey is almost over. I need to get back home and hug my wife and kids, and tell them how much I love them!